Blood, Sweat *and* Welfare

Blood, Sweat *and* Welfare

A HISTORY OF WHITE BOSSES AND ABORIGINAL PASTORAL WORKERS

MARY ANNE JEBB

UWA PUBLISHING

First published in 2002, reprinted in 2014 by
University of Western Australia Publishing
Crawley, Western Australia 6009
www.uwap.uwa.edu.au

This book has been supported by the National
Council for the Centenary of Federation and the
Australian Historical Association.

Centenary of Federation
1901-2001

A Centenary Library
of Australian History

National Library of Australia
Cataloguing-in-Publication entry:

Jebb, Mary Anne.
    Blood, sweat and welfare: a history of white bosses and Aboriginal
    pastoral workers.

    Bibliography.
    Includes index.
    ISBN 1 876268 61 1.

    1. Aborigines, Australian—Western Australia—Kimberley—Social
    conditions. 2. Aborigines, Australian—Western Australia—Interviews.
    3. Aborigines, Australian—Western Australia—Kimberley —
    Employment. 4. Aborigines, Australian—Western Australia—Public
    welfare. 5. Agricultural laborers—Western Australia—Kimberley.
    6. Kimberley (W.A.)—Social conditions. I. Title

994.140049915

Produced by Benchmark Publications, Melbourne
Consultant editor: Jane Hammond Foster, Perth
Series design by Robyn Mundy Design, Perth
Cover design by Ron Hampton, Pages in Action, Melbourne
Typeset in 9½pt Garamond Light by Lasertype, Perth

this book is dedicated

to the memory of my brother

Ben Smith

CONTENTS

ACKNOWLEDGEMENTS

This book brings together the threads of people's memories and written historical records from archives and libraries. I am forever grateful to the storytellers from the north Kimberley who were patient and generous. As their stories unravelled I grew increasingly incredulous that there was room in their lives for a laugh and a yarn, let alone for working with me on my book. I soon learned that this willingness to share, laugh and work is an enduring characteristic of survivors of the Kimberley pastoral frontier. Their views and their words helped to give the written records life and meaning.

Thank you to the storytellers whose words appear in this book: Campbell Allenbrae, Daisy Angajit (Beharrell), Evelyn Bidd, Jack Dale, Jack Dann, Dot Delower, Ned Delower, Jilki Edwards, Maggie Ghi, Maggie Gudaworla, Harry Howendon, Mick Jowalji, Jack Jowan, Billy King, Pat Lacy, Peter Lacy, Rita Laylay, Willie Lennard, Rosie Mamangulya, Freddy Marker, Barbara Midmee, Wallace Midmee, David Mowaljarlai, Morndi Munro (Morndingali), Weeda Munro (Nyanulla), Fred Russ, Susie Umungul, Betty Walker, Sammy Walker, Ginger Warrebeen, Banjo Woorunmurra.

It is too hard to name every person who has helped to make this book possible, as it grew out of a doctoral thesis accompanied by five years' residency in the Kimberley. Many friends, family members and colleagues went out of their way to encourage me to write and to assist me with field trips, looking after storytellers, proofing, editing and discussing ideas. I am particularly grateful to: Maryon Allbrook, Anne Atkinson, Valda Blundell, Therese Carr, Craig Chappelle, Kim Doohan, Sarah Giles, Sue Gillan, Anna Haebich, Daryl Kickett, Joan McKie, Simon Neville, Howard Pedersen, Kate Smith, Leonie Stella, Patrick Sullivan, Beverley Treacey, Mandy Ungundan, Daniel Vachon, Anthony Watson, John Watson, Peter Yu and Sarah Yu.

Gus Bottrill and Ailsa Smith gave hours of their time researching and photocopying items and then sending them to me in the Kimberley. Thank you.

While producing the PhD thesis that laid the foundation for this book, I was supported and encouraged by Murdoch University supervisors Lenore Layman, Bob Reece and Carol Warren. Their assistance is gratefully acknowledged. Editorial suggestions for publication from my examiners, Peter Read, Henry Reynolds and Nancy Williams, were very useful.

I have been helped on innumerable occasions by staff at the Derby Library, the Battye Library and State Records Office of Western Australia, the Kimberley Land Council and the Aboriginal Affairs Department Library Perth. Sue Beverley, Jenny Carter, Thea Corbett, Gerard Foley and Tom Reynolds deserve special mention for their patience.

A publication subsidy provided by the Western Australian History Foundation gave me the necessary inspiration to move the manuscript from a PhD thesis to a book. A Federation Grant from the Australian Historical Association also assisted.

I am deeply appreciative of the understanding and encouragement from my husband, Malcolm Allbrook. Thanks also to our family, Charlie and Sarah Jebb, Nick Allbrook, our son-in-law, and our grandchild Patty Jean Niyandi.

STORYTELLERS AND KEY CHARACTERS

Campbell Allenbrae Born about 1922 on Kurunjie station. Father and mother worked with Afghan sandalwooders. Head stockman at Kurunjie late 1940s and early 1950s. Wife Dargie, stockwoman on Kurunjie.

Jack Dale Born about 1920 near Mt House station. White father, Jack Dale of Queensland. Mother Dolly Dale. Travelled in the bush during 1920s with grandfather. Trained for stockwork at Mt House. Contract head stockman in 1950s and '60s. Chairman of Imintji Aboriginal Community 1984–91.

Maggie Ghi Born in the bush around 1920. Father and mother removed her from Kurunjie homestead and hid her in the bush. Around 1930 captured by Rosie Mumungulya and Jack Campbell from Kurunjie station. Camp cook and stockwoman. Worked contract musters to Wyndham for Scotty Salmond in 1940s and '50s.

Maggie Gudaworla Born about 1912 Mt Barnett region. Moved with mother to Mt House about 1924. Returned to Mt Barnett with missionaries about 1936. Stockwoman.

Harry Howendon Born about 1914 in the bush. Fred Merry named him about 1922 at Mt Barnett station camp. Drove sheep from Fitzroy to Munja in early 1930s. Stockman at Mt Hart. Founder of Dodnun Aboriginal Community, Mt Elizabeth station.

Mick Jowalji Born a few years before Scotty Saddler and Jowalji's father occupied Tableland lease in 1920. Head stockman at Tableland. Travelled with Jowan on shooting incidents in late 1920s and early 1930s. Chairman of Yulumbu Aboriginal Community, 1995.

Jack Jowan Born about 1910. Left with Jack Connaughton and Aboriginal uncle as a boy. Worked in Mt Barnett region during 1920s. Moved to become stockman at Tableland station. Chairman of Tirralintji Aboriginal Community, 1989–94.

Mary Karraworla Born about 1905. Taken from the bush by Jack Carey after father shot about 1919. Accompanied Carey throughout violent 1920s in Mt Barnett and Gibb River region.

Billy King Born about 1920. White father William King. Head stockman for Mt House 1947–72. Manager of Mt Barnett station and chairman of Kupingarri Aboriginal Corporation 1989–96.

Rosie Mamangulya Born in the bush. Mother captured for work at Kurunjie where Rosie grew up in 1920s. Stockwoman and homestead camp boss at Kurunjie station. Tracker for Jack Campbell in 1920s when he explored Drysdale River region looking for people to work at Kurunjie.

Scotty Martin Came in from the bush to Mt Elizabeth in 1949 aged about eight. Became head stockman in 1960s. Chairman of Dodnun Aboriginal Community.

Barbara Midmee Born on Tableland station late 1920s. Stockwoman and cook. Sister of Mick Jowalji.

Morndi Munro (Morndingali) Known also as Billy Munro. Born at muster camp on Napier Downs station around 1912. Father captured by police in 1880s, mother captured at Barnett police station about 1908. Head stockman of Napier Downs, Kimberley Downs and Meda 1955–72.

Weeda Munro (Nyanulla) Wife of Morndingali. Born in the bush near Mt Joseph in King Leopold Ranges about 1914. Grew up and trained for stockwork on Mt Hart station. Renowned stockwoman. Father Wundigul.

Larry Murphy (Mobby) Born about 1900. Father speared and killed. Jack Carey's assistant. Stockman at Gibb River station until death in late 1960s.

Fat Paddy (Ngulit) Born 1890s near Mt Barnett. Confronted and escaped from Jack Carey about 1919. Stockman at Mt Barnett and Napier Downs.

Police Paddy (Wundigul) Captured near Mt Hart by police about 1905 to become tracker at Mt Barnett. Stockman and assistant for Mick O'Connor, Fred Potts, William Chalmers and Felix Edgar. Convicted for murder and gaoled 1927–32.

Susie Umungul Born in the bush about 1910. Rescued by Mary Karraworla from massacre of family group. Built first bark hut on Gibb River station. Noted horserider and saddler.

ABBREVIATIONS

AADL	Aboriginal Affairs Department Library
AAPA	Aboriginal Affairs Planning Authority
AD	Aborigines Departments files (including Native Welfare)
ARAD	Annual Report Aborigines Department
AWU	Australian Workers Union
BL	Battye Library
CAR	Commonwealth Arbitration Commission Report
CNA	Commissioner of Native Administration
CNW	Commissioner of Native Welfare
CoP	Commissioner of Police
CPA	Chief Protector of Aborigines
Col Sec	Colonial Seceretary
CSO	Colonial Secretary's Office
DO	District Officer
DOLA	Department of Land Administration
DSS	Department of Social Security (Commonwealth)
GG	*Government Gazette*
NB	Researcher's Note Books
NDG	Northern Division General (Native Administration files)
NWD	Native Welfare Department
PC	Police Constable
PD	Police Department file, Battye Library
PF	Personal File
PGA	Pastoralists and Graziers Association
RM	Resident Magistrate
SS	Social Services
UAM	United Aborigines Mission
US	Undersecretary
WA	*West Australian* newspaper
WAPD	Western Australian Parliamentary Debates
WAVP	Western Australian Votes and Proceedings

The map of the Kimberley on the following spread is copyright *Australian Geographic*, adapted by Claire Hunt.

The Kimberley

AREA ENLARGED

0   100   200 km

GEOGRAPHIC ART : RAYMOND SIM
AUSTRALIAN GEOGRAPHIC CARTOGRAPHIC DIVISION
Adapted by Claire Hunt (2001)

INDIAN

OCEAN

Bonaparte Archipelago

Cape Volte

Montague Sound

Bigge Island

York Sound

Mitche Falls

Augustus I.

PRINCE

Kunmunya Mission

Kunmunya Aboriginal Reserve

Koti Bay

Coffee Royal site

Hall Point

RES

Doubtful Bay

Montgomery Islands

Buccaneer Archipelago

Collier Bay

Walcott

Munja

Inlet

Isdell F

Lombadina Aboriginal Reserve

Cape Leveque

Federal Downs

Wotjalum Aboriginal Reserve

Oobagooma

King Sound

Pender Bay

Mount Hart

Lacepede Islands

Beagle Bay

WINDJANA GORGE NATIONAL PARK

Napier Downs

Cape Baskerville

Beagle Bay Aboriginal Reserve

Derby

Meda

Coulomb Point

Mowanjum

GIBB

RIVER

Kimberley Downs

TUNNEL CREEK NATIONAL PARK

GREAT

NORTHERN

HIGHWAY

Broome

Gantheaume Point

Roebuck Bay

Cambalin

Fitzroy Crossi

Fitzroy River

Lagrange Bay

GREAT NORTHERN

GREAT   SANDY   DESERT

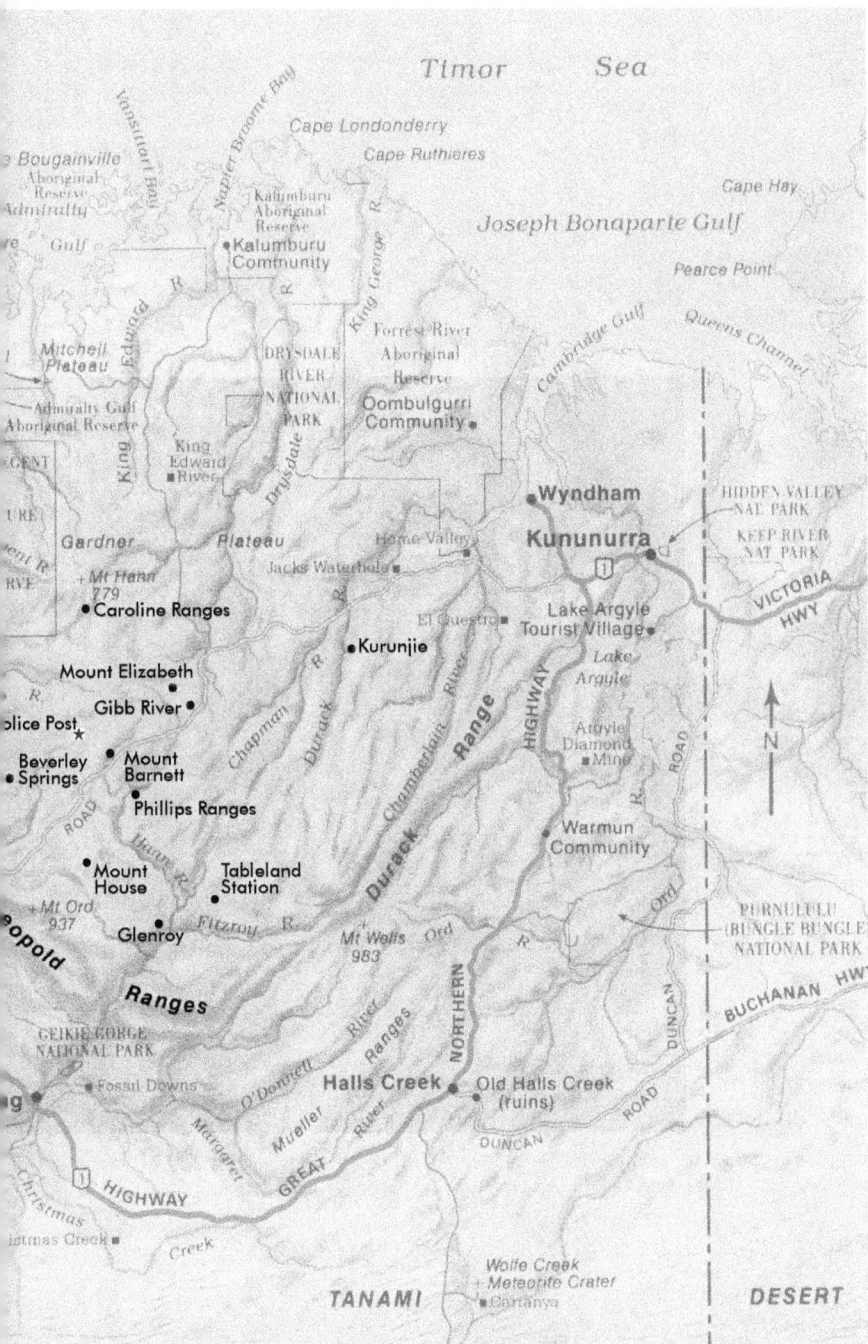

Timor Sea

Cape Londonderry

Cape Ruthieres

Cape Hay

Bougainville
Aboriginal
Reserve
Admiralty

Kalumburu
Aboriginal
Reserve

Joseph Bonaparte Gulf

Gulf

Kalumburu
Community

Pearce Point

Mitchell
Plateau

DRYSDALE
RIVER
NATIONAL
PARK

Forrest River
Aboriginal
Reserve

Cambridge Gulf

Queens Channel

Admiralty Gulf
Aboriginal Reserve

King
Edward
River

Oombulgurri
Community

Gardner

Plateau

Home Valley

Wyndham

HIDDEN VALLEY
NAT PARK

Mt Hann
779

Jacks Waterhole

Kununurra

KEEP RIVER
NAT PARK

Caroline Ranges

El Questro

Lake Argyle
Tourist Village

VICTORIA

HWY

Kurunjie

Lake
Argyle

Mount Elizabeth

Gibb River

Chapman

Durack

Chamberlain

Range

Argyle
Diamond
Mine

Police Post

Beverley
Springs

Mount
Barnett

HIGHWAY

ROAD

Phillips Ranges

Haun

Durack

Warmun
Community

Mount
House

Tableland
Station

Mt Ord
937

Fitzroy

Mt Wells
983

Ord

PURNULULU
(BUNGLE BUNGLE)
NATIONAL PARK

Glenroy

Ord

Leopold

Ranges

River

Ranges

NORTHERN

DUNCAN

BUCHANAN HWY

ROAD

GEIKIE GORGE
NATIONAL PARK

Fossil Downs

O'Donnell

River

Halls Creek

Old Halls Creek
(ruins)

Mueller

River

GREAT

DUNCAN

ROAD

Margaret

Christmas

HIGHWAY

Creek

istmas Creek

Creek

Wolfe Creek
Meteorite Crater
Carranya

TANAMI

DESERT

N

INTRODUCTION

The region, the project and the people

I N the northern ranges of the Kimberley, European pastoral settlement began in 1903, with a second phase of intense settlement from 1920. The recent settlement in this region meant that some of those who had experienced both 'first contact' and the arrival of welfare were still alive into the 1990s. They were children of the frontier who had survived the two mass movements in Kimberley history: the move towards pastoral stations in the 'early days' of the twentieth century and then away from them in the 1960s and '70s.

This book places Aboriginal life story narratives in a wider historical context, drawing on written archives and a range of oral testimonies about the origins and development of the pastoral system in the north and central Kimberley. It examines Aboriginal pastoral workers' life stories within the broader economic and political context which affected the process of incorporating northern ranges people into the Australian nation.

In the 1960s a model of culture change from contact to 'intelligent parasitism', developed by the influential anthropologist A.P. Elkin, became the basis for arguments against paying Aboriginal pastoral workers a wage equal to other workers. Presenting the case against equal pay within the pastoral industry to the 1965 Commonwealth Arbitration Commission, John Kerr painted a dismal picture of Aboriginal people's inevitable demise into welfare dependency through lack of employment and reversion to inflexible cultural traditions.[1] He argued that Professor Elkin's article on 'intelligent parasitism' showed that Aboriginal people cooperated with pastoral 'Bosses' only so far as they were culturally able. Kerr also argued that they neither desired European material objects nor wished to place pastoral work above their own religious and cultural interests. Aboriginal people were actively engaged in the pastoral industry because they had to be. Kerr told the commission that:

> parasitism represented an adjustment from one form of parasitism to another, but it is intelligent because those who engaged in it, whilst wishing to preserve their own way of life, depart from it only in the most limited way, depart from it only to an extent which is just sufficient to enable the settler or pastoralist to carry on his property and to give them certain articles which they desire in return.[2]

Elkin's analysis was used to support Kerr's argument on behalf of pastoral interests that in Aboriginal culture there was a 'lack of interest in consistent work' and an 'inability or unwillingness to look after the future'.[3]

After the hearings, the editor of *The Australian* commented on how this case, more than any other in the history of arbitration, brought to light 'fascinating' anthropological and cultural information, which demonstrated convincingly that Aboriginal people were not worth equal wages.[4] Cultural traditions had been interpreted publicly and politically to the disadvantage of Aboriginal people. The 1965 wage hearings and later amendments, and related hearings in 1966, '67 and '68, received extensive press coverage.[5] The ensuing debate turned on arguments that undermined Aboriginal people's economic importance to the industry and that, unlike *terra nullius*, are yet to be revised.[6]

The mass migrations of the 1960s and '70s transformed most station 'mobs' into unemployed or underemployed town camp dwellers. By 1971, small reserves on the outskirts of Kimberley towns, which had catered for between twenty and forty people in the 1950s, held up to 300 residents who had previously lived on pastoral stations. These overcrowded and unserviced fringe camps were thought to contain people displaced from station employment by the decision to enforce equal wages for Aborigines in the pastoral industry. But one of my contentions in this book is that the social and economic foundations of the old rationing system, on most of the stations in the northern Kimberley, were crumbling before the award wages decision and its application in 1969. The 'eviction after award wages' theme underestimates Aboriginal agency in the migration process and fails to take account of their changing social and economic requirements and the pull of welfare support and amenities. It glorifies the period of 'settlement' on stations and reinforces the myth of the 'lazy native', which under-pinned public debate and Arbitration Commission discussions in the 1960s about the inclusion of Aboriginal workers within the Pastoral Industry Award.

Pastoral paternalism framed the majority of Indigenous people's experiences in the Kimberley, much of the Pilbara, and other parts of northern Australia.[7] The northern communities along the Gibb River Road in the Kimberley have enabled me to examine the practice and complexities of this paternalism in the context of the very recent transformation in relations between management and 'mob'. I have been able to explore the multifaceted interactions between Aboriginal people, management and government which developed on pastoral stations from first contact to the 1960s, when welfare and wages reached Kimberley stations. Importantly, these northern stations are also a reminder that many of those who experi-enced first contact were alive or only recently deceased in the 1980s and '90s when I was carrying out my study, and their children continue to manage social and economic relations forged on a very recent frontier.[8]

Ngarinyin station people and the Gibb River Road

Derby is a small country town in the far north of Western Australia 2,300 kilometres from Perth. There are two roads across the Kimberley, both of them over 600 kilometres long. One, the main sealed road, goes east from Derby along the Fitzroy valley, linking the ports at Derby and Wyndham with the areas of first pastoral settlement and the gold rush in the 1880s. The other, the Gibb River Road, was surveyed from 1954 and constructed for beef trucks in the late 1960s.[9] It goes north-east across the ranges.

When you travel along the Gibb River Road, you follow a well-worn path past station signposts: Meda, Kimberley Downs, Napier, Mount House, Beverley Springs, Mornington, Mount Barnett, Mount Elizabeth, Gibb River and Kurunjie. You drive over the Napier Ranges, the King Leopold Ranges, and further north-east into the Caroline and Packhorse Ranges. There are row upon row of almost vertical faces of ancient and jagged rock that stand between the flat lands of the Fitzroy valley and Ngarinyin country. At first the land is covered with short grasses dotted with occasional flat-topped hills with boab or bottle trees growing out of the sides, and small Unggumi trees shaped like large television antennas stand out on the plains leading into the foothills. There are native pines and pockets of palms filling cracks in the sides of the hills, where water will trickle or even rush if there's a heavy wet. Near Mount Barnett and deep into ranges country, the vistas are spectacular and the waterholes clean and surrounded by reeds and flat granite rocks. The box trees with their dark trunks give the impression of a wooded understorey, an unusual image for the spinifex and red dust of northern Australia. The wet season, from December to April, is also the hottest season. It is hot, very hot, for most of the year.

From 1989 until 1994 I visited communities along the Gibb River Road to research the complex historical relationships which were negotiated from first contact in the northern and central Kimberley ranges between pastoral Bosses and Aboriginal people and then with Welfare. Howard Coate, who had travelled across the ranges since 1934, took me north on his weekly evangelizing trip to the Aboriginal communities who were returning to reoccupy land.

We would stop at Sadler's Creek Crossing and sit in the water in the middle of the road to eat sandwiches, cool down and literally wash the dust out of our eyes. It was a seven-hour rough road trip to Mount Barnett, then called Kupingari Aboriginal Community. Coate also stopped at the Imintji Community, a small lease excised by state government grant from the Mount House pastoral lease and occupied by Aboriginal people. He began his Bible reading in Ngarinyin language and then sold second-hand clothes. By 1996 the road had been reconstructed and river crossings laid down. Wilderness tourism flourished, and more than 3,000 campers visited Bell Gorge, near Sadler's Creek, in two months.[10] By then only fools sat in the middle of the road for more than a few minutes during the tourist season.

The Gibb River Road enhanced mobility and thus the range of influences, services and activities open to Aboriginal people in the northern and central ranges. The Mowanjum mission truck, from the reserve outside Derby, arrived at Mount Elizabeth station for wet season ceremonies within weeks of completion of the roadworks across the Phillips Ranges in 1969.[11] In recent years, Aboriginal communities have based themselves near the road, either near the old station homesteads or at sites that maximize vehicle access from Kalumburu on the north coast to Derby in the south. The road, despite being a recent phenomenon cutting across old station cart tracks, walking tracks and dreaming tracks and linking language groups, provides a contemporary regional identifier for the people occupying the area north-east of Derby.[12] The region is also known as 'over the ranges', popularized in the 1930s by Ion Idriess's books *Over the Range* and *Outlaws of the Leopold*.[13] Banjo Woorunmurra, co-author of *Jandamarra: The Bunuba Resistance*, stated that he and his contemporaries were 'ranges cowboys'. These are not identifiers that north Kimberley Aboriginal people often use for their cultural markers, but they are part of the history of contact in the northern Kimberley, and significant factors in the nature of pastoral development and relations with Indigenous people.

The majority of the older Aboriginal informants to this research are identified as a cultural entity by their Wandjina-Ungud religion.[14] They also spoke or understood Ngarinyin language and from 1996 were increasingly being represented as a distinct socio-political entity, the 'Ngarinyin people', with 'Ngarinyin country' being the central and northern ranges area north of Derby.[15] They spoke mostly Ngarinyin language, but they also spoke or understood neighbouring languages: Unggumi, Nyigina, Bunuba, Kija, Worrora and Wunambal. However, in this book I have not focused on storytellers' Indigenous language, religious underpinnings and clan-based social system, but rather on their post-contact historical relationships and negotiations with Europeans, and the structures in which they became enmeshed as they moved in and out of the pastoral station system. I chose to work mainly with people who spoke Ngarinyin because this was also a practical point of entry for me as a researcher. It placed limits on the language variables for the fieldwork process, and it took me into the areas north of Derby where people continued to live and work with the 'Boss' and 'Missus' on pastoral stations. It was not only helpful but necessary to understand some Ngarinyin language, to be able to stay in their communities and hear the names and places which are scattered throughout all older people's narratives.

Older storytellers usually spoke at least three languages, including one from their mother's or father's side or from their having moved into a different language region with a marriage partner for work or as a result of institutionalization. All storytellers spoke Aboriginal English in addition to Indigenous languages. Identifying as a part of a station 'mob' sometimes, but not always, coincided with land and language identifiers. Storytellers living at different stations were connected through the landowning system. Most storytellers knew where their country was, who owned it and who was looking after it.[16] In addition, most informants had occupied or lived near their country as pastoral workers. Morndingali, or Morndi Munro, with whom I worked intensively for two years to produce his collection of station narratives, *Emerarra: A Man of Merarra*, spoke five languages and could 'hear' at least three more.[17] His mother was a Ngarinyin speaker and landowner from near Mount Barnett, and his father spoke his 'private language', Unggumi. His grandmother, who trained him in important social obligations and taboos when he was a child, spoke another language, possibly Umide, which is no longer heard in the Kimberley. His father's brothers, who taught Morndingali to work on the station, spoke Bunuba. They all worked at Napier station. Morndingali also moved to work in the desert and learned some Walmatjarri, taking part in ceremonies there and hoping to be given a wife from that area. But when asked who he was, he was Emerarra, a man of his father's and grandfather's clan country, Merarra, which runs north along the Isdell River to a point where salt water meets fresh water near Walcott Inlet.[18]

At the Derby reserve and the stations north along the Gibb River Road, there were people who had come onto the stations as children and who had experienced the period of Welfare intervention and migration of the 1960s and '70s as significant members of the station workforce. In 1989 Willie Lennard and his family had only just arrived from Meda station after around fifty years of work there. The new manager burned down the house and sent them to town.[19] At Karmalinanga reserve I worked with Morndingali, his wives Weeda Munro and Daisy Angajit, his son Jack Dann and wife Rita Laylay, Jack Dale and his wife Biddy Rinjaworla, Freddy Marker and his sister Maudie Lennard, Ginger Warrebeen, Wallace Midmee and Mabel King.

David Mowaljarlai assisted often with discussions and formal interpreting of Ngarinyin. He was part of the Mowanjum Community, fifteen kilometres from Derby at the start of the Gibb River Road. Two hundred and fifty people speaking one or more of the related languages Ngarinyin, Worrora and Wunambal live at Mowanjum. The older adults are mostly people who were moved to Derby in the 1950s from their isolated coastal missions, Kunmunya, Wotjulum and Munja. Their various countries are from 150 to 600 kilometres from Derby. The next community east along the Gibb River Road is Winjingare, a small excision on Napier station owned by Morndingali and his family.

The Imintji Community is another small one-mile-square excision, 230 kilometres from Derby, north of the King Leopold Ranges on the Mount House station lease. In 1989, when I made my first visit, about sixty people were living in recently constructed houses, tents and tin shelters. There was a reliable water supply and electricity, but no school, no store and no on-site administrative support. A state welfare authority officer visited weekly with stores and pension money. The chairman, Jack Dale, had worked at Mount House station and then moved in the 1950s to do contract mustering on nearby stations. In 1983, Dale argued with the manager at Beverley Springs and joined his relatives from Mount House, Tableland and Silent Grove to form an Aboriginal community at Imintji, alternatively known as Sadler Springs. At various times over the next four years, Jack Dale looked after me in the Mount Hart, Beverley Springs, Silent Grove and Mount House area, pointing out aspects of the country and sharing many life story experiences for the purposes of my research and for his private collection. From 1994 to '98 I lived in Derby and continued to refer to him and his wife Biddy Rinjaworla for advice.

Tirralintji Community members also stayed at Imintji during the wet season. Tirralintji was a bush camp, with plastic and steel-framed shelters and a solar-powered cool room, 100 kilometres to the east of Imintji, with rough access through the Mount House lease during the dry season only. The community was a family group of approximately twenty-five ex-workers from Tableland station led by Jack Jowan and Mick Jowalji, the ex-head stockman. Jowan, Jowalji and Jowalji's sister Barbara Midmee, along with their spouses, were first-generation station workers. Barbara Midmee was a classificatory daughter to Morndingali and my constant source of advice on bush foods, fishing holes, station work and early days stories. Her niece, Betty Walker, became community chairperson in 1992. This core group refused to leave the Tableland area when, in 1983, they walked off from the homestead camp to a bush site forty kilometres towards Mount House. In 1990 they were still there, living on bush resources and stores brought out by a community welfare officer. In 1992 Commonwealth funding provided them with permanent shelters at the Imintji site and a new truck. They had never come to town to live, and in November 1994, after acquiring title to the Tableland pastoral lease under the name of the Yulumbu Aboriginal Community, they were adamant that they would never have to. Jack Jowan remained at Tirralintji in his bush hut with two daughters and their husbands and children.

Mount Barnett station is 100 kilometres north of Imintji, along the Gibb River Road just north of the Phillips Ranges, and

312 kilometres from Derby. It became also known as Kupingarri, after it was resettled in 1989 by traditional owners. Many of the older people referred to Mount Barnett as the 'mission' because UAM missionaries camped there in the 1930s and later worked teams of Aboriginal people to build the existing homestead. But it was never an official mission. There I worked mostly with Maggie Gudaworla and Billy King, the chairman and station manager.

Billy King was head stockman at Mount House until 1972. He helped old traditional owners Joe Jorda and Dutchie Bunggurt return to their clan land at Mount Barnett. Bunggurt had been forced to leave his area in the 1920s and take refuge at Kunmunya mission. He moved to Derby with the Mowanjum mission people and then to Imintji. Bunggurt was Harry Howendon's older brother and remembered seeing the police when they first came to Mount Barnett pre-1910. Maggie Gudaworla was a highly respected linguist, storyteller and custodian of songs and law, and contributor to most of the anthropological studies conducted in the previous twenty years in the Mount Barnett region.[20] She was Morndingali's classificatory wife and corrected some of his stories after I read them to her.

In 1989 approximately sixty people lived in the old Mount Barnett station shelters about 100 metres from the homestead. Two white employees managed the store and the accounts, and gave general advice to the community. During my field visits along the Gibb River Road from 1989 to 1994, the community grew dramatically to resemble a township. It was moved from the station homestead site to a more accessible position south of the Barnett River and adjacent to the Gibb River Road. It had a government school, clinic, large store and fuel station, 260 members, nine white staff, a tourist camping area at the main gorge and waterhole, and a range of new houses. In 1992, 6,424 tourists visited the camping site.[21] It was also a working pastoral station. Billy King moved into the old homestead as station manager and chairman of Kupingarri. Morndingali's eldest classificatory son and custodian for Merarra became chairman of Kupingarri in 1997, with his wife as the female chairperson.

Gibb River station is 100 kilometres from Mount Barnett along the Gibb River Road, with the Mount Elizabeth turn-off almost halfway between these two communities. The station was bought back in 1989 for the traditional owners, and the old head stockman, Alphie White, was made chairman in 1994. On my first visit to Gibb River station, the community lived in the old iron 'blacks' camp', without access to running water, electricity or a store. By 1994 there were eighty members living in new housing and a single men's quarters, all serviced with power and water. There was a store for basic foods (ice-creams, lollies, bread and packaged meat were sold from the old Missus' verandah) and a new Catholic primary school. It was also a working pastoral station. There I worked mostly with Maggie Ghi, Rosie Mamangulya, Maudie White and Susie Umungul, who were all born in the bush and came into stations as children. The previous owners of Gibb River had moved into town, except for one son, who was the mechanic, and his wife, the bookkeeper. This couple weathered the transfer of ownership to the community and became paid employees on their old station.

At Gibb River, Mount Barnett and Mount Elizabeth, I worked with Campbell Allenbrae, ex-head stockman of Kurunjie station, another 100 kilometres east of Gibb River station towards Wyndham. He taught me the small amount of Ngarinyin language I was able to master, translated interviews in Ngarinyin language, discussed and recorded his own station stories, assisted Morndingali at the reserve with his book, and was my primary caretaker during my stays there in 1990, '91 and '92.

In 1989, when I began my research, the living and working conditions at Mount Elizabeth, Mount Barnett and Gibb River were representative of other stations across the Kimberley until the 1970s. They were dominated by a homestead, with a nearby store and what was once called 'the blacks' camp' made up of small corrugated iron sheds. Mount Elizabeth showed least signs of physical change. Just beyond the workers' camp the tiny pensioner huts were all empty; all the old pensioners who had come to the station as young men with the old manager had died. The middle-aged 'girls' wearing loose printed cotton shifts were quietly sweeping the house while an older woman swept leaves in the garden. They worked for the Missus and the Boss. Men in cowboy-style clothing moved among horses at the yards just metres from the homestead, watched by young children swinging from the yard rails. At four o'clock people began to move towards the station store, where the Missus booked up food, tobacco, cool drinks and clothes. The women who worked in the house washed every afternoon before they visited the store, then moved on to the late afternoon housework. The smell of scented soap filled the storeroom verandah. In the evenings, small groups sat by camp fires while an old bushman, Dicky Udmorrah, and the traditional owner for the homestead area, Harry Howendon, sang songs and told stories. The air was permeated with the scent of local pine, called 'kooroo' by Aboriginal people, split from old fence posts and placed on milk tin lids near each camp to keep them free of mosquitos. The inevitable camp dogs moved about in search of scraps or plates left on the ground or on the old wire beds which doubled as shelves.

During my research it became clear that many of the station people saw Mount Elizabeth as a refuge from the social problems of town, and they shared some of the manager's resistance to outsiders. While this resistance can be viewed as enhancing management's control of 'their' group, Indigenous people also had an investment in it. After sitting through the noise, confusion and frequent violence of Derby town reserve, I was impressed with Mount Elizabeth's comparative peace and cultural self-sufficiency: its huge shade trees, peacocks, children and teenagers playing music, old people with their packs of dogs, and especially the regular and spontaneous storytelling and music-making. I also noticed that when social security representatives came to the station they went straight to Pat Lacy, the Missus, not to the camps, and she provided the necessary information. She had put time and effort into managing social security and a range of service deliverers to make the transition from rations to a Commonwealth-funded Aboriginal community coexisting with a private pastoral lease.

The Boss still went out with the muster camps, still picked up workers and sat at the sheds with the 'boys' tinkering with vehicles, plaiting nylon ropes and hatbands, and talking about the weather and the stock. He had significant knowledge of sites on the lease, passed to him by old Aboriginal men. But Pat Lacy was expressing profound doubts that the group would survive contact with certain aspects of the outside world, particularly grog.[22] She gave many examples of the deterioration in living standards, health and group discipline, and the new language of greed and violent conflict that came with the shift away from the station manager's protection and their now unrestricted access to vehicles. She was distressed at the changes in people she had 'looked after' and managed for twenty years and her husband had known intimately since he was a small child.

With the provision of outside services, management's protective and domestic role began to alter, and they were faced with the possibility that they were now only a temporary resource about whom the community was ambivalent. The managers at Mount Elizabeth, especially the Missus, were confronting the double-edged sword of paternalism built on acts of kindness within unequal power relations and distinctive cultural systems. They were faced with the burden of having been intimate strangers for thirty to forty years. Pat Lacy's statements echoed those of the plantation owners in America over 100 years before: 'It is the slaves who own me. Morning, noon, and night, I'm obliged to look after them, to doctor them, and to attend to them in every way.'[23] The Missus was struggling to reconcile underlying tensions and conflicts that had been created by the pastoral system in the northern ranges since first contact in 1903.

Change had been slow at Mount Elizabeth partly because of the physical isolation from towns and government welfare agencies. The thirty-five-kilometre stony track from the Gibb River Road, 380 kilometres north-east of Derby, was not accessible for five months of the year. But a range of other factors, including the nature of the industry, government policies and the social organization of the Indigenous people, also contributed to the conservative nature of the community and their Bosses.

'Gardia coming'[24]—oral history and 'fieldwork'

This book is particularly concerned with the interactions between pastoralists, Aborigines and the state, in an area where welfare arrived only recently and white station personnel wrote very little.

Consequently, oral sources are vital for understanding what happened. By far the majority of the people who lived in the north and central Kimberley and formed the station communities were Aboriginal. Their oral testimony forms the basis for this research. However, while attempting to show the importance of oral sources to the inclusion of Aboriginal people and poor or fringe whites in Australian history, I am not assuming that one form of information is inherently more authentic than the other, or more or less reliable.[25] Aboriginal oral sources require analysis and contextualization, just as written documents do.

I have drawn on information from twelve key storytellers who worked on stations north of Derby. Extensive taped interviewing and notations on discussions and observations recorded in field notebooks were collated to build select biographies. By 'select' I mean that I had specific questions I wanted to answer, dealing with recollections of the period of meeting a white Boss, becoming a worker, the introduction of welfare and wages, and the move off the stations.

I have tried to avoid oppositional modelling of contact relations which relegates Indigenous people to either victim or resistance status. Equally, it is fruitful to view the emergence of welfare in the north as an extension of a colonial relationship in which Aboriginal people are active and interested but less powerful. In the sphere of local relations and everyday occurrences, the colonizing project is never complete domination, nor entirely successful: 'distinctive forms of Indigenous sociality and politics contribute in a crucial way to the dynamics of accommodation and resistance constitutive of colonial history'.[26] The broader economic and political context, which affected the process of incorporating northern ranges people into the Australian nation, can be understood by examining, through individual contacts and biographies, the patterns of alliances with Bosses and the impact of welfare on those relationships. The impact of welfare and bureaucracy on Aboriginal people's capacity to speak about traumatic pasts is also taken into account.

Working with older Kimberley Aboriginal people means that complex rules of ownership of information govern who will tell

Faces from the past: some of the storytellers

1 *Weeda Munro.* Copyright Kevin Shaw
2 *Daisy Beharrell.* Copyright Kevin Shaw
3 *Campbell Allenbrae.* Copyright Rod Taylor
4 *Jilki Edwards.* Copyright M.A. Jebb
5 *Barbara Midmee.* Copyright M.A. Jebb
6 *Scotty Martin.* Copyright M.A. Jebb
7 *Banjo Woorunmurra.* Copyright Howard Pedersen
8 *Dickie Udmorrah.* Copyright M.A. Jebb
9 *Billy Munro (Morndingali).* Copyright M.A. Jebb
10 *Jack Jowan.* Copyright Rein van de Ruit
11 *Jack Dale.* Copyright Rein van de Ruit
12 *Mick Jowalji.* Copyright Rein van de Ruit

6

7

8

9

10

11

12

stories and what they will tell. Not all information was easily understood—in fact, a great deal was inaccessible. While there are some
songs and creation stories that are immutable, oral testimony is very
much alive and dynamic in the Kimberley region. Some narratives
recorded for this research related to events or activities without a
chronological frame. Most, however, named characters, events or
places which, through juxtaposition with written records and other
oral interviews, placed the narrative within a chronological frame.

The standard oral history 'interview' is complicated by the
cross-cultural context.[27] Many tapes have more than one speaker and
alternate between discussion and monologue.[28] Others were conducted under trees, near rivers or in camps with dogs and children
playing and fighting nearby. I advocate this approach because it
enables speakers and their peers to overcome different cultural
modes of expression, language and uses of oral narratives. It also
helps me to provide culturally appropriate questions and responses
to storytellers, and facilitates the passing on of stories to other
Aboriginal people within the research process.

Older Aboriginal people often used terms like 'half-caste' and
'full-blood' but without the prejudice imbued by the system of laws
and institutions that spawned them. Throughout the book I have
continued to use these terms to describe differing experiences or
policies based on caste, without placing them in parenthesis. Aboriginal people also used 'Welfare' to mean all outside government
agencies—the Aborigines Department, Native Affairs, Native Welfare
and Child Welfare. 'Boss' and 'Missus' are capitalized because they
are used by storytellers as titles for the manager and his wife.

The referencing style in this book follows standard empirical
systems. For oral information and observation, I have indicated
names and dates of taped conversations or names, page numbers
and dates from my field notebooks. Names of people are included
in the text unless I have been instructed by the informant or their
immediate family to delete them. This capacity to control elements
of the product was part of the research contract with storytellers,
who automatically own the copyright on taped information.

By utilizing oral testimony and working with Aboriginal
people in a collaborative manner, I was consistently drawn from a

narrow period and focus—the social impact of equal wages on station workers in the Kimberley in the 1960s and '70s—towards a wider range of life story narratives. Interviewees told and retold stories of an earlier period, when they were children or before they were born, as explanatory devices for their collective history. They talked about aspects of their work on the stations, 'holidays' in the bush, living conditions and their contacts with the Native Welfare Department in the 1950s. These early days narratives became a framework to explain their changing relationship with the Bosses and the pastoral system.[29] I have also researched these stories to date them and to establish the identity of some of the people involved. The research shows how individuals struggled to negotiate and manage their interactions with Europeans and the various government agencies associated with the pastoral industry. It also shows how individuals continued to negotiate and manage their economic dependency, so that they were 'waiting' at the reserve in the 1990s rather than being 'stuck' there.

Ion Idriess and the archives

The written records that helped to establish a chronological framework for events and changes in the relationships between police, pastoralists and Aboriginal people in the region also provided documentary evidence for patterns of pastoral development, and for official government policies concerning police, pastoralism and the protection of Aboriginal people. They supplemented oral testimonies and in some cases added new and important information about deaths, disappearances and removal of children.

Written documentation includes files from the various government departments which had an interest in surveying, settling and servicing the region north of Derby. The police were the major source of written historical information from 1903 to 1948. After that period, there are about 400 Kimberley region files from the West Australian Departments of Native Welfare and Aboriginal Affairs, which embrace what were seen to be welfare issues for the towns and the 100 pastoral stations.[30] They provide a detailed record of the introduction of welfare services to Kimberley pastoral stations, covering the introduction of equal wages in the pastoral industry and Commonwealth social security benefits.

Other written sources for the period before 1948, when Aboriginal Affairs developed a patrol system into the northern region, include observations from missionaries and anthropologists. The coastal missions at Kalumburu and Kunmunya and the government ration station at Munja attracted scientists researching Aboriginal culture, religion, languages, health and physical characteristics.[31] The majority of white people who made the history and formed the station communities in the northern ranges region either did not or could not write. Fortunately, Frank Lacy of Mount Elizabeth station was an exception.

Of all the documentary sources, Ion Idriess's *Over the Range* and, to a lesser extent, *One Wet Season* created the most interest amongst storytellers.[32] These books paint a benign picture of the settlement process in the north Kimberley in the early 1930s. Set in Ngarinyin country and the stations north of Derby to Gibb River, they include some of the storytellers, their relatives and white Bosses as characters. Idriess's image of the wild northern ranges fired the public imagination about the northern Kimberley, and, despite sometimes offensive caricatures of Indigenous people, he made useful historical observations on paternalism. His books are particularly helpful for understanding something of the culture of the 'early days white men' who lived on the fringe of white society and chose 'over the ranges' as their domain.

> Although the East and West Kimberleys are now settled the country over the range is not. Although the tribesmen are fast entering the 'iron age' (and alas fast vanishing under disease) old Felix always has a revolver handy—must never be without one when he leaves the house; for some of these Aboriginals are 'sulky feller'. The danger is aggravated when the *munjons* come down from the hills.[33]

While it is tempting to dismiss Idriess's perspective of life in the ranges area as an anachronism that is mostly insulting to

Indigenous people, his books are useful social documents for developing a picture of a fringe community. They are also essential for understanding the enduring public image of, for instance, the 'wild girls of the hills'—a label he attached to Weeda Munro and her sisters who were the stockriding team at Mount Hart station in the 1930s. *Over the Range: Sunshine and Shadows in the Kimberley* appeared in November 1937 and sold 10,000 copies in a fortnight.[34] By December 1937 it was in its fourth edition and was still being printed in the 1950s.

Idriess avoided writing anything which suggested that immorality, exploitation or avoidable conflict occurred between settlers and Indigenous people.[35] His biographer, Beverly Eley, who had access to his private journals and correspondence, suggested that he wanted to protect his mates and acquaintances from gossip and innuendo, and from being blamed for wrongdoings to Aboriginal people. He was an image maker as well as a documenter of his travels and recorder of oral history. His images of the north encouraged southerners' pride in the white men (and very occasionally white women) who settled it for the sake of civilization and the Australian nation. In doing so, he wholeheartedly embraced the ideals of the pioneer myth which celebrated white men's determination, bravery, foresight, endurance, resourcefulness and heroism in the grand colonial project of civilizing and occupying a vast and dangerous land. In the same vein, he utilized the conventional imagery of colonial writers whose work excluded Indigenous people from a role in the future development of the north, portraying them as exotic, manipulative and childlike. And like other writers of the 1930s and '40s, he lamented their passing as an unavoidable by-product of progress which resulted in different types of people coming into evolutionary competition rather than active conflict with each other.[36]

Despite the overriding tendency in Idriess's works to infantilize Aboriginal people, he was enthusiastic about incorporating them as identified characters who occupied places they had named, rather than a silent backdrop in an empty land. He also characterized them as belonging to a domestic sphere. Although the Indigenous family was presented as inferior to white civilization, Indigenous characters were socially related to one another within a family framework that was recognizable to readers.[37] They were not just the 'Natives'—they were fathers, uncles, wives and children. He also extended and varied the pioneer myth by introducing and examining mounted police practices and the peripheral white men in the colonial project: the stockmen and bushies who became 'chronics' (drunkards) when they got to town. This interaction and dialogue between white men and Aboriginal people is particularly evident in *Over the Range* and *One Wet Season*. Here Idriess expanded from his focus on the lone hero, the mounted policeman, to include the not so heroic but still active and interested trackers, 'nomad whites' and Indigenous people resisting a European regime.

When Idriess arrived in Derby in 1934 to observe the mounted patrols, he wrote to his publishers that although there were only a handful of white men in the north Kimberley, the region and the characters were colourful and exciting.[38] These were 'the badlands' north of Derby where few outsiders would travel. They had the ingredients for Idriess to stir suburban interest—Australia's own wild west made more exotic by the 'stone age' people. Descriptions of Derby wharf, the township, the police station and lockup, Aboriginal trackers and the native hospital, where lepers were held in a wire compound, are all vivid pictures of a small frontier town with a population of about 200 white people and few motorized vehicles. The characters at the Port Hotel were drunks and storytellers who had arrived in town for the wet season. There they spent their cheques and waited for the season to break, when they would return to the stations. These are the men who slip through official histories, the 'loners' who follow frontiers from Queensland, the east Kimberley, the Pilbara and even further afield.

Although Idriess utilized standard colonial images of the good and civilized whites versus the 'stone age' and essentially bad blacks, the ranges provided him with a geographic and metaphorical boundary where extraordinary events and relationships could be rationalized. At the same time he was committed to silences which collapsed the process of settlement in the region into the period and picture he described. Preceding events, as well as issues of direct white violence, terror, fear, coercion or sexual intimacy between

Old stockmen and characters from over the ranges came to Derby for the wet season. Copyright Battye Library, 66500P

black and white were not central features of the scene. But, as Idriess described it, the ranges region was not an uncontested picture of harmonious settlement by white pioneers: it was 'unsettled' and consisted of tensions and struggles for all the characters.

William Chalmers, co-owner of Mount Hart station was, according to Idriess,

> a great worker and a quiet shrewd man ... Occasionally a bit wild, hardly to be wondered at in the then untamed country with its primitive environment and its wild men both white and black. And the only women were wild women.[39]

The white men of the ranges remained unsettled, living in bark huts with earth floors, talking to their dogs and without white wives. They had a tenuous link with the classical image of a successful white pioneer.

> Mount Hart is a frontier station; hard to realise that such still exists in Australia. The homestead was really one big shed, bare walls, open doors placed so that at a glance any one moving in the country behind or in front can be seen. The only window has a heavy wooden shutter that at a touch drops into place ... everything is rough strong and serviceable ... Handy on the walls are guns and rifles; the needed belt with heavy revolver is slung across the table.[40]

Without white women, Idriess's white men on the frontiers of civilization acted out a romantic drama with the land. However, in the ranges region the majority of white occupants were not primarily engaged in dominating the land or becoming landed gentlemen and husbands.

A relationship of control without intimacy or extreme outbursts of violence was carried into white men's transactions with Aboriginal women. For the men in this region, the criteria of a white man's civility were not having a 'bush black' for a wife and not losing control of your temper. Idriess was careful not to portray Aboriginal women as wives or potential wives, but they were not excluded from his picture of the north. That would have involved an extraordinary fiction, for Aboriginal women and girls were to be found wherever there was a white man's hut. There were very few children in the bush in the 1930s and more men than women,[41] but on the stations there were many women. The fact that they were never placed in a white man's bed was consistent with the dominant European view which excluded them from that realm of domestic intimacy and was backed by legislation aimed at preventing cohabitation.

The only man whom Idriess described as having several children and two wives was also described as brutal, cruel, fearless and unwilling to cooperate with police, trackers or station whites.

Oomagun moved in the Mount Elizabeth and Gibb River area in the 1930s. Idriess stated that he smiled and spoke softly when white men approached and appeared 'slightly amused, but not interested':

> If all aboriginals had his mental as well as physical strength, Authority would have a hectic time in first catching the wrong doers, and then in proving anything against them.[42]

Like Ernestine Hill in the Northern Territory, Idriess arrived in the north to write about the struggles of the settlement process without blaming any white people or damaging the image of Australia as a developing and 'fair' nation.[43] But in the northern ranges, the Derby pub and police records, Idriess found relationships and practices which underlined the notion of an active struggle between Europeans and Indigenous people, and between white men and the environment, evocative of violent and unsettled times. He reassured his huge readership that this phase of unsettled relationships was passing. The white nomads, like the Aboriginal people, belonged to a transient stage. He salvaged the nomad whites who occupied the frontiers by portraying them with police as protectors who were assisting Aboriginal people to negotiate the impact of civilization while introducing an element of control into their lives. At the same time he reinvented the mounted policeman as a combination of the bushman and Anzac hero. While Idriess suggested that there were problems emerging in the 1930s over marriage arrangements, he focused on the struggle between Aboriginal men and women, rather than recognizing a wider and more significant manifestation of contact experience and the potential social and economic impact of a small number of white men.

Idriess wanted to present even the nomad whites as honourable men, but this picture was not supported by oral evidence and Idriess himself calls it into question. *Over the Range* describes groups of Aboriginal men moving from station to station and in the bush in the early 1930s, but Idriess overstated their capacity to injure white men, encouraging dramatic tension by condensing thirty years of contact history into a 'moment' that did not exist. The struggle to retain and train Aboriginal women was an important factor in developing a station workforce. But the actual methods of capture and control were completely missing from the ideal picture of settlement and from Idriess's more expansive view of interactions between white men and Aboriginal people in the 'unsettled' northern regions. Idriess was silent on the value of Aboriginal women to white men, except for their capacity to work, and thus failed to acknowledge the potential for conflict derived from their alliances with white men. He also failed to associate the 'outlaw groups' who were moving from station to station in the 1930s with Aboriginal women's captivity on the stations, a theme which will be explored in later chapters.

CHAPTER ONE

Battle for the New Country, 1903–1914

[W]e are dealing with a question which requires a very firm hand: the natives in these northern districts far outnumber the whites, and being for the most part wild, unreasoning creatures, it would lead to a great disaster should they once get the idea that they can overpower their employers ... my work is mainly for the benefit and protection of these natives and not for any harsh repression, yet I consider that firmness exercised in a manner which they only understand will in the end be more to their benefit than a weak toleration of their lawlessness.

Henry Prinsep, Chief Protector of Aborigines, 1906[1]

AS the newly federated nation of Australia moved into the twentieth century, the West Australian government opened the land north of the King Leopold Ranges, Ngarinyin country, for pastoral leasing. Between 1903 and 1909, Ngarinyin people of the Kimberley ranges experienced an intense wave of police activity to suppress resistance. Ngarinyin storytellers Maggie Gudaworla, Harry Howendon, Jack Jowan, Mick Jowalji,

Morndi Munro and Rosie Mamangulya were born towards the end of this period. They lived to retell their parents' tales of survival and meeting the 'early days' white men who occupied their country.

In addition to the oral tradition, written historical information about events and relationships with white men during the time can be found in records from the Isdell police post near Mount Barnett station, from its inception in 1903 to its closure in 1914.[2] Police and trackers associated with this post patrolled or travelled through the region from Derby to Gibb River in the north, raiding camps, arresting people and removing many to gaols in Derby, Broome and Roebourne. The police at the Isdell post concentrated their activities on the area of land that surrounded the pastoral leases at Mount Hart, Mount House, Mount Barnett, Isdell River and Grace's Knob. Their role was to help white stockmen extend the boundaries of European occupation in the Kimberley into 'the new country north of the King Leopold Ranges'.[3] At the same time they were also patrolling and safeguarding the older leases to the south, nearer the Napier Ranges.

Although, in this period, relationships between white men and Aboriginal people were circumscribed by matters of life and death, not everyone was in the same danger. Some people found protection from the exigencies of white occupation in their relationships with white stockmen and the police parties who assisted in the pacification process. By learning the rules of occupation, they found a place that assured their survival and laid the groundwork for their children's incorporation into the station system. This is not to suggest that these relationships were based on mutual respect or complete unity of interest: the circumstances in which they were made and maintained involved instances of violence, coercion, social dislocation and fear. They became, however, more than loose associations between victims and aggressors. These white men also kept some people alive, introduced them to the world of work, and occasionally fathered and maintained their children and members of their families. This complex dynamic between violence and protection formed the basis for paternalism, which was as an enduring characteristic of station culture and life with a white Boss.

First contact in Ngarinyin country

In 1837 Sir George Grey led a British expedition to the north Kimberley coast, hoping to complete the first overland surveys from the north to the new Swan River Colony, a few thousand miles to the south. He was also to provide information that might lead to colonization by the British, who wanted to extend their annexation of the eastern coast to the whole of the continent.[4] Supported by the Royal Geographical Society, Grey was instructed to gather botanical information and specimens, and to 'familiarize the natives with the British name and character'. He managed to travel from Prince Regent to the King Sound along the coastal strip, but not to the Swan River or further inland into Ngarinyin country, due to 'overwhelming' Aboriginal opposition.[5] Nevertheless, Grey described the country near the coast as well watered and fertile with good prospects for pastoral settlement.

The first long-term contacts between Europeans and ranges people came in 1864, when pastoral interests from Victoria sailed across the top with women, children and sheep to begin a settlement at Camden Harbour. This extraordinary attempt failed after two years, with deaths of all the stock and some settlers and Aboriginal people. The settlers left the region to the Indigenous occupants in 1866.

In 1879 another push was made by a colonial exploration party from the Swan River settlement in the south, headed by Alexander Forrest. He remarked on the 'endless rugged zigzags of the cliffs' that forced his party to give up in 'despair' from crossing the ranges and entering Ngarinyin country.[6] The party was approached by a group of about fifty armed men who left after being given some flour and sugar; on returning later that day, they were frightened off with gun shots instead. As the party moved along the southern edges of the King Leopold Ranges from Mount Matthew to Mount Hart, Forrest remarked on the beauty of the pools and waterfalls in the region, and on its occupation by Aboriginal people:

> Native fires are very numerous about here, which shows that, although this country is entirely unsuited to Europeans, it is well adapted to the support of native existence,

The endless rugged zigzags of the cliffs of the King Leopold Ranges. Copyright M.A. Jebb

Bell Creek Falls, within the King Leopold Ranges.
Copyright Simon Neville

the natives in these high lands being in greater numbers than in the good lands below.[7]

Ngarinyin country was subject to speculative leasing in the 1880s as the Kimberley was bought and sold to various entrepreneurs, but it was not occupied by pastoralists and their cattle until after the turn of the century. On the southern fringes of Ngarinyin lands, pastoral occupation in the 1880s and 1890s followed the Robinson, Lennard and Fitzroy Rivers, where Unggumi, Nyigina and Bunuba people lived.[8] However, the ranges which had stopped Forrest from entering Ngarinyin lands in 1879 continued as a barrier to pastoral expansion until 1898.

Police patrols went into the King Leopold Ranges during the 1890s chasing alleged thieves and cattle killers. In 1892 patrols near Mount Broome on the south side of the King Leopold Ranges officially killed six Aboriginal men in retaliation for the deaths of two miners. The last Aboriginal men executed in Western Australia were taken from the King Leopold Ranges after extensive and determined patrols from 1897 to 1900.[9] The conflicts between police and Indigenous people would have had some impact on the people of the central lands, with groups or individuals moving into neighbouring country to exploit resources and for comparative safety. But these movements and interactions were not on the same scale for Ngarinyin people as those that occurred with the initiation of the Isdell police post in 1903.

Introduced diseases probably preceded the police post, but it is difficult to say what effect these had. Frank Hann, who explored the region in 1898, made no mention of illness among Indigenous people, but he was not permitted to see many of the women, children or old people. The police mentioned venereal disease in 1907, four years after the stockmen and police arrived in Ngarinyin country.

Individual prospectors may also have moved close to the central ranges in their search for gold. But until after 1905, prospectors were concentrated in and around the Mount Broome goldfields on the southern boundary of Ngarinyin country, where Bunuba, Unggumi and Nyigina intersected on the south side of the King

Leopold Ranges. After 1905 individual stockmen also prospected in the area as an adjunct to station work. Some had joined the gold rush to the Kimberley in the mid-1880s, while others accompanied Queensland and Pilbara pastoralists to open new ground. Their holiday-time specking took them outside lease boundaries and the official pastoral frontier to small camps at waterholes and creek beds. There is no evidence that these white nomads, drifting along creeks and ranges, travelled too far from the known goldfields or pastoral leases, or had a dramatic impact on Ngarinyin people. Many of the white men who came into Ngarinyin country after the turn of the century came from leases in the earlier settled districts. They brought trackers, who were also called 'private boys', and Aboriginal women with them to assist their occupation. The pattern of moving with white men had already begun for these Aboriginal people. Their initial contacts and relationships with white men probably followed a similar pattern to that which emerged in the northern ranges.

The northern ranges —'too good to be idle'

The King Leopold Ranges continued as a barrier to further exploration until May 1898, when the adventurer, pastoralist and prospector Frank Hann travelled through the area to explore, survey and report on its pastoral and mineral potential.[10] Hann, like the majority of other explorers and surveyors, took Aboriginal men and women with him. Two Aboriginal women, one with the inimical colonial name Minnie, and four Aboriginal men, who were from either Queensland or the Northern Territory, moved through the ranges country, starting at Derby and travelling north as far as Gibb and Charnley Rivers.

Hann followed the course of the Hann, Gibb, Adcock, Barnett and Isdell Rivers, naming them and hills, creeks and mountains after friends, acquaintances, relatives and government officials. Even Minnie, his long-time assistant, had a creek named after her. He named the Isdell River after his friend and benefactor James Isdell, who had rescued him from ruin the year before while prospecting in the Nullagine district. Hann viewed Isdell's kindness as a sign that he was 'a real white man'.[11] Isdell later joined the Aborigines Department and was the first Aboriginal protector to travel through the northern ranges area in 1908. Prospectors, pastoralists, explorers and adventurers were proud of their whiteness and its associated qualities. Many men, like Hann and others who came to settle the north after the turn of the century, struggled to observe a strict division between white and black and lived secret lives as husbands to Aboriginal women on the frontiers of settlement.

During his exploration of the northern ranges, Hann often recorded sightings and evidence of Aboriginal occupation. From May through to August he noted an extensive array of tracks, camp sites and fires. At Mount Clifton, just north of the prospecting camps, he saw more tracks than he had ever seen in his previous travels from the east Kimberley to the Pilbara.[12] On the Isdell River, near Isdell Gorge, the 'blacks were exceedingly numberous [sic], but whenever one of our party came into view they fled'.[13] On the Edkins Range, north of the King Leopold Ranges and west of Grace's Knob near where the police post was later situated, Hann was surprised by the density of the Indigenous population. He noted 'tracks and camps in every direction', managing to take one group by surprise:

> I got right onto them before they saw me, when they all bolted, some catching up their spears. I got some fine spear heads in that camp … left a tomahawk and some other things in camp in place of the spear heads I had taken.[14]

At the foot of Mount Caroline on the south side of the Phillips Ranges, in the centre of Ngarinyin country, he came across thirteen established graves. The next day he returned to camp to find his 'boys' using a skull for target practice, having raided the graves.

Contacts between Hann's party and Indigenous people were clearly not friendly, nor could they be called a meeting of wary but peaceable strangers. Hann expected to be attacked and was 'well armed'. He reported on several occasions shooting at groups of men who appeared on hilltops to watch the party. At a gorge near Mount Hart he noted:

> The blacks were on the main range to our left and very cheeky. They thought they had us. I put a few shots over to them which blocked them for a time. We had to go through [the] gorge. Had the blacks come on us there was no help for us as they could see us and we could not see them.[15]

When, on another occasion, a 'great number' of people shook their spears and yelled at the party, he and his 'boys' fired several shots in their direction. At Mount Clifton, nearer the prospectors' camps and in company with several other white men from the Lennard River stations, Indigenous people came towards them and Hann noted having 'got one black-fellow'.[16] It isn't clear whether this was a hit or a capture.

Capturing Aboriginal women was not unusual for Hann.[17] The women who accompanied him in the north Kimberley also prospected for gold, cooked and hunted for food. Thanks to his Aboriginal assistants he had a constant supply of fish, duck, kangaroo and possum as he moved from waterhole to waterhole in the cool season weather. During his tour of the north he 'hammered' one woman for undisclosed transgressions but did not increase the size of his group. The captured man or woman may have given information and then been released, or moved off with the white men from the Lennard River stations.

Hann was excited about the pastoral prospects in the area north of the King Leopold Ranges. He commented that he

> had no idea the country was so good. I never saw such a better watered creek in my life ... No one could believe there was such a good track and such good camps in the middle of the range. I never saw such a place or any one else, I believe.[18]

In 1898 he took up a large lease of 793,000 acres near Mount House, after drawing a sketch of the country and lodging a payment with

Dr House, the Derby resident magistrate and namesake for the new pastoral lease.[19] The lease was transferred to Joe Blythe the same year, who added it to others. Further north of the King Leopold Ranges, Hann again commented in glowing terms on the natural watercourses and deep pools, good grazing land, unusual pastures of box wood on the plains surrounding the Barnett, Gibb and Harris Rivers, and useful stands of pine on the ranges. He came to the conclusion that although the people of the northern ranges were, in his opinion, a 'better class of blacks' than those of Queensland, 'such country was much too good to be idle as a mere hunting ground for wild blacks'.[20]

Station workers and prospective leaseholders for the northern country—Blythe, G. Calder and A. Rose, who occupied leases on the south side of the King Leopold Ranges—made excursions into the northern ranges area after Hann, but did not move cattle there until 1903.[21] Alexander Sadler, known as Scotty Sadler, also explored

Frank Hann reported in 1898 on the attractive country over the ranges that consisted of pockets of boxwood trees and grassed plains. Copyright Kevin Shaw

north from Fitzroy Crossing to the north-eastern fringes of Ngarinyin country.

The push to extend pastoral settlement 'over the ranges' received official support from the West Australian government in 1901. In the same year, F.S. Brockman led an exploration party from Wyndham to the west coast, passing through Mount Elizabeth and Mount Barnett.[22] He recorded few contacts with Indigenous people but noted extensive evidence of occupation and some characteristics of Aboriginal life drawn from observations of cave paintings, camps, walking tracks and belongings that were abandoned on the approach of the exploration party. Brockman advised the colonial government to reserve land near the coast for a prospective township at Camden Harbour for later settlement of the northern region.

White nomads—a law unto themselves

The extension of pastoral occupation across the King Leopolds from the turn of the century until 1920 did not result in permanent homestead settlements of the Fitzroy and Ord River districts, nor port facilities at Napier Broome Bay, as had been mooted in 1901 after the Brockman survey. Brockman's report on the pastoral potential of the north Kimberley led to speculative leasing but not to 'settlement'.[23] It involved small herds, barely enough to meet the stocking requirements of 100 head of cattle. There were groups of two or three white stockmen, accompanied by police and their Aboriginal assistants, living in bush camps and occupying pockets of land surrounded by high and rugged ranges. It was an isolated and remote pastoral frontier. From 1903 to 1914 the stockmen and their assistants moved around their leases from camp to camp and built and rebuilt huts at various locations, or moved from lease to lease as they changed hands.

The owners of the pastoral leases were predominantly companies (M.C. Davies and Sons, Joe Blythe and Sons, Rose Bros and J.A. Game) which were extending their existing holdings to out-stations in well-watered pockets of land further north enclosed by ranges and not in need of fencing. Felix Edgar formed a partnership with William Chalmers at Mount Hart, and G. Calder's name appeared on maps as a lessee, but his cattle belonged to James Rose or to Game. He took over Blythe's Milliwindi station, the southern section of Mount House, in 1910. Owners like James Rose (recorded in police patrol reports as Major Rose because of his Boer War service) travelled regularly to their isolated bush holdings. Calder's (or Isdell) pastoral camp was the most permanent and was often visited by police and groups of stockmen in the period from 1903 to 1910. Calder himself was made a justice of the peace to work with the police.

The first decade from 1903 was dominated by the pacification of Indigenous people. The police and stockmen who came into the country in this period were on the periphery of pastoral settlement. They came with guns and few stores or items for exchange, preoccupied with reducing the capabilities of Indigenous people to hinder or threaten future pastoral occupation. They wanted eventually to surround themselves with a small group of specially selected workers, drawing on bush populations for seasonal and more intensive tasks such as mustering, fencing, building yards and creek crossings, or clearing land.

The system of European justice operating in the Kimberley after the turn of the century involved the arrest of whole groups of Aboriginal people, securing them by neck chains and marching them 'to the nearest magistrate or justice of the peace, who completed the formalities by sentencing all and sundry to two or three years' imprisonment'.[24] This system of arrest and gaoling provided stockmen and police with the means to pacify Indigenous people and begin to train them for work. It was regarded as a more civilized version of justice than the earlier method of dispersals and summary punishment used in the 1880s and '90s, in which the police and pastoralists attacked and sometimes injured or killed Aboriginal people who were attempting to escape, allowing none of them to front a bench for trial. Instead, they were being 'protected' from summary justice and brought to trial for an officially designated offence.

Unfortunately dispersals and violent confrontations between Aboriginal people and police and stockmen continued into the 1920s in the northern ranges within the more formal system of trials and gaoling. Indeed the act of arresting alleged cattle killers was often violent and in itself punitive.[25]

Situations were often dangerous for Aboriginal people, as armed police patrols surrounded and raided bush camps at dawn. There was a tendency in the decade up to 1905 for police not to report instances when things 'got out of control' and 'warning' shots hit people.[26] With the Roth Royal Commission in 1904 and a separate inquiry in 1905 into alleged abuses of Aboriginal people by police and trackers from the Isdell camp, the mode of arrest and accompanying violence came to light.[27]

In the northern ranges country, arrests were accompanied by punitive actions which, together with the system of arrest and gaoling, laid the groundwork for entry into the pastoral system. Aboriginal men and women were first captured under the umbrella of arresting cattle thieves and were then released to stockmen as workers.

In April 1902, Brockman's recommendations to reserve land for a township at Camden Harbour were placed before the Minister for Lands. A month later the government advertised that pastoral lands in the hinterlands near Mount Elizabeth and the Gibb, Charnley and Hann Rivers were reopened for selection from July 1903.[28] In 1902 the Police Commissioner reported that he had no need to increase policing in the Kimberley because 'cattle killing' incidents were under control.[29] In August 1903 he announced that 'police protection' would be provided for the new settlers because the land had only recently been explored and was isolated.[30]

The Police Commissioner was advised by the Kimberley police to send two parties of constables and black trackers to converge on the region from east and south, but he refused to provide such a large force without extra funding. Walter Kingsmill, the Colonial Secretary, convinced cabinet to set aside £1,000 in the estimates for a police post to be situated at Grace's Knob, just south of the leases owned by Rose and Game. From that point the police would patrol the 'new country' over the ranges at Mount Hart, Mount House and further north around the Isdell, Gibb and Hann Rivers.[31] Rose's stock was to arrive in the district by October, and the police camp was required to be operating by that time to patrol the area to the north of the proposed station and assist with its occupation. The post was 300 miles from Derby, and the police party had to transport all their provisions for an initial six-month period.

Constable Jack Wilson, previously at Turkey Creek, was chosen to lead the party of three constables and four Aboriginal trackers. There is no record of the exact reasoning behind Wilson's appointment, but he had gained experience of a frontier situation when he was stationed in the Halls Creek area. Wilson proved to be a ruthless operator who led a thorough campaign against Ngarinyin people, both as a policeman until 1905 and as a stockman at stations in the north until his death in 1939. As a policeman he made an extraordinary amount of money out of ration fees for prisoners and trackers, as well as the extra pay for 'special duties' at a frontier posting in the east Kimberley before taking up the Isdell post.[32] Wilson became the subject of embarrassing allegations in two separate inquiries and had retired from the force by the end of 1905.[33] But he did not leave the area. He became one of the white Bosses who was central to the incorporation of Ngarinyin informants into the pastoral industry and was 'the little iron man' in Ion Idriess's book *Over the Range*.[34]

Jack Wilson was one of the rough early days whites who came to rely on an Aboriginal wife and children for his own survival. His stepdaughter was Daisy Beharrell (Angajit) who recalled in Munro's *Emerarra* how Wilson had lived and worked with her mother and provided food and donkeys for her when she was a child.[35] She did not view him as a bad man but knew he was one of the men who 'cleared' the bush people. Wilson's identity in oral discourse is as a stockman and white Boss, not as a policeman. He was named by storytellers along with other stockmen—Billy Skinner, Dick Sullivan, Jack Connaughton, Jack Dale, Jack Gallagher, Scotty Sadler and Jack Carey—who worked together to 'clear the country' of bush people from Mount Hart, Mount House, Isdell River and Mount Barnett after the police camp closed in 1914.[36] Storytellers were sure that these men were employed by station owners further south to clean the country of people. Each one of the storytellers either lived with or was related to one of these white men or their Aboriginal wives.

The Isdell police camp was initially staffed by Constables Wilson, Napier and Forbes, accompanied by four Aboriginal trackers, Onearra (Turkey Creek), Bobby (Fitzroy Crossing), and Toby and Charley, who had worked with police at Derby and Fitzroy Crossing. While it is difficult to establish where the trackers came from prior to their association with police, oral testimonies record trackers in this period coming from Fitzroy Crossing and Turkey Creek into what was new country for them.[37] According to written records, the trackers did not speak the language of the northern groups beyond the Phillips Ranges—primarily Ngarinyin. Onearra, who was Wilson's assistant and the most notable of the trackers at Isdell, could communicate with people around Mount House and east towards the Fitzroy River.[38] He probably spoke Bunuba and Kija.

Police were dependent on black trackers and often left patrol work to them while they waited at camps or with the horses if the country was accessible only by foot.[39] The police records rarely show this complete reliance on the trackers, nor the extent to which they were left to their own resources while pursuing other Aboriginal people or accompanying them to towns for court hearings. After 1905, trackers were not supposed to carry firearms but very often did. Their role in the pacification process was crucial to the success of police and stockmen's attempts to subdue resistance and select potential workers. Their relationships with local people were complex. Sometimes it was clear that the trackers performed their tasks with deadly efficiency, tracking, chaining and pursuing people who tried to run away. At other times it was apparent that trackers themselves ran away from police and were brought back along with the prisoners. They were also likely to be blamed by police if things went wrong.

By December 1903, when the police party arrived at Isdell station (variously called Calder's, Isdell Downs, Grace's Knob or Scented Knob), Calder claimed he had 100 of Rose's cattle on the river and reported that no Aboriginal people had visited the river frontage since he had arrived. The police camp was initially positioned only four miles from Calder's, but it was moved about ten miles north to the Manning River. This gave the police party easier access to the people and the country near Mount Barnett, where Dick Sullivan established a stockman's camp late in 1904 for Rose Bros. In 1905 W. Fitzgerald, an agricultural specialist who had accompanied Brockman in 1901, revisited the area with a survey team, including Charles Crossland and Hepple Browne, to survey the leases at Mount House and further north to Gibb River and to report on the region's agricultural prospects. The West Australian government also offered a £300 reward to whoever could locate a cart access road through the ranges to the northern leases. Mick O'Connor, a stockman who was in the northern ranges to manage the Mount Barnett lease, was assisting the party as guide in the hope of receiving the reward.

Fitzgerald reported that 624,500 acres of good pastoral land were served by the Isdell River and its tributaries. He also said that on the Isdell itself there were 287,000 acres of cultivable land, adding that although 'most of the finest land North-east of the King Leopold Ranges is held under pastoral lease, it is to be regretted that with the exception of one or two lessees no effort has been made to stock it'.[40] Despite this, Fitzgerald reported in 1905 that the 'troopers' at the police camp 'were kept busy by the blacks'.[41] By 1909, the police reported that there were still only about 100 cattle on the Mount Barnett lease, although the leases at Mount House and Mount Hart were better stocked.[42] The small herds driven over the ranges to the Isdell and Barnett Rivers, and the immediate response of government to fund a police camp nearby, suggest that the initial exercise of stocking the country was cautious, if not experimental — even designed to provide a small preliminary reason for pacification with police assistance and judicial support. Ngarinyin people paid a high price for the presence of a small number of cattle and even smaller numbers of white men.

The campaign to remove Aboriginal men

From 1904 to 1908, police and trackers from the Isdell camp captured, detained and escorted to Derby no less than 283 men and fifty witnesses who were, in all except a few cases, women. These are minimum figures taken from records that, for at least 1904 and part of 1905, were lazily kept.[43] The numbers include several instances of repeat arrests: some people who were released after twelve months' imprisonment were back in custody after only a few months in the bush. Some of those who were arrested, removed for witness duties or became trackers in the early 1900s were related to the storytellers of the 1990s, and their land affiliations were well known. Many were again mentioned by Ion Idriess in the 1930s when he went with the police on a patrol 'over the range'. They were labelled then as outlaw bands, twenty years after dealing with this first frontier.

Police Paddy (Wundigul), Weeda Munro's father, was a tracker at the Isdell police station during this early period. Toolwonoor was arrested and gaoled from Isdell but returned to his country to become one of Idriess's 'outlaws'. Ludmurra was arrested and gaoled twice between 1904 and 1908 and became one of Idriess's outlaw 'generals'. And Bolva, Weeda Munro's sister and a witness for cattle killing, was again secured in the 1930s on one of the patrols referred to by Idriess.[44] Several of the white men who came to the region after 1903 also survived and stayed in the northern ranges to become Idriess's characters and early days Bosses, including Jack Wilson (the little iron man), Fred Potts and others.

Table 1 shows the intensity of the campaign in the early period to remove Aboriginal men from the region. Sentences were usually from three months to three years for cattle killing and stealing offences. Not all arrests resulted in gaoling. In 1905 the Derby resident magistrate, Dr Wace, refused to charge eighteen prisoners because he believed there was insufficient evidence.[45] Wace was a strong critic of the system of justice that operated in the north Kimberley. He labelled cattle killing trials a 'farce' and took a firm stance against several of the local white men and police whom he believed abused their authority.[46] He was particularly critical of the combination of Constable Wilson and Calder (the justice of the peace and pastoralist) and the methods of arrest at the Isdell station.[47] Wace's efforts to protect Aboriginal women in the newly occupied north Kimberley resulted in the magistrate from Cue being directed by the Commissioner of Police in 1905 to inquire into the goings on at the Isdell post. Wilson resigned from the force shortly afterwards.[48] By the end of 1908 there were ninety-two Aboriginal men in Carnarvon, Broome and Wyndham gaols who had been arrested by Isdell police and successfully prosecuted for cattle killing.[49]

Table 1: Arrests from Isdell police station, 1904–08

Year	Month	Prisoners	Witnesses
1904	July	11	4
	Sept	8	3
1905	August	17	4
	Sept	13	4
	Oct	12	2
1906	January	12	4
	Feb	9	2
	April	17	6
	July	16	3
	Nov	10	
	Dec	19	3
1907	Feb	12	2
	May	11	2
	July	13	2
	September	11	
	Oct	17	4
	Nov/Dec	18	3
1908	Feb	13	2
	March–Dec	44	
TOTAL		**283**	**50**

Compiled from PD1588 special item, Isdell Police Station Journals 1903–1908.

The social impact of the campaign of arrests and gaoling was significant. Police arrested and removed only men who could sustain the long walk to Derby and who were likely to offer resistance to the colonizing enterprise. It severely reduced the numbers of men

*Phillips Ranges men: Morndingali stated that the men in
the above photograph were from the Phillips Ranges and
were, from left to right (with one man not discernible),
Kuwalli Tommy, Burrun Jack, Marmandoo, Kuntjilli,
Rajilla Rudlow, Tulawangu Walter, Tilyangu Spot
(Morndi Munro, NB4, pp. 27, 30, July 1990). Barrun,
Marmandoo and Rajilla are named in chapter 3 as
members of the 'outlaw bands'.*

Copyright Battye Library, 21051P

in bush communities, destabilizing the economy and increasing
women's vulnerability and dependence on white men. After only
three months in the district, the police reported coming across a
group of one man and 'several' women who were moving north
over the King Leopold Ranges to 'avoid the Fitzroy police'.[50] The
impact of the loss of men from the hunting communities was noted
as early as November 1905, when a police party tracked and caught
a group of four women and six children in the act of killing a cow:

They had broken the cow's hind leg and had the beast down on the ground and were throwing stones on the cow's head, the beast almost dead when the women saw me and they said me hungry fellow. There was no male natives with these women. They said the male natives belong to them was in gaol.[51]

As the arrests increased, the incidence of women travelling alone or in groups with one or two men also increased. In March 1906 police reported that they had tracked a large group of men, women and children, but on raiding the camp the next morning they had found eleven women and 'some children' who stated that the men were 'frightened' and went away during the night.[52] In June the police noted that one man who had just returned from gaol was travelling with nine women and a group of children, while days later they caught up with another group of only two men and several women and children.[53] In October 1906 they raided a camp of five men and twelve women. The following month they raided a camp of three old men ('too decrepit to walk') and twenty-six women. Fifteen men who had been with the group had left three days earlier to evade police. They were tracked north to Charnley River, captured and gaoled.[54] In 1907 the police found six men hiding in the Isdell Gorge who had recently been released from prison.[55]

In September 1907 a group of 'several old women' hunted alone, setting fire to the bush as they travelled to prevent the police from following them. Fires destroyed the feed for the horses and made tracking more difficult and conditions unpleasant and dangerous. Although these fires were an important form of resistance for Indigenous people, they may have been lit out of season and unusually destructive. It was thus a desperate strategy. In 1907 fires were raging out of control across the district from Mount House to the Isdell River and Mount Barnett.

Control of women and children

In January 1905 the police called in at Dick Skinner's camp which he had set up just north of the police camp on the Barnett lease owned by Rose. Skinner and his white assistant O'Malley had two Aboriginal women, Morbur and Woolinginna, in the camp. One of the women reported that a boy, about eight years old, had been lost in the bush and 'eaten by bush blacks'.[56] After three days' travelling, the police party was 'approached' by two other women who said that the boy was travelling with them. According to evidence given by the boy, the woman at Skinner's camp was his mother and had told him to stay away from the white man and travel with the bush people. She had led the boy away from Skinner's camp, tracked the bush group, which consisted of three men and six women, and told him to join them. She had concocted the story of him being eaten to enable him to leave Skinner. A month later, the police reported that the women from the bush group had joined Skinner's camp and the boy had moved on with another group. Skinner asked the police to continue looking for the boy and to force the women to leave, as their presence in the camp would soon bring a larger group and ensuing 'trouble'. The police escorted the women for three days, then warned them not to go near white men's camps.

Skinner and the police continued to hunt for the boy, travelling hundreds of miles in search of the 'runaway'. Although Skinner had clearly lost control of this young boy, he eventually gathered a workforce around him. The early Isdell police records were seldom explicit about the degree to which control of children and women was contested or the police feared by local Aboriginal people. Their record of the 'approach' of the bushwomen to inform the police party of the boy's whereabouts was later recorded by Fitzgerald in 1905 as a raid involving Calder and police: 'the men bolted up the trees while the women threw themselves flat on the ground, threw sand over their heads and howled like dingoes'.[57] It was not the quiet approach and cordial exchange of information suggested by the police report, but an incident that added to the culture of terror on the frontier.[58]

The two women at Skinner's camp were drawn into a sphere of limited protection, which distinguished them from bush people and decreased their chances of being dispersed, chased or taken to Derby as witnesses. Only four months before the police had dispersed the bushwomen and heard evidence from Skinner's woman, Woolinginna, she had herself been a bushwoman (and apparently wanted her son to remain with the bush people). Her association with Skinner was supported by police and the system of arrests.

In May 1904 police journals record tracking a large group of men and women north of the Isdell police camp to Gibb River.[59] The tracks indicated that a large group of Aboriginal people had herded cattle away from the river frontage and then split the cattle into two groups. After a dawn raid of the camp, the party 'secured' Woolinginna as a witness to cattle killing and the man she travelled with, Carwell, as the alleged offender. She travelled first to Isdell police camp, then to Derby to testify against Carwell, and she was then escorted back to the Isdell camp. After that she stayed with Skinner and tried to continue her son's contact with the small groups moving in the bush.

Aboriginal women's association with police, trackers and white men in the region began in a climate of fear and sudden change. Women were not arrested for cattle killing but were removed for months at a time for witness duties. Their return to the bush and their families was not guaranteed. In May 1905 separate patrols yielded female witnesses Nimbandi and Morbur, and several male prisoners. The witnesses travelled with the police party from May until August, picking up other prisoners and walking to Derby. Throughout this time the police were drawing daily ration allowances for the women. In late August, on the return trip from Derby, the police recorded releasing the women to 'their tribe', who were known to be in the bush south of Calder's Isdell station.[60] However, the women did not leave the police party as was suggested in the journal. They continued with the police, herding a group of goats, which they had cared for since leaving Derby. According to the police, the women were 'offered further food if they helped with the goats', and they chose to stay.[61] The next year Woolinginna was again recorded as living at Skinner's and Morbur at Calder's camp accompanied by another woman. They had come in from the bush while in the custody of the police. Such choices were clearly determined by the campaign of arrests, frightening dawn raids and removal of men to gaols.

In February 1905 Dr Wace assisted one of the women witnesses, Nimbandi, to make a formal complaint against the police and Calder, alleging instances of murder of prisoners and rape of female witnesses. Wace was irate that a man like Calder could be given the role and responsibilities of a justice of the peace.[62] Roth's 1904 inquiry had already resulted in embarrassing publicity about police actions in the Kimberley. He pointed out the absurd lack of protection afforded by the 1898 Aborigines Act, which permitted an 'outrageous' state of affairs.[63] For the Isdell police it was a relatively easy and lucrative business to catch a group of prisoners and witnesses, travel with them for three weeks to gaol and then accompany the witnesses 300 miles back to the region. In particular, from evidence given by Constable Wilson, Roth had concluded that police made a profit from their ration allowances for prisoners and witnesses, which was shared out amongst station personnel. Over a period of four months in 1904, Constable Wilson had been paid £192 for rationing prisoners and witnesses.[64] Wilson admitted that women witnesses and trackers may have had sexual intercourse while the women were in custody, that police had gaoled children and intimidated witnesses, and that for much of the ranges district there had been no interpreter who could speak Ngarinyin.[65] Police had also failed to supervise armed trackers.

Nimbandi's allegations and the Troy Inquiry

The inquiry into Nimbandi's allegations was undertaken by ex-policeman Patrick Troy, who had become the mining warden for Cue. Troy travelled to the region in May 1905 and interviewed Nimbandi, the police and Wilson's tracker Onearra, who was implicated. Troy's inquiry was relatively unbiased and provided evidence of police 'cooking' their journals to enhance their allowance claims. It offered clear evidence of the potential for abuse and punishment by police or members of the police party.[66] Nimbandi's allegations and the Troy Inquiry, together with Roth's evidence about Isdell police station and Constable Wilson, provide an unusually comprehensive documentary picture of events in the region. Although Troy concluded that Nimbandi's allegations of murder and rape were not proven, her statement was a rare officially recorded complaint from an Aboriginal woman against police and white men's practices in her country during the period of pacification.

Nimbandi began her statement in a similar way to the storytellers in the 1980s, by naming her 'country'. She came from the Phillips Ranges, and her 'special place' was also the centre of the violence, Ungadinda, the waterhole at Manning Gorge where the Isdell police camp was situated.[67] Nimbandi was thought to be one of the sisters from Kupingarri country, near Mount Barnett, who first came to police and trackers. The name 'Nimbandi' may also have been a functional word. *Nim uminde* means to remember or get back the thought.[68] As a custodian for Ungadinda she had a right to know and speak for the country.

Nimbandi said that her first husband had been killed by sickness (singing) by Aboriginal men from Meda station. After her husband died she moved to live with his brother who was arrested and gaoled. They were travelling together when the police picked them up. She stated that Calder and Wilson had raided their camp and shot three young men who were trying to escape. That evening they were all chained to trees. Two of the police, Wilson and Forbes, and one of the trackers, Onearra, sexually assaulted three of the women while they were chained. They received damper at night and kangaroo during the day. Nimbandi alleged that, after raiding another camp, the police shot an old man while he was lying on the ground on a piece of flattened bark. At each raid, several of the men escaped.

Nimbandi's statement was made in Derby through an interpreter who, according to Troy, was unreliable, did not speak her language and suggested the answers. Troy set off on horseback with Nimbandi to investigate the site of the alleged atrocities. He picked up Duncan, a station worker at Balmaningarra (near the Napier Ranges, renamed Kimberley Downs) who was recommended by the manager to act as interpreter. The area was not his country but he was believed to speak enough of the language for the purposes of the inquiry. Morndingali called Duncan his uncle and an Unggumi man. He may have spoken Ngarinyin from his mother's side. He also became one of Idriess's characters, playing a central role in the murder of an Aboriginal man from Grace's Knob in 1919.[69]

Nimbandi led Troy to the Isdell police camp and surrounding region, and to the scenes of the alleged murders and rapes. Onearra, the accused tracker, accompanied them. At each site Nimbandi attempted to act out the events that had occurred there. At a site about ten miles from the police camp, where Nimbandi showed him the paperbark on which the old man had been shot and killed, Troy found no traces of blood or a body. He concluded that as there was no body, there was no evidence: 'given the remoteness from whites it is improbable that any concealment of a body would have been thought necessary'.[70] Troy found that while Nimbandi contradicted herself during the inquiry and her previous statements, the police and tracker Onearra agreed on the main elements of the allegations: that no stockmen rode with the police party and therefore they could not be accused of combining into unlawful posses. Nor were there any murders, beatings or rapes. They were supported by A.E. Love, who had travelled with Wilson and Onearra through the Gibb River and Mount Elizabeth area in 1904 in search of a pastoral lease. Love testified that, during the trip, Wilson had made it clear to him that he 'was averse to dealing harshly with natives'.[71]

Despite his inability to rely on Nimbandi's evidence, Troy indicated that he held doubts about the truthfulness of the white men in the northern ranges. He found that tracker Onearra had given evidence of camp raids and rounding up escapees that fitted more accurately with the scenes of broken spears and scattered camp sites than the story given by Wilson. On his arrival at Calder's camp, Troy found that Mick O'Connor, one of Rose's stockmen from the Fitzroy valley, had left Derby the day before him and arrived in a very short time to warn the others of Troy's imminent arrival. Calder avoided any contact with him at all. He was away from the camp on both of Troy's visits and made no attempt to give a statement. Two women were at Calder's camp, one of them Morbur, the witness from 1904 who had also allegedly been raped while detained. Troy believed the women were being detained against their husbands' wishes.[72]

After a few days retracing the patrols and alleged incidents, all the trackers disappeared. Troy continued with Nimbandi as the tracker but without any means of communicating with her. He returned to Derby, and within three months Constable Wilson resigned from the force. He became a prospector and itinerant worker for the various lessees and stockmen in the central ranges region, travelling with his Aboriginal wife, who was 'picked up' from her country at Mount Barnett during the period 1903–14. She was Daisy Angajit's mother, Winnie Wilson.[73]

The month after the Troy Inquiry, patrol reports began to follow a new procedural format. They began, 'After going into camp', and included details of alleged offenders 'freely admitting' to the offences, being taken to the site of the offence and giving details of the stolen property in their possession. The owners of the stolen property were named, but there was no mention of brands. Considering the problems of surveying the country and the lack of fencing, it is unlikely that police knew where the boundaries were or whether cattle were inside one boundary or another, or on vacant crown land. What they did know was that Aboriginal people tended to stay near waterholes and in inaccessible pockets of land connected by known tracks.

One of these tracks followed Harris Creek, which allowed access from the northern areas of Gibb River and Mount Barnett to the southern area of Mount House. Although it was a strategic place for hiding and moving between countries, the frequency with which Harris Creek turned up in the existing records as the site where alleged cattle killing offences took place, and where bones and ground ovens were found, suggests that the evidence was being recycled. On one occasion, Constable Napier recorded that, despite having no proof, he was 'morally certain that it [the meat found in ground ovens at Harris Creek] was the property of Rose Bros owners of Isdell Station'.[74]

From 1905, police recorded instances of white men showing them where offences had occurred and naming the owners of the property. Their involvement in raids was not recorded, but it was unlikely that they held back while the police party raided camps. Given the increasing numbers of arrests from 1906 to 1908, it seems that the police continued to write up patrols after arrests were made by trackers working without supervision, continued to misunderstand and frighten witnesses, and continued to share profits from ration allowances. It is also doubtful that the police significantly modified their methods of arrest, but they did attempt to record standard procedures—and Jack Wilson no longer wore a police uniform.

Conditions in the northern ranges were obviously not conducive to standard police procedures: it was a 'first contact' situation in rough terrain and a well-populated region. For the first year of white occupation there were only three white policemen with four black trackers, and four or five white stockmen with Aboriginal assistants. The police travelled under the guidance of trackers who were new to the area. For numerous raids, they recorded escapes and their inability to follow tracks because of rain or inaccessible terrain. Although police and white men were armed and had Aboriginal assistants, the local Aboriginal people were in their own, extremely rugged, country.

Escalating tensions

In 1905, the second year of European occupation, the numbers of white men, trackers and 'private boys' increased rapidly, and so did the recorded conflicts between them and local Aboriginal people. While Troy was investigating Nimbandi's complaints, Crossland, Browne and Fitzgerald arrived to survey and explore the central ranges district.[75] They occupied the region for four months, travelling with a group of eight white assistants and at least four Aboriginal assistants. Two Aboriginal women also travelled with the party to mind horses, but they were not officially recognized as members of the group. Fitzgerald, who had come to report on the region's pastoral and agricultural prospects, noted the intensity of Aboriginal occupation indicated by walking pads around the country, smoke signals and evidence of rock paintings and old camp fires. He always carried a loaded revolver but recorded having to use it only once against Aboriginal people. In general, local people avoided contact, but some groups watched the survey parties and travelled close by, while two small groups exchanged spearheads and information for tobacco.

Fitzgerald's description of relationships in the region showed the prevailing tensions and the potential for loss of life. He did not approve of two of the white men, intimating that there was something amiss when these men had given statutory declarations about the ownership of cattle at a trial in Derby. He also described an attack on his colleague's party by a group of Aboriginal people and Calder's previously cited raid on a camp of Aboriginal men and women near the Charnley River, who ran and hid and were clearly terrified.[76] On another occasion he found a stockman, Delaney, at Mount Barnett, 'scared' by a group of sixty Aboriginal men, women and children who had come towards his camp and then moved only a short distance away into the bush.[77]

In the Phillips Ranges, where the police had already been operating for over twelve months, Fitzgerald became separated from his party and was attacked:

[I] saw a number of native smoke signals on Phillips range which is opposite and these were shortly afterwards followed by the native 'coo' from among the rocks close by me. As I was armed with a heavy service revolver, I examined this as guard against eventualities. Soon after this I saw two blacks stalking me each armed with three spears. The younger one evidently meant mischief and although there were numerous breaks in the cliffs through which I could have descended to the lower ground, there was a risk of being speared in attempting it. Ultimately [I] came to where the cliffs gave way to a sharp slope and as the young black was about 60 yards behind me, and would evidently make a rush at me immediately I began to descend for the purpose of trying to score a hit, I decided on testing his intentions. I held up my hand for the purpose of proving I carried no arms. He replied by hissing and shaking a spear at me ... My antagonist as I suspected, appeared about 3 yds from me with a spear shipped for my benefit, and appeared for the moment to be non-plussed at my disappearance. I at once fired at him, when he gave a yell and went down. He immediately jumped up and bolted, apparently shot through the shoulder. To my astonishment 9 other natives made their appearance but they were 100s of yds away.[78]

The police at Isdell had only been permitted four trackers, who had all decamped during the Troy Inquiry. Constable Napier followed Onearra and Toby, two of the 'runaway' trackers, to a bush camp near Fitzroy Crossing, where he once again enlisted them. He wrote that they were 'perfectly willing to return'. From there he sent a telegram to his superiors asking for trackers from Roebourne to be sent to Isdell, possibly to overcome any likelihood of conflicts of interest for north Kimberley trackers. Napier had been involved in the capture of Jandamarra in the 1890s, when a Roebourne tracker had proved more successful than any from the local area. Despite the trackers not speaking the language of the northern groups, they developed allegiances and obligations with local people which were complex, dynamic and difficult for the police to comprehend. They began to take wives from the area and extended their family networks. According to Napier, the trackers refused to go with him to 'strange country' without taking other men for 'company', so three others were hired as Napier's private boys and rationed from his allowance.[79]

While Napier was in Fitzroy, Constable Forbes went south towards the older pastoral leases on the Lennard and Barker Rivers to enlist men who were known to the manager at Balmaningarra station — Munday, Peter and Paddy. Munday ran away within twelve hours: in the 1930s Idriess named him as a member of the outlaw group who refused to 'settle'.[80] The manager's private boy tracked Paddy into the bush and he was also enlisted.[81] There was no written record of Paddy's attributes in this early period, but he was an assistant to several white men and was later suspected of killing a white man in 1916. He was also gaoled for killing two Aboriginal men in the 1920s and became one of Idriess's main characters. Weeda Munro, his daughter, stated that he was a young man living in the bush when his brother, who was private boy for a teamster carrying stores to Balmaningarra station, 'picked him up'.[82] Paddy, or Wundigul, was not always a great help to the police or his later Bosses and, after only a few months of service to the Isdell police, 'ran away' with a police revolver, leaving the police officer stranded in the bush.[83] He later returned, but what he did with the revolver was not recorded. This was possibly the police attempting to cover up the fact that they allowed armed and lone trackers to wander the bush. Their marked nonchalance was out of character in comparison to their panicked response to later instances of bush people stealing or carrying weapons. The police had only limited control over a tracker like Paddy, who developed a fearsome reputation among both his own people and whites.

The numbers of trackers and white men in the district had increased markedly by mid-1905. There were stockmen's camps at the Isdell and Barnett sites that now included extra men for building stockyards. Seven trackers and three police worked from the Manning Gorge camp, located between the homestead huts. Crossland, Browne and Fitzgerald and their party of trackers, white assistants and Aboriginal women split into two to comb the area and survey it. Troy was also moving in the region, completing his investigations. In addition, there were visiting parties of stockmen and private boys from southern leases bringing stores and mail to the out-camps. The police camp was never attacked, but in 1905 Fitzgerald and the police recorded two instances of armed men stalking them.[84] Fitzgerald shot his attacker, but the police did not record shooting anyone. Constable Forbes had been forewarned by his trackers, who intervened to save him:

> ... a party of male natives following my horse tracks towards my camp. These natives had their spears in their womeras ready to throw. The trackers then concealed themselves in the rocks and watched the bush natives until they were getting close to my camp and then seeing

that the natives intended throwing the spears by the way they were acting and also heard them saying so, they then gave me the alarm by singing out. The bush natives then ran away. I only succeeded in catching two as the country was rough. All the others got away.[85]

What the police did record was a process of escalating tension and conflict between bush people and police, which they used to justify police presence and the aggressive campaign of arrests. The records also provide evidence of neighbouring groups moving into the areas occupied by white men and cattle to continue ceremonial practices and possibly to share some introduced foods and materials like tobacco, flour and pieces of cloth and glass.

The boundaries of protection and ownership between bush and station were beginning to emerge, with women and children the first to be identified from the local groups as belonging to a particular white man or tracker. Police also began to distinguish between known and settled groups of Aboriginal people and groups or individuals who threatened the colonizing project. The removal of even a few of the men and the control of one or two women had an immediate impact on a group's capacity to maintain itself, physically and socially, but some people escaped and others became known to police and white men as non-threatening.

Certain bush people became familiar to stockmen, moving between bush and station, and negotiating with them in order to stay in the bush, and stay alive. Their role, which developed over time, was to look after herds in the bush, keep them away from the ranges and boggy areas, protect them from other Aboriginal groups, and eventually provide a pool of labour when more than a core group of four or five workers was needed. In return they received, according to oral testimonies, occasional meat rations and some tobacco when they came into camp.[86] Negotiations of this kind were made by senior men or women who were, according to informants, 'Ernod' or 'Ngowerung': leaders of clan groups who held the authority to make such decisions.[87] In this early period, negotiations took place at Mount Barnett, and then at other stations in the region from the 1920s to the 1940s, as land was occupied for pastoral purposes. In every case a woman and children from the group stayed with the white stockmen while the decision-maker continued his life in the bush. When police raided the bush camps, the stock-men identified their bush people, and they were released from custody.[88]

In September 1905 the police recorded a rare instance of not arresting six men and eight women who were camped in the region, near water being used by cattle. Nimbandi had been picked up at this camp twelve months before and had given it as her country in her evidence to Troy. This group's relationship to Nimbandi, Morbur and Woolinginna may have helped them. These women and others from the area continued to live with white men and trackers, increasing their range of skills including English language and their capacity to protect their own close relations. Constable Napier reported that

> all appeared to be very quiet and as I saw no stolen property in their possession I did not molest them. I don't think they had been molesting stock in any way as there was a mob of Isdell cattle close by their camp that was very quiet and they appeared to have been there some time, they having strayed away from the Isdell Cattle Station.[89]

Local people's relationship with police could also be influenced by the trackers, who were in powerful positions. The Fitzroy trackers who assisted with the pacification process also became enmeshed in local obligations and relationships. They maintained wives from the region while they worked for the police. Some of the trackers used their power to identify alleged prisoners in order to have husbands removed to gaol so they could take a wife without being punished. When husbands returned to their country after years of imprisonment, they could find their wives with other men—Aboriginal or white—and some fought to get them back.[90]

The women who cooked and washed for the police also looked after groups of old people who came into the camps because they were starving. They prepared kangaroo and damper to supplement fish from nearby creeks, and gathered fruits and goanna for them.[91] Alignment with trackers could increase chances of survival and sharing the very limited supply of rations that could be transported across the ranges on pack mules and horses.

Many groups who did not enjoy protection from arrest, nevertheless continued to move across the country to maintain significant ceremonial practices. These movements and gatherings challenged the new rules of coexistence with white men. The main concern in the police journals was expressed in military terminology, describing Indigenous groups combining to oppose them or adopting a strategic response like stealing guns and ammunition, destroying property, lighting fires to decrease police mobility or herding stock into remote and well-hidden pockets of range country. Young men in particular were consistently identified by police parties and stockmen as potential antagonists and were not secure in the region. Boys were therefore often integrated into pastoral work when they were very young.

In September 1905 Constable Napier reported that he had been 'distinctly' informed by men he had recently arrested that 'the natives from the Drysdale River country and from the Fitzroy were going to come and kill all the whites, then kill the horses then finish the cattle in this district'.[92] Police insecurity was magnified by the size of the groups gathering in the region and compounded by a robbery at Mount Hart camp in late 1905, when guns and ammunition were allegedly stolen. The police recorded finding at a site on the Barnett River a number of cow heads, large numbers of broken spears from the attack on the cattle and twenty-two ground ovens — clear evidence of a feast. They attempted to follow the group north towards the Drysdale River but were cut off by fires lit by the group as they moved north.[93] A week later, the stockmen at Isdell station reported that a group of sixty Aborigines, not including women and children, had gathered near the Isdell out-camp. A police party of one constable and five trackers surrounded and raided a camp in the area and reported finding a civilian coat, matches, tobacco and strips of blanket. These, police were told, had been traded with them by people moving north from Mount Hart station towards the Isdell River out-camp. The system of trading and exchanging

knowledge and items across the country was expanding the numbers of people implicated in crimes against European property. In
this case, eight men were arrested.[94]

While escorting the prisoners to the Isdell police post, the
patrol raided another camp:

> A large number of natives were in the camp and a great
> number got away judging by the number of beds that
> I saw where natives had slept. I feel confident in saying
> that fully 80 male natives and more than that number of
> females had occupied the camp. The bush natives broke
> from the patrol party and got into the rocks and the
> trackers went in pursuit of them to try and turn them
> back where upon the bush natives turned on the trackers
> by holding their spears up and shaking them, also
> challenged the white man along with the trackers to
> come to the rocks and get them, as I had 8 natives
> arrested I was unable to accompany the trackers to try
> and make other arrests.[95]

In the Phillips Ranges another group were 'talked into'
coming into the police camp by Onearra, who tracked the ranges
with private boys but without a constable. Two men carried
materials allegedly stolen from Bobby Brown's Mount Hart camp: 'a
dark grey tweed coat, crepe shirt, ½ yard of print, wood chisel,
about ½ lb of 4 inch tin nails, a piece of fencing wire'.[96] They were
arrested and gaoled along with several other men who were also
implicated in the robbery or who had received stolen property.

The police were aware of ceremonial gatherings in the region
and on one occasion were apparently convinced there was no
threat. In December 1905 and January 1906 the police had continued
to track groups of people across the region, arresting some and
gathering information on the whereabouts of the stolen rifle,
shotgun, and two revolvers and ammunition. Then, north of the
Napier Ranges, the police party was notified of a 'strange' group of
Aboriginal people thought to be from Mount Hart to the south of the
region in the King Leopold Ranges. They were occupying the

northern end of the station lease. The camp was raided but nothing to associate them with the robbery was found in their belongings. The trackers, who had originally been picked up in that district, informed the police that the group of about thirty men were from the north side of the King Leopold Ranges towards the coast, and 'that they were there at the invitation of Balmaningarra natives to take part in circumcising 6 native boys and as soon as the ceremony was over they were going back to their country over the range'.[97] Balmaningarra was a designated trading and exchange point in the Wunan system—the religious, social and legal imperative that connected the smaller groups across the north Kimberley. This group were on sacred business and were also senior affiliates of trackers Paddy and Peter, who accompanied the police on that raid.[98] The men were released.

By February 1906 the guns and ammunition had still not been found. Corporal Buckland and Inspector McCarthy visited the region, and the police took on two extra private boys, as the four trackers and three private boys were found to be inadequate. One of the extra men, Coombool (pronounced Gumbil by informants), was 'secured' for work after appearing in the records six months before as a prisoner arrested for cattle killing at Mount Barnett. Coombool claimed a wife from the women at the police station — Nellie, or Yuulut, who was tracker Paddy's classificatory mother. This made Coombool Paddy's classificatory father.[99] Paddy was now working with the police in his own country, accompanied by his son and wife.

More camps were raided in March and April, and possessions from Brown's camp were found. Mick O'Connor, who had taken charge of Isdell station for Rose Bros, accompanied the police on the patrols. In one camp, to the north of Isdell police camp, the police found a 'new rasp, 2 new horseshoes, some new fencing wire, a billy can, some pieces of cream shirt, piece of old dungaree pants, a piece of rope and a potato tin'[100] — the spoils of unattended white men's camps.

The trackers and police camps now included men and women who could communicate with groups throughout their patrol area, and their recorded information on movements of individuals began to include destinations and names of men leading the groups. The level of information seems to deepen with new Aboriginal recruits and more experience in the ranges with Ngarinyin people. The police were informed that the weapons were in the possession of a group who were travelling north towards Charnley River. But the prisoners' chains were full, so no attempt was made to follow them. Seventeen prisoners were delivered to Derby, and, without the sympathetic Dr Wace to scrutinize the charges, all were convicted of cattle killing and given maximum sentences of three years with hard labour.[101]

In June 1906 the police party raided and arrested men at a camp in the Packhorse Range, a small range between the Isdell and Barnett Rivers. Among them was Telyon, labelled the 'ringleader', who informed them that he had stolen the gun and, after using all the ammunition which he had carried away from the hut in a 50lb flour bag, had buried it. The other guns were supposedly with two separate groups led by men who were also labelled as ringleaders. One was Carwell, Skinner's woman's husband, who was now labelled an outlaw and moving outside the parameters of pastoral protection where his wife was. The female witness secured from this raid was Manuworla (transcribed on different occasions as Menowella and Mandowalla in the records) who became tracker Paddy's wife and mother to Weeda Munro.[102]

On 20 June the police raided a camp in Manning Gorge consisting of one man just released from gaol and a number of women and children. On the 24th they moved north between the Barnett Gorge and Charnley River near Mount Elizabeth. There they surrounded and raided a large group of men, women and children. A loose page of the Isdell journal records the clash:

> Native camp covered from 2 to 3 acres a large number of male and female natives when the natives saw the patrol party they made a general stampede most of male natives having spears, womerahs in their hands some had both spears and womerahs. They rushed to South where PC Johnson and tracker Toby were stationed and seeing the PC and tracker there, turned and rushed to other side

> where trackers Onearra and Paddy was. Here some of the
> natives threw spears just missing the trackers, some
> escaped others turned and ran towards where PC Forbes
> was on North side of camp where he was engaged
> handcuffing 2 natives together when one native who was
> running in his direction speared me in two places.[103]

The page was torn off at this point, unlike any of the other pages. Perhaps because of the scrutiny afforded to the station, the records were changed and the section recording killings of Aboriginal people was destroyed. The following page states that nine men were arrested. But a report in the *Hedland Advocate* more colourfully titled 'Nigger Shooting' stated that on 24 June 1906 Constables Forbes and Johnson were attacked while making arrests. Forbes was wounded in the chest and arms but reported shooting and killing his aggressor.[104] The shootings were not fully reported in the Aborigines Department Annual Report. In 1906 Chief Protector Henry Prinsep congratulated Constable Forbes for his patience while under attack but expressed his concern that thirty-nine men had been gaoled for three years for attacks on cattle at one isolated pastoral station alone. Although he agreed that 'the crimes were committed in very wild country, where it is necessary to show the efficacy of British law to these untutored savages', he believed it was time to consider feeding them beef at ration centres.[105]

Raids on bush camps in the northern region in 1906 marked the violent culmination of months of escalating tension. They pointed to the potentially disastrous and certainly frightening consequences of resisting European occupation of the country. The potential for loss of life or injury was clear, and the fear and anxiety were carried into oral tradition as a part of life for Indigenous people since before storytellers were born. They stated that a massacre occurred at Manning Gorge when the police station was there and that a separate massacre of a large number of people occurred near the Charnley River.[106] The details of names and places were not available for these specific events, although a story was told to me as I was driving, and therefore not taped or noted, of a man called Nipper throwing a spear at Forbes which hit him in the chest. The spear had no point so Forbes carried on. These stories were part of a generalized struggle between police and bush people. For instance, Phillip Krunmurra, who was the son of Charcoal the 'outlaw general', and Maggie Ghi, who was a child in the 1920s, made the following statements:

> *Phillip Krunmurra:* Ungadinda from that old police station. Yeah. That time now. That policeman he was a bit rough too.

> *Maggie Ghi:* Olden day policeman he been proper rough man because blackfella been rob longa policeman house, from a whitefella. They didn't lettem [white people] to come here. They didn't let to come here anyway. They bin havem big fight, blackfella and whitefella long that country![107]

Krunmurra's namesake, 'Crowanmurra', appeared on the police lists in 1906 as a male witness secured at Manning Gorge who had been among the group threatening to combine and kill the whites in the area. Indigenous resistance to white occupation is a constant theme in oral tradition.

Maggie Gudaworla and Harry Howendon were both born prior to 1914 near the Barnett station camp when the police camp was at Manning Creek. Howendon gave only a little information specific to that time, when his father was incorporated into the station workforce:

> Nother old police station been up to Nikol yard sitting on top the main river. Police station been there. Early days police station. All that way, gaol house [all the people] finish. I been little bugger when that police station [was at] Nikol yard ... My father never tell me. He been Mount Barnett [station] all day. After when he been run away they always bringim back house, 'til [I] was born.[108]

Gudaworla, whose namesake appeared on the police lists, described the police station era as a time when old people camped near the police and their trackers and received rations. Her mother was Woolinginna (pronounced by Gudaworla and other informants as Worlunyinna), also known as Maudie. She was Skinner's first woman from the Barnett area. Her aunt was the cook at the police camp and a tracker's wife. Gudaworla's stories of the police station era focus on the ration camp and old people starving in the bush. Billy King's mother and sister were also at the Isdell police camp. His aunt lived with a tracker, Wunnarra, who may have been Onearra. She moved to Mount House station, where Billy King was born in about 1920 to another ex-policeman and stockman, William King.

From late 1906 to early 1908 patrols of one or two policemen and six trackers ranged across the country from Isdell to the Fitzroy River, arresting men and securing witnesses who were camped at gorges and waterholes or hiding under cliff faces. Complaints were laid by stockmen and managers that cattle had been killed or chased on the leases. They combined with police to form posses and set out for camp sites and waterholes where they identified cattle bones or ovens, some not used for months. On three occasions men were arrested for being in possession of 'ornaments' made from bullock tails which they said had been given to them by other groups.[109] The system of arrests included people who had received stolen property even though the owners of the property could not be identified. Arrests from Isdell police camp were responsible for ninety-two of the 229 Kimberley men in gaols at Roebourne, Carnarvon, Broome and Wyndham in 1908.

The travelling 'protector' and a change in policy

By late 1908 the practice of arresting and gaoling Aboriginal people for killing or eating stolen beef was estimated to cost £20,000 per year. This was an expensive exercise for pastoral expansion into an area in which few people in the south had an interest. The government began to question a system that protected remote, understaffed and understocked pastoral leases. It had also invested large amounts of the departmental budget in isolating diseased Aboriginal people on Lock Hospital islands off the coast of

Carnarvon.[110] There was at this time a shift in public attitude towards the need for greater government intervention, which included issues like public health and the increasing incidence of venereal disease among Aboriginal women. Science and the state were uniting in their 'interest' in Aboriginal people. In 1907 the Chief Protector, Henry Prinsep, tried to argue that on the basis of new scientific evidence, which suggested that Aboriginal women who had a white child became infertile, there was a need for increased funding for the Aborigines Department, as well as support for policies that prevented white men living with Aboriginal women, 'in order to keep up the splendid supply of labour now available in the Northern region'.[111]

The change in policy was also brought about by the adverse publicity from the Roth Inquiry in 1904, Troy in 1906 and Professor Klaatz in 1907, who claimed that Kimberley Aboriginal people 'regarded every white person with dread' and that 'police officers were likened to dangerous animals'.[112] Public concern about the Canning Stock Route Inquiry in early 1908, and the police shooting of an Aboriginal woman in the Halls Creek area, placed the government under further pressure to intervene and reduce conflict in the newly occupied ranges areas of the north, central and east Kimberley. In response to calls from Kimberley residents for more police and tougher methods like flogging and dispersal to farms in the south-west to stop cattle killing, the Colonial Secretary reminded pastoralists that there were already twenty-seven police, twenty-nine trackers and 107 horses working from Wyndham alone.[113]

In 1908 evidence was given during the Canning Stock Route Inquiry that surveyor Rudall had never heard of the practice of exchanging gifts with Aboriginal people for their assistance. His method was to run them down and force them to find water.[114] Criticisms of the West Australian government were made by federal counterparts, and questions were officially put by the British government about the Canning Stock Route Inquiry. In the same year Frank Hann, who used similar methods to Rudall's to capture his assistants, found himself the subject of extreme public criticism, and gruesome descriptions appeared in the *Kalgoorlie Sun* of Hann 'flogging' Aboriginal men in order to steal their wives.[115]

The government also changed its policy on arresting and gaoling alleged cattle killers, in an attempt to curtail the spiralling costs of rationing Aboriginal people who were arrested, gaoled and increasingly moving into police ration camps or stations. In 1908 the travelling inspector of Aborigines, James Isdell, was engaged to check Kimberley stations and ration camps to ensure that rationing was necessary and not open to fraudulent practices. At the same time, he was charged with the protective duties enshrined in the 1905 Aborigines Act: ensuring that employers of Aboriginal people had permits, that no abuses against them occurred, that Aboriginal women did not cohabit with non-Aboriginal men and that children fathered by white men were removed to missions.[116]

James Isdell's report on the northern stations showed that by 1908 white men at Mount Hart, Mount House, Isdell, Barnett and Grace's Knob leases had permits for a small workforce—usually of one or two private boys, three men and three women from the area—plus one or two boys under sixteen and camps of old people and young children.[117] These were members of the core group who stayed near white men with occasional visits to the bush. White men lived in huts of bark and stamped earth built by Aboriginal people. At Mount Barnett, there were large numbers of old people and children living in a nearby camp. They were unable to survive in the bush because their male relatives were either in gaol or had left the area. There the old people survived on fish and the occasional 'handout' of bones, offal and kangaroo. Isdell suggested that the government should provide rations for the old people by paying the manager, Mick O'Connor, for beef. Any other rations like flour, tea or tobacco could not be supplied as the managers would not transport them the long distances from Derby for Aboriginal people. Isdell reported that he saw no half-caste girls at the station home-steads and those people who were working under permit were 'fat and happy'. His inspection of the stations north of the King Leopold Ranges was not repeated by an officer of the Aborigines Department until 1950.

Isdell reported that in the Mount Barnett and Isdell River area there were few young men left on the stations, and that of the few who moved in the area and were not attached to stations very few had not spent some time in gaol.[118] The system of punishing cattle killers was not working. In fact, he suggested that Aboriginal men in this region were 'very bad and treacherous' and that they enjoyed their stay in gaol, even asking him if their wives and children could accompany them. In the context of the women being left alone and at the mercy of other groups, individual whites and police trackers, or starvation, gaoling may have helped some Ngarinyin people to survive, despite the dislocation and absence from their country and extended families. Isdell also warned that Aboriginal women would soon replace men as cattle killers and that the idea of gaoling women would cause embarrassment to the government. He wrote:

> In a few years we will have the unusual spectacle of the women doing the cattle-killing, and the men sitting in camp waiting for their bit of steak. If a mob of women are arrested, brought in on the chain, tried and sentenced to a term of imprisonment, how they will have to be dealt with will be a difficult problem for any future Government to decide; and the general public are sure to take a big hand in it.[119]

Although costs were primarily responsible for the change in government arrest policies, issues of protection and the destructive impact of colonization were also canvassed in reports and debates which led to the setting up of reserves for Aboriginal people living in remote regions.

In July 1909 Isdell warned the Colonial Secretary and the Chief Protector of Aborigines that in some areas, particularly the east Kimberley, the environment and people's access to resources had altered so drastically that they needed beef to survive.[120] Simply reserving land for their use would not provide enough meat to keep them there. His suggestion for the formation of a government-run Aboriginal pastoral station between Fitzroy Crossing and Halls Creek was accepted, and in 1910 Moola Bulla was established and expected to accommodate up to 1,000 people. The Chief Protector was instructed by the Colonial Secretary not to have uniformed police on the reserve as 'a uniformed policeman, in the eyes of the natives, is the greatest enemy he has, and the less we have to do with uniforms the better it will be for all concerned'.[121] He was also told not to forget the value of handing out tobacco as an incentive to stay near the ration depot and to break bush people's spears if they continued to kill cattle. He believed the Moola Bulla reserve would attract people from outlying areas, even those over the ranges to the north, and therefore assist pastoral expansion in the new country beyond the Leopold Ranges. Chief Protector Gale also tried, with little success, to find an overseer who could work with Aboriginal people but who did not have the 'habit too common amongst stock-men in these parts of abusing natives and calling them names'.[122]

In 1911 the one-million-acre Marndoc reserve on the north-east coast was also established as a reserve where Aboriginal people would be protected from contact with white people and where they would not need rations. A Benedictine mission (1908) at the mouth of the Drysdale River and a Presbyterian mission (1912) at Kunmunya on the north-west coast were also established in this period. Moola Bulla and Marndoc were long distances from the central ranges and provided an alternative means of survival only for people who were on the fringes of Ngarinyin country. The missions were also peripheral to interactions and relationships with white men in this very early period.

The impact of changing policies on police practices was first evident in the northern ranges in 1909, when the Isdell police followed up a report from Billy Skinner that hundreds of Aboriginal people were gathering on the Mount Barnett lease between the Manning, Barnett and Hann Rivers. Skinner was one of the first stockmen on the Barnett River and had reportedly been living with Woolinginna from at least 1905. When the police investigated Skinner's complaints in 1909, they found camps, ovens, broken spears, half-eaten calves and dead cows distributed over a wide area, 'right out in the open, in the middle of the cattle run'.[123] At Bella Creek, which runs into the Hann River, the wire stockyard had been destroyed when all the wires from sixty-three panels were removed. Heavy stockyard wire was in demand for spear making. It was expensive and difficult to replace because it had to be packed out on horseback from the towns and through the Fitzroy stations also owned by Rose Bros. Towards Hann Gorge and Mount Elizabeth the police found an area of broken trees and tracks where animals had bogged and been speared, and 'under a shady tree, there were sticks placed across two rails making a table on which the beef had been laid'.[124] This site was where Skinner and his assistants had 'come onto' the group and scattered them while riding the boundaries of the Barnett lease.

The police confirmed Skinner's report that there were at least 100 people involved in the feasting and destruction of the stock-yards. They tracked and raided various groups of old people and women, who said they were meeting for a corroboree on top of Manning Gorge not far from the police camp, but found only small numbers of men. The Barnett station bush people, who were supposedly no longer a threat to pastoral occupation, had joined with visiting bush people from the north and helped to kill cattle and destroy the yards. The police made no arrests on any of the raids because of 'lack of evidence'.

In 1910 another incident went without any arrests, despite the police, who were accompanied by Mick O'Connor, finding '15 cattle tails, fencing wire cut into pieces and made into spears'. They were apparently outnumbered by 'a number of male natives coming towards [them] with spears, in open order and appeared to be sneaking into our camp'.[125] The same patrol reported that there was a good area of 10,000 acres which could be used for an Aboriginal reserve and that the pastoral leases near Mount Barnett, Mount Elizabeth and Gibb River, which had been owned by Rose Bros, held less than 100 wild and frightened cattle.

In February 1910 Bobby Brown, the overseer for Felix Edgar at Mount Hart, reported that he was in danger of being forced off the station by Aboriginal people. The incident was reported in the *Hedland Advocate* under the heading 'Natives Take Possession at Mt Hart':

> Natives have taken possession of the station, and the cattle have all gone. One hundred natives at the old yard, Barker River; over thirty showed fight; broke a number of their spears. Cattle must be brought away or natives shot.[126]

The article stated that 'feeling was strong' in Derby that police needed to provide better protection or pastoralists would abandon their stations. But the police were changing their practices. They refused to muster an official party to respond to the alleged cattle killing, arguing instead that Brown was known to be 'excitable', that the police did not believe cattle killing actually took place and that the station was insufficiently manned by white men to deserve police protection.[127]

Government inquiries into allegations of incorrect arrest and gaoling procedures and fraudulent rationing claims were under way by late 1910.[128] This was reported in the northern press and followed up in 1911 with a story about Brodie, the 'honest' Derby policeman who helped to release alleged cattle killers from prison, and threats to publish embarrassing details about ration profits being shared around the Kimberley by storekeepers and police.[129]

The push to open the country through an intense campaign of arrests gradually receded, with no further arrests for cattle killing in that district between mid-1910 and 1915. This term coincided with C.F. Gale's period as Chief Protector of Aborigines. Gale was an ex-northern pastoralist who tackled the issue of the government subsidizing station ration costs as well as the system of arresting cattle killers. He also instructed police to arrest only the ringleaders in cattle killing cases,

> instead of arresting all and sundry natives who happened
> to be eating some of the beast killed by their comrades.
> The whole party were generally convicted on the admis-
> sion of their guilt; an easy enough matter to obtain from
> practically uncivilised natives.[130]

The following year Gale reported that the number of arrests for cattle killing had decreased by 197. In response to government rations being withdrawn on stations, some managers in the Murchison, Gascoyne and Pilbara regions refused to provide rations for old people on their stations, taking limited responsibility only for young workers. This was the first sign of conflict between the government and pastoralists over who was responsible for Aboriginal people from pastoral leases. Gale wrote to all pastoralists employing Aboriginal labour to enlist their support to provide rations for old Aboriginal people on their leases. He reported in 1910 that he hoped for assistance, especially from those who,

> having borne the heat and burden of the early pioneering days, assisted mostly by native labour, realise their obligations to those natives who have grown too old for further service, and who are the parents or relatives of the younger employees, by providing them with the necessaries of life at their own expense.[131]

Ration costs were cut by half in 1910. They became the subject of ongoing tensions between the government and pastoralists for the next fifty years.

In 1911 the Aborigines Act of 1905 was amended to lessen the likelihood that Aboriginal people would be gaoled for cattle killing and to provide legislative support for greater government intervention in Aboriginal people's lives. They could no longer provide evidence of their own guilt, and owners of the stolen cattle or those laying the complaint were required to appear in court.[132] Stockmen refused to travel the distances, and police began to scrutinize their complaints.[133] The per capita ration allowance was also withdrawn and replaced by a system of prepaid stores, thus removing the profit incentive.[134] By 1912 there were only three men left in prison who had been convicted of cattle killing offences. Chief Protector Gale suggested that a permanent solution to the problem could be found by deporting the ringleaders' wives and families from the regions, thus eliminating future resistance by 'breaking up' the groups. The First World War intervened and Gale was sacked in 1915. But the idea of detaining wives to control the whole group became an important part of local relationships between European Bosses and Aboriginal people.

Between 1910 and 1914, the Isdell police post was an unofficial ration camp where old people received blankets, flour and kangaroo meat, while younger relatives worked on nearby stations. Police also provided medicines to some of the men and women who were reportedly suffering from venereal disease. About fifteen people from the Isdell camp who were suspected of carrying venereal disease were sent to Derby and then on to island hospitals off the coast of Carnarvon, a thousand kilometres south.[135]

Finances for extending settlement within Australia came under further pressure with the beginning of the First World War. From 1914 police were instructed to again cut costs by limiting their use of trackers and ammunition. Superiors in Perth were warned that police would not want to patrol with only one tracker and would not move across the ranges alone. The police station at Isdell was closed, as were the police out-camps throughout the Kimberley, the system of supporting pastoral settlement shifting to occasional patrols from Derby, Fitzroy Crossing and Turkey Creek.[136] At that time, only four leases north of the King Leopold Ranges were occupied, and only one, Glenroy, had an owner residing on it, ex-policeman Spong, who had engaged Jandamarra in clashes during the 1890s.[137] Isdell Downs was 'about to close', and Mount Barnett was 'soon to follow suit' due to the poor condition of the soil and grasses.

According to the police report that had led to the closure of Isdell police camp, the local Aboriginal people still speared a few cattle but were no longer 'wild' and a threat to white men's lives as they had been in 1903.[138] They had also suffered from an epidemic of malaria and widespread venereal disease.[139] In 1916 the new Chief Protector of Aborigines, A.O. Neville, tried to have the police station reopened as part of his plan to establish a chain of ration depots across the Kimberley. But the Commissioner of Police did not want to commit his troops to the task and told Chief Protector Neville that he should 'open a ration station not a police station'; he was not going to direct his men to feed and administer medicines to Aboriginal people.[140] Neville did not open a ration station in the northern ranges, nor did he have protectors other than the occasional police patrols to report on the region.

The First World War depleted the Kimberley of white stock-men, and several of the younger men who had occupied the northern leases when Rose, Blythe and Game owned them joined the armed services.[141] The pastoral stations continued to be occupied by even smaller numbers of white men, who surrounded themselves with Aboriginal workers and enforced their own form of rough justice and discipline. It has been suggested that by 'about the beginning of the First World War', the northern ranges leases were 'settled'.[142] This accords with the police rationale for closing the Isdell post. However, oral testimony, together with police patrol journals and incident reports after 1914, suggests that the closure of the police camp ended the official campaign of arrests for cattle killing but did not significantly alter the climate of fear and potential for violent clashes between stockmen and Indigenous people. Struggles over the control of women and workers resulted in continued conflict and some killings. The ranges were not settled.

CHAPTER TWO

'Stone blind in their need of Christ': the early days Bosses, 1915–1930

A FTER the police closed the Isdell post in 1914 the relentless campaign of gaoling and dispersing large groups of unknown bush people stopped. It was replaced by a more discriminating process of reward for individuals and small groups who were allied to a white Boss and severe and swift punishment of those who refused to acquiesce. From 1915 to the early 1930s, stockmen and managers in the central and northern ranges were assisted by occasional police patrols, with peaks in official activity in 1916 and 1922 after white men were murdered. On these occasions police made extensive and coordinated raids on bush camps over a wide area.[1] Patrols on the coast near Drysdale mission in 1920 and to Kunmunya mission and north to Cape Voltaire in 1921 were also made in response to alleged murders of white men, although bodies were never found.[2] For most of the time white stockmen were responsible for occupying and settling the region without continuous police assistance or scrutiny into the methods they used. Fred Russ, whose father settled Gibb River station, remembered the early days as a time when 'You were a law unto yourself up there. The police wouldn't have cared.'[3]

From 1919 to 1925 cattle killing incidents continued to be reported in the north and central Kimberley, resulting in arrests and gaoling of about ninety Aboriginal men.[4] A severe drought in 1924 was followed by the massacres at Forrest River in 1926.[5] Chief Protector Neville responded by establishing the Munja government ration station on the coast in 1926 to prevent Aboriginal people becoming a threat to white men and their cattle by moving onto pastoral stations. The role of the police changed from arresting large groups of Aboriginal men to dispersing them from pastoral leases, destroying their dogs and spears, and arresting leaders or individual 'trouble makers'. Some of the nomad whites also found themselves outside the boundaries of acceptable behaviour and in conflict with police, who occasionally enforced the 'protective' clauses of the Aborigines Act against their interests. In general, relationships between white men and Aboriginal people remained extremely fragile, with conflict over Aboriginal women increasing. The result was that on a number of occasions the killing of a white man precipitated government intervention in the form of terrifying raiding parties to 'resolve' the conflict.

Violence and the threat of it continued to circumscribe relationships between Aboriginal people and white men, but greater familiarity and experience led to increasing security for the small numbers of people who were able to work, share land, women and children, and assist white men with other Aboriginal groups. For some women and children survival was more certain. But this pattern did not apply evenly to the region over the Leopold Ranges, and some individuals and groups found themselves outside the managers' protection, despite having assisted them earlier. For them it was a return to chaos. In the north, beyond the King Leopold and Phillips Ranges, another phase of pastoral expansion in the early 1920s brought renewed violence and dislocation to the region.

The lateness of this expansionary exercise meant that older informants had experienced it and could provide detailed accounts of their experiences. Their narratives, together with written sources, show that the peaks of official police activity evident in written records were accompanied by a localized process of accommodation which had a significant impact on their chances of survival.

They also show that white men's behaviour, regardless of whether they were settling new country or not, was unpredictable. Finding a good and reliable Boss was a difficult and risky business. Only a few stations in the northern region developed in this period into large homestead camps, with the material trappings of a successful pastoral enterprise and a highly structured, work-based regime. The majority of Ngarinyin people experienced a protracted period of instability, which intensified from about 1919 through the 1920s as white stockmen struggled to establish their own pastoral leases in marginal and isolated country around Mount Barnett, Gibb River, Mount House and east to Ellenbrae and Tableland stations. By the early 1930s, many of them had failed to develop a pastoral station and turned instead to peanut crops, prospecting, selling dingo scalps, sandalwooding, contract droving or labouring for the few stations in the region that could afford to pay for labour. They also turned to each other, exchanging dog scalps for stores, especially tobacco. By the mid-1930s when Ion Idriess travelled in the region, the manager at Munja ration station on the coast described the area north of the King Leopold Ranges as the 'underworld of the Kimberleys'.[6] Missionary visitors more kindly described the white occupants as 'stone blind in their need of Christ'.[7]

The period from 1915 to the early 1930s is referred to in contemporary Ngarinyin discourse as part of the 'early days', when informants and their families were 'getting used to' white men and forming their first relationships with a white Boss. Within the early days stories there is a subset of narratives and biographical information which revolves around the actions and impact of a white man called Jack Carey, who worked on the pastoral leases north of the Leopold Ranges from 1915 to 1929.[8] According to available written sources, William John (Jack) Carey was born in 1892 and was a young stockman in the north Kimberley in 1915 and a pastoral leaseholder at Gibb River station from 1922. He was declared unfit for the armed services because of malaria when he attempted to enlist in August 1918 aged twenty-six.[9] The *Nor'West Echo* reported on 22 August 1925 that Jack Carey had had an accident in a motor vehicle on the way to Halls Creek. Fred Merry took over at Mount Barnett as manager in the same year. Although Carey was rarely mentioned in official records and was completely absent from Ion Idriess's account of the white men of the northern ranges, which included men with whom Carey lived and worked, his activities were firmly entrenched in oral history. Young and old know a portion of the Jagari (Jack Carey) story.[10] As Morndi Munro (Morndingali) said:

> Not too many gardias like Jack Carey. [He] been a bad man, proper bad man. No gardia been like him. I don't know about Ned Kelly but Jack Carey we know … I know that man I seen that man … Police never try to caught him. I don't know how come. He must have his own Law. He done that all the way down, cutting man ankle, cutting man shoulder, chuck a salt on the people, made'm crawl around taking all the pain. Died there. Put a chain around them and chase'm in the water. Make'm swim and killem. That what he done. All that story about Jack Carey. That story is all around the place, I tell you, all around you can hear that Jack Carey, big story … Only bloke can beat him, that Ngulit.[11]

Within oral tradition, Carey was a significant historical figure because of his immediate impact on some storytellers and because he was representative of the worst aspects of relationships between Indigenous people and early days white men. In a clan-based contact history, Jack Carey stands apart from other early days whites as a significant individual whose actions were directly linked to the dispersal and near-extinction of the primary custodians of land near Gibb River, Mount Elizabeth and Mount Barnett. Carey the white man killed, maimed, threatened and 'cleared out' the area. But he was not alone. The narratives include information about other people, black and white, who lived and worked with him and who came into conflict with him. They contain a range of detailed information about small groups' attempts to negotiate with white men and with each other. They also extend into the realm of magical interactions between the clan's 'wish man' or *banmun*, Ngulit, and Jack Carey, police and trackers.

The stories of resistance and trickery through magic are perhaps the most important aspect of the narratives for Ngarinyin storytellers. People grew intensely interested and animated when Ngulit and his activities were mentioned. Ngulit, rather than Jack Carey, is the most significant actor in their history. As a representative of the deepest aspects of Ngarinyin law, he can never be defeated and his death in the Derby leprosarium in 1944 was 'not really him'.[12] Many of Ngulit's extraordinary feats and accomplishments refer to a realm of interactions and responses which inform this research but lie outside its analytical scope. What is important here is Carey's representation in the narratives as having broken the emergent rules of confrontation and negotiation of the early days. His status in the narratives as being different from other early days white men provides a descriptive focus for understanding the limits of expected behaviour after the police had left the Isdell police post. Carey represented a break with the emerging pattern—a reference point in a new ethic.

The policy of 'protection'

During the period under review there were few external constraints on white stockmen's relationships with Aboriginal people throughout the Kimberley and even fewer in the northern ranges. The overriding ideal enshrined in the West Australian 1905 Aborigines Act was the development and expansion of the pastoral industry, with Aboriginal people remaining on pastoral stations under the benevolent control of European managers and stockmen. While the Act gave the Chief Protector the right to remove Aboriginal adults to any district or institution if he believed it was in their interests, Aboriginal people under an employment permit were exempt from the removal clauses.[13] In practice, the Act was aimed at minimal interference in station relationships unless there were half-caste children or extreme cases of abuse. This was primarily an economic response from the government to avoid the cost of rationing dispossessed people or non-workers on pastoral stations. It enhanced pastoralists' access to an Indigenous labour force and placed them in the position of controlling Aboriginal people's capacity to live in or near their country as well as managing their integration into the station system. It was based on the belief that Aboriginal people were better off on the stations, where they would be integrated into pastoral development and kept away from the vices of prostitution and alcohol which existed in towns and mining camps. On pastoral stations they would participate in an employment system of self-contained communities, dividing their time and energy between the station and the bush, under the supervision of managers and white stockmen. Stockmen would be assisted by occasional visits from the police who carried out the protective functions of the Aborigines Department under the 1905 Act. These included ensuring employers held an employment permit signed by a protector of Aborigines and discouraging them from cohabiting with Aboriginal women.

During his time as Chief Protector, from 1915 to 1940, A.O. Neville made occasional attempts to regulate station relationships in the Kimberley but met with determined and effective resistance from the pastoral lobby which dominated parliament and resented government intervention in its affairs.[14] He therefore ended up concentrating on the institutionalization of adults south of the Kimberley and half-caste Aboriginal children throughout Western Australia. Neville also made several attempts to establish inalienable reserves and ration depots for displaced Aboriginal people, and to introduce a form of wages for northern pastoral employees.[15] It was in 1916, when Aboriginal labour was at a premium due to the First World War, that he attempted to introduce a system of wages for pastoral workers. This was rejected after a change of government the same year, and was again turned down by cabinet in 1922. Further attempts in 1925 and '27 never reached cabinet because of pressure from the pastoral lobby led by A.A.M. Coverley, MLA for the Kimberley. In 1928 a proposal for wages in a draft Aborigines Bill was deleted in cabinet, again due to pressure from northern pastoralists who 'objected to the Bill because it gave the Department too much power to interfere with their affairs'.[16]

Neville's capacity to intervene on pastoral stations was severely limited by lack of staff and finances, as well as the political necessity to concentrate on the south. Parliamentarians' support for a policy of non-interference in the Kimberley merely added to his problems. The Aborigines Department was hopelessly underfunded for the task of 'protection' of people in isolated areas. And when Neville took up the Chief Protector's position in 1915, the department had only a vague idea of how many Aboriginal people occupied the Kimberley region.[17] During his time in office a travelling inspector was appointed for the Kimberley, between 1924 and '29.[18] The travelling inspector's tasks were: to reduce the numbers of Aboriginal people on rations, and thus the cost to the state; to report on the missions and government stations at Moola Bulla (1910) and Munja (1926); to collect part-descent children for missions and government institutions; to oversee court cases involving Aboriginal people; and to report abuses of the permit system. The travelling inspector visited Broome, Derby, Fitzroy Crossing, Wyndham and Moola Bulla, with occasional visits to stations along the Fitzroy valley. He did not visit the stations in the hinterlands north of the Leopold Ranges, relying instead on word of mouth from permit holders, the Munja manager after 1926, the mission at Kunmunya and police patrols.

The 1905 Act instituted a system of work permits intended to provide minimal protection for Aboriginal workers through government supervision of the types of people who became Bosses. The system was weighted in favour of pastoral employers, requiring only that the Boss supply 'substantial, good, and sufficient rations, clothing and blankets, and also medicines and medical attendance when practicable and necessary'.[19] An Aboriginal person under permit was liable to prosecution for leaving his or her place of work, refusing to work, neglecting to fulfil required tasks, or deserting or quitting his work 'without the consent of his employer'.[20] It legalized the practice of police returning 'absconders' to stations, without formally asserting pastoralists' responsibility for rationing the old or infirm. That was left to managers and stockmen in exchange for limited interference from the state in employment contracts and conditions, or in the methods used by stockmen and managers to train and retain a workforce.

In the remote Kimberley, pastoralists were allowed to employ under a general permit. This could cover whole communities who were listed without names under the headings of workers, male and female, indigents, children and half-castes. Just who the workers were was unknown to the department, as pastoralists were required to give only the total number of 'natives employed'. Even the local police had little knowledge of which Aboriginal person came under which permit agreement. When James Isdell inspected stations in the northern ranges in 1908, he issued the first general permits to the managers at Mount House, Isdell Downs, Mount Barnett, Mount Hart and Napier stations to cover seventy-six Aboriginal employees: thirty-two men, thirty-six women, two boys and six girls under sixteen years.[21] The only 'single permit' on which the employee was named was issued at Mount House for a Queensland Aboriginal assistant named Queensland Charlie.[22] General permits enabled pastoralists to expand and contract their workforce as required and gave the employer legal backing to enlist the assistance of the police to round up employees. Brown at Mount Hart was issued with a general permit by Isdell in 1908 so that he could 'employ some more bush natives' as he came across them.[23] The practice of raiding camps for workers was called prospecting for children. Even as late as 1940, when the Fyfe Royal Commission inquired into conditions in the northern pastoral industry, the commissioner recommended continuing the system of general permits. This allowed pastoralists to take on 'excess' labour or a pool of labourers to accommodate the variation in the workforce as people moved away to the bush or became ill or disabled.[24] General permits were also more economical than single permits, with a maximum fee of £2 per year for an unlimited number of Aboriginal people. Single permits, at 10s per person per year, were only economical for self-employed wagon drivers, cooks or yard builders who had one trained Aboriginal worker whom they wanted to make sure no one else poached.

In 1913 there were 748 Aboriginal men and 530 Aboriginal women recorded as working under permit in the Kimberley. By the end of the First World War, the total number had risen to 2,279.[25] In 1930 1,041 Aboriginal people were employed in the Derby region alone, under thirty general permits.[26] The rise was due to the increased demand for labour as white men enlisted for service in the First World War, and to more intense supervision of the permit system after the arrival of A.O. Neville as Chief Protector in 1915. Neville instituted a more rigorous system which cancelled all permits on 30 June each year and stipulated that applications had to be viewed by the magistrate in Derby. Previously, employers only applied once to a policeman or to their neighbour, who could be a protector or justice of the peace, and the permit could be transferred to the new leaseholder as a land and labour package.[27]

In the northern ranges in the 1930s there were general permit holders at Gibb River, Mount House, Mount Hart and Kurunjie, which were the main pastoral work centres, but very few single permits. Apart from the new restrictions, permits could be a problem for some stockmen and employers when the police performed their protection duties of checking on all permit holders. Police visits might draw attention to living conditions and white Bosses' relationships with Aboriginal people. Permit holders were sometimes threatened with cancellation of their permits if they were reported by police or fellow stockmen to be living with Aboriginal women. It was the anti-cohabitation clauses which emerged in this period that became the main reason for government attempts at 'protective' intervention on stations in the northern ranges, rather than concern over the climate of fear and intimidation in which labour was recruited.

This system of protection through permits placed white stock-men and managers in the position of overseeing Aboriginal people and reporting to police patrols if there were problems beyond their control. But cases of abuse of permits came to the Aborigines Department's attention only occasionally from 1915 to the early 1930s, and they were rarely successfully prosecuted. In the northern ranges it was possible to stay outside the permit system because there were so few inspectors or protectors pursuing the department's protective obligations under the Act. Neville's scrutiny of the permit system did not challenge many permit holders or address violence on the stations over the ranges. However, it brought occasional cases of excessive brutality to light and increased pressure on single white men to deny that they employed Aboriginal women and to hide their sexual relationships with them.

Taming and detaining workers

Mick O'Connor, who was known to Ngarinyin storytellers as Migana, was a stockman at Isdell Downs from early 1905 to 1915 when the police camp was officially closed. In 1908 Travelling Inspector Isdell had suggested that O'Connor be given a general permit as well as a ration allowance to provide beef to the old people who were moving into camps for food. For twelve months after the decision was made to close it, the police camp also operated as a ration depot, with beef provided for twenty-two people. Maggie Gudaworla, who was born about 1912 near the Mount Barnett police camp, was adamant that her mother, father, uncles and aunts were not ration camp people: they were workers who stayed with stockmen. The ration depot at the police camp was for old people, while workers stayed with O'Connor. Maggie's aunt lived with the police tracker and cooked the old people's food. By the time the police abandoned Isdell camp, Gudaworla's parents and some of their affiliates had moved into the sphere of white men's assistants by becoming stockmen and stockwomen, trackers or cooks. Gudaworla's description of Mick O'Connor, their first white Boss, was typical of most informants' contradictory portrayals of early days Bosses: a 'bad man but a good manager'. He fed some people, dealt harshly with everyone and was capable of killing.

After the police camp closed, O'Connor moved to occupy the vacant police hut where old people and women remained. The women tried to leave the camp, and here Gudaworla describes O'Connor's methods of taming two of her 'aunties' for station work:

> Old man Migana (Mick O'Connor) … that's the Boss belongin to early days. He's cheeky one too … when twofella girl been get away, leavim kitchen. Two fella cook there. Alright two fella bin go way now. That on top that hill [Mount Barnett]. Whole lot, big mob go way. All the girl. Alright he bin go gettim horse and he bin climb up that right longa house, that police man route. Police station already gone. They bin makim longa Isdell first time, now they bin go there longa gorge [Manning

Gorge]. Migana there now. He live there, kitchen. Right sit down there. He bin climb up there. Migana chasim all about close up longa house, that on top way. He bin catchim twofella, tie im up twofella. Fire em all round, grass ... [crying]. Two fella bin sit down longa chain. He bin burnem round. Twofella bin cry. They bin ... [crying].

Right he bin takem twofella now, gotta chain, home, Mount Barnett. Right twofella bin sit down there. One day, right he bin take im out twofella [from the chain] go longa kitchen ... He never killem, 'cause that two girl bin young yet. He bin want to keepem twofella. Every boy bin married em girl there, all the time.[28]

In 1915 O'Connor moved away from Mount Barnett to occupy his own small lease just south of the Leopold Ranges at Mount Joseph. He moved again in about 1916 to another small lease at Paddy's Paddock north-east of Mount House. Mount Joseph was bought by M.C. Davies who owned the neighbouring lease, Kimberley Downs. O'Connor was one of the 'smallholders' of 'salt beef and damper days' referred to in Bolton's study of the Kimberley pastoral industry. They survived by selecting a pocket lease between or next to larger stations, branding strays from the larger leases and then selling out to the leaseholders after making enough of a nuisance of themselves to get a reasonable price.[29] They travelled with at least one Aboriginal woman and a male assistant, and expanded their workforce by using people who moved in the bush.

Police Paddy, or Wundigul, and his wife Manuworla joined O'Connor at Mount Joseph and then moved on to work at Mount Hart after O'Connor went east out of Wundigul's country. Weeda Munro was a child when her father and mother worked at Mount Joseph with O'Connor. Gudaworla's aunt and her tracker husband moved to Mount House after the police station closed but continued to 'holiday' in the area. Morndingali's mother had been taken from Mount Barnett by her husband when he drove a herd of cattle from Napier Downs to Grace's Knob for James Game to stock the lease. Billy Skinner was left at Isdell Downs, the furthest north of the pastoral camps, dealing with the people who had survived the first period of occupation in the Mount Barnett and Gibb regions and who were not removed to towns or other stations with police and stockmen. He estimated that there were approximately 300 Aboriginal people living between Isdell and Mount Hart station camps.[30]

In 1915 Skinner came to the notice of the Chief Protector after he was charged with the manslaughter of a young Aboriginal man, Billy, or Chameron, at Isdell Downs station.[31] Skinner had come north as a stockman working for Rose Bros and formed the first camp at Mount Barnett in 1904. Maggie Gudaworla's mother, Worlunyinna, or Maudie, was captured by police as a witness. She left with Skinner in 1905. Her brother Donkey, or Marmandoo, was a young boy at Skinner's camp when the incident occurred. Gudaworla's narrative about Skinner killing her uncle mirrors the events detailed in police records.[32] In 1915 Skinner was manager of Isdell Downs for James Game with two white assistants, one of whom was Peter Backsen, who provided Idriess with stories in the early 1930s when he lived in a bush camp north-west of Isdell Downs.[33] Skinner was arrested and charged by Constable Napier on patrol from Fitzroy Crossing where he had been stationed after the closure of the Isdell post.

Evidence from witnesses and the accused established that Skinner and Backsen had gone to the stockworkers' camp, about 100 yards from the white men's camp, to remove Dolly, or Dadai, from the stock 'boys' who were 'fooling about' with her. Backsen fired shots above their heads with his revolver; Skinner carried a rifle. She stayed the night in the white men's hut and the following morning was 'frightened' by one of the stockmen into running away from the hut. Skinner followed her to the camp. He was armed and surrounded by dogs. His dogs fought with the stockmen's dogs, and Chameron hit Skinner's dog. At this, Skinner hit Chameron who then picked up a stone and threatened Skinner. In turn, Skinner fired a warning shot and then fired at Chameron's neck. In April 1915 Skinner was acquitted of the charge without putting up a defence. Chief Protector Neville, acting on the advice of Crown law that a 'glaring miscarriage of justice' had occurred, and the fact that Skinner was known to be a very heavy drinker, cancelled his permit to work Aborigines.[34]

Skinner went back to Isdell Downs after the court case and continued to manage the station until early 1916, when he came into conflict with the police and lost control of his trained workers and the camps of bush people nearby. The patrol was part of an expedition of two parties made up of police, white stockmen and at least seven trackers. They swept through the region from Napier Downs station to Federal Downs station and the Mount Barnett area in search of Rinjalngu, or Spot, the alleged murderer of a white man, George Aukland.[35] O'Connor had known Aukland for many years, having worked with him to establish Isdell Downs. O'Connor, Jack Dale, Jack Carey and other white station workers accompanied the police at different stages of their patrol. Aukland had been murdered at Federal Downs camp in late 1915. Federal Downs was west of Mount Hart and north of Napier Downs; it was a small lease taken up by Derby butcher and storekeeper, McGovern. Aukland and his white assistant occupied the lease, living in a small wooden hut. It was alleged that Aukland had threatened to shoot Spot after chaining his wife, Maudie, to the verandah post. Maggie Gudaworla's narrative of this incident stated that Maudie, not her husband, killed Aukland.[36] And a report in the northern press stated that the murderer found his wife manacled to the bed in the company of George Aukland.[37]

The patrols searched camps throughout the region, shooting 104 dogs and engaging in a stand-off with Aboriginal people at a large granite rock called Mundooma. The journals of this expedition correlate with Ngarinyin people's stories of two massacres on the northern boundaries of the Napier Downs lease which occurred in the aftermath of Aukland's death.[38] One, at Limestone Spring, involved only police, while the other, at Mundooma, an easily distinguishable granite rock, was said to have been led by Police Paddy, or Wundigul, Weeda Munro's father. He was picked up by the police party from Mount Hart station in late 1915 for the purpose of tracking the alleged murderer.[39] The police journals do not record any killings or injuries to Aboriginal people, but particular trouble spots are mentioned which are also the alleged massacre sites, suggesting that some violent encounters occurred. The reports state euphemistically that on one occasion a group of twenty-five people were 'frightened somewhat' by the dawn raid which resulted in twenty dogs being killed.[40] On another, at a large granite rock, it took the police and trackers two hours to persuade people to stop throwing rocks at them and come down to be questioned.[41]

The police patrols moved north until they were one mile from Skinner's camp at Isdell Downs. Here they raided a camp of 166 people, shot and killed seventy-six dogs and chained forty people to trees, but they missed Spot, who was in the camp but escaped with his wife Maudie. The patrols camped in the area for four days, but their journals do not record what happened during this time. On 9 January the police received a message from Billy Skinner that he had Spot and Maudie at his station camp. Spot's legs were badly bitten by Skinner's dogs. Maudie and Spot walked to Fitzroy police station and then on to Derby.

Spot was well known to Skinner, who worked him at Mount Barnett in 1907 and knew he was part of the extended station group that moved between Mount Barnett and Mount Hart.[42] He was not a trained horseman but one of a group of local people who travelled on foot between two or three leases in their clan countries, carrying messages between white men's camps, reporting on the condition of waterholes and assisting white men with specific labour-intensive tasks. Leases did not have large numbers of horses, which were expensive and subject to disease. Instead managers relied on bush-walking groups who were semi-integrated into their work regime and were known to be living in their own country and therefore unlikely or unable to leave. The key was ensuring that people came to camp regularly enough to be of assistance. In 1915 Spot had been picked up at Mount Hart station by George Aukland and taken outside his familiar country to Federal Downs. According to Skinner,

Opposite: Some families managed to accommodate white men's needs and continue to meet and walk in their country between waterholes in the King Leopold Ranges and white men's camps. This photo was taken in about 1920. Courtesy WA Museum, photographer W.R. Easton

Spot had been handed over to Aukland by Constable Napier, and it was this interference in forcing him out of his country that had caused Aukland's death.

Spot was given a light sentence on the grounds of provocation. The Chief Protector did not want to return a 'murderer' to his country to create more trouble, so Spot and Maudie were sent to work at various places in the south-west, including the Perth police stables and a farm.[43] They were still in the south-west of the state in 1919 and may have been sent to Moore River settlement which opened in that year.

Skinner's complaints about the police in 1916 were fuelled by a grudge against Constable Napier for allowing him to be charged with Chameron's murder and standing by while he lost his permit to work Aborigines. Skinner's allegations present a picture of the double-edged nature of violence and dependency, fear and protection, which developed on the northern frontier. He stated that no Aboriginal person over the King Leopold Ranges would steal from a white man's camp or 'had done for years'. He always carried a revolver in camp and had been expecting conflict with his stock-workers as they had been getting 'cheeky' since the police had left Isdell.[44] He may have relied on a third party to write his letters as each one has a different style, and Resident Magistrate Elliot of Derby recorded comments on one of the letters, which suggests that he had written it. Elliot came into conflict with police in 1919 when he tried to cancel a stockman's permit on the grounds that he was a known 'combo' and 'living like blacks'.[45] The stockman, R.P. Griver of Liveringa station on the Fitzroy River, had written to the Chief Protector complaining that Aboriginal women across the Kimberley were not being adequately protected from prostitution. Magistrate Elliot then investigated the stockman, not liking what he found. He was particularly disturbed about Griver participating in a mourning ceremony over the death of his half-caste son. This was a sign of 'going native'. The police defended him to the Chief Protector as a good character, the case was withdrawn, and he was allowed to continue working with Aboriginal people.

The discourse of white racial superiority and need for purity is an interesting theme among these men who were performing the difficult task of living on the margins of empire. 'Going native' was not only a euphemism for living with an Aboriginal woman as husband and wife: it referred to empire—civilization—being overcome by the bush and becoming savage. Griver had danced naked in the bush, which seems to have upset the magistrate more than his having a half-caste son. Further comments from Jas Gallagher in the *Longreach Leader* in 1932 detailed Gallagher's views on practices of forcing Aboriginal people into a station workforce: these were based on his experience working on a station in the west Kimberley from 1927 to '32.[46] He argued for a degree of necessary violence to the extent of occasional killings by boundary riders to protect themselves and stock. He stated that the real problem was when white men 'went native', took a woman from a 'tamed' and trained 'boy' and then had to kill him because of jealousy. His comments were strongly denied by the Chief Protector, but they point to relationships that are supported by oral historical narratives and police files about the north Kimberley.

In one long letter written to Chief Protector Neville after the 1916 patrols in response to Aukland's death, Skinner accused the police of chaining any Aboriginal man or woman they could lay their hands on; forcing evidence from witnesses by threatening to kill them; sitting in camps while trackers were away for days at a time; starving witnesses; threatening to enforce laws against particular white men, and prosecuting 'cattle killing' on the basis of 'evidence' which was in fact old bones from beef rations.[47] He also suggested that killings had taken place on the 1916 patrol by two white stockmen, Bert Bowers and Charlie Taylor, who travelled with the police doing their 'dirty work' for them. The resident magistrate who assisted Skinner with the letter annotated it with the comment to the Chief Protector that if the allegations were only 50 per cent true, they needed an inquiry by a man like G.T. Wood. Once Crown prosecutor and resident magistrate of Broome, Wood later acted as royal commissioner into the massacre allegations on the Marndoc reserve in 1927.[48]

Constable Napier, in rejecting Skinner's allegations, stated that the region was a known trouble spot where 'several' Aboriginal people had been shot by police in self-defence and where policemen had been speared and injured.[49] The sergeant of police added that the officers were protecting Dolly from Skinner's attempts to cohabit with her and also protecting the two stockmen who were frightened they would be killed on their return to Skinner's camp.[50] He added that Napier had about as much to do with Aukland's death as 'Julius Caesar' and that the facts of the case were that 'Aukland in order to cohabit with Spot's gin handcuffed her legs together. Spot saw what happened and smashed the side of Aukland's head in.'[51] He also stated that Napier had resigned from the force and joined the Australian Imperial Force late in 1915. The police dismissed Skinner's allegations as mere grudges by a man who was illiterate and often drunk, and whose real motive for killing was jealousy over an Aboriginal woman. For Chief Protector Neville, Skinner was the type of white man from whom Aboriginal people needed protection: poor, prone to violence and drink, and cohabiting with Aboriginal women. He was, in the parlance of the time, in danger of 'going native' and crossing the boundary of publicly acceptable behaviour for white men.

The loss of a permit to work Aboriginal people had an immediate impact on Skinner. He was demoted from manager to head stockman and paid £2 instead of £6 per month.[52] Station owners who had nodding regard for the protective clauses of the 1905 Act and the permit system employed managers only if they had a general permit. Without a permit they could not manage a station, as they were not legally entitled to control an Aboriginal workforce which was vital to pastoral development. In 1918 Skinner was again reported by police for continuing to employ Aboriginal people when he had been banned from holding a permit because of the incident when he shot Billy at Isdell station. Two years later he was again in charge of Aboriginal people, this time at Oobagooma station. Skinner's manager had a permit to employ Aborigines and spoke personally to the resident magistrate in Derby, who wrote to the Chief Protector recommending no action on the grounds that 'Skinner's unlucky shot [of 1916] was unintentional, just to frighten'.[53]

Skinner's main problem was that he lost Aboriginal workers in whom he had invested time, energy and rations (and perhaps more in the case of Dolly, who worked in the white men's hut). He depended for his livelihood as a stockman or manager on his ability to find, train and keep Aboriginal workers. When Napier arrested him in 1915, he removed his most trusted female worker, Dolly, and the two core male stockworkers who had 'lived with him for years'. Skinner had 'got them out of the bush when they were young, [and] took a lot of trouble in learning them to work'.[54] Dolly was escorted to Derby by Napier's party and handed to Mrs Blythe. She was then released to travel with Scotty Sadler to Mount House, where he had established his own small pocket lease, Isdell Junction, between Mount House and Mount Hart stations. According to the police, this was her country.[55] Dolly moved on to become Jack Dale's wife and in 1920 gave birth to Jack Dale junior. The other two men were sent to Fitzroy Crossing with a fourteen-year-old boy from Skinner's camp.

After the police raid near Skinner's camp in 1916, Bert Bowers, who was travelling with the police and had a pastoral lease partnership in Isdell Junction with Scotty Sadler, took seven Aboriginal men and five women off the police chain to build up his own workforce. The police defended this as justified under the 1905 Act, as the Aboriginal people concerned said they did not belong to any other white Boss and Bowers had 'as much right to them' as Skinner.[56] Skinner was furious, writing:

> If I could not get natives to work for me or stay with me without having to get policemen to chain them up and hand over to me, I would carry my swag out of the country. Those people are all new settlers out here—any how those natives have all run away now. This treatment to blacks is only trying to make them bad. I don't think they will be any come here again for many a day, they got such a shaking up.[57]

He added that he had not made a cattle killing report since 1910, had assisted in capturing Spot for killing Aukland and had handled the large populations of Aboriginal people without police assistance: 'It looks to me if a man cannot get or keep natives without their [police] assistance that he should not be given a permit.'[58]

Skinner, like other stockmen and managers in this newly occupied region (and possibly throughout the pastoral north), maintained a fragile balance between coercion and accommodation in order to extend his influence to other groups of Aboriginal people. He tried to avoid continuous rationing of camp people or stimulating open conflict and resistance, which had dominated the earlier period when the police were stationed on his doorstep. White stockmen relied on an Indigenous system of authority and sustenance to develop the station, and on core workers for labour and assistance in managing local groups. Their core workers required the manager's accommodation to a range of their own social and economic activities, such as exchanging items with visitors and leaving the station camps to attend ceremonies. The camp of 166 people near Skinner's group of eighteen people at Isdell station in 1916 were known to Skinner and had visited before. When they came to visit they exchanged rations, clothes and items like glass and tin with the camp workers, as well as providing him with a pool of potential workers with whom he had been dealing for six years. In return, the core workers continued their separate sphere of ceremonial and social obligations with the additional resources of the station to encourage good relations with their neighbours.

On the occasion of the raid, Skinner had just released one of his trained stockmen, Charley (named Warramallener in the records), for a corroboree, giving him flour and tobacco and instructing him to 'come back when the fun was over.'[59] Charley and his wife were chained after the police raid in 1915 and removed by Bert Bowers to work further south at Isdell Junction with Scotty Sadler. Charley's removal stripped Skinner of a trained stockman and hunter who could shoot and spear game. It also changed the social dynamics of the camp and the relationship between the camp and bush visitors. Charley was no longer able to negotiate with bush people on Skinner's behalf. Removing key men challenged local authority systems and left Skinner unprotected and unaligned.

A 'family' of workers

Establishing a core group of labourers and gathering others from the bush for labour-intensive tasks was not easy. Scotty Sadler and Bert Bowers formed a partnership in 1915 on the Isdell Junction lease between Mount House and Mount Hart. Bowers brought his skills as a carpenter, stockman and general labourer to their pastoral enterprise.[60] He also brought valuable items like tools, saddlery, horses and mules. But the men had difficulty finding and keeping Aboriginal workers to develop the station. Sadler had brought his Aboriginal wife to the Isdell Junction camp, along with her brother, younger sisters, mother and father, and a young half-caste boy called Sandy from a Fitzroy River station. Only his wife, Coomie or Coombilya, and Sandy stayed with him for long periods; the others ran away to their home station soon after they had camped at the prospective homestead site, Imintji Springs (site of the present Imintji Aboriginal Community). With this small workforce, Sadler and Bowers built a hut and horse yard. They exchanged their specialist pastoral skills — spaying, branding and cutting cattle — with neighbouring stockmen and contractors for horses, mules, stores, cattle and the use of neighbours' yards. They started with thirty cattle, exchanged with O'Connor for mules and horses, and by 1917 they had 1,000 cattle, which the police alleged contained more than their fair share of animals from neighbouring leases.[61]

Coombilya and the boy Sandy travelled with Sadler, cooking, collecting wood and water, tailing horses, roping and assisting white men to cut, spay, dehorn or brand. In exchange, they received rations, which allegedly included extras such as soap and lollies for Coombilya.[62] They could also ride and help with musters if the neighbouring stockmen did not have enough labour of their own.

In general, men, women and the child Sandy dug post holes and foundations for the hut and carted stones, water and sand. There was no marked gender division of labour, and children also performed a range of tasks, which made them valuable assistants. They carried water, dug holes, watched horses and cattle, delivered messages to other managers and stockmen, and helped with domestic work. Women and children were less physically capable of resisting stockmen and running away on their own into the bush, and, if trained from a young age like Coombilya and Sandy, they were able to communicate with white men as well as being familiar with work requirements. Girls were taken as wives at a young age, while boys were working as stockmen by the time they were fourteen years old. Children were also future core workers on whom station managers could rely for support and assistance with pastoral work and with other Aboriginal groups.

According to the manager of Mount Hart, it was recognized practice in the region that only one white man per station worked on musters with an all-black team of workers.[63] Neighbouring stockmen and contractors visited Sadler and Bowers' camp regularly on their trips into and out of town with stores for the northern camps at Isdell, Mount Barnett, Mount House and Mount Hart. They all travelled with at least one Aboriginal assistant whom they occasionally left with Sadler or Bowers to help at the station or with a muster. They recognized specific Aboriginal people as belonging to certain white men and assisted each other to retain them if they ran away and went to other camps without permission from their Bosses. They were 'held' by giving them tobacco or rations until their Boss arrived.[64]

To develop the station, Sadler and Bowers needed more labour for tailing cattle, yard building and fencing to stop cattle wandering into heavy scrub or pockets in the nearby ranges. Bowers accompanied the police on their raids of camps in the Isdell region to recruit labourers, taking men and women off the chain to start his own workforce at his station. However, he managed to retain only one man and woman, who also ran away at the end of 1916. In February 1916 the police reported that Bowers was travelling in the region of the Margaret River 'trying to get Natives but was unsuccessful'.[65] Sadler went to Mount House and returned with a group of men and women. Two of the men ran away and Sadler followed, but there is no record of what transpired. Sadler made another attempt to find extra labour in early 1917, described here by Coombilya:

> Next day Scotty get em Horses & he & Peter go away. He
> take em two fellow pack horse & two fellow riding horse.

Scotty tell me he go away look out more Blackfellow to
help build em yard & tell Me & Nellie to look after Station
& dig more post holes.[66]

In February 1917 Bowers disappeared. Police came from
Perth to investigate, but the case was never resolved. They concluded that Sadler had the motive and cability to kill Bowers, but
there was no body and only a confusing trail of allegations against
Aboriginal people.[67] Wundigul, or Police Paddy, was named by three
Aboriginal witnesses as the murderer. He was one of a group of at
least fifteen Aboriginal men and women who met at a main waterhole during their wet season break while managers were away in
Derby. The station camp and store was watched by a white
stockman and old people, while mobile senior men and women
who were also workers travelled to meet their contemporaries from
other stations. Three men and women from Mount Hart met five
others from Mount House and then moved to a bush meeting place
where Munday and his group were camped. Munday had run away
from the police in 1905 when they tried to enlist him as a tracker for
the Isdell police camp.[68] He was named by Idriess as a black
bushranger wanted by police for murdering an Aboriginal man.[69]
Two of the other men had worked as trackers for the Isdell police
and were now incorporated into the station system as workers.
Another was Queensland Charlie, who was the only Aboriginal
person under single permit in 1908. He was a key worker at Mount
House, having been integrated into local social systems and given a
wife and responsibility for a particular tract of country.

According to the witnesses' statements, Bowers had approached
the group, sought help to unload his packs and then asked for one
of the women in exchange for food and tobacco. Her husband
refused, and Wundigul led the attack on him, throwing his body into
the waterhole and taking the stores. The station manager of Mount
Hart, Frank Gardiner, defended them, giving details of the group's
country and likely route during the wet season and stating that they
could not possibly have been in the area where they supposedly
killed Bowers. The police interviewed them again, with the result
that they all stated that the police tracker had threatened to shoot

and burn them if they didn't admit to the offence. The police accepted their statements and they were all released.

In fact, this group could have been at the pool where Bowers was supposedly killed, as it was not more than two or three days' walk from Mount Hart station. This suggests that in this case the manager did not wish to have them implicated because of their value as station workers. Indeed, ten years later, regardless of the official outcome of the murder investigation, Chief Protector Neville added the killing of Bowers to Wundigul's list of offences when he was gaoled for killing two Aboriginal men.[70]

The investigating officer nevertheless suggested that Sadler had encouraged the story, possibly even started it.[71] Sadler was labelled a 'combo' and castigated by the police because of evidence from Coombilya that he had made her kill three of their half-caste babies and forced her to hand two other babies to women at another station. Sadler replied that he did not have a direct hand in the deaths of the babies.

Jack Dale's mother, Dolly, later told her son stories of Bowers' disappearance. She had been removed from Skinner in 1915 by Constable Napier and had then travelled with Sadler to the Mount House area. She became Jack Dale senior's wife and camped with him at an out-camp of Mount House station, twenty-five miles from Sadler's Isdell Junction camp. She told how Bowers and Sadler had been fighting over their methods of training and detaining Aboriginal workers, and on the day of the disappearance they had had a violent fight. Sadler told police that on two occasions Bowers had caused workers to run away. Just before Bowers disappeared, he had tried to stop Sadler 'thrashing' the boy Sandy for making a mistake while yard building.[72] This kind of interference was intolerable to Sadler, who had moved to dissolve their partnership.

Although Sadler was never formally charged with the murder, the police, acting on the Chief Protector's instructions, removed the half-caste boy Sandy and took him to Moola Bulla government station in 1918. In 1938 a second half-caste boy was removed from Sadler, despite his correspondence with the Chief Protector pleading that the boy would become a useful worker if he remained and protesting that the policy of removing children was biased against small leaseholders.[73] The boy was young Jack Carey, whose father had by that time left the Kimberley.

Half-caste children were problematic for white stockmen. Biskup referred to one instance of a pastoralist in the east Kimberley boasting that he had no trouble getting workers because he bred them himself.[74] This seemed a logical way to expand a station workforce, but it was not one that many people would admit to, nor was it successful in the northern Kimberley. Billy King and Jack Dale, who were both born about 1920 to stockmen who worked in the Mount House region and lived with Aboriginal women, named only about ten other half-caste children who lived in the north or who were removed from there to missions in the 1920s and '30s. The presence of one or two light-skinned children in small camps where there was only one white man could lead to further questioning by police if they decided to act on rumours started by disgruntled or jealous stockmen. There was also the social stigma of having half-caste children, which resulted in most white fathers denying any responsibility for them. On northern Kimberley stations during this period, all children were part of the workforce as well as part of an Aboriginal community living in camps and the bush. They were valuable labourers and future trained stockmen and stockwomen. It was a rough environment, however, where an education was un-likely and where there were no white women to bring a semblance of civilization deemed appropriate to a child with white blood.

This did not mean there were no half-caste children born in the northern ranges, or that they were given up easily to missions and government stations by their fathers or by stockmen and managers. For instance, Jack Dale, William King and former policeman Jack Wilson all had half-caste children and tried to keep them.[75] During the few years in this period when a travelling inspector was placed in the Kimberley to increase official interven-tion in the region, the Chief Protector instructed police in 1925 to remove young Jack Dale and warn his father to stop cohabiting with Dolly.[76] Jack Dale senior was a contractor who relied on Dolly and her classificatory mother and father to work for him and to help him enlist Indigenous workers from the bush for yard and road building. He had been in the north Kimberley since 1910 and had established a small brush-roofed camp at a spring on the Mount House lease. From there he took his small team of Aboriginal people out to various jobs, fencing or yard building. The police informed the Chief Protector that Dale had agreed to send the boy to school when he was six and would hand Dolly over to her tribal husband, Left Hand Spider, immediately. Dale took his son and wife to the Phillips and Packhorse Ranges further north of Mount House to avoid police and collect dingo scalps, but he returned to work at Mount House in 1926 when Dolly joined her Aboriginal husband. In June 1926 and July 1927 police patrols called in at Mount House station and asked the manager whether Dale was continuing to cohabit with Dolly. They reported to the Chief Protector that she was living with Left Hand Spider but made no comment on the child's welfare until his father died in 1928.

From 1926 until his death in 1928 while working on Mount House Station, Dale tried to stop his son living a camp or bush life with his mother or Aboriginal family, but he would not release him to police for placement in a departmental institution or mission.[77] He spoke to his son about sending him to the Dale family in Queensland and providing him with an education, but drinking and violence dominated his life. He shot his son in the ankle to stop him camping with his grandparents, nearly killed him on another occasion after tying him to their camp roof as punishment for trying to run away to his mother at Mount House stock camp, and then died in front of him after a violent fight with another stockman at the Mount House main camp in 1928.[78] By the time the police patrol visited the station again, Dale's body was buried. They accepted the manager's statement that no one was to blame, although young Jack Dale spoke English and may have told them what he had witnessed.[79] The white stockmen had already given Jack's grandfather flour, tea and tobacco to take young Jack away from the station until the inquiry was finished.

Billy King's father also died, but the child did not come to the attention of the police until Dale's death in 1928. Neville instructed police not to interfere and remove the boys unless they were being mistreated, as it was girls rather than boys who needed to be removed from stations.[80] He believed that both boys' welfare was secure under the protection of the manager at Mount House station, where they would be integrated into the workforce. The Blythe brothers owned Mount House, which they worked from their neighbouring station, Fairfield. When the truck was sent out to Mount House for the first time in the late 1920s from Moola Bulla government pastoral station, where half-caste children were taken for training, both boys were warned by the manager to hide at a nearby waterhole.[81] Jack Dale remembers watching the protector walking around the waterhole looking for them while they hid and waited. Part-descent girls, on the other hand, were removed and sent to missions or government stations, where it was hoped they would not be at risk of sexual abuse or of producing more half-caste children and where they would receive training as domestics. The boys in particular were valuable station workers, and where there were large numbers of white stockmen (or, as in the case of these boys, their fathers were dead) paternal responsibility could be shifted or hidden. It was more socially acceptable for white men in this period to integrate children from the camps or the bush into a station regime than to accept the responsibility of fathering a half-caste child, risking police visits and questions in addition to the shame of rearing their own part-white child in a rough bush camp.

After the First World War, stockmen returned to the north Kimberley to establish their own leases and assist old mates. Mount Barnett, Gibb and Kurunjie stations were occupied by new owners Fred Russ, Dave Rust and Scotty Salmond; Isdell Downs was owned by Sidney Kidman; and further west Oobagooma, Federal Downs, Secure Downs and Mount Hart were working stations and out-camps owned by men who had shares in butcher's shops in Derby. Leases north of Mount House were occupied by Jack Smith and Bob Maxted, and other stockmen who worked for Blythes, MC Davies or Rose Bros. Glenroy station, north-east of Mount House, was owned by ex-policeman Spong and worked with the assistance of ex-policeman Jack Wilson. Tableland station was also new, and access was through Mount House.

By the mid-1920s Mount House had become the centre for wet season gatherings of local white men from surrounding stations. The old cooks, teamsters, boundary riders, carpenters and stockmen met at Mount House, which was at the end of the cart track from where stores and mail were collected. After Mount House, stores had to be carried by the donkey teams or packed out on mules or horses. On occasions the revelry was fuelled by home brew and other alcohol, secreted in drums of flour and other stores so that fellow stockmen and donkey team drivers did not steal it. The men gambled and drank for days. According to Jack Dale and Billy King, the camps of Aboriginal workers went bush to avoid the drunken brawling and target shooting which ended the wet season breaks and put them at risk. The scenes described by informants of gatherings at Mount House were mirrored in the pub brawls and antics in Idriess's *One Wet Season*.[82] The difference was that the revelry turned violent and 'characters', like Jack Dale's father, were killed in front of their own children.

'Tales told by natives'

This picture of early days conditions on stations over the ranges extended to other stations in the west, central and north Kimberley. There was little protection for Aboriginal people. Two incidents of the government attempting and failing to intervene in gross cruelties towards workers occurred in 1924 and '25 at Kimberley Downs station, sixty miles from Derby and on the police patrol track to the northern stations. The first concerns the disappearance of an Aboriginal woman who allegedly died while attached by a rope to the manager's saddle.[83] The travelling inspector, who had been appointed in 1924 after a gap of thirteen years, struggled to overcome distance and resistance from police and white men to investigate the case, but the witness went missing and no body was ever found.

In 1925 he had more success and brought a case of neglect against station manager Harry Bannon, who held the employment permit for Kimberley Downs.[84] An Aboriginal woman had been shot in the leg when a stockman fired from the verandah towards the camp to force her to come to the homestead camp. The woman's injury was not reported, and without medical treatment or assistance she died. Bannon had his permit withdrawn for six months. The owners, M.C. Davies and Son, moved him to Napier Downs station further from Derby, where he was manager until 1934 when Ion Idriess visited. The Aborigines Department tried to prevent the man who fired the shot from working with Aboriginal people, but it was continually frustrated by a lack of resources and a system that was not aimed at protecting Aboriginal people at the expense of white men's employment prospects. In 1930 the Chief Protector ordered police to ban him from working with Aborigines, but the instructions were withdrawn after pressure from the minister and MLA for the Kimberley, A.A.M. Coverley. He argued that it was 'persecution', that no charge had been proven and that the original allegation of cruelty was based on inadequate evidence — 'tales told by natives'.[85]

Morndingali was about twelve years old and living with his father, mother, uncles and extended family at Napier Downs when Harry Bannon became manager in 1926. He remembered old people disappearing and believed they were shot or left in the bush camps and refused food at the station because they were no longer 'useful'.[86] He and his older brother were in relatively secure positions because their father and uncle were already trained stockmen and leading hands at the station. Morndingali's father had assisted with the occupation of Mount Barnett and Isdell as a stockman who drove cattle to the northern leases. He returned to Napier Downs from Mount Barnett with Nurgaworla, Morndingali's mother, who was a cook at the police station, having been captured by police.[87] On Napier they worked at muster camps and, from their son's stories, appear to have been comparatively secure. For instance, Morndingali described how, after his birth at a muster camp, the manager had insisted the family return to the station to protect the new baby.[88]

By the early 1920s Morndingali was being trained to be a stockman and had an established position within the core working group at Napier Downs station. Despite experiencing a range of punishments, from kicking to threats that he would be shot if he didn't work quickly and efficiently, his childhood was not circumscribed by the intense physical uncertainty that prevailed on stations north of the Leopold Ranges during the 1920s. From his stories and written sources, he came closest to losing his life on wet season breaks when Aboriginal inter-group disputes were settled.[89]

What Morndingali did grow up with were detailed narratives of atrocities and disturbances which occurred during his childhood and teenage years in and around his mother's country north of the Leopold Ranges near Mount Barnett. There, the pacification process intensified as stockmen expanded the boundaries of pastoral settlement into regions that had not been previously settled by white men or, in cases like Mount Barnett, showed few signs of pastoral occupation—a few wild cattle, a hut, a yard and Aboriginal people who still occupied the leases. It was this expansionary context that produced the legendary Jack Carey stories.

CHAPTER THREE

'Taught to kill':
soldier settlers and the
station 'family'

A FTER the First World War the government instituted a
policy of extending settlement into the northern
regions, where pastoral occupation had been inhib-
ited by rugged ranges, lack of access to ports and continued
resistance from Aboriginal people. The committee appointed to
advise the government recommended that 'material development' of
the north was needed, regardless of its incompatibility with the needs
of Indigenous people's 'spiritual welfare'.[1] Occupying the north was
also a strategic concern, as the Dutch, Germans and Japanese began
to show interest in the region following the war.[2] This prompted the
federal and state governments to turn their attention to developing
the area, and so the idea of expanding the pastoral industry over the
ranges into Ngarinyin country was reignited.

In 1921 William Easton led an official expedition into the
northern district to survey the area from Walcott Inlet north to Napier
Broome Bay, 'with the object of locating the most suitable site for a
new port to serve the large tract of vacant country lying between the
King Leopold, and the Durack Ranges'.[3] Easton portrayed the
'numerous' Aboriginal occupants, who watched him but never made

contact, as skilled bush people with a strict family-centred social structure and remarkable capacity to exploit the abundant natural resources. He suggested that they would not 'cause much trouble' if they were not interfered with,[4] adding that it was:

> practically essential that men settling this country should have had previous experience of similar work, as there will be innumerable hardships to be borne, and much isolation. A knowledge of natives and their customs is necessary, as the natives, even if friendly disposed, would soon gain the ascendancy of an inexperienced man.[5]

The push to expand pastoral occupation was bolstered by the soldier settlement scheme, introduced in 1919. The scheme allowed smallholdings to be thrown open for reduced rents and was encouraged by the opening of the Wyndham meatworks in 1919. The Department of the North West was established in 1920, and A.O. Neville was made secretary, with his Protector of Aborigines duties split at the 26th parallel so that he could concentrate on the north.[6] He was also responsible for employing ex-servicemen.

Jack Carey, Fred Russ, Dave Rust and Scotty Salmond all worked as stockmen at Mount Barnett in 1919 and 1920, and applied for leases under the soldier settlement scheme. Carey applied for two leases, one near Gibb River and one on the Barnett River.[7] His application was initially turned down because he had not actually joined up, producing only a rejection certificate. But a pastoral board member supported his appeal, and he took over the Gibb River lease late in 1920. Carey and Russ shared costs until 1925, when Russ took over the Gibb River lease. Dave Rust applied as an ex-serviceman for land east of Mount Barnett, which he named Kurunjie station.[8] Salmond and Rust had been in the 10th Light Horse together, and before the war had been Kimberley stockmen for Fitzroy River pastoralists. They were all experienced stockmen with limited resources, developing stations on the fringes of pastoral settlement. They joined others like Fred Easton at Sale River on the coast south of Kunmunya mission, Scotty Sadler who expanded his holdings to Tableland, and Jack Connaughton who had owned small and marginal pastoral ventures in the northern ranges for years. They attempted to expand their workforces and establish their authority over Indigenous people, occupying leases by a combination of intimidation and reward for select communities and individuals prepared to accommodate white men's requirements. Oral sources indicate how fragile relationships were, with individuals attempting to negotiate a settlement with a white Boss by sharing land, women, children and labour resources.

After the police investigation into Bert Bowers' disappearance, which had resulted in the half-caste boy Sandy being removed for his protection, Scotty Sadler sold his Isdell Junction lease to Sidney Kidman, and in 1919 moved further east to establish Tableland station. He sold out in the early 1950s but occupied the station as a stockman or assistant until he hanged himself in 1966, aged ninety-two.[9]

Protection and fear

Sadler had moved to Tableland with a group of people he had collected from the Mount House lease. The senior man of that group, Biriraiyidmi, known to white men as Monkey, showed him the way from Imintji Springs to the Tableland lease and a permanent waterhole, which was also a significant site for which he was custodian. Biriraiyidmi and his family became the core group from which Sadler built a labour force. He left his son, Mick Jowalji, with Sadler to be trained as a stockman and one of his wives to be trained as a house girl. Mick Jowalji became head stockman and much later, in 1995, chairman of Yulumbu Aboriginal Corporation, which bought the Tableland station lease.

In the early days of the station, Biriraiyidmi came into the station camp to work for short periods, just enough to get tobacco or trousers, and then he would move off again. Occasionally, rather than working, he would come into the homestead camp only to claim tobacco and other items, which his wife, sons and others were obliged to give him. Sadler knew of these visits and would tell him to hunt cattle out of certain range areas and take only one for himself and his group. The group who moved with Biriraiyidmi were probably other wives, children and old people who were not needed at the homestead camp.

Biriraiyidmi had the authority among his own people to come into the station and tell the workers in the homestead camp when and where there would be a ceremony and if they were obliged to attend.[10] He could translate that authority to assist Sadler with his labour requirements, bringing a workforce together for specific tasks. He also brought a neighbouring senior man into the station system so his young son could be trained as a stockman. On one occasion Sadler told Biriraiyidmi to gather men and women from the bush to transport roofing iron across the Leopold Ranges for the Tableland station homestead. With two people on each end, piles of iron were carried across the ranges to the Tableland camp. The men and women also assisted with the building and were rewarded with tobacco and rations and allowed to move back to the bush. Biriraiyidmi's grandson, Wallace Midmee, retold the incident:

> They carry iron through the gorge, camp, pickim up, carry again. They never damage them, they keepim clean, they frighten. They wipe im clean. They climbed up that jump up and come in to Scotty. Puttem down slowly, layim down.[11]

The working relationship between Biriraiyidmi and Sadler was circumscribed by the threat of being removed or harassed by police or stockmen. He had started working with Sadler when he was taken off a police chain which held a large group of alleged cattle killers. This incident seems to have occurred in 1919 when about thirty Aboriginal men were arrested near Mount House for killing cattle. That year, the number of cattle killing convictions rose to forty-seven, mostly from the central and west Kimberley region.[12] As one patrol brought the prisoners to Derby, they passed Sadler's camp and he was able to remove Biriraiyidmi. He, in turn, extended that favour to other groups throughout the 1920s, encouraging them to become part of the station system:

> *Mabel King*: Policeman chase people bring em into station.

Wallace Midmee: Some time they take em long way out. Tie em up, bring em in the station. Call my grandfather 'Who this?' Scotty Sadler tellem. 'Oh yeah this bloke work for me.'

One time my grandfather been tied up there. Scotty Sadler saw him: 'Let this fella go.' He stayed for a few days and took off. Nother time, policeman had about twenty bloke tied up. Grandfather said 'This my countryman.' Scotty let the lot go. Scotty said 'You mob want to work?'[13]

Mick Jowalji recalled his father's role as settling down other groups for their benefit:

Scotty Sadler makin that place. My father he was the Boss. Like a big Boss. Everyone been come in longa him. My father been bringem in whole lot. Make it easier for them and makem good manager, settle em down, don't want to go.[14]

Men and women who were not identified as workers and were suspected of interfering with cattle were not safe, despite being related and known to the survivors in the camps. If stockmen and managers identified them as strangers and a potential threat, punishment and dispersal could be swift and violent. Jowalji described one incident when Sadler's white stockman heard of cattle killing on the lease nearby at Glenroy station. He rode out from the homestead camp, across the creek where the house girl was washing the manager's clothes, told her to return to the camp, and then moved on to the bush camps:

He been come out longa all about.

'Ah Boss here, Boss. Oh yeah. What we can do for you?'

'Makem paddock, makem fence.' All that good way, manager been say.

This lot been get away from mob, livin la river.

Gardia been go sit down waiting there for might be five hour, he been sit down.

And he been walk away from this mob and go sit down on top longa side, longa hill.

He been all day watch us. He see him one fella been just come in now, come lotta spear, my cousin brother. Missed him. Second bullet right here, under the rib. Forty four.[15]

Even Biriraiyidmi was not entirely protected. When he tried to leave the station and move away from the area with his wife and other children, he was shot in the leg and had to rely on the intervention of a stockworker who could speak English for protection. His daughter, Barbara Midmee, who was born after 1920, described one incident when her mother tried to leave the camp:

And old Scotty Sadler too, he been murderin one … We land up on the river. My mother been cooking la station. Me fellas been go.

My father been look. 'He come us.' That mob of dog. 'What for you follering me?' He bin tellim.

He bin sickem out dog longa dad. My mother bin carryem up me and my father been on top. This nother one [a stockman who had joined them from the Mount Barnett region] he walk, running all the way, take em back old fellas.

And he bin shootim my father in the leg, Scotty Sadler, he been shootim my father. My mother been takim mefellas bush. Long way, [her]self.

And we been waitin longa bush and he [the stockman] been comin up. Him been tellim [Sadler] 'What for you want to. What for you been shootim this old man? He got big mob of family, you'll have to let im go.' He bin tell im. My father got no English much and my mother.[16]

Biriraiyidmi's children lived on Tableland until they were forced to leave in 1984 after an argument with the new owners.

Jack Jowan moved to Tableland station after his first white Boss abandoned his small lease in Jowan's country, just east of Mount Barnett near the Chamberlain River. His first Boss was Jack Connaughton, who was a stockman in the northern ranges and leaseholder from 1920 to '25 for leases variously called Hann River, Echo Hills and Berri Werri, all in the central ranges region. He was also named by the police as being in Carey's company at Gibb River in 1921. Frank Hann had met him in the Pilbara in 1897 when Connaughton was prospecting for gold. He had two 'wild blacks' on the chain to show him water.[17] Jowan had been about eight years old when his father left him and his mother[18] with Connaughton and his Aboriginal assistant, Alungguwari, at Berri Werri station. Alungguwari, later known as Berri Werri Charlie, was Jowan's classificatory father and brought him up as Connaughton's special boy. In that capacity, Jowan saw and was involved in many instances of 'hunting bush people'.

Jowan and Jowalji's stories cover an area of land from Gibb River station and Mount Barnett east to Glenroy and Tableland station. They refer to managers and stockmen working together to punish people for cattle killing, attempting to run away or removing women from the homestead camps who had been identified as white men's women. While riding with their Bosses, Jowan and Jowalji had seen Aboriginal people being shot. But their narratives did not all tell of decisive victories or clear-cut boundaries between white and black. They recalled one incident when they were helping white stockmen to round up bush people. As they were tracking men, they shot a kangaroo. The shot alerted the stockmen to their whereabouts and to the men they had been tracking:

> *Jowan*: We been hunting blackfella all round bush, bring em back.
>
> *Jowalji*: Me and you go. Getta rifle. Boss been go make a camp. Me and you climb up trackem all the blackfella. Me two fella police boys long time. We been youngfella.
>
> *Jowan*: I tellim 'Don't shoot, don't shoot.'
>
> *Jowalji*: I been hungry, I want to shoot that kangaroo, but this one say, 'Don't shoot. By and by hearem we.'

> *Jowan*: Too late they been findem we, all gone. All
> been gone. Boy called Willie, two gardia put a revolver
> and shoot. He never take notice that boy, walkin away.[19]

Jowan commented that it was a 'cruel business', while Jowalji stated
that he didn't know why Scotty Sadler had spared him.

> Oh long time rough. I don't know how come my Boss
> been save me. I been grow up and stop longa him.
> Mefella, my sister, Barbara, this one father belonga him
> [Tableland Anji, deceased] and Jock and Sandy and me
> here, one dead sister … Big family.[20]

Jowalji's youth and capacity to work, and the fragile but longstanding contract between Sadler and his father, ensured his survival
and continuing occupation of his country. His mother's role as
cook in the homestead camp and mother to a number of children
reinforced their comparatively privileged position.

During his childhood Jowan had worked with the soldier
settlers when Carey was at Gibb River.[21] He referred to Carey's treatment of bush people as part of the settlement process in which
white men killed bush people. He described Carey's cruelty as
exceptional but not the fact that he killed. When Jowan was about
twelve, Carey called at Connaughton's camp and reported that bush
people were lighting fires in the Mount Barnett region. He left the
camp with two Aboriginal men, George Dulnoor and Toby
Naninggoorrt, and their wives in search of the trouble-makers.[22]
Connaughton instructed Jowan to take a message to Fred Russ at
Gibb River station. He travelled alone on a mule with a tuckerbox of
food as his payment. As he took a back track, the mule bolted into
the bush to a small waterhole on the Hann River. There he saw
bloodied water and mud and evidence of recent killings. He rode on
to Gibb River main camp and delivered the message. Russ warned
him not to go near the waterhole on the Hann because it had been
poisoned and there were dead dogs in it. Jowan rode back with a
message from Russ to Connaughton, who read it aloud, apparently
not worried about the contents, which told of men being killed by

Carey on the Hann River and their bodies thrown into the water-hole. The next morning Connaughton rode with Scotty Salmond and young Jowan to another waterhole, where they waited until daylight and then raided the Aboriginal camp. One man was shot in the back while the women were left hiding in the pandanus palms in the water. Jowan remembered the incident:

> Alright we seeim one old man been run. Mine Boss been lookin at that road findem him. 'Here Jack you want to have a shot?'
>
> 'No. I can't shootem my own body,' I been tellim.
>
> 'You gotta do it,' him been tell me.
>
> 'No,' I been tell im. 'No.'
>
> ... He want me to shootim that old man that run. I never like shootim. I been tellim 'You can shootim.' Alright he been knockim here [in the back near the shoulder blade] fall down ... Big solid man.
>
> Ah poor fella.
>
> 'You gottim?' Two fella [stockmen] talk like that.
>
> 'No I got one there. But this one don't matter, him little bugger.' Gardia, this Gardia been tellim 'Takim la water chuck him in.'
>
> I been longa that two man. I never like Scotty Salmond and Jack Connaughton.[23]

Salmond himself described the first years of occupying Kurunjie and Gibb River as a time of 'vigilance' and 'courage', when he and Dave Rust were 'stalked' and attacked by 'savage Kimberley tribes' who retreated, 'dragging their dead'.[24] When Salmond died in 1957, his obituary in the *Northern Times* honoured him as one of the pioneers of the most isolated regions in the Kimberley, whose 'courage and uncanny bush craft caused the natives to call him "devil devil" of Kurunjie'.[25] Ngarinyin storytellers used that title for Salmond in the 1980s and '90s. Like Jack Carey, Salmond seems to have encouraged his reputation for being able to frighten Aboriginal people. Salmond added that in the early days of pioneering Kurunjie, the early 1920s, he had been told by police that the 'savage natives would kill [him] in a fortnight' and he would not receive police protection.[26] Although patrols were infrequent, he stated that the soldier settlers did receive some police assistance and that he took part in 'official and unofficial punitive expeditions'. He did not describe exactly what happened on these occasions, except to say that he chased, chained and frightened people and kept a pack of savage dogs to protect him and his camp.

In 1921 patrols set out in response to the alleged murders of Bass and Smith between Cape Voltaire and Kunmunya mission on the coast. There is no record of the patrols moving as far east as Kurunjie, but they may have been some of the unofficial punitive expeditions in the north Kimberley to which Salmond referred.[27] Three patrols set out, from Derby, Broome and Fitzroy Crossing, with two trackers each. They were all heavily armed. The report suggests that they moved easily to the coastal mission to capture the alleged murderers and witnesses, and returned through Mount Hart to Derby without incident. Four years later Constable Pollett described the 1921 patrols to the local doctor in Derby, stating that four police and eleven trackers rounded up 270 Aboriginal people near the west coast and saw extreme cases of sickness.[28]

The southern portion of the Marndoc Aboriginal reserve in the east Kimberley was thrown open for soldier settlers in 1922.[29] John Hay, who had worked as a stockman for leaseholders in the north Kimberley before the war, took over Nulla Nulla station as an ex-serviceman on the southern portion of the reserve. In 1926 he was speared by an Aboriginal man after a dispute over an Aboriginal woman. The police party's response to Hay's murder formed the basis for the Wood Royal Commission into alleged massacres of Aboriginal people.[30]

The 1921 patrols, and another in 1920 to the far north coast and nearby islands, were described by the Commissioner of Police in 1932 as examples of dangerous mounted police work. These patrols, which were to the north-west of Ngarinyin country, contributed to the fear and dislocation in the whole northern Kimberley, as did the Marndoc reserve massacres in 1926 on the eastern regions of Ngarinyin country.

Prospecting for children

At Kurunjie station Scotty Salmond formed a settled relationship with at least one senior Aboriginal man, who visited his camp for many years, working occasionally but living mostly in the bush. He operated like Biriraiyidmi at Tableland and Peter Yamiga at Mount House, making frequent visits to the white men's camps for rations and to check on his group. Other men and women joined him and his white assistant, Scotty Menmuir, and were trained into pastoral work. Rosie Mamangulya and Susie Umungul remembered starting the camp at Kurunjie, while Maggie Ghi came into the camp when she was a young girl in the 1920s,[31] and Campbell Allenbrae was born in the camp in the early 1920s. They spoke specifically of the spearing of Yellow Harry (Harry Annear) in 1921 and the police patrols avenging his death as the beginning of a 'war' between Aboriginal people and white men:

> That bloke Yellow Harry started the war. Jack Carey was working the other side, Barnett and Gibb. They used to meet up with Jack Connaughton and Scotty Salmond. Jack Carey used to tell Scotty, 'This is a good one for station.' Scotty was new from Scotland. They had just a few cattle, not much. First place, Jack Connaughton and Scotty were going to make a place at Berri Werri, but Scotty started Kurunjie, different one.[32]

Salmond also made specific mention of Harry Annear's spearing by an Aboriginal man. Salmond was contemptuous, stating that his spearing was his 'own fault' for stealing a young Aboriginal woman and then not being vigilant or quick enough to shoot a few people from the attacking party. Salmond summed up the situation:

> It was no good being noble and dead. The natives had been brought up knowing nothing but killing. In spite of the wailing and singing over dead relations a life meant nothing to them. All they could understand was savagery and strength. Even now strength is the only way to get

their respect. We'd just come back from a war in which we were taught to kill. And when it came to a showdown we were the stronger.[33]

Harry Annear was a half-caste who was assisting pastoral expansion. According to police records, he travelled north in late 1921 from Sadler's Tableland station to look for new country and for children for existing leases.[34] According to storytellers, he was prospecting for children to bring south to the pastoral leases. He was heavily armed, carrying two rifles, two revolvers and 400 rounds of ammunition, 150 lent to him by Jack Connaughton. He travelled with three Aboriginal women, two of whom he had removed from a bush camp; they were chained to trees at night to prevent them escaping. The Aboriginal husband of one of them was camped at Connaughton's station on the Hann River when he heard that Annear had moved into the bush with his wife. He followed and speared him. Annear then shot himself in the forehead.

When the police found the body, it had been mutilated around the genitals. The guns and ammunition were missing. Police parties from Fitzroy Crossing and Wyndham, accompanied by Jack Wilson, Jack Connaughton and Jack Carey, converged on the area, raiding camps, shooting dogs and chaining witnesses, from Gibb River to Tableland station and east to Kurunjie and Durack River. One of the policemen reportedly took ill, and he and Jack Carey moved off on their own towards Tableland station. At Connaughton's lease adjoining Mount Barnett they rounded up all the Aboriginal people and questioned them. At Mount Barnett itself they rounded up ninety-four Aborigines after a raid on one camp. One police party continued raiding camps east towards Durack River. At a gorge on the Durack River a large group of men, women and children were surrounded, and, according to the tracker's statement to police, some people 'fell down'.[35] Cambell Allenbrae, who lived at Kurunjie and lost relatives in the conflicts after Annear's death, stated that the patrols across the ranges in 1922 culminated in a large massacre at Durack River Gorge.[36]

The Annear incident and police response has been referred to by Neville Green as part of a continuing 'pacification' process, which culminated with the Marndoc reserve massacres in 1926.[37] Police party raids in 1916, '22 and '26 were significant events, which erupted on each occasion because a pastoral worker had been killed or injured following a dispute over an Aboriginal woman. They marked points at which negotiation and accommodation between small groups of Aboriginal people and individual white men had broken down, and the police joined white stockmen to contain resistance and enforce punishments. Each incident involved the police searching for a known Aboriginal man who had worked for white stockmen. They were not simply pursuing 'bush blacks' but were taking part in a process of dividing and separating out those people who were willing to comply with white men's requirements, which included their controlling access to certain Aboriginal women and children.

According to Ngarinyin people, Annear and Jack Carey were 'boundary riders' and 'prospectors' for new leases and for children to train for the stations. Annear's female assistant also stated to police that 'Harry been go down longa that country to look out boy to look out longa horse, he been wantem boy to work longa station.'[38] Children continued to be a valuable resource in this second wave of settlement. Campbell Allenbrae described the process as it was told to him by his father:

> Scotty Salmond and Jack Carey were talking about what they can do. Take young boys and girls, give them tucker and tobacco. But those old people didn't like it, they threw it away. Flour they kept for corroboree paint. Tea, they put it in a billy can. 'No don't eat it, that thing is blown.' Sugar they reckon, 'That's river sand, rubbish. Throw it away.' Scotty Salmond used to put flour in paper bark, tie it at the end and put it in a cave. Everywhere Scotty Salmond and Jack Carey gave tucker, but early days blokes didn't like it.
>
> After a while these young fellas [who] were getting trained, told the old people, 'Don't make humbug with that flour. For eat, make you full up guts.' My Dad was telling them that in all that Durack country, and my

brother-in-law. My Dad was with the whitefellas in the first place. 'Eat that tucker, we eat it, don't throw it away.' That's what he told the bush fellas.[39]

Scotty Salmond had removed Campbell Allenbrae from an Afghan sandalwooder, who camped near Kurunjie station in the 1920s. He stayed with Salmond and eventually became head stockman at Kurunjie in the 1940s. His mother and father divided their time between sandalwooding with the Afghans and working with Salmond at Kurunjie station during the 1920s and '30s. The 1905 Aborigines Act excluded 'Asiatics' from employing Aboriginal people, which put them at a disadvantage when it came to retaining labour.[40] Salmond strictly controlled the boy's contact with his relatives who moved in the bush. But, as Allenbrae stated, many of his closest relatives had been dispersed or killed at the Durack Gorge massacre, so if Salmond had wanted to track him after running away, he only had to go to the Afghans' bush camps, where his parents and grandparents were staying. This left him without many options.

Jack Carey—breaking the rules

Around the same time as the Annear incident, the rules of occupation and coexistence were collapsing in the Mount Barnett region, leading to a crisis for the landowners of Kupingarri, Gunbungarri and Ngorru Ngorru near Mount Barnett and Mount Elizabeth. Maggie Gudaworla's mother and father moved to work the Mount Barnett lease with Fred Russ and Jack Carey in about 1919 and stayed through the early 1920s when the stockmen were trying to establish their own stations. During this period her clan affiliates experienced a slow reversal in their fortunes and exclusion from a white Boss's protection.

The group included stockmen and women who had been trained since the early 1900s by the first white stockmen in the region over the ranges: Skinner, O'Connor, Dick Sullivan and other white men at Mount Barnett, Isdell and Grace's Knob. They had been affected by the campaign of arrests and dispersals when the police camp was at Isdell, and many, like Allungguwari (Berri Werri Charlie), Morndingali's mother, Billy King's grandmother and Wundigul's wife, had moved into the stations and established their position as workers: 'All those police boys [and] policeman kill all the people and they want to work on station.'[41] Others continued to move in the bush and visit station camps like the one at Isdell when Skinner was manager. Ngulit, the 'magic man' who had escaped from Carey when he worked the region near Mount House and Beverley Springs, continued to move in the bush between Mount Barnett, Isdell, Grace's Knob and Mount Hart. On one occasion, when he was threatened by two trackers who travelled with the Fitzroy police patrols, he magically led his two wives and one old man out of danger and called up a storm to prevent them being followed.[42]

Before moving with Russ to Mount Barnett, Gudaworla's group had been able to rely on protection from the managers at Isdell Downs. Her mother was Skinner's first woman, and when he was replaced by Fred Potts in 1916, she and her husband and a small group continued to move in the region, visiting the Isdell Downs camp and their own country at Mount Barnett without fear of harassment. Potts lived in a small camp with an Aboriginal woman, her husband and children, and a group of old people. He fed the old people and, according to Gudaworla, stopped the police removing her father after a raid on their bush camp. Ngulit may have been able to escape through his own magical powers, but Gudaworla's father and mother, like many other Aboriginal people, relied on the social obligations of relatives who were aligned with white men to ensure their survival.

When Carey first came to the Isdell region in about 1915, the Mount Hart manager gave him the task of assisting Fred Potts in out-camps on the lease. According to oral sources, he shot and burned a group of bush people who were visiting the boundary area between Isdell station and Mount Hart.[43] Gudaworla stated that Potts ordered him to leave the area because he was a danger to the trained and settled Aboriginal people who also moved in the bush socializing with visiting groups: 'manager bin huntim away. "Go on, you go way. You might shootim my boy," he tellim'.[44]

On a separate occasion Gudaworla and her family were again moving in the bush between their clan land at Mount Barnett and Grace's Knob station when they decided to visit the workers at Grace's Knob to ask for tobacco. Potts was manager there and had been joined by Wundigil, his wife Manuworla and their children. Weeda Munro was among the children, and two other classificatory daughters were also with Fred Potts. Their mother, Ludbuworla, sister to Manuworla, was Potts' Aboriginal wife. Her husband, Babaij, was, according to Maggie Gudaworla, shot and killed by Jack Carey near Berri Werri station and thrown into a waterhole. Wundigil patrolled the lease with Fred Potts:

> Wundigil and Fred Pott[s] come up, want to put mefella on the chain. Daddy said 'Wundigil here!' He leavim Daddy mine and three boys because he full cousin for my father. Weeda mother, Manuworla, he pickem up Mount Barnett.[45]

Weeda Munro was a baby when her father and mother lived on Mount Hart with Fred Potts, and she grew up there to become a trained stockwoman.

In 1925 Potts was sent to the Mount Matthew out-camp to watch cattle and Aboriginal people. George Layman owned the Secure Downs lease to the west of Mount Hart, and Frederick Easton owned Sale River, also called Avon Valley station (which became Munja government ration station in 1926). They stocked their leases with cattle and wanted police support to control the Indigenous people who were moving in the region. They had some help from a 1924 patrol which raided a camp four miles from Easton's hut and removed the 'ringleaders' to Derby after Easton had pointed them out. Easton himself was acquitted of stealing cattle from Isdell station in 1924, much to the amusement of the local press, which described the managers' confrontation:

> The Manager of Isdell rode up, jumped off his horse, rushed at the accused, with a cocked and loaded revolver in his hand, and holding it within a foot or two of the

accused's head, ordered him to hold up his hands. He then searched the accused, his swag and packs for firearms, taking a revolver and gun away, giving his native boy the former and putting the latter in his own pack. Couldn't have been better staged—by a Yankee 'Deadwood Dick' screen actor.[46]

In 1925 there were more reports of 'trouble with natives' from Easton, Layman, Potts and others in the western ranges area. The police were told not to lend too much support:

Cattle killing attributable to not enough white labour employed. At Walcott [Sale and Secure Downs] about 4,000 head roaming about a million acres. They can afford to lose 30 head a year, but they cry for help at one loss by natives. Natives do nearly all the work.[47]

Fred Easton drowned in 1926, amidst a minor controversy in which it was claimed that he had been poisoned by his own Aboriginal domestic. His lease was bought by the government and became Munja ration depot and government pastoral station.

In 1927 Potts lost his permit to work Aboriginal people after Wundigul shot and killed two Aboriginal men who worked at the recently established Munja government ration station on the coast, while they were moving in the region of Mount Matthew. The disappearance of the two men and stories of the killings were reported to police by Reid, the manager at Munja. Evidence at the hearing suggested that Potts had given Wundigul the gun and told him to go and clear the bush blacks from the nearby waterhole. Both the police file and Wundigul's daughter, Weeda Munro, stated that the killings were retribution for the death of her teenage brother, who had been watching cattle with another young boy and died after falling from his mount.[48] Potts was aware of Wundigul seeking retribution for the death. His actions may have been motivated by an internal system of justice and morality, but they also came at a time of increasing tensions in that region after Mount House lessees opened a new out-station at Mount Matthew, in the western end of the King Leopold Ranges, and police refused to ride out from Derby when stockmen asked for help. Wundigul's actions contributed to the process of clearing bush people who were moving from Munja station to Mount Matthew.

When Carey and Russ moved to Mount Barnett in 1919, Carey continued to endanger Indigenous people who were identified as stockworkers or were semi-integrated into station work. He took a group of people from Mount Barnett camp east towards Berri Werri station, and shot and killed a man so he could have his wife, Mary Karraworla. He returned without the camp people. According to Gudaworla, Fred Russ would not let him have any more workers and sent him to Gibb River with Karraworla and a young man called Mobby, or Larry Murphy. Larry had been brought up by white men after his father was killed by spearing.

Such activities were not recorded in written records, although oral sources describe a dreadful range of violent incidents following Carey's attempt to settle Gibb River station between 1919 and 1924, resulting in members of Gudaworla's clan group gradually disappearing or seeking refuge elsewhere. For instance, Ngulit moved south towards Napier Downs station after magically avoiding Carey's attempt to shoot him while he was chained to a tree. Two old women were shot while fishing at a waterhole. A group of men were shot and drowned after accidentally dropping a box of chickens in the Hann River on their way from Mount Barnett camp to the new hut at Gibb River station lease. A young man sought refuge at Kunmunya mission after fighting with Carey and threatening to kill him, and one young woman, Susie Umungul, became Dave Rust's wife after Carey shot her father and threatened to kill her.[49]

Gudaworla's mother continued to work for Fred Russ at Gibb River station until Carey shot her daughter, a young girl, about 100 yards from the homestead camp, and they decided to leave. Gudaworla remembers being told by her mother that her sister was dead and they were fleeing. She was carried on her parents' shoulders to Mount House, where they joined Gudaworla's aunt who lived with the ex-tracker from Isdell station. Carey had broken all the established rules of the early days. He had gone too far. He killed old people, women and a child, and people assisting him with work. The act of 'sitting down' next to a white man's camp for food and protection was worthless.

After Gudaworla and her parents left, Carey discovered that three stockmen had left the goat yard open. He shot them all. They were all clan members of Kupingarri, Gunbungarri or Ngorru Ngorru. Russ returned and ordered him off the property, apparently at gunpoint. Carey's wife moved into the homestead camp as Russ's wife, and Mobby continued as part of Russ's stock camp at Gibb River station to draw on his protection for his involvement in past atrocities he had committed with Carey. Carey moved on to Table-land station with Scotty Sadler and Jack Wilson and was reportedly involved in a vehicle accident in 1925 near Halls Creek, possibly on the way to Wyndham and out of the Kimberley.[50] Ngarinyin story-tellers state that Jack Carey was shot by other white men, wrapped in canvas and drowned. This has not been confirmed, despite a great deal of searching of probate, death and police records.

The Carey narratives and related incidents during the 1920s uncover a range of temporary and fragile alliances between Aborigi-nal people and white men which increased people's security only marginally. From Gudaworla's perspective (one repeated by other informants), Carey was different from other early days white men because he killed women, girls, trained workers and people who signalled their preparedness to 'settle' by camping near the home-stead. From written sources and other early days stories, it is evident that Carey was also part of a wider process of 'settling' the northern ranges. Like his contemporaries, he had an Aboriginal wife, child and assistant who had been brought up by white men, and he was quick to use a gun to threaten people who challenged his authority. Carey differed from other white men in his propensity for cruelty and his willingness to transcend the boundaries of white men's behaviour. In the process of breaking the rules of workforce protection, he entered the separate sphere of Aboriginal people's interactions. He spoke Ngarinyin and walked naked in the bush, carried a bundle of spears in which to hide his gun, used his wife to meet and call in bush people, hid near waterholes and in rocky outcrops, painted himself with white ochre, hung a corpse in a tree near a known walking path, used a rasp on people's feet, cut the ankle ligament, sat with men at a ceremony, then salted their newly made cicatrise wounds. His power to find people, track them and trick them was so unusual that he, unlike any other white stockmen in the northern ranges, was said to have some form of magical power himself, similar to the all-encompassing lightning powers of the north Kimberley.[51] He had become savage and immoral. He increased the terror of the early days by appropriating and exploiting Aboriginal people's secret sphere of fears and obligations, and confused the established boundaries between white and black. Billy King, Peter Lacy at Mount Elizabeth and Fred Russ agreed that Carey symbolized and exaggerated Aboriginal people's fears of all white men for years after.[52]

In escaping from Jack Carey, Ngulit increased his status almost to that of a legend. The long and detailed narrative told by several storytellers describes him evading Carey, despite being chained to a tree with a gun pressed to his forehead. His powers over life and death extended to an ability to heal people and to escape from police and trackers. Ngulit's powers of resistance were also evinced by the stories of his being able to steal tobacco from white men's storerooms and locked tin trunks, and deliver it to his group who continued to walk in the bush or who were camped at another station.[53] Tobacco, a powerful commodity strictly controlled by white men, was used in exchange for work and sex, and as a key tool in the maintenance and training of a station workforce.

Captive wives

Each small group who could claim a reliable white man as protector and Boss was closely connected to an Aboriginal woman who lived with that white man. Informants often referred to their early days white Bosses as their 'fathers'. In some cases, like Jack Dale, Arthur Wilson and Billy King, they claimed they were biological fathers. This designation reflected the significant role of the Boss as protector, material resource and authority figure to the informants. It also accommodated white men's relationships with a significant man who called the white Boss his brother, sharing land, resources,

women and children. Even Carey, who threatened most Aboriginal
people he met, protected and rationed a small group of people who
were sisters and close relatives of his Aboriginal wife, Mary
Karraworla. Harry Howendon survived and became a stockworker
at Mount Barnett because Carey's wife was his aunt. When Carey
came across Harry's mother and father in the bush, his wife claimed
them as family:

> Only mine old father, he [Carey] been find im in the bush.
> He take im in the house. Because he been marryem sister
> for [of] my mother. They been take im la house Mount
> Barnett, leave im there. Old woman been carrying me
> and my sister, me two fella been go. Leave me fella.
> Ah ... give it me fella tucker, clothe, ration. He been good
> to my old woman. Cause he been have [her] sister.[54]

After Carey left Gibb River station in 1925, Howendon and
his family became the core working group for Fred Merry, who took
over as manager at Mount Barnett. Howendon's sister was Fred
Merry's woman and, like other female assistants to white men,
intervened to stop her younger brother being hurt:

> *Howendon*: Oh he a rough man. When me been little kid,
> you know, and when me been doin work me properly
> way, he come up put a whip longa me, chasem me longa
> horse. Chasem me all around, right round, I go round. I
> start cry. When I been kid you know. Mummy and Daddy
> longa home. Only my sister, that's all. [S]he arguing with
> him. My sister argued with Fred Merry for me, like.
> *Question*: Did he listen?
> *Howendon*: No. From there he taken me now right up
> to camp. He give me hiding properly there. My sister
> come up. Damper, [s]he chuckem longa head longa old
> Merry, makin im stop. [55]

Merry then went on to save young Howendon's life when a bull
charged him. The family and one other small group from Gibb River

moved with him to the coast in 1931 and featured in Idriess's *Over the Range*.[56]

Carey's wife, Mary Karraworla, was also responsible for rescuing another young girl and close relative, Susie Umungul, who was taken into Gibb River station and later lived with Dave Rust at Gibb River and Kurunjie stations.[57] Informants recalled the story of Susie's rescue as the time when Jack Carey told his wife that she would be shot if she didn't help him. Other stories recount instances where Mary Karraworla lied to him to protect people.

Susie Umungul and Rosie Mamangulya helped build the first station huts in the early 1920s, becoming stockworkers as the stations developed in the 1930s and '40s. Both women moved into station camps after their fathers were killed. They also saw their 'promised husbands' shot and killed, one by a white man and the other by his half-caste assistant.[58] They and other older women from the northern stations described their first contact with their white husbands as a process of being chosen from the station camps when they were pre-pubescent girls. They received limited ration privileges as a white man's wife, and, like Mick Jowalji's father, there were times when they went into the bush to help white men find new country and bring young women, men and children into the camps to settle them down for the station.

Maggie Ghi was younger than Susie Umungul and Rosie Mamangulya and stayed in the bush with her parents for a few years after Gibb River and Kurunjie station huts were established. She was a young girl in the 1920s, living with her father and mother on the fringes of Kurunjie station and travelling between Afghans' camps, where they exchanged dog scalps for rations. Her first contact experiences reveal the process of entrapment used by the white men, and their assistants and women, to force her into the camps.[59] When Maggie Ghi was about ten years old, her father and mother went to Kurunjie station camp, where relatives, like Rosie Mamangulya, were already part of the core group, living and working with Scotty Salmond and partners Dave Rust and Scotty Menmuir (called Minderoo by storytellers). Her parents did not stay for long, deciding instead to sneak into the white men's camp, remove her from the verandah and take her to the bush in the east

Kimberley.[60] They were taking Maggie away from Scotty Salmond's camp to meet their obligations to her promised husband, who was waiting in a bush camp near the Pentacost ranges in the east closer to Wyndham. Maggie recalled the incident:

> Mmm. They bin come and pickem up me, now, my mother and father. 'We'll have to go now, followim up,' they reckon. We bin travellin night time, not day time. All about on top hill. We bin run there ... longa that Afghan camp, Jaana [Sahanna] camp.[61]

Maggie Ghi's promised husband died from being speared before she was able to become his wife. After her parents returned to their country, her mother died, and Maggie and her father, who were travelling in the region between Gibb River and Kurunjie, were tracked and brought into Kurunjie camp. She was initially tied to a bed, then slowly introduced to her new husband, Salmond's Aboriginal assistant, and also to the white men and work:

> *Maggie Ghi*: I followem twofella here [Rosie and Susie sitting with her at the interview]. My mother been lose [died]. Take me longa whitefella now. Because I never know whitefella. My father never know whitefella, he didn't know, I didn't know. We been sit down there, bushman. [laughs] Bush black fella. My Daddy been sit down bush black fella properly. We humble way. We been go take me fella to Scotty Minderoo, old bugger.
>
> *Rosie Mamangulya*: That his [Salmond's] mate.
>
> *Maggie*: Right up longa brother.
>
> *Jilki Edwards*: All come from one country.
>
> *Rosie*: Yeah he come from Kotlen [Scotland].
>
> *Maggie*: Gotchaman [Scotchman].
>
> *Jilki*: Dave Russ, Scotty Salmond, Scotty Minderoo all from Scotland.
>
> *Maggie*: That the first white man [she met]. Old bugger Scotty Minderoo. He tellim me 'Go on you work this one'

[actions for washing plates]. He married little bit me, not too much but [everyone laughed].[62]

Salmond's Aboriginal assistant had been 'grown up' by Salmond with his mother and sister Rosie Mamangulya, who was also one of Salmond's special female assistants. Their mother had come into the camp from the bush with two children. She was not Salmond's wife, but her daughter, Rosie, claimed to be 'married' to him, although the term covered a range of liaisons.[63] Rosie Mamangulya was also 'married' to Jack Campbell, Salmond's assistant, who was of Afghan and Aboriginal descent.[64] Rosie stated that she was Jack Campbell's tracker and wife when they went looking for land and workers in the Drysdale River area north of Kurunjie and Gibb River stations. It was Rosie Mamangulya and Jack Campbell who tracked and captured Maggie Ghi and her father and brought them back to the station and tied her to a bed. Rosie's group from Kurunjie reclaimed her for the Aboriginal assistant, while her father was allowed to sit and receive rations. She was not forced into marriage immediately because she was too young and 'frightened'. She was then brought round to the idea of having a husband by older women in Salmond's camp, who were all close relations to his Aboriginal assistant:

> *Maggie Ghi*: Some day we go, that mate mine Biddy, she friendim me all the way. Meantwofella go and sit down longa him now, talk talk long him. That man I bin talking la him now.
>
> 'You stop here now, my brother now. And don't come back,' [s]he tell me. 'No me'n you gonna go back.' From there I bin stop longa him.
>
> … I bin camp there, longa that olguman, mother blong to Rosy, Dolly his name. [S]he tell me 'You cook Ngarla for him, meat, you know. And tea. Take im for him, give it long him. And he sit down there.' [S]he told me that.
>
> *Question*: She trained you?
> *Maggie*: Yeah [s]he trainem me all the way …
> I bin think about it now 'I'll have to marry that man.

He do anything for me.' ...

Biddy now, 'Can't stop single.' [S]he bin say, 'You gotta marry.' ...

[S]he bin tellim me like that. He gotta look after me. 'He gotta get you anything, like meat anything, he gettim. And you gotta do it like that again.' He tellim.

Right I bin think about it now. Finish now, I married now.[65]

Their marriage did not cause conflicts with other groups, perhaps because her promised husband died and her close relatives were already at the station and assisting with her new marriage. It also suited the manager, Scotty Salmond, who began the process of training Maggie Ghi to become part of his team of male and female stockworkers and domestic assistants. The stockworkers and assistants were intimately associated with one another and relied on the Bosses for their survival.

When the police patrols came to Kurunjie in the late 1920s, white stockmen were warned of their arrival and sent the women to the camps:

> *Question*: Where did Dave Rust pick you up?
>
> *Susie Umungul*: He been pick me up here [Gibb River] takin me that way longa old station Ungudinda [Mount Barnett]. We been go that way then, longa Kurunjie. We been sit down there.
>
> *Maggie Ghi*: Him been living there longa Dave Rust when policeman come out and standing up longa black-fella. 'Go that a way.' Send longa camp.
>
> Police man go way, [we] go back longa house [all laughed].[66]

As there were no half-caste children in the Kurunjie and Gibb River camps in the 1920s, the police took no action.

Mick Jowalji and Jack Jowan described some of the desperate conflicts that emerged between 'full brothers' over women who were captive in a white man's camp:

Mick Jowalji: And nother one, this white man wife, black girl, him been like a that [walked close to her and whispered]: 'You give me tobacco.' And gardia been look back like that. He see him talkin with that girl. White man belonga wife.

'Alright get them horses we go long river, big river.' They been go down big river, these two brothers. This nother [brother] been get away. He know that he [the white man] might do something.

But this one [brother] been tell him 'He's alright Boss, he good one. He been tell im you, get that mule and me and you go here longa river.'

Alright plant [other stockmen and horses] can go back, right back to station.

He been take him there, that mule, proper quiet, he can't move. Him been take long that big waterhole, get him there, finish, shoot. [67]

On a separate occasion, Jowalji's uncle from a bush camp tricked his other uncle at the station into a trap to remove his wife:

Mick Jowalji: And one fella, he bushman again, he been come here longa station. And he been tellim this other young fella, stockman bloke, he been tellim 'Ah I been come up pickem up you two fella. We'll have to get away, bush, leave em manager.'

'Alright.' …

He got no wife nothing, he single man, he been trickin this nother uncle. So rollem up swag and get going. 'Oh well better camp here.'

'Alright make a big fire.' That cold weather …

He been get away from station too. Bushman been pushem out. Makem to go way from station. Right la rock, bashed im on la head. Never get lookin. Broke em all, smashem all the spear. Smashem, finish he get that wife, take im way, that new man been Boss now take it wife bush. [Everyone laughs] Bad people long time you know.[68]

This may have been a new and destructive development in response to changes in Aboriginal men's access to women who had moved into the station sphere amidst the instability created by disease, gaolings and restrictions on movements outside the stations or the station workforce. Aboriginal men could not simply move out of their area to find another wife. If they did, they risked breaking their own law and seriously disrupting the pattern of ownership and caretaking of the land. As a result, a woman's residence at a station influenced her husband's capacity to stay outside the station.[69] Once women were captive with a white man, there was a ripple effect to other family groups and neighbours who relied on them for wives.

The combination of official and unofficial violence against Aboriginal men who attempted to approach or claim Aboriginal women in white men's camps led to an ongoing resentment:

> *Morndingali*: All round this cattle station country. Every-where white men were having black women. They didn't have too many white women, they were going more for black women. They put it over the black fella.
>
> *Campbell Allenbrae*: We couldn't fight. He would just take that girl away and she's got a little fella from him. They were pretty rough with those girls. I know you were handling things alright this side [to Morndingali] but my country Kurunjie, they were really rough gardia.
>
> *Morndingali*: Oh Christ yeah. That's the top end. There were no policeman there, that's bush country and they did what they liked. Shooting men when they were sitting down eating tucker. If they challenged them when they were taking the young women away, shoot the man and take the woman.[70]

The shortage of wives and restrictions on access of any kind to Aboriginal women also led to Aboriginal inter-group conflict over women who were camped at the stations. This was occasionally settled by spearings and injuries at ceremonial gatherings, or by direct raids on a station camp of the kind described by Ion Idriess at Mount Hart and Kunmunya in the 1930s. When Idriess described the 'outlaw' Possum stealing young Weeda Munro from the Mount Hart camp and from her father Wundigul, he failed to include the manager Frank Gardiner in the conflict.[71] Possum was her promised husband, while Willie, the Aboriginal assistant to the owner William Chalmers, also claimed her. However, Frank Gardiner had chosen her as his homestead girl, and neither the bushman nor the assistant was permitted to claim her. 'Gentleman' Gardiner, as Idriess called him and as he was known to other white men at the time, chained her to the bough shed verandah and fired shots above her head as a warning never to leave his camp.[72] She was with him when he died in 1934 when Idriess was in the Kimberley researching his books.

The balance of force and coercion was complex. (Weeda was a captive to the stockmen and manager, despite her father being the manager's assistant.) It was not, as Idriess suggested, a simple case of white men protecting Aboriginal women from the abuses of the black outlaw gangs who roamed the bush.

Some stockmen took refuge at stations from punishments by other Aboriginal people and were protected by their association with a white man. From 1915, when police were withdrawn from the Isdell post, they were also instructed not to make arrests in inter-Aboriginal marriage disputes because of the 'tribal' nature of the offence and the complexity of the evidence, making it unlikely they would get a conviction.[73] This placed the onus on managers, stockmen and assistants who could speak English to report deaths or injuries and to provide evidence for the police. The patrols could then be used to remove rival husbands, white or black, and to pursue bush groups who threatened the stability of the stock camps.[74]

For example, in 1925 Fred Merry asked for police assistance to arrest six named men who would not 'settle down' at his camp or at Mount Barnett and who threatened his stockmen and his authority in the region.[75] One of his stockmen was living at the station for protection after being involved in a wet season killing over an Aboriginal woman. Merry did not mention that this stockman also lived with an Aboriginal girl at the Mount Barnett camp. Her alliance with him restricted her access to her promised husband, and may have been significant in the early disputes near his camp after

1924.[76] He suggested that the group of resistors were killing cattle and coming into his camp while he was away. The police investigated his complaint, and arrested and gaoled six men for cattle killing but considered the murder a 'tribal matter so took no action'.[77] By removing large groups of cattle killers, they had also removed the problem of inter-group disputes which threatened Merry and his stockmen. The shame of living with an Aboriginal woman may well have been hidden behind calls for police to settle cattle killing problems, when they were primarily problems of access to wives.[78]

Other Aboriginal men, such as Mobby (Larry Murphy) and Wundigul were used by white men like Jack Carey and Fred Potts to disperse bush groups with whom they and their affiliates were fighting. Mobby also used Carey to take Ngulit's wife and other women.[79] After Carey left the Gibb River region in about 1925, Mobby was punished for his role as assistant to the white man. He travelled with his contemporary, Charcoal, or Ungundongerri, through the region from Gibb River to Kunmunya mission and the coastal stations at Sale River, meeting at bush camps and settling disputes. Reverend Love at Kunmunya described the period of 'revenge killings' between people from the inland and those taking refuge at the mission.[80] Storytellers spoke of the 'Dambun wars' when the 'glass spearhead' people came from Kunmunya to steal women and land from Gibb River.[81] They were chased away by the manager, Fred Russ. The *Nor'West Echo* also reported in 1926 that there were 'tribal wars' in the region near Kunmunya.[82]

This process of resolving past crimes of women-stealing and revenge killing continued for more than two wet seasons, and according to Charcoal's son, Phillip Krunmurra, was the subject of the message sticks shown to Ion Idriess and displayed in *Over the Range*.[83] When Constable Lawrie O'Neill picked up Charcoal and others in 1932 for taking part in violent retributions over women, he was removing men and women who, over a period of several years, had been responding in part to disputes that had emerged during white occupation in the early 1920s. Mobby refused to accept his responsibility for the killings of the early days but accepted punishment for breaking Ngarinyin law in relation to other men's wives. He and Carey's wife, Mary Karraworla, became Fred Russ's trusted assistants and worked at Gibb River or Mount Barnett until their deaths in the late 1960s.[84] Russ recalled how his father and his Aboriginal assistant, Joe White, 'survived' because of the 'little group' of people, Mary, George, Nipper, Quartpot and Mobby, who were forced to align themselves with the Boss for their own survival.[85]

Arrival of the missionaries

In general, the government failed to protect Kimberley Aboriginal people from cruelty, and rarely discussed the possibility of coercion or exploitation in the pastoral system. Instead, it provided legislative and police support for managers and stockmen to control the process of integration of Aboriginal people into the pastoral system, with few constraints on the methods to achieve those ends.

Newspaper reports in 1926 of the 'wild tribes' of 'Derby's outback', where white men were in 'constant danger of losing their lives', were labelled as 'ridiculous' and 'libellous' by the member for Roebourne. Plans to settle British migrants in the north were being negotiated at the time.[86] The Aborigines Department and the government hoped that the 700 Aboriginal people who were thought to be living in the ranges between Mount Barnett and the coast would quietly move to Munja, ninety miles away, where they would be fed on beef and trained to raise crops of peanuts.[87] About 150 people worked occasionally for the manager, Harold Reid, and his wife in exchange for regular rations, but their forays into the bush and stations further inland continued.

In 1927, after twelve years as Chief Protector and inspired by the public outcry over the Forrest River or Marndoc reserve massacres of 1926, A.O. Neville wrote a strictly confidential minute to the Attorney-General:

> I can definitely assert that throughout the North there is
> still much amiss in the relations between blacks and
> whites. Numerous though the reports are, only a small

portion of what is wrong is ever reported officially to the Department.

It is well known by those associated with the North that there are definite principles employed by those engaging in nefarious practices, which result in the degradation and assist in the extermination of the black race. Then, again, under the existing conditions of employment in the North, the Aborigines are far too often regarded as the chattels of the white employer, and while actual cruelty is not alleged, coercion is undoubtedly used to enforce the employer's wishes, not only as regards working but also in regard to the disposal of women and dependents, savouring on a system of semi-slavery.[88]

In 1928 Neville travelled with the anthropologist A.P. Elkin to Munja, via Mount Hart station, staying for only a few days and, as his biographer said, finally taking part in a true adventure in the wilderness.[89] The following year, an Aboriginal reserve was gazetted at Mount Hann abutting Mount Elizabeth and Gibb River leases. Nevertheless, Neville saw no protective role for missionaries when the United Aborigines Mission sent Tom Street into the north Kimberley in 1929 to evangelize the 'untouched tribes' on the Mount Hann reserve. He also refused to give them land or government support, and instructed police to check on their activities to ensure that they were not gaining a foothold in the north by masquerading as pastoral leaseholders.[90] J.R.B. Love and the Presbyterians were on the coast at Kunmunya, Reid was at Munja, and the Catholics were on the north coast, and that was enough. Neville's attitude was that, regardless of how well-meaning the missionary, the 'government should be first in these areas'.[91]

The missionaries Tom Street and Howard Coate stayed in the region for the next ten years by negotiating with leaseholders for the use of their land in exchange for work which was done with the assistance of a large group of Ngarinyin people who came to their camp. Like the majority of the white men in the region, they relied on an informal system of exchange with other white men who occupied leases without large herds of cattle, or who just occupied old camp sites and struggled to survive.

In the early 1930s the Depression placed further pressure on poorer leaseholders and owners of marginal land. Sidney Kidman sold his leases at Isdell Downs, and Kurunjie was temporarily closed while Dave Rust and Jack Campbell assisted Fred Russ at Gibb River and Salmond sought work at Munja.[92] The work was a failure for Salmond and resulted in him having to repay the Aborigines Department for rations he had lent to his friend, Fred Merry—who in turn swapped them for dingo scalps with doggers at camps in the northern ranges. Among them was Jack Wilson, the ex-policeman still in the north Kimberley.

Correspondence surrounding the missing stores at Munja alluded to Salmond having 'gone mental'. Reid explained Salmond's condition as possibly a combination of drink and war injuries. Salmond was not charged and paid for the missing stores from wages due. His letters to Reid explaining the situation gave an indication of his desperate straits and the social isolation of itinerant white workers. By the time he left Munja he was tempted to 'take the short cut'—suicide. He referred to being in a bad state, with drink his 'biggest enemy' and the bush, 'as usual', the only cure for his troubled disposition.[93] The issue that most troubled Salmond was the accusation from the manager at Munja that he 'thought nothing of cohabiting' with Aboriginal women.

Chief Protector Neville responded by calling for the cancellation of all general permits to men who lived only from dogging or itinerant labour. But as Reid told him, men in the northern ranges knew the Aborigines Act but police rarely visited or checked on them, and he was not able to either.[94]

By the early 1930s the Ngarinyin population was severely depleted, despite having the protection of rugged ranges and a government and religious mission in neighbouring territory. While the country supported groups of bush people, the populations at station camps and missions had few children.[95] Diseases would have had some impact too, as epidemics of influenza, malaria and leprosy were recorded in this period at Kunmunya, Munja and in the towns.[96] The manager of Gibb River station told his son of visiting camps of dead and dying people in the 1920s who were being decimated by influenza.[97] Cases of venereal disease had been identified at the Isdell police camp as early as 1907. Salmond stated that the problems he had experienced trying to settle Indigenous people down had dissipated by the early 1930s because there were so few people left in the region.[98]

Violent confrontations between police, white men and Aboriginal people added to the picture of decimation and decline, as did violent internal dispute settlement which occasionally resulted in death by spearing. By the early 1930s, when UAM missionaries began the unofficial Mount Barnett mission, their call for an end to the 'evil' practices referred to internal disputes. Idriess, like the missionaries, also focused on disease and moral decay within the Indigenous population to explain their decline, without taking the impact of white settlement into account. Fred Russ, Mary Karraworla, Mobby and others sat down at the missionaries' camp at Mount Barnett with members of the groups who had been forced to flee their country but were returning with the missionaries. This meeting, according to Gudaworla, signalled their move back to their land and an end to the extreme violence of the 'early days'. She recalled the missionaries' arrival from Mount House to the Mount Barnett and Gibb River area:

> 'One fella Boss there with gardia. Watch this one. Might be gardia.' Mefella [my relatives] been talk. Alright he been go now. He been go back [and bring] old man brother [Fred Russ's 'brother' Mobby] and Mary Karraworla.
>
> 'What this one, he gardia, headstockman?' he tellim. 'No that's a missionary, he gotta preachem you fella by and by, night time.' he say. 'He learnem you fellas. Where you fellas killem self, all this bad.'
>
> Old woman Karraworla say 'That a missionary, missionary.' [S]he been say. Everywhere this way ration camp. 'Missionary, missionary.'
>
> All right we been sit down now.[99]

CHAPTER FOUR

The big round-up:
the leprosy campaign
and its aftermath

A CAMPAIGN of leprosy patrols from 1934 to '45, which focused on rounding up bush people, put pressure on northern people to settle with a pastoral manager and conform to station life. Government policies in the '30s and '40s, which directed that managers rather than the state provide rations to whole communities of Aborigines, added to this pressure. Bush populations therefore declined in the late 1930s as patterns of occupation contracted towards station homesteads, out-camps and missions, and a pastoral routine was established.

Leprosy and other diseases were important factors in population decline and the history of the north Kimberley, along with the closing of missions and ration stations immediately after the Second World War. The stigma of leprosy and regional isolation measures, such as the 'leper line' in 1941 which prevented Aboriginal people's movements outside the Kimberley, were also factors working against pastoral development in the north Kimberley.[1]

The leprosy patrols—collecting suspects

Police patrols made extensive sweeps across the north, raiding camps and removing groups of bush people who were suspected of carrying leprosy. Aboriginal people who moved between Munja, Kunmunya and the pockets of bushland in the northern ranges, and who were not incorporated into a station workforce, became the focus of the campaign, although station people were also caught up in it. They were isolated at the Derby Leprosarium, known as Bungarun to Aboriginal people.[2] Of the estimated 1,134 admissions to the leprosarium from its inception in 1936 to its closure in 1986, approximately 513 people came from the northern ranges.[3] Several of the men and women who were labelled as trouble-makers by police and Europeans in the early 1930s and mentioned by Idriess in *Over the Range* were captured by the leprosy patrols between 1938 and '43.[4] Senior men and women were among them, such as Ngulit, Charcoal, Mobby, Yuulut and Marmandoo, who had been with police at the Isdell camp at the time of first contact and involved in retributions in the Gibb River region in the early 1930s. Their containment in the leprosarium added to the dispersal of northern people outside their country and away from relatives on the stations. At the same time, the institutionalization process brought members of previously dispersed groups together, encouraging the spread across language and clan groups of stories like that of Ngulit's escape from Jack Carey and the police.[5]

The leprosy campaign provided the conditions for contact between government officers and northern bush people, and became the main form of outside intervention on northern stations. It was conducted in such a way as to reinforce the early days pattern of police raids and removal of bush people, rather than introducing a form of government assistance and protection for Aboriginal people. Leprosy and the collection campaigns, together with government policies aimed at segregating blacks on pastoral stations, constrained Aboriginal people's movements and contacts with anyone outside the immediate confines of the station and the Boss. The leprosy campaign pushed people into the stations, separated non-workers from workers and undermined the authority of senior men and women over younger workers.

Police patrols in the early 1930s, like the one led by Lawrie O'Neill in 1934 which became Idriess's focus for *Over the Range*, brought leprosy in the north to the attention of the government and the public.[6] At that time, the Health Department did not know how the disease was transmitted, and residents of Broome and Derby panicked. Even the district medical officer warned that any alleged case of leprosy in the towns would be hunted into the bush by townspeople or police and thus needed to be removed immediately.[7] Between 1933 and '37, 147 new cases were diagnosed. Numbers rose sharply in 1936 when Reid from Munja, Reverend Love from Kunmunya, the travelling medical inspector Dr Davis, and four trackers made a special patrol of the coastal region around Munja, Kunmunya and north to Vansittart Bay, west of Kalumburu. About forty-two people were collected from camps in the region.[8] Reverend Love reported to the Native Affairs Commissioner that the patrols were frightening Aboriginal people and keeping them away from the mission.[9] Separate patrols of stations close to Derby resulted in seventeen people being removed from Kimberley Downs and six from Meda station.

In 1937 Davis made a special patrol into the central ranges region north of the King Leopold Ranges, an area which was 'hitherto untouched' by leprosy patrols.[10] He collected only three people from the stations at Mount House and Mount Hart, reporting that it was 'not always easy to get natives to submit to examination'. He was also uncertain of the extent of disease among people who had left the stations prior to his patrol and were hiding in the bush. Some managers were so antagonistic toward Davis' 'interference' that he had been prevented from seeing their station groups. This had happened at Napier Downs station, when Harry Bannon was manager. Morndingali recalled the exchange:

> When the first doctor, named Doctor Davis, came around the country, I was a working man then and Doctor Musso came after that. Davis came to Kimberley Downs and Napier, put us in a line and took our clothes off, trying to examine us for leprosy and things like that. Harry Bannon was manager. He was rough on that doctor,

rough on policeman too. He said, 'Before you come trying to do that, you come ask me. That boy is working with me, I know if he's sick. I'll send him to hospital. But he's not sick now. What are you trying to take the clothes off him? How would you like standing there naked? I'm the Boss, if he's sick he'll tell me and I'll send him in for medicine.' He used to tell Doctor Davis and Musso too. Half the time they never came to examine us, used to leave us alone.[11]

Davis reported to the government that the 'rumours' that Aboriginal people on stations in the northern ranges were all 'sick and dying' were unfounded. He believed the main problem was that people did not have enough to eat, which resulted in a very high mortality rate. He felt it was 'remarkable that there was not more evidence of malnutrition'.[12] This, coupled with untreated injuries from horse falls and 'fighting', increased the number of disabled Aboriginal people on each station. The further north he went, the more Aboriginal people's health improved because they had better access to bush foods.[13]

The methods of capturing leprosy suspects were the same as those used for suspected criminals: a policeman and two or three trackers surrounded a camp and, at dawn, raided the camp and put suspects on the chain. Shots were fired into the air or at dogs to stop anyone running away. The entry in police files for 18 January 1936 reads: '... natives very wild, nine rounds of ammunition expended to quieten camp, had difficulty making natives come together, in all we rounded up 31 natives only 1 getting away'. And again on 9 September 1936: 'Raided camp fired 15 rounds of ammunition to quieten the camp, natives very frightened and attempted to get away—got all the camp 27 natives in all amongst whom was the witness.'[14] The police parties visited all stations, out-camps and miners' and doggers' camps from Meda to Kunmunya. They travelled to Mount Hart, which was abandoned, and to the old camp near Mount Hart homestead, which was also empty after the death of another nomad white, mica miner Syd O'Sullivan, alias Dan Ryan. Grace's Knob and Echo Hills were occupied occasionally by doggers

Bob Muir and Peter Backsen. The police raided nearby camps and bush camps in the area to locate leprosy suspects and attempted to resolve future law and order problems by shooting forty-one dogs in three camps and an 'excess' in a fourth.

Cases of leprosy (and granuloma) continued to increase in the coastal region in 1938. Reverend Love at Kunmunya advised Neville that the incidence of leprosy was 'alarming' and influenza 'disastrous'.[15] Police Constable Cooper undertook a patrol of the northern region from May to July 1938, to 'evacuate leprosy suspects'. He also investigated complaints from Fred Merry at Sale River station that his sheep were being speared, and that he had been threatened by an Aboriginal man named McGinty who had approached his camp while he was away and demanded stronger tea from Merry's wife.[16] (White Bosses were not used to even the slightest suggestion of answering back.) Cooper was assisted by two trackers, Kicker and Paddy, with additional help from private Aboriginal assistants and Protector Reid from Munja.

Cooper did not believe Merry had secured or shepherded his sheep and felt he had exaggerated the number killed by Aboriginal people. He arrested seven of the men involved in the incident but did not transport them to Derby for trial. Instead he arranged for them to be rationed at Munja station, on condition that they stay away from the white men's camps at Sale River where Merry was, and Marie Springs where, in the early 1930s, Bob Thompson had started his small agricultural lease to grow peanuts. He did not realize that Thompson had placed his camp near a significant sacred site because it attracted potential labour.[17]

Cooper's report contained unusually detailed ethnographic information about the movements of people in the region, their ceremonial practices and obligations to exchange meat with visiting groups, and locations of men's and women's sacred sites. One section of his report reads:

> Dandalmooroo is a sacred ground where they perform their ceremonies. In January last the 15 referred to above [men] were employed by the headman of the Sale River tribe to bring pieces of painted wood and a corroboree

which they call 'Croker' from Munja Stn natives to Sale
River. It is the bounden duty of the headman to supply
those employed with food on their arrival for the service
performed. Dandalmooroo is situated within one and a
half miles from Merry's homestead and the game is killed
out of that area. As there were a few station bred sheep
close at hand, the carriers demanding their dues, and no
other game for miles around, sheep were killed to satisfy
them. Only the men are allowed to visit Dandalmooroo.
The sheep were cooked and parts of the meat was taken
to Moonyuloo and given to the women there.[18]

These insights may have been pointed out to him by members of a
team of visiting anthropologists who were based at Munja at the
time of his investigation.[19] They showed that white occupation in the
region was sparse and—although it had not stopped some
Aboriginal people's movements across the country from as far as
Mount Barnett and Gibb River to Munja, Sale River and Kunmunya
— the population in the bush and on stations was in decline and
under continuing pressure from patrols and disease.

At first the police patrols failed to locate leprosy suspects
who took refuge on Augustus Island or dispersed and hid in
sandstone ranges where their tracks could not be followed. The two
senior men, McGinty and Nipper, who were described as 'creating a
bad influence on the others', were not located; only twelve adults
and two children were collected for the Derby Leprosarium. Four of
the adults, two men and two women, were found on the return
journey at Scotty Sadler's old camp near Mount House. One couple
had run away from Kunmunya to avoid the leprosy patrols there.
The other couple were hunted off Napier Downs by Harry Bannon
to protect his workers from the spread of disease.[20] The man who
was identified by Cooper as Nullun was Ngulit, the 'magic man' who
had escaped Jack Carey in the 1920s and continued to move
between stations in the early 1930s. Harry Bannon was himself
diagnosed with leprosy in 1942 and moved south to Woorooloo
sanitorium. He joined Bob Thompson, alias R. Steele, owner of the
small agricultural lease at Marie Springs, who had voluntarily

submitted for treatment in the Derby Leprosarium directly after Cooper's visit in July 1938.[21]

At the end of 1938 Davis reported that leprosy was spreading from the coast, but he was still unsure of the extent of the disease because of the number of people who had escaped previous patrols and were hiding in the bush. Bob Thompson's diagnosis confirmed fears among police and non-Aboriginal residents that white people could catch leprosy, and Derby police refused to make another patrol into the ranges without a doctor.[22] Davis called for a 'more efficient and drastic' approach to the northern region to 'survey every native bringing them all in'. Thus the region would 'be rendered clean with every hope of future settlement'.[23] A conference between government ministers and departmental heads in February 1939 also heard the disturbing news that white station people were sending their families away from the region and threatening to abandon their leases.[24] Davis' suggestion for a more 'drastic' approach was therefore taken up.

In 1939 two patrols, each of two policemen, at least three trackers and a doctor, set out from Derby and Wyndham to inspect and collect leprosy suspects throughout the north.[25] The western patrol tracked and raided camps, pursuing one group of ten people for four days until they were finally detained on chains. The group had been warned by two women and two children from Munja and had fled into the bush carrying one old man on a sapling stretcher. They were among forty-five people detained at Munja following the patrols. Twenty-four of them who could walk were admitted to the Derby Leprosarium.[26] The two patrols met at Gibb River and raided three camps in the region. From one camp McGinty and his wife, who had escaped Cooper's patrol in 1938 and travelled in the Gibb River and Mount Barnett region, were both detained as lepers. Yulbu, who was Weeda Munro's sister and a stockwoman at Mount Hart until it was abandoned in 1937, was caught by the patrols at Walcott Inlet. She and three other people escaped from the patrols and were not recaptured. As the patrol returned to Derby it picked up Nurgaworla, listed as Marianne Nilguawun, from Napier Downs station. Nurgaworla was Morndingali's mother, who had been captured by police when they were stationed at Mount Barnett

Leprosy patrols.
Copyright Battye Library, 4421B/7

between 1903 and 1914. She became a cook at the Isdell police camp and was taken south to Napier Downs where she became Tom Munro's (Linyit's) wife. She died in the leprosarium in 1944.

Resistance builds during the war years

The statistics from the leprosy patrols show that by 1939 there were only small numbers of Aboriginal people, between seventeen and twenty-seven, resident at each northern station with a total working population of about 150. There were larger numbers of people being rationed at missions and government stations (143 at Kunmunya and 154 at Munja) and moving between camps. However, they were greatly reduced from previous estimates.[27] In 1939

Reverend Love at Kunmunya reported a marked and worrying decline in the mission population due to disease and drought in the region. He believed that the situation in the bush was even worse than at the mission:

> We have expected in past years visits of people from the bush in numbers up to one hundred at one time. These visiting parties are much smaller lately. Reports have been brought in of deaths of people whom we know and doubtless there have been others of whom we have not heard.[28]

There were only fourteen children amongst the 200 people who visited Kunmunya mission in 1939. By 1941 there had been only forty-four births at the mission in twenty-three years.[29] The situation was similar at Munja, with the manager and official protector Harold Reid reporting that the number of people attending the station were down from 300 to 150, with very few children or pregnant women in the group.[30] After Thompson, Merry and other smallholders abandoned their leases in 1939, Love was alone at Kunmunya. He wrote that there was:

> no profitable industry at present in view in this part of Australia. If there had been, the country would have long ago been taken up by white settlers. White settlers have tried and all have so far failed.[31]

Love left Kunmunya in 1940.

In late 1939 and 1940 Davis made a 'determined effort' to clear the inland region of the King Leopold Ranges, and north to near Mount Barnett and Gibb River, of leprosy suspects, including those who had escaped previous patrols. He travelled for two months with police and trackers, detaining a further thirty-two people at Munja ration station.[32] Commissioner Bray instructed Reid to lead a raid on the UAM camp at Mount Barnett where Maggie Gudaworla and her family were staying with the missionaries Tom Street, Ern Faulkener and Howard Coate. Reid warned him that the methods of raiding camps could cause embarrassment if they were made public:

> I would have to approach this camp with my boys under cover of darkness and take up our positions surrounding the camp and wait for break of day before making a move, would then rush the camp and endeavour to hold everyone in it. It's a risky game and one has to have a rifle to bluff the natives into submission and there is always a chance of some daring native putting up a fight and one could be jammed into using a weapon to protect his life …[33]

He added that he did not have the resources in men or horses to undertake the patrol, and if he went, he would need to leave the leprosy suspects and rationees unattended at Munja. He sent a tracker, Casey, to lead the police patrol, but Casey ran away after realizing that he was also a leprosy suspect, and the police went into the camp without a tracker to guide them or interpret.

The missionaries' camp at Mount Barnett was raided, but only four women were captured, a small group of men escaping to the nearby hills.[34] Constable Mason wrote that the missionary Howard Coate had told Aboriginal people they did not need to leave the area because he could provide the necessary medical treatment. This disturbed the doctors at the leprosarium and added to the Native Affairs Department's increasing antagonism towards the missionaries, who had been in the northern ranges since the early 1930s.[35]

Despite continuing opposition from Neville, and from the Benedictines who ran the Kalumburu mission, Tom Street, Ern Faulkener, Howard Coate and William Heggie persisted with their evangelizing for the UAM. They also established a small unofficial mission camp in the Mount Barnett region in 1933 and an out-camp of Sunday Island mission on the west coast, south of Munja, in 1934. Their passionately held beliefs were expressed in regular items which appeared in the *UAM Messenger* during these early years, reporting on the struggle to overcome government resistance and an extreme lack of resources for their enterprise. Tom Street wrote in 1934:

Having spied out the land, it is time to possess it for the Lord and build up a work for him. Station boys at Gibb River know so little English we could not use them for interpreters. Knowing nothing of God, these poor, ignorant, Satan bound souls naturally are not conscious of Sin against Him, nor their need for a Saviour. Never before has there gone into this range country seeking these lost sheep for the Lord. No wonder that Satan does his utmost to keep the light of the glorious Gospel out of this stronghold of his.[36]

Howard Coate and Ern Faulkener worked as itinerant missionaries during the 1930s, living in a similar manner to the doggers and poorly resourced station owners and managers in the northern region. They exchanged flour, tea, bush meat and cloth with local Indigenous people, in return for their assistance to build huts and yards and their attention to Bible readings. Howard Coate followed Reverend Love's method of evangelizing: he learned and utilized Indigenous languages, eventually translating large sections of the Bible into Ngarinyin and becoming a renowned but reluctant expert in north Kimberley Aboriginal languages.[37]

At the time of the leprosy patrols in late 1940, the Mount Barnett camp was described by police, and Reid, as a collection of trouble-makers, wife stealers, escaped lepers and runaway workers from surrounding stations.[38] Reid noted that it was also a known meeting place for station people on 'holidays' from Mount House and Gibb River. The UAM missionaries did not come into conflict with local station owners or managers over the control and main-tenance of Aboriginal workers, as was the case further south near Udialla, La Grange and Moola Bulla. When the missionaries came to Mount House in 1934, the manager instructed Gudaworla's brother, Marmandoo, to accompany them north. Gudaworla joined them in about 1935, having travelled north from Mount House towards Gibb River where her relatives were working for Fred Russ. Thirty other people also moved to the missionaries' camp in about 1935, after Isdell Downs station was abandoned.[39]

Bob Muir, who owned the Mount Barnett and Grace's Knob leases, came to an arrangement with the missionaries, allowing them to camp on his leases in exchange for rationing workers when they were not needed at his camp. Fred Russ at Gibb River assisted the missionaries by permitting his workers to visit during their breaks from work. Russ's son believed the camp at Mount Barnett swelled to at least 200 people during this period of reoccupation with the missionaries.[40] Marmandoo stayed with the missionaries throughout the late 1930s until he was collected by a leprosy patrol in 1942. In April 1940 Coate bought Muir's leases, but the pressure from police leprosy raids and lack of resources forced him to abandon the camp, and he joined the armed services.[41] His contemporary, Ern Faulkener, continued evangelizing in the north from Mount House station, where he used his carpentry skills in the building of the Mount House homestead as well as carting mail and stores from Derby across the ranges. Coate returned after 1946 to work along the Gibb River Road from Derby.

After the 1940 leprosy patrols Travelling Inspector Davis resigned and enlisted in the armed services. Before he left, he revised his earlier assessments of the limited nature of leprosy, reporting that it was endemic in the northern ranges and may have been since 1930.[42] In 1941 a wire compound was built at Munja to hold leprosy suspects, but inmates continued to escape and many died. In 1942, after Japanese air raids on Broome, panic spread among Kimberley residents, and about thirty people escaped from the Derby Leprosarium and travelled north to Munja. There they were placed in the wire compound, but some escaped into the bush when there was the prospect of being shipped to Derby again.[43]

Mabel King, born in the bush near Munja in about 1938, told a story of running from the police on the Munja reserve when she was very small. Her father would not settle at Munja or on any pastoral stations, and they were walking in the bush when a police patrol saw them. She was swung onto his shoulders in a hessian bag and bumped about until they had escaped capture.[44] She was transported to the leprosarium in September 1945, when she was estimated to be seven years old, among a large group of people including her mother, younger brother and sister.[45] She was released shortly after and moved to Mount House station in about 1950, where she became Billy King's wife and worked in the Mount House homestead.

By 1944 Munja was reputedly little more than a 'holding place for lepers', avoided by Indigenous people and needing regular injections of departmental money.[46] The Commissioner of Native Administration decided to close it in 1944, and four years later most of the Munja residents were transferred to the care of the Presbyterians at Kunmunya. At this point several of the workers and their families moved to Kimberley Downs and Napier Downs, where they were integrated into the labour force to work with Morndingali and his brother, father and uncles. Morndingali remembered the last days of Munja when he had been enlisted by Reid to work at the wire compound and track runaways and sick people in the bush:

> They was dying. We carting with a two [wheel] cart, little cart, little steel wheel cart. We used to cart them fellas in that hill. And they're there all been bury up before they got to Bungarun. They died there ... We used to drag them fella dead body take em down to the hill there in the bit of a ... they got a bit of a ridges there, we had to bury them there. And that's when that Munja used to broke down. They was frightened that wash away might come from all that stuff might comin back to the home so they give that place away.[47]

Further leprosy patrols in 1943 and '45 brought the number of northern ranges people isolated at the leprosarium between 1938 and '45 to 153 adults and fourteen children under the age of sixteen. Forty-four were recorded in the leprosarium admission books as more than fifty years old. Old Charcoal, who had escaped from O'Neill in 1932, was recaptured in 1934 and described by Idriess as a fearsome and respected man who would not cooperate with whites. He escaped from the leprosy compound at Munja and was still 'at large' in 1945.[48] Police reported that he was travelling in the region north of Gibb River station with twenty-five other escapees and suspected lepers from the Leopold Ranges and the coastal areas around Munja and Kunmunya.

While they were in the leprosarium, Aboriginal inmates adopted a range of strategies to continue ceremonial and social obligations, both inside the institution and on the outside. Charcoal's son, Phillip Krunmurra, described a formal ceremonial retribution planned from the leprosarium, which took place during the late 1940s near Gibb River station, over 300 kilometres north.[49] Jack Dale and David Mowaljarlai described dances and initiations involving the old men, with the Bosses' overseeing the ceremonies. Nevertheless, leprosy and the isolation process continued the dispersal process which had started with European colonization of the north Kimberley. The removal and isolation of senior men and women in the leprosarium not only separated them from younger stock-workers on the stations, but also undermined the protective role of the government ration station at Munja and Kunmunya mission and the Mount Barnett 'mission' camp.

The methods of collecting leprosy suspects resulted in a protracted period of tense and punitive relations between police and northern bush people. During the Second World War, the Native Affairs Department (occasionally called the Aborigines Department because of old file headings) was instructed to close all coastal ration points, collect all 1,450 Aborigines not employed on pastoral stations in the Derby region and concentrate them at points 100 miles inland.[50] Otherwise, according to Brigadier Hoade, 'practically all natives would be liquidated by the enemy before they left these shores. The labour problem after the War would then be most difficult.' The Chief Protector warned that there were 'practically no' departmental staff in the Kimberley and that if the armed services went out with guns, it could develop into a 'nigger hunt' as Aboriginal people tried to evade capture.[51] The plan was abandoned, although police patrols of the northern region in 1944 and '45 did occur.

Constable Carr led a patrol across the north from Wyndham to Kunmunya to collect leprosy suspects and shoot camp dogs.[52] Armed trackers killed one man and injured another, and an Aboriginal woman released chained prisoners, who then set fire to the constable's saddles and gear, leaving him to walk north to Kalumburu mission. The ensuing inquiry recommended no action be taken as the police felt the evidence from Aboriginal witnesses was confused — typical of people who had 'exceptionally poor' memories for detail and who forgot the past quickly. There was also no evidence of 'wanton cruelty'. Carr was reported as having 'good relations with the natives' and missionaries, while the tracker Dampier, who allegedly fired the shots, was described as one of the best in the Kimberley, placing police work above all other obligations:[53]

> The reason for his unpopularity among the natives in the district appears to be the fact that he puts his police work before everything else and has no scruples about locating and assisting to arrest any native, wanted by police, and will go to any lengths to ensure the capture required. He has no fear of any repercussions which may be meted out to him by the tribes or natives concerned. As far as the police are concerned he is an ideal boy and would be very hard to replace.[54]

The report also stated that the nature of patrol work in isolated regions left police dependent on trackers, who were likely to receive a 'hostile reception' on raiding camps:

> Furthermore, in the case of a scattered camp, it eventuates that a police party becomes a number of individual raiding parties and police accompanying the trackers just cannot see everything that goes on. A camp may cover a couple of acres of country and with scrub and trees intervening it is not in the Constables [sic] power to observe and control the whole of the actions of the trackers. They get their orders before starting but after that are hardly seen until such time as the camp is rounded up and assembled in one spot … If all patrolmen in the north were to report truthfully I feel sure that they would admit the same difficulties and also that unless they arm their assistants they would not get the cooperation which is needed to make the work a success.[55]

Constable Carr continued to patrol the north in early 1945 without further incident. He reported that the area north of

Kunmunya and Gibb River station held only camps of old, sick and starving people from that region and from further south, who refused to go into missions or stations.[56] He rounded up eighty-seven people in one camp at Prince Regent River and 140 in seven other camps in the far northern region, but most escaped. He did not pursue them, reporting instead that they were starving, blind and sick, and in need of departmental assistance.

The Native Affairs Department re-employed Lawrie O'Neill as a travelling inspector in 1944 and instructed him to report on the situation in the far north.[57] He suggested that Carr had exaggerated the problems for bush people. He recommended that there was no need for departmental assistance because people chose to live there, were accustomed to surviving on very little at certain times of the year and, as there were few children in the bush, the problem was not ongoing.[58] He added that there were probably young people with the old and sick but they had escaped detection and would return to assist the others once the police left. O'Neill pointed out that if the department chose to intervene to collect leprosy suspects, it would need an expensive campaign from sea and land and different methods of collection. Although police officers were paid a ration allowance for each Aboriginal person as well as a 'risk of infection allowance', O'Neill suggested that they required further inducement to make them 'sympathetic to natives' and prevent 'dogging expeditions' and their trading in dog scalps:

> [T]his latter is quite important as I am certain that fear of having their dogs destroyed is one of the reasons why the natives are hard to contact in this area ... fear of being taken away from their country ... chaining of sick natives and walking them sometimes hundreds of miles plus the killing of their dogs first is not much inducement to them to either give themselves up or to betray their fellow tribesmen.[59]

The police inquiry into the shooting incident found that there was no evidence of police trading in dog scalps and argued that packs of dogs had been a long-term problem for pastoralists, forcing managers like Dave Rust at Kurunjie to 'move people on' who were travelling outside the missions.[60] The Commissioner of Native Affairs argued in correspondence to Inspector O'Neill that camp dogs needed to be shot to stop them building into hordes that ate old Aboriginal people's food.[61] The commissioner refused to grant further subsidies to missions to feed people who were moving between the bush, the missions and the stations further south. He stated that the 'happiness of the bush natives in their ordinary bush habitat is important in my opinion and I have no desire to encourage them to indolent habits in camps alongside missions'.[62]

The dog scalp vermin bounty peaked in 1945 at 13,889 for the Kimberley.[63] At £1 per scalp, they were a valuable commodity, offering a trade more predictable than agriculture and easier than growing cattle or sheep. Oral testimony did not record anyone selling or exchanging scalps with police, but police were killing hundreds of dogs in camps on their patrols and there was certainly room for trade.[64] Aboriginal people's fear of police killing dogs was also drawn to the Commissioner of Native Affairs' attention by Scotty Sadler at Tableland station. [65] In 1944 the police shot the station camp dogs, then scalped them in front of their owners. Scalps were openly traded by Aboriginal people with missionaries at Munja and Kunmunya, station Bosses like Frank Lacy at Mount Elizabeth, and itinerant miners and beachcombers, in exchange for tobacco and rations.[66] Jilki Edwards described how she and her mother and father stayed outside the northern missions of Kalumburu and Forrest River during the war by trading scalps with missionaries and with white men who worked on the roads.[67] Jimmy Kelly, a stockman and station manager in the ranges region during the war and after, recalled how some men would cheat on the vermin bounty by 'knocking off' Aboriginal people's dogs.[68]

A combined police and medical patrol of the Prince Regent River was planned but abandoned in 1946. In 1947 responsibility for leprosy patrols was transferred to the Health Department. The Commissioner for Native Affairs described the northern Kimberley in 1947 as 'still very wild'.[69] Police continued to be involved in occasional patrols, and chains were used to hold leprosy suspects until at least 1949. In that year, a small group of suspects was chained to the pine tree outside Mount Elizabeth homestead camp, and young Scotty Martin was handed to the manager's wife, Theresa Lacy, to save him from the walk to Mount House where the truck met patrols and to begin his training as a stockman.[70]

Although the introduction of antibiotics and penicillin in 1949 brought leprosy carriers more hope of a cure and dramatically changed the prognosis for venereal disease sufferers, the number of people in the leprosarium peaked in 1951. Even after that, there was no drop in numbers to indicate that people were being treated outside or released from isolation. Aboriginal people were kept in isolation at Bungarun longer than was medically necessary if they were 'normally resident in an inaccessible area' or unable to fend for themselves and showing signs of disease.[71] There was no alternative for most Aboriginal people in need of medical supervision and rations.

'Benevolent supervision'

During the 1930s and '40s government and northern managers' interests converged under a policy of nonintervention, which left the sustenance and training of station people to managers, with occasional visits from police and leprosy patrols. The Moseley Royal Commission in 1934 set the tone for policies and legislation during this period, rationalizing the exclusion of full-blood station people from social and economic changes that may have caused them to leave or object to their employment on pastoral stations.[72] The commission was called partly in response to government and local Europeans' fears of leprosy.[73] Reports of abuses on northern pastoral stations in the *Anti Slavery Reporter* in London and Melbourne, and a case brought by the Australian Workers Union in Derby in 1932 to pay Aboriginal people wages, added to the pressure on the West Australian government to review policies and practices concerning Aboriginal people.[74]

Commissioner Moseley visited towns, some accessible central Kimberley pastoral stations, and government settlements at Moola Bulla and Violet Valley in the east Kimberley. He did not travel over the ranges, confining his observations of Kimberley pastoral stations to those in the Fitzroy Valley and near towns. From these contacts he rejected any need to establish a policy of government intervention on pastoral stations, agreeing with the 'saying of experienced people in the North' that the 'more you leave a native alone the better it is for him'.[75] He was adamant that suggestions of forced labour and slavery were untrue, that the 2,000 or more Aboriginal people living on seventy or eighty pastoral stations in the Kimberley were 'happy', and that the policy of noninterference should continue:

> I have seen numbers of these station camps, and have seen no sign of unhappiness in the natives. During the day the men work the run, the women—or some of them—are employed in or about the homestead. The old or infirm and children, where they exist, are kept by the station. At an early age the children begin a training which makes them useful ... Bearing in mind the number who do nothing, it is not a cheap form of labour, but it suits the pastoralist who, by looking after the old people, keeps the young people on the property and has labour when it is needed. It would be difficult, if not impossible, to obtain white labour when such labour is required only during a portion of the year.
>
> It is a life of freedom in that the native is under no obligation to remain on the station if he desires to go elsewhere. He has no such desire—he is in country to which he belongs and given fair treatment—which in my view he undoubtedly is—he wants nothing better.[76]

Moseley's report portrayed station owners as benefactors to a station community who lived as near as possible to their 'natural state', 'in the country to which they belong', and worked in an appropriate environment 'in the bush amongst stock'.[77] It was a conservative report, which also reduced Aboriginal people's employment status to one of mendicancy: pastoralists were doing Aboriginal people a favour by 'allowing them to remain' while undertaking the difficult task of utilizing a workforce that was 'naturally lazy' and resistant to overwork.[78] Moseley argued that in order to maintain the current situation on pastoral stations, whereby private individuals provided for the welfare of Aboriginal people, they should be excluded from training programs to bring them to a 'higher degree of living' and precluded from receiving wages.[79]

Moseley recommended a similar hands-off policy for all isolated Aboriginal reserves and missions, thus reinforcing the Native Affairs Department's existing stance, which focused state assistance and intervention on half-caste children at missions and government institutions.[80] He made specific reference to the region north of the Leopold Ranges in his recommendation for changes in court procedures for bush people who were disadvantaged by the current system of arrest and trial.[81] In June 1934, while in Derby conducting his enquiries, he presided over the trial of Charcoal and Nipper for the murder of an Aboriginal man, Burrin, in the region between Gibb River station and the coastal settlements at Munja and Kunmunya. These men had been collected by Lawrie O'Neill during the patrol on which Idriess based *Over the Range*.[82] Moseley categorized them as being at the extreme end of the scale of civilization: 'the bush native who has seldom seen a white man'. He recommended that the government extend the Mount Hann reserve, which was only eighty kilometres north-west of Gibb River station, to 'preserve country for them where water and game are to be found for their use and leave them to their natural life' but with no additional rationing provisions. This was the same area, north of Mount Elizabeth and Gibb River station, that had been recommended for reservation in 1909 by the police. The additional land extended the Mount Hann reserve to 1,520,000 acres for the use and benefit of Aboriginal people.[83] It was rarely referred to again in reports or patrol journals, and was degazetted in 1954. The leprosy epidemic and patrols, and the government's refusal to provide a rationing point nearby, undermined the aim of the reserve to allow Aboriginal people to live without contact or conflict with whites.

Moseley acknowledged that his recommendations would not sit well with ethnologists—people like A.P. Elkin and Phyllis Kaberry. They were drawing public and scientific attention to the value of Aboriginal culture in the Kimberley and the need for the state to prevent the depopulation and deculturation process that accompanied colonization, by providing rations and medicines in isolated regions.[84] Kaberry made a public appeal to Moseley in 1935 to continue the feeding station at Violet Valley in the east Kimberley, to assist Aboriginal people's cultural continuity.[85] In 1934 and '35 she visited the east Kimberley to carry out field research for her study of Aboriginal women's role in their society.[86] She argued for a state-supported system of non-interference in tribal ceremonial and social life, for protection from 'molestation by police', and economic support through rationing, rather than policies that attacked Indigenous practices as 'devil worship'.[87]

Kaberry saw Violet Valley as a good example of a feeding station which supported people unable to work on stations. She recognized the divisions that were occurring between bush and station, and the dire straits of those people who were not identified as core workers and not rationed adequately. She was present in January 1935 when 400 people from the bush and surrounding stations gathered at the ration station to hold ceremonies. They gathered there because they knew there would be food and tobacco, that their dogs would not be shot, and that they would be permitted to continue their ceremonial practices. According to Kaberry, the latter concern was 'the crux of the matter'.[88] Kaberry was careful to point out that the ration station did not interfere with the economic interests of the surrounding pastoral stations, as the people who gathered there were not needed on stations. Those people from stations who gathered for ceremonies came during the wet season when they were on 'holiday'.

Moseley did not support Kaberry's argument that ceremonial gatherings should be supported and protected by the state. He recommended that Violet Valley and Munja ration stations should continue so long as they did not pander to what he saw as Aboriginal people's natural laziness: only those who worked should receive rations. The Mount Hann rationing point, which had been mooted and scuttled in 1916, foundered once again.

Most of Moseley's recommendations and additional clauses to the 1936 Native Administration Act focused on continuing an informal system of pastoralists rationing Aboriginal people in exchange for work, and on not increasing the already low levels of government intervention. The one area where he supported increased government involvement on the stations and in the northern Kimberley, and where he received a sympathetic reception from government, was leprosy collection and treatment, along with the formation of an Aborigines Medical Fund for Aboriginal people on stations. He had been shocked at the number of deaths that occurred among Aboriginal people in the Kimberley while he was making his inquiries. He was later to find out that a severe epidemic of malaria had passed through the Kimberley in 1933.[89] This followed continuing reports of widespread 'influenza', which was held responsible for the deaths of people in towns, missions and stations in 1919 and 1920, and from 1929 to '36.[90]

To meet pastoral interests, the 1936 Aborigines Act introduced a voluntary Aborigines Medical Fund for station people. It involved an annual £1 fee for each permanent worker, which covered all their Aboriginal dependants, 10s for trainees, 5s for casual workers and a maximum payment of £50 per single employer.[91] Thus employers with a general permit and 100 Aboriginal people paid £50. Costs of travelling to the 'native' hospitals in Derby and Wyndham were to be born by the employer. The fund replaced employers' workers' compensation liabilities for physical loss due to accident or injury for Aboriginal workers. It also abolished fees for permits to employ Aboriginal people for one month and reduced permit fees for casual employees of over one month.[92] Each employer who worked an Aboriginal person under the permit system was obliged to provide sanitary conveniences, bedding and a mosquito net 'if so required', and 'suitable substantial and sufficient food and drinking and bathing water'. Blankets, boots and clothing could be supplied 'in lieu of wages'.

The Regulations of the Native Administration Act 1936, which were gazetted in 1939, continued the policy of anti-cohabitation on pastoral stations. Section 86 prohibited both the employment of unmarried Aboriginal women at homesteads where there was no white woman present and the employment of any married Aboriginal woman away from her husband.[93] Despite opposition from the pastoral lobby to any changes to the Aborigines Act that increased government intervention on their properties, Commissioner Neville managed to insert a strongly worded clause stating that: 'No child under fourteen shall work or be hired for labour under any conditions without the consent of the Commissioner.' He also inserted a clause making payments to the Aborigines Medical Fund compulsory. These clauses passed through parliament in 1939 when A.A.M. Coverley, member for the Kimberley and leader of the pastoral lobby since 1924, was made Minister for Native Affairs. He reassured pastoral interests that the regulations and interference in employment conditions depended entirely on the minister and would be exercised 'only if circumstances required it'.[94]

The issue of cohabitation between Aboriginal women and white men on pastoral stations had been raised by Moseley in 1934. He expressed his 'amazement' at the small number of half-caste children on pastoral stations and at the inconsistency in attitudes and practices of Kimberley residents. On one hand they stated that it was unwise to be 'familiar with natives' because the 'natives lose respect for the white man who fraternises with them', yet on the other they condoned widespread sexual intercourse between European men and Aboriginal women.[95] He suggested changes to the 1905 Aborigines Act to increase the fine for cohabitation, but he was especially concerned to change the attitudes of white men in the Kimberley to 'instil a feeling of repulsion at the practice of cohabiting with native women'.[96] In 1935 Chief Protector Neville made some attempts to restrict white men's access to Aboriginal women by withdrawing employment permits issued to doggers and men of their 'type'. However, as noted in the previous chapter, the protector at Munja, Harold Reid, warned him that the Act was almost impossible to police in the northern ranges.[97] There were very few white women occupying homesteads or camps, and Travelling Inspector Davis reported that he excused some employers from complying with government guidelines because they were too isolated to be expected to abide by the regulations.[98]

Neville resigned in 1940, expressing his disillusionment with pastoral interests in his book *Australia's Coloured Minority*.[99] He argued that Aboriginal people's natural propensity to stay in the country on which the stations had been built was exploited by employers, who provided only for their 'bare existence', 'destroyed' family life, robbed them of women and then 'discarded [them] in old age'.[100] He did not mention that he had helped to develop departmental policy which left rationing to station managers, frustrated missionary assistance to Aboriginal people outside pastoral stations and anticipated the almost certain 'extinction' of full-blood people:

> It is apparent that full-blood aboriginal labour will disappear before very many years have passed, and it is my hope that the rising generation of coloured youngsters, many of whom are being at least partially trained, in Departmental institutions and missions, will be able to take the place of its full-blood predecessors. More intensive training should take place and replace the feeling expressed by some employers that an 'educated native is a no good native'.[101]

Before Neville resigned, he filed a note for the new commissioner, F.I. Bray, which was submitted to the Fyfe Royal Commission into the beef industry in the same year. It suggested that the 'real problem' in the Kimberley was that some Aboriginal men were 'intelligent', realized their value as employees and were not prepared to work for nothing unless their families were also cared for by employers.[102]

Fyfe's commission was mainly concerned with profitability and associated economic issues in the pastoral industry, particularly the devastating drought in the Murchison and complaints from pastoralists that there was a serious shortage of labour, 'white and other'.[103] The war, mining and other industries, and road and general labouring work made it 'extremely difficult for pastoralists to obtain satisfactory white labour for station work at award rates'. At the same time, departmental rationing points at Moola Bulla, Violet Valley and La Grange Bay south of Broome were providing station groups with an alternative source of rations and destabilizing the station workforce.[104] Fyfe heard complaints from pastoralists that missions were also taking employable Aboriginal people away from stations.

Pastoralists complained to Fyfe that 'increased obligations on employers created by legislation lessened the freedom pastoralists have had in past years'.[105] The Department of Native Affairs was blamed for doing 'more harm than good, particularly in the direction of making the native employees independent and difficult to manage and retain'.[106] Fyfe pointed out that the Commonwealth Arbitration Acts meant more complex contracts for employers than agreements and supervision of Aboriginal employees under state Aboriginal Affairs legislation. He supported the permit system, which enabled Kimberley pastoralists to take out general permits for managing a pool of labourers instead of having to identify an individual worker. On Commissioner Bray's advice that 'thousands' of Kimberley station people did not understand the value of money, Fyfe recommended that, although a system of wages might be needed in future to retain select workers, 'the time was not yet ripe' in the Kimberley. He rejected suggestions from the Pastoralists and Graziers Association for indentured Asian labour, opting instead for 'the preservation and education, within certain limits, of the native population'.[107]

Fyfe was impressed with Davis' evidence that a serious decline in the Aboriginal population and the high incidence of untreated bone breakages, which maimed workers for life, contributed to labour shortages. Bray added that the incidence of serious injury to workers was so high that 'actually we gave up recording them'.[108] Fyfe recommended that the Aborigines Medical Fund and the medical patrols be retained to prevent the 'complete loss of this class of labour':

> The efficiency of native labour and the amount of it available and likely to become available in the future, are important factors from the pastoralists' point of view, ... as they are dependent on the health and preservation of station natives ...[109]

Fyfe's recommendations were similar to those of Moseley sixteen years previously: to contain all full-blood Aboriginal people on stations and limit industrial developments in the Kimberley, and to make no significant changes in living conditions other than cleaning up some of the station camps and continuing the Aborigines Medical Fund.

There was very little change in government policies during the war. In 1945 Commissioner Bray outlined the state's Aboriginal Affairs policy by repeating sections of the recommendations from the 1937 Commonwealth and State Ministers Conference. The conference was influenced by the ideas of A.P. Elkin, to bring all Aboriginal people, including those classified as 'full-blood', who were in missions and on stations under a government policy umbrella. It created a three-tiered categorization of full-blood people: 'detribalized' living near towns, 'semi-tribalized' living on pastoral stations, and 'uncivilized' living in a 'tribal state'.[110] The employment and education policy for 'semi-tribalized' people on stations was aimed at the continuation of the system of 'benevolent supervision' by station owners and managers, and the continuation of the system of seasonal employment with holidays in the bush. To prevent the movement of people categorized as 'unemployable' away from the stations, a policy was adopted by the conference to provide small reserves in their tribal areas near stations. Here, the 'unemployable' could live and those employed at stations could 'repair' in order that they might continue 'as nearly as possible a normal tribal life' and 'unobjectionable tribal ceremonies'. Station people's 'ultimate destiny' was for employment that was 'lucrative' but did not 'bring them into economic or social conflict with the white community'.[111] The subject of wages was to be the responsibility of the states. The conference also decided that Commonwealth Age and Maternity Allowances should be extended to those people who were less than full-blood, on the recommendation of the state Departments for Native Affairs, and paid to departments, not individuals. Full-blood people on northern stations were not included in the scheme; they continued to rely on the station economy and the Boss.

The West Australian government did not move to create reserves on or near station land where it would be responsible for rations and medical care, as had been agreed at the 1937 conference. However, it did introduce the Aborigines Medical Fund and embrace the policy of containing and segregating Aboriginal people on stations under the benevolent supervision of managers. In 1945 Bray explained that the department's policy of nonintervention applied to all 'tribalized' Aboriginal people on reserves:

> Purely tribal natives who live in the desert areas under primitive but healthy hygiene laws have reached only a low standard of civilisation, and as most of these natives are outside our control no further mention is needed of them.[112]

The 'semi-tribalized' category of full-blood people on stations had been changed to 'semi-civilized'. For them there was a commitment from the commissioner to encourage station owners to make limited changes to living conditions, such as insisting on sweeping humpies and burying rubbish once a week. Other improvements, like lavatories, were dismissed as 'not much use', and, while recognizing that some full-blood Aboriginal people on stations were skilled workers, Bray did not include them in any policy changes aimed at introducing wages, huts or education to pastoral stations. They were categorized as 'better types of semi-civilized full-bloods'. State government policy for Aboriginal people on stations was that they

> be kept under benevolent supervision in regard to employment and social and medical services in their own tribal areas, and education is not particularly necessary for them. Nor is education necessary for tribal or un-civilised natives. They should be safe-guarded in their tribal areas, and there is a doubt in my mind as to whether it is even necessary to disturb their social state by attempts at Christianity. Rural and pastoral pursuits are considered to be the most suitable avenues of employment for native labour. Socially they appear to be much happier in country districts.[113]

'Full-blood' marginalization

Throughout the official debates about Aboriginal people's employment status, and the pros and cons of state intervention, government officials assumed that full-blood Aboriginal people were better off on stations than they were in institutions or ration depots. Moseley had made it clear in 1934 that he recommended nonintervention partly because the station system supported groups or families on or near the land on which they had been born. The children 'where they exist are taught from an early age to be useful', while women and older people performed occasional duties in return for their keep.[114] But in 1937 Neville warned members attending the Commonwealth Conference on Aboriginal Affairs that institutionalizing Aboriginal people did not necessarily lead to better health. He stated that he was 'not proud' of the government's ration scale and refused to give details, adding that at missions, pastoral stations and government settlements it was

> neither sufficient nor of the right kind. It lacks the very things that the people need. The natives in our State exist on four articles, meat, tea, flour and sugar. For the most part they do not get enough meat.[115]

While Commissioner Bray voiced his concern in 1940 that some station people were unable to supplement rations with bush food, he did not institute a system of government support to pastoral stations. He stated that there were two classes of people on stations:

> namely, those who can be employed and those who cannot. The latter are accommodated in special camps and are considered the responsibility of the station as well as the employed natives.[116]

The other members of station camps were pensioners who had been injured or grown old in station employment. In the Kimberley, the Native Affairs Department restricted rations to people who had come in from the desert or who were 'not attached' to a station; it 'made every effort not to ration natives who were born and reared on pastoral holdings but it must be recognised that game and hunting grounds have been depleted'.[117] The system of rationing, which was supported by the government, was for children, pensioners and the sick and injured, categorized as dependants of employed people on the stations: 'In short, the Department considers the pastoralists to be responsible for the natives who have been born, reared and employed on their holdings, including the pensioners.'[118]

Although the 1936 Regulations of the Native Administration Act prohibited the employment of any Aboriginal child under the age of fourteen, Bray was aware of their importance to pastoralists because employers had refused to allow some half-caste children to be removed to institutions or missions. He admitted that the department had no idea of the number of children on pastoral leases but was confident that the 'established custom' of station owners looking after everyone on the stations was unlikely to change in the Kimberley. Those pastoralists who had attempted to eject non-workers from their leases, he said, had also lost access to the children and regretted it: 'pastoralists are beginning to realise that it is to their advantage to care for and keep native children on their holdings as a means of recruiting labour in years to come'.[119] Because government policies were developed to include half-caste children as a state responsibility, full-blood children were excluded from policies: they were part of a station camp and a future employment resource whose training and sustenance were the manager's responsibility.

Bray's rejection of increased state intervention was consistent with decisions made in 1944, when Justice Kelly heard a case brought to the Commonwealth Arbitration and Conciliation Commission by the Australian Workers Union, for inclusion of full-blood Aboriginal people as station hands in the Pastoral Industry Award.[120] Kelly rejected union claims that full-blood Aboriginal workers were being exploited by employers because they were increasingly filling responsible positions without pay or official recognition, and at the expense of white waged labour. He upheld submissions from pastoralists to previous hearings in 1932 and 1938, and the Fyfe

Commission in 1940, that Aboriginal people needed supervision, that they were few in number, that money would be of no use to them, and that their living standards and values were lower than those of white people. He stated that money would be an 'embarrassment' to them. He noted especially that the people of the Kimberley were not 'civilized' enough to be included in standard employment provisions and that 'local' interests knew how to deal with the variation and nature of their employment relations. This assessment was based on information from Fyfe's Royal Commission of 1940:

> I take the view that we are under a moral obligation not to hasten the extinction of these people. Deprived of their hunting grounds they are entitled to look to us for food and such clothing and shelter as they require. But it would be foolish...and even cruel to pay them for work they can do at the wage standards found to be appropriate for civilised 'whites'.[121]

Justice Kelly was not willing to accept any union claims that they were acting in the interests of Aboriginal people. As Aboriginal people were not permitted to join the Australian Workers Union until 1964, there was some basis to his decision.

National arbitration cases and awards applied only as state exclusions were lifted through Aboriginal Affairs legislation. In 1944 West Australian state awards were introduced which provided only limited wages and conditions for Aboriginal farm workers in the south-west land area, or through Citizenship Rights legislation enacted in the same year. This exclusion of the north from state awards also excluded Aboriginal people in the north from federal awards. In the same year the Commonwealth's attempts to include Aboriginal Affairs in its constitutional powers failed at a referendum. This meant that, until changes in the provisions of state Aboriginal Affairs legislation in 1963 and the successful wage cases from 1965, pastoralists and the state departments continued to have responsibility for enunciating and carrying out what was thought to be in the best interests of Aboriginal people on northern stations. It also gave these parties the power to define full-blood Aboriginal people as only partially incorporated into the economic life of the Kimberley. Their role as workers was diminished, and their lack of access to alternative forms of support outside the stations and the managers was maintained. This increased the importance of 'Welfare' when Native Affairs, and later Native Welfare, eventually moved to influence Aboriginal people's working and living conditions on Kimberley stations in the 1950s.

CHAPTER FIVE

The struggle for authority: settling down

> They been shootem all the people. And people been left
> to goin in the station and trying to work for gardia. Make
> himself sensible a bit. Tryin to pick up all the experience
> from gardia side. And they been learn about gardia more
> then. And before we been born we had to follow them
> foot track to them old people. People alive today, we
> work a different way, 'longside gardia. We couldn't be
> different, we had to follow the work, we've got no other
> life, couldn't do it.
>
> Morndi Munro, 1990[1]

THE distinction between working for white people and
following the foot tracks of the old people was an
important part of the accommodation process for
Aborigines. During the 1930s and '40s, the pastoral work routine
was becoming increasingly structured and time-consuming in the
north and central ranges. Bush populations were contracting, and
station populations were developing a pattern of wet season
'holidays' when essential ceremonial meetings occurred.

This chapter explores key aspects of the working relationships that were negotiated between stockworkers and their Bosses.
Although force and potential violence continued to influence those
relationships, they were becoming more complex in their inter-
dependence, exchange and accommodation to work. Aboriginal
people's movements revolved around white men's camps, and
individual Bosses were left to their own devices to integrate work
with the cheapest form of payments available to them to maintain
some workers at the camps.

Anne McGrath's study of pastoral stations in the Northern
Territory to 1940 notes some of the characteristics of station life
which encouraged Aboriginal people's independence and cultural
continuity.[2] These were also apparent in the north Kimberley. Fishing and visiting waterholes, hunting and collecting bush foods and
medicines, travelling across country on musters, sharing information
with younger workers, checking on sites of significance, speaking
language with contemporaries, sitting at camp fires retelling stories
or listening to grandparents, sharing rations and learning to ride
were all activities which allowed for the transmission and integration
of existing secular knowledge. They were also the focus of
informants' nostalgia for station life. The reward for complying with
pastoral work requirements could mean a secure source of rations
for small groups of men, women, old people and children, and a
degree of independence at work and on 'holidays' in the bush.
'Holidays' relieved managers from rationing Aboriginal people for
periods throughout the year and during the wet season, while food
gathering from the bush and nearby waterholes supplemented
everyone's diet, including the stockmen's and managers'. Time for
ceremonies was more difficult to integrate into a pastoral routine
and had to be relocated to designated 'holiday' periods during the
wet season.

There were limited privileges for station workers within a
system where food and security of occupation depended on the
managers' patronage. Fear of losing their place on the stations
where they had access to rations and relatives framed informants'
early working lives, adding to the Bosses' power over them. It also
shows how senior people's authority to direct activities in their

country, like time for 'holidays', had to be renegotiated in the light of the Bosses' work requirements and their dependence on rations.

The pastoral context

Unreliable rainfall, fires, Kimberley horse disease, distance from ports and towns, pests and fluctuating cattle prices all worked against consistent or large profits in the northern Kimberley cattle industry. This meant that there was little pastoral expansion during the 1930s and '40s beyond the leases which had been established during the 1920s. Gibb River, Tableland, Mount House and Kurunjie stations remained isolated outposts of pastoral settlement, while the neighbouring lease at Mount Barnett was intermittently a mission, a doggers' camp and an out-station for other leases. In the north of the region, between Gibb River and Kalumburu mission on the far north coast, doggers and beachcombers visited from Broome until the Second World War.[3] For a short period in the early 1930s they were joined by Bert Haldane, who tried his hand at agricultural development on a small lease north of Kunmunya. To the west, between Munja (the government pastoral station) and Kunmunya (the Presbyterian mission) two smallholders, Fred Merry and Bob Thompson, attempted to develop mixed agricultural leases.

By the beginning of the Second World War, these enterprises had failed. Bob Thompson contracted leprosy and Fred Merry took his new white wife and child to a safer and less isolated environment. Mount Hart homestead in the Leopold Ranges was also abandoned in the late 1930s after the death of the owner and the suicide of the manager Fred Potts, who had previously been banned from employing Aborigines after allegedly giving Wundigul a gun to shoot bush people.[4] Mount Hart was reoccupied for short periods as an out-station of Mount House. Mount Elizabeth was taken up in 1946 by Frank Lacy, while Mornington, Echo Hills and other small leases were worked from larger neighbouring leases or by poorly resourced men who relied on dogging or itinerant work to survive. Further south of the Leopold Ranges, Napier Downs and Kimberley Downs continued to be run by managers working for absentee owners M.C. Davies and Son, who had owned the leases since the turn of the century. The numbers of white stockmen and managers also declined during this period as pastoral settlement foundered. When an army unit was formed from local whites to defend the northern region, all sixty white men in the north were utilised, despite their being older than hoped for a fighting force.[5] Many of them were the old nomad whites of the 1920s settlement period.

With the exception of Fred Merry's small coastal lease at Sale River, where he experimented with sheep from 1936 to '39, the northern Kimberley pastoral industry was entirely based on cattle. Pastoral leases had a small number of fixed yards and very few fenced paddocks, herd management being limited to spaying non-breeding cows. The open range system relied on natural watering points, which were replenished yearly by torrential rains between December and March. By late November only permanent waterholes remained as the river system evaporated and some waterholes became boggy or stagnant and a danger to cattle. To manage the herds' access to water, a form of cattle shepherding was necessary. Aboriginal family groups camped near waterholes and kept cattle away from boggy areas, or groups of workers were sent out from the homesteads to watch and move cattle for days and sometimes weeks at a time.[6]

The muster took place for four to five months during the dry and cooler months. Preparations for muster began in March with horse breaking and replacing and restoring leather ropes, harness and saddlery. Each muster involved groups of approximately fifteen men and women on horseback moving around the leases for weeks or months at a time, herding cattle, branding, dehorning, castrating males and spaying females. Some of this work was completed without a holding yard. The cattle were herded into a group and individual beasts selected, secured with hand-made rawhide ropes and worked on in the open. Each muster gradually picked up mobs of cattle, clearing out pockets in the ranges and moving on with the herd. When the herd was large enough for shipment, the droving teams of about fifteen riders and a cart with cook and horse tailers picked their way through the ranges to the ports of Derby, Broome or Wyndham. In the rough ranges country, without paddocks, holding yards, artificial watering points or, in many places, even steel wheel cart access, the industry depended on horseriders to survive. It also depended on Aboriginal people to perform a variety of tasks to develop the homesteads, clear tracks, build and clear yards, maintain and make station equipment, watch and manage cattle, and muster herds for market.

Each homestead and pastoral lease, regardless of size and distance from towns, was accompanied by a 'blacks' camp', where a core group of workers, pensioners, children and injured or sick adults lived in bark or spinifex humpies for long periods throughout the year. In 1932 the owners of Mount House asked the Aborigines Department to remove more than 100 old and infirm people to a ration depot because they were not working but were being rationed. The Chief Protector did not respond, leaving the station owners to sort out the problem.[7] After the crisis associated with Jack Carey and the early days, Mount House became a centre for a large group of refugees and dispersed people from Bunuba, Nyigina, Unggumi, Ngarinyin and Kija language groups. Maggie Gudaworla was a child in the camp, while Jack Dale moved between the camp, the bush and the homestead as his fortunes changed. Gudaworla's mother, like many other older women, worked around the homestead, carrying water for the gardens, homestead and camp, and tailing and milking goats, while their children were trained for stockwork. In about 1935 Gudaworla's father and mother moved back to Mount Barnett with the UAM missionaries when the crisis of the early days was over and they could 'settle down'.

The size and make-up of station camps fluctuated over the year. Population and employment figures kept by the Aborigines Department were general estimates for the Derby West Kimberley region and, as the commissioner stated in 1941, are of 'doubtful value' given that there were no travelling inspectors between 1930 and '39 and no prescribed system of counting.[8] Reports of station populations in the northern region from the leprosy and police patrols between 1937 and '39 showed an average of twenty working adults on each lease, with additional children and old people bringing the resident station 'mob' to between twenty-five and forty-five people.[9] Such small numbers of people suited managers, who did not want to ration non-workers or manage large camps where internal obligations overrode those to the Boss and work. They concentrated their training and rationing efforts on children and the small groups of people who had been incorporated into work during the early days or who were born on the station.

The anthropologist Phyllis Kaberry believed that a small station camp of only twenty people was unlikely to be socially sustainable.[10] She observed and documented a range of practices in 1935 on Bedford Downs station, next to Tableland, which led her to conclude that Aboriginal people lived a full and rich economic and ceremonial life when they were travelling away from stations, missions and ration depots during the wet season breaks. Kaberry stated that it was difficult to say how much movements and practices had altered since European contact. But she noted that some change had probably occurred with pastoral work, as bush people who were not part of a station workforce gathered during the April to July period for initiation and mourning rituals, while station people only gathered in large groups during the wet.[11]

While Morndingali, Banjo Woorunmurra, Harry Howendon and Maggie Gudaworla all described instances of singing in the station camps and checking sites while droving or on muster as a part of their station lives, they did not mention sacred or ritual activity during work. Morndingali described a definite separation of work and ritual on the stations to protect the processes of Aboriginal law:

> Not that time, we used to hang onto the white man work. We never lookin at that Law. We didn't want to interfere with the blackfella way trying to do the culture and all that. But we done that in the holiday time, when we had a holiday when we out in the bush, when we got a ration bag and all that. Manager don't got us in the work that time. We can done what we like with all this culture, talking more about culture and this holiday place and try and meet up some ceremony place, trying to mix up with the people trying to corroboree around there. We didn't have no white man work didn't been onto us, we used to

hang onto our Law, [ex]changing corroboree or might be
new corroboree to take it and show other people. And
they give us nother corroboree from them, like that. And
when we going back to the work we never even worry
about the Law, blackfella Law, we used to hang onto the
work and all that.[12]

The intense and secret nature of some of the ceremonies, as
well as the need to incorporate specific people from neighbouring
stations or outlying regions to meet existing obligations, meant that
they could not be performed during the work season without
disrupting the work routine.

Jack Dale travelled in the bush and between stations in the
Mount House and Mount Hart region from 1928 to the mid-1930s,
when he was a child.[13] For several years after his white father's
death in 1928 he walked with his grandfather, grandmother, mother
and Aboriginal father from station to station, following ceremonial
and social obligations and staying on the fringe of the station
system. His narratives help explain the gradual process of negotiation and accommodation that occurred in the late 1920s and early
'30s in the northern ranges, and managers' attempts to regulate
workers' movements away from the stations to meet social and
ceremonial obligations.

Jack Dale's grandfather was an important Ngarinyin man
living in the Mount House region and senior to the stockmen on the
station. He had escaped police patrols during the 1920s and retold
chilling stories which instilled a fear of police and white men in
Jack. Nevertheless, he was known to managers and stockmen in the
region and continued to move between station camps, sneaking in
at night and hiding in riverbeds during the day. He was reasonably
fit (he carried Jack across rivers or up steep ranges), but he was not
a working stockman on whom the managers depended for their
labour. He and other old men and women worked occasionally,
chopping and carting wood, carting water, gardening, making bread,
assisting with road making, cutting posts and a range of other
labour-intensive tasks. According to Jack, his grandfather's role was
to oversee and ensure the continuation of ceremonial obligations to

the land and to other groups. Other senior men from neighbouring stations shared similar responsibilities.

In the early 1930s, Jack Dale's grandfather was instructed by a senior affiliate at Napier Downs, Peter Yamiga, who lived in the station camp, to bring a large group of men together for a ceremony for one of the younger Napier Downs stockmen. He walked for weeks during the dry season from Leopold Downs station across the ranges, camping at sites at Mount Ord, Mount Eliza, Mount Bell, Mount Matthew and Bell Gorge, following an established path for that particular ceremony. In the northern part of Napier Downs lease, another large group had travelled south from Munja government station and were waiting to exchange corroborees and take part in ceremonies and dispute settlements. Morndingali, his brother Tim, a male cousin, his father and three uncles were stockmen at Napier Downs and were instructed by Peter Yamiga to attend the meeting. Jack Dale's Aboriginal father, Spider, was also a stockman at Napier Downs and went north for the ceremony. He had been taken from the bush in the early days, around 1910, by Alec Thompson, who was manager at Kimberley Downs in the early 1930s when Idriess visited.[14] According to oral testimony, Thompson had been present when Spider's father was shot by stockmen. The boy had been removed to Mount House, where he was trained for stockwork, and then moved with Thompson to Napier Downs where he stayed after Harry Bannon took over as manager in 1925. Thompson moved on to Kimberley Downs in the early 1930s to settle with a white wife,[15] the only white woman living on a station north-east of Derby in the ranges region. Idriess wrote that she understood the 'golden rule' for wives not to ask questions or pry into 'little irregularities' on the station. Both Jack Dale's and Morndingali's father and uncles, and their female relations and spouses made up the core stockworkers for Harry Bannon at Napier Downs station. They all left the muster camp during the night to attend the ceremonies, which effectively put a stop to the muster.

Over the following week there were initiation ceremonies and dispute settlements, including a spear fight involving Weeda Munro's father, Wundigul. He had been gaoled in 1927 and released in 1932, a year or two before the meeting, and had now come to make a claim over his wife, who had been living with an ex-police tracker and worker for Mount Hart while her husband was in gaol. Wundigul may also have been facing ritualized punishment for the murder of two men from Munja, for which he was gaoled in 1927. While the large group waited for men and women from stations to the north, they were interrupted by Jack Goodall, one of the early days white men who lived north of the King Leopold Ranges surviving on the dog scalp bounty with some specking for gold on the side. He committed suicide in 1939 after coming to the attention of the police for a severe assault on an Aboriginal man.[16] Jack Dale recalled Goodall's white beard and hair as he approached the camp and squatted by the waterhole to wash his face:

> Old Jack [Goodall] … Big tall fella with a short nose [laughs]. Anyway he come up first thing in the morning, look around. Everyone look around. 'Here's a policeman here,' they reckon. 'It's a policeman here. Come on.' Everybody scattered everywhere. They went, went bush, climb up the hill. My father too, stepfather was climbing up the hill. He climbing up the hill, he left me behind him … I wasn't smart enough to keep up with them. And I pull up halfway. I singin out 'Come on policeman we here.' I said 'We up here. They left me. They left me.' I said 'Policeman we here, on top of the hill. Come up here.' I reckon [laughs]. Anyway my father sneak back again, he grab me and he took me up there and he give me a good hiding for singin out to the police.
>
> It wasn't a policeman. He was just a bloke was doggin, see. But we thought he was a policeman, I singin out for policeman. 'We here, we hidin all the way on top of the hill.'
>
> Right that was finished. He come up with a pack-horse and give us a flour … for the whole camp. We had a good feed, he was a good bloke. Then we went down to this place where my uncle got cut with a bottle, cuttin him.[17]

Harry Bannon followed the Napier Downs workers to the dancing ground but did not interrupt the ceremony. He returned to the muster camp and waited for the stockworkers' return:

Jack Dale: We had a big camp there. They had a big dance, big corroboree. And old Bannon's lookin for all this mob. This was his two good boy. His [Morndi's] uncle [Dooly] and my stepfather [Spider]. They was a right hand blokes for Bannon. He look all over. I think he was camping in the dry bank in some where. And then he went across, he know this big meeting ground for every Aboriginal and he come up there. He stop up right up on top of the hill, high hill and he left his horse behind him where we can't see him. And he sneak up on his hands and knee up to that tree. And he want to see. He's lookin down there and he had no glass [binoculars or telescope] and I s'pose he couldn't see properly with one side. He come out bit more but he had a hat on. He come out bit more for full head. Well they spotted him from down the camp there, from the fishing ground. And they said 'Hey Bannon there, stop quiet now.' Oh everyone got frightened, they reckon he gonna shoot them, you know? We all jumped into the water. Jump in the waterhole to get out of him. When he seen that happen he just got on his horse and went home.[18]

The senior men and women decided to break camp soon after the ceremonies and directed their group's return to the stations to avoid any trouble with the manager:

Jack Dale: We split up and Peter Yamiga told my grandfather to take the mob back for job [to Mount Hart], that grandfather mine. The two of them was talking about 'We don't want to fall out with the white man, take the stockboys back to Napier.' Peter wasn't a working man but he took all the stockboys back to Napier. They didn't want any problem with Bannon. They couldn't tell

Bannon the reason the stockboys left, otherwise he wouldn't let them, otherwise they get killed. They ran away from Bannon for this Law. If they didn't go for their Law this other mob from two sides would kill the [black] Bosses. When they went back to Bannon [and said] what they got away for, he said they shouldn't get away from work. They said they went holiday. Gardia wouldn't believe.

Peter was living in the camp when Bannon was there. He wasn't a working man, but he got his rations, he was a pensioner. Bannon didn't know he was a Boss, he mightn't have had him there if he knew. That's what they used to do, gardias. If they know there was a Boss in camp lookout for Law, they'd get rid of him. They never hunted him off, died of old age.[19]

Peter Yamiga, Jack Dale's grandfather, and other senior men and women who were classified as pensioners at a station camp were responsible for the workers' attendance at ceremonies, but their dependence on the manager and younger men and women limited their authority. After the ceremonies Jack Dale's Aboriginal father, Spider, refused to return to the muster camp at Napier Downs. He stayed in the region of Mount House and Mount Hart in the ranges with his wife and young Jack Dale, living from the bush and supplemented by rations passed to him by relatives on the stations. According to Jack, Spider wanted to keep his wife away from the stations, where his access to her would be challenged by Aboriginal as well as white men.[20] William Chalmers, part-owner of Mount Hart, and Bob Maxted, owner of Mornington station north-east of Mount House, sent rations of flour and tobacco to him to entice him into the station to work and to help feed the young half-caste boy who was living 'wild'. Spider was not chased by police or managers but always approached station camps at night or hid nearby until a message or rations were brought to him. He worked for a short time with Bob Maxted and Jack Smith, who had taken over sections of Kidman's leases and renamed them Mornington. Then he moved to Mount House and settled down to join the stockwork team. Jack Dale was about thirteen years old at the time (mid-1930s) and began his training for stockwork.

Wundigul did not return to Mount Hart station after the ceremonies in the north of Napier Downs lease. His aggression had brought his immediate relatives into damaging disputes with other groups, as well as triggering police raids of their bush camps. Jack Dale recalled his grandfather trying, and failing, to stop Wundigul from taking revenge against the man who had usurped his position while he was in gaol. Jack Dale agreed with Idriess's representation of Wundigul in the early 1930s as 'nearly out of control' and threatening to kill white and black people on Mount Hart station.[21] Jack's grandfather was senior to Wundigul but had great difficulty controlling him. Eventually he convinced Wundigul to leave the region and move north towards his wife's country south-east of Mount Barnett. He and his wife moved north to the Phillips Ranges, then west to Munja government station, and in the late 1930s returned to Napier Downs, where his daughter Weeda Munro was working as a stockwoman.

This direction from the senior man of the region was made for the protection of the majority of people in the Mount Hart and Mount House region. Wundigul had become a 'trouble maker', who would be pursued by police if they came across his camps or tracks and was a danger in the station camps.

Learning who's Boss

The younger stockmen for whom the ceremonies were being held north of Napier Downs had been trained since childhood to work on the stations and were completing essential components of their training in their own law. Some stockworkers were separated as children from their families by managers for long periods to inculcate in them the skills and authority structure of the stations. Morndingali, who had been brought up as a stockman on Napier Downs station, referred to a transition in relationships between Aboriginal people and white men as a change from 'bush' to 'middle time'. Aboriginal people were no longer labelled as 'bush niggers' or 'wombas' but as 'boys', 'blackfellas' and 'black gins':

My name now, today you call me Aborigine, that's a different name, that's a new one name. We used to be Womba ... Nigger, we are bushmen you see. Now today, new name.

'Ah, where's that boys?' That lately name, half a name, middle. But in the first place that was a Womba.

'Where's them blackfellas?' That our name. That's how manager used to call us. 'Where's the blackfellas? Tell them fellas to come up.'

... And woman they used to call em 'Where's the gin? Where's the black gin? Where's the black lubra?' That's the name.

... Well poor fellas, we been trying to come and put all that name, come close onto white man. [22]

To encourage the transition from 'bush niggers' to station 'boys' and 'gins', managers engaged in a system of rewards and punishments, which was referred to by informants as learning their

Some station camps over the ranges in the 1930s were no more than bark walls with a stamped earth floor, but they could still have servants. Copyright Ion Idriess Collection

'discipline', getting their 'experience' and becoming 'sensible'.[23] The learning process began when they were children. It involved a range of punishments, including beatings, kicks, verbal abuse, being tied to a tree, boys and men being forced to wear a dress, shots fired above their heads, and food and water being withheld. Children worked as horse tailers, cleared yards, assisted with goat-herding, housework and gardening, delivered messages to muster camps and neighbouring stations, and watched cattle on the river frontages when the muster teams were resting. They learned the skills of station work and the overriding rule of the stations: to move quickly when the Boss was around and never to question his commands. The core workers entered a privileged sphere of rations and comparative security.

Aboriginal girls and women in the north Kimberley worked in the homesteads and in the stock camps, as well as riding for stockwork. Maggie Ghi described her initial training and how this

Cattle work at Mount Hart Station, 1930s.
Copyright Ion Idriess Collection

gave her the independence of having a place with a white man and freedom from being punished for making mistakes. After running away from Kurunjie station, she and her mother hid in the hills until the manager's offsider claimed her as his wife and taught her to ride:

> We been la bush on top and this same man again your brother, come up now. He love me now. Put me long a yowerda [horse] now. That yowerda take me all round. I don't know riding. Proper bushman, wild one. He stockman. He mustering there all around. He put me longa horse now. They been tie me up [to the horse] and put me long yowerda. I didn't know that yowerda yet. Proper Munjung [bushman], nothing. They tell me puttim on trousers. I never like it on trousers. I got a dress …
>
> I been frightened longa that bullamana [cattle]. I been stand up that tree [hid in a tree]. I don't like much. I been

Aboriginal stockwomen at Mount Hart station, 1930s, Weeda Munro on right. Copyright Ion Idriess Collection

This woman (now deceased) was trained by Fred Potts, and worked with Weeda Munro at Mount Hart Station in the 1930s. Female stock teams were a characteristic of ranges pastoral work. Copyright Ion Idriess Collection

sit down now. Gardia tell 'You been boil the billy now,' Scotty Salmond. I go and get wood. And make fire. And get a water now. He train me for that. 'Puttem longa billy longa fire.' … Good Boss too. He cheeky one too. He cheeky fella alright. What he been tellim anybody, they never do proper work he come up with a whip and make em all about work. Start em all about, that the way. Not shootem, with a whip … We been get a rotten hiding, I tell you. From whip, from that boot too, he kickem mefella. We been learn makim damper, makim bread, cookim meat, makim custard, makim soup soup, makim anykind custard, corn flour, everything. Well we been start to cookim now. Gardia never talk long mefellas

Open range cattle work without yards.
Copyright Ion Idriess Collection

now. We been get learn now. I know everything. He
been leave it to mefellas do.[24]

Campbell Allenbrae from Kurunjie station explained that his
removal from his mother and the Afghans for whom she
occasionally worked was his manager's attempt to stop him getting
'silly' and 'spoiled', and to give him a place on the stations as Scotty
Salmond's 'boy':

Campbell Allenbrae: ... old Scotty pick me up and 'Oh
never mind might be spoiled.' Old Scotty was reckon I
might be spoil a little bit, with the Afghan. 'I better take
you away from them.' When I was only that much [about
ten years old], I get away from mum and I gotta horse
work now. Learn me how to do something all the time,

good everything. I gotta do something good all the time … He trained me with his idea. He don't want me to get silly. Anyway if I'm get away from Scotty well I'm not anybody, I don't interest in work. Because I was in that old fella Scotty, well he trained me different way, his way of work or whatever he do. And I do my work just like him. That's way I learn to work. That old man all the time learn me how to work. I get understand from him and I learn to work what he want to tell me to work. I go by him, go by old Scotty.

Question: What did your father think about that?

Allenbrae: Old father was thinking 'Ah well, he might take him off me or he might go for good.' …

He said 'Ah well you might take him.' And one time he had an argue with him. 'What you gonna do?'

'Well he's mine now,' old Scotty reckon. 'I gonna take him for my boy now.'[25]

After a period of separation from his family and training in pastoral work, sufficient to ensure Allenbrae returned to the camp and did not run away, he was permitted to participate in his initiation ceremony during the wet season holiday break. Despite the displacement of his father's authority over him and a persistent fear of being beaten or having food withheld, Allenbrae was not deterred from undertaking his initiation ceremonies:

Well I tell Scotty 'Ah well, I gotta go do my Law.'

'Alright,' he said. Send me way. Put me out, give me tucker, everything for holiday. Mum with me. We go out in the Law ground. When I finish that, my Law finish, right I go for nother two week. Come back one week time. I was okay, I come back right again. 'Ah well, he alright,' he say. Old Scotty send me out for doing that business … Give us tucker and tobacco …

No he don't stop me. When I finish that one, everything, well I'll be out there all the time doing all sort of what he want me to do, saddling, leather work, whip work, all that business. Making bridle, reins, girth, blanket, surcingle, all sort of thing. Pack saddle, all that.[26]

Other men and women who were being trained in stockwork at Tableland, Gibb River, Mount Hart and Napier Downs during the 1930s described a similar pattern. They were released after Christmas, with rations, to complete ceremonial obligations and meet other groups at 'holiday' camps. Then they would return around April to begin work.[27] If they were identified workers, they received a ration bag of flour, tea and sugar to supplement bush foods. But this was expected to last for weeks during the wet season. If the season was very wet it was difficult for large groups to gather and move about. Rations ran out, and managers refused to provide any more. A trained and settled group of workers integrated 'holidays' into station work and were rewarded with unencumbered access to the lease and rations for a portion of the year. The police were no longer needed to round up the core workers:

> *Question*: What about the police? Why wouldn't they come chasing you?
>
> *Morndingali*: What they gonna chasin me for?! I got no trouble with him. I used to work on the station. I used to go for holiday. The station manager used to send me with a ration.
>
> *Question*: Why they chasing this other mob [Jack Dale's family]?
>
> *Morndiingali*: ... Because they running away. Cart other mob to the station, tryin to put him in the work and tryin to get him to work. They got away from the station, tryin to sneak away. All this Aborigine fellas, they used to walk away from a white man to work for couple a while there ... they didn't try to stand the white man. They used to work for a little while and they was start off for work and they was try to get away in the night and walked away from a place. They never try to get through the manager.
>
> Why I been get used to? I used to go and put announce; I used to give him my month notice or a week

notice, before I gonna pull out. That what I used to learn
about, when I was first start of it. That's why I used to get
all this experience out of white man, that what I use to
do. And I'm here now, gettin old. I was workin for station
till I get old. I didn't try to live out in the bush and try to
make myself run away from a station. And police didn't
chase me, put a chain around me. I wasn't a man tryin to
get away from my station manager. I used to workin for
hard man that used to work me, with a dry bread and a
corn beef, that's all ...[28]

The camps of ration people, like Peter Yamiga and other
senior men and women, received food from their relatives or from
the managers in exchange for work, but they risked being 'hunted
off' by managers if they threatened the stock or the social relations
on the stations. Harry Howendon told stories of sneaking into
camps from the bush until the 'Queenslanders' came to the north
Kimberley during the Second World War to Mount House, Mount
Hart and Napier Downs:

We sitting up every night time. Never come outside. We
want tobacco, we sitting down longa stock camp. Gettem
tobacco, we go way night time. That the rule we been
havem before. Sneaking all round here ...

When Queenslander been coming this country, none
we been walk outside [we didn't walk around]. All the
Queenslander [said], 'Oh you fella can come in any time
la house.' Oh we big mob of spear, everything we longa
house talk talk long all the stockman. Any tobacco we
been want im and go back. We been live the bush ... All
the stockmen stop back them manager. That the rule we
been havem before. This time we come up, we talk talk
talk la stockmen, stop with them.

They say 'You can walk here now.' Everybody can
walk outside, bushman come in and that just walk up to
house. Not like the olden time all that Fred Merry, and
Fred Russ and Dave Rust and all that, Scotty Salmond. We

been always sneak up … All the Queenslander been come up, oh we can walk about outside. They can meet you in the river, you can feed.[29]

Harry Howendon, Dutchie Bungarrt and Dickie Udmorrah were also 'hunted' from Munja government station in the early 1940s and moved to camps with Queensland doggers in the central and northern ranges.[30]

Frank Lacy's journals provide a rare, albeit brief, written description of hunting both bush people and individual 'trouble makers' from the Mount Elizabeth lease in the late 1940s and '50s. In 1946 Lacy selected two young women, one senior woman and two old men from the Gibb River camps to develop Mount Elizabeth station.[31] Mary Karraworla was the senior woman. She had been Jack Carey's wife in the 1920s and Fred Russ's wife in the 1930s while she assisted her relatives to come to terms with the UAM missionaries, and she was now helping to establish Mount Elizabeth. Lacy also had two Aboriginal men with him from the south-east Kimberley who had travelled and worked with him for twenty years, but he needed more workers to establish the station. Like other managers in the north, he tried to negotiate a settled relationship with bush visitors by exchanging tobacco with them for dingo scalps or occasional work. But they left the camps without warning and camped among his cattle. In January 1949 he noted: 'Bush blacks here. I raided camp and got two. Broke up weapons and gave them about more dead [cattle] junction middle creek.'[32]

In 1950, '55 and '68 Lacy again noted having hunted people from the station.[33] In February 1955 an Aboriginal man with five wives, who walked with them in the bush from Kalumburu to Mount Elizabeth and called in occasionally for tobacco, led a group of 'bush blacks' into the station camp to remove the workers for a ceremony. Lacy hunted them off, which led to 'trouble' in the camp and the workers threatening to 'run away'.[34] Within days, two working men and women from Lacy's camp walked off at night to follow the groups for the ceremony.

Throughout the 1940s and '50s Lacy's workers cut timber, cleared tracks, built yards and watched cattle but they also left the camps without warning to meet others at a nearby gorge or socialize at Gibb River station camp. He gave out rations for 'holidays' with instructions to return at a set date but consistently sent one of his long-term assistants or young boys to bring people back with the offer of fresh beef or a stick of tobacco. A loose note slipped into his diary for January 1950, reminding him to read Frank Hardy's *Power Without Glory*, sat poignantly between entries that expressed his frustration at his failure to control all Aboriginal people's activities on and nearby the Mount Elizabeth lease.

The Bosses' offsiders

Station managers across the north Kimberley, like Harry Bannon at Napier Downs and Frank Lacy at Mount Elizabeth, relied on the younger men's and women's horse skills, their limited English language and their ability to manage community members in the camps. They were the Bosses' offsiders, who translated the managers' orders, occasionally carried guns to kill kangaroos or cattle for the camps, assisted with the training of some of the workers, wore clothes, and received additional items of cloth and tobacco during the work season. Attaining a leadership position on the stations was not simply a matter of being chosen and trained by the Boss to impose order on the others. Their authority as the Bosses' offsiders was integrated into relationships and obligations in both the camps and the bush.[35]

Multiple leadership roles developed on all the northern stations to integrate work with the existing authority system deriving from Aboriginal land and law obligations. Jack Dale described his Aboriginal father, Spider, and Morndingali's uncle, Dooly, as leaders only for work, not for law. While Morndingali's father, Linyit, was leader for the country on which the station was located and was also a good horseman, he was not the leader for work because he could not speak English:

> *Jack Dale*: They [Spider and Dooly] used to be the favourite blackfellas. In them days all these old timers

they used to have one good man or might be two. They work on that two to tell the rest of them what's going on and what to do. They the leaders, they lead the rest of them. That the sort of job they used to do these good boys ...

Question: Was Dooly, you know, before you talked about your two grandfathers, they were like leaders?

Jack Dale: That was Aboriginal way. Dooly was leader gardia way. These really old fellas they leader tribal Law and that sort of thing. Dooly was a leader in gardia side. These old fellas they couldn't ride a horse or anything. These good man, old Bannon had that for leader. Every place they work, they had their own leaders but the gardia had their own leaders again. That's in gardia way ... They had the Law right through all the time. When white come in, that's when they started on this after Christmas they go in the Law. This was before Christmas when we walked off. They were supposed to be working chasing bullocks. That's the way [why] Bannon used to go and follow them good boys, he never hunted them.[36]

Patterns of inheritance and comparative privilege emerged within the station system for core workers and their families and for part-descent assistants who had accompanied the Bosses to the north during the early days. At all the stations in the north, men and women who had been assistants or children during the early days became the core workers affiliated with the Boss and the station in the 1930s and '40s. Part-descent workers were known as managers' offsiders on the majority of stations in the north (Joe White at Gibb River, Jack Campbell at Kurunjie, Billy King at Mount House, Joe Butcher at Mount Hart and Sandy Harris at Tableland). However, they were accompanied by a leader for the 'boys', who was not necessarily chosen by the Boss. Peter Lacy recalled that only the oldest man in the camp, Jumbo, who had travelled from Halls Creek to the northern region with the manager, could sack workers; his father did not.[37] But work orders only came from the manager's offsider.[38]

Fred Russ remembered the overriding power of the old men, Quartpot, Nipper and Murphy (Carey's offsider, Mobby), at Gibb River station to hunt off any strangers or outsiders who threatened the stability of the station group or their position there. According to Fred Russ junior, punishment from the old Aboriginal men was more frightening to Aboriginal people than punishment from the manager, old Fred Russ:

> the young ones had no choice, nowhere to go. Older ones would chase off a bloke from another station. They were frightened of punishment from their side more than Dad's side.[39]

Managers from Mount Elizabeth, Gibb River and Meda stations all gave examples of their failure to influence the selection of the manager's offsider; internal obligations prevailed above their own attempts to choose a leader for work. There were limits to the manager's authority.

Morndingali occupied a privileged position at Napier Downs station. His father and uncle shared positions of leadership which integrated work with law, while his grandmother was Ngowerung, woman leader for law and the senior 'house girl'. She passed on her position as 'house girl' to her daughter, who used to sneak extra food from the kitchen to Morndingali and his brother throughout the 1930s until she was taken to the leprosarium. He had also inherited special skills and accompanying songs from his father, which he used to sew and heal horses and mules, adding to his status within the system of working for white men.[40] Despite Harry Bannon drawing a gun on Morndingali when he didn't move quickly enough in the stockyards, he described his father Linyit, or Tom Munro, as the tougher disciplinarian of the two men. But Linyit rarely openly challenged Bannon's authority, telling his son privately, 'Don't listen to that white man, you do it your own way.'[41] His authority lay in his leadership for law, which was not destroyed but displaced by the pastoral routine and the manager's dominance of the work sphere.

A skilled and settled group of workers

When Ned Delower replaced Harry Bannon as manager on Napier Downs station in 1938, he found himself in charge of a skilled and settled group of workers led by Dooly, Linyit and two older women. Delower had no previous management experience. He was passionate and successful as a racehorse trainer and jockey at local Kimberley race meetings, but he was not fond of droving or mustering:

> You'd kill a bullock today and between the heat and the blowflies, you had to throw it away after three days ... In March, wet and miserable and hot and blowflies and mosquitoes and all the rest of the Kimberley pests that are around ...
>
> When you're pushing 1,500 head of cattle you're not thinking of poetry, you're dead thirsty, there's little puddles of water there but by the time the cattle go through, it's just mud ...
>
> That's a miserable job droving, day after day—ten or twelve, eight mile, all depend on your waters, camps. Blimey ... It's so monotonous, just so monotonous. I never enjoyed droving. And they [Aboriginal people] can be monotonous, just sit there and doze all day. Then do your night watch on top of it.[42]

During the Depression, Delower and Tom Ronan had 'bagged it' around the east Kimberley and Northern Territory, reciting and discussing Australian bush ballads.[43] From 1935 to '37 Delower had worked as head stockman on a Fitzroy River station before being offered the position of manager at Napier Downs. As station manager in 1938, he received £6 per month plus keep. A white stockman received £2 10s and head stockman £3 10s. Wages had not altered since 1915 when Billy Skinner had complained to the Chief Protector of Aborigines that losing his permit to work Aboriginal people had caused his demotion from manager to stockman and a subsequent drop in income.[44]

Jim Kelly, who owned Oobagooma station in the late 1930s and was a stockman in the 1940s, described tobacco as 'wages', adding that camp people were 'only too anxious to work' because 'the tucker was cut off and everything like that for them'.[45] In the station camps, tobacco and food were used as a form of payment for specific tasks, while drovers received extra items for their work off the stations. Kelly recalled the system of payment during the 1940s:

> On the road whites got four pound a week. The blacks got thirty shillings spending money, they'd get naga red cloth for the gins (sort of a dress for gins) a pair of trousers and hat, something like that. They got as much tobacco as they wanted.[46]

This created a division between workers and non-workers based on their receipt of regular rations and their access to clothing and training for specialist work in the muster camps, homestead and droving teams. Banjo Woorunmurra remembered the divisions on Mount House station between ration camps and workers during the 1930s when he was a young stockman. His mother was head 'girl' in the homestead:

> I was a young fella. My father, when we have tea, the white man, he like me this old man. He said 'Son when you grow up you'll be the man to work on the station. You can go droving.'
> And I listen to what he was telling me.
> Alright, I look back, old man come up.
> Aborigine fella he come up sit down there. And this Gardia fella he sing out to them 'Hello bro, here tobacco.'
> 'That's all they good for, they give emself tobacco.'
> I sitting down there listening that story what they talk about.
> I been grow up, I been watching their footstep this white bloke, how he been work. And I come round that side. I seen this other one Aborigine fella. 'Ah that's how

they been work. When I grow up big man I doing the same.' That was my thought.

Alright when they come, old gardia say 'I think you're big enough to ride horse boy.' I'm happy. Old man give me the horse, give me two horses. Righto I got two, I been work. He tell me this white man, he said 'Listen, you do it what I tell you. You take orders. What I want to say, you take it.'[47]

Billy King recalled playing cards on the Mount House verandah, eating at the stockmen's table and having access to the homestead when he needed it, like 'part of the family'.[48] In 1950 the manager asked for King to be exempted from the Aborigines Act.[49] He was advised that King should himself write to the Native Affairs Department, submitting two referees and stating that he would live 'according to European standards, and disassociate himself altogether from tribal customs'. Despite being a privileged worker, with clothes, accommodation, work, rations and access to the homestead verandah, Billy King, like other half-caste stockmen in the north Kimberley, could not read or write and would not dissociate himself from 'tribal customs'. Only the leprosarium altered that for people who were removed for long periods from a young age. They nevertheless did the work of head stockmen during the 1930s and 1940s—without the wages.

Delower did not require paid assistance at Napier Downs in the late 1930s and early '40s, nor at Oobagooma from 1944 to '49 or at Tableland where he was manager from 1956 to '68.[50] At Napier Downs he managed existing authority structures, asking Dooly to name the best riders and organize the 'boys', and Dolly to keep the kitchen 'girls' working.[51] Dooly nominated his two nephews, Morndingali and his brother Tim, as the best riders for training racehorses and working stock, thus entrenching their position with the new manager. At Tableland station Mick Jowalji, the eldest son of the man who led Sadler to the station site and the first of the 'boys' to be trained since childhood, became 'head boy' and horse breaker on the station. His brothers and sisters and their close relatives were all protected and trained for work. Jowalji and the group of stockmen and women were working with camels as well as horses. As Delower had no experience with camels, he left them to the Aboriginal workers. He was dependent on Aboriginal labour.

In 1944, when Delower worked his own lease at Oobagooma station, he was drawn into a cattle stealing incident involving Jim Kelly, who had previously owned the lease.[52] In response to a rumour that the police were going to cancel all permits across the northern ranges stations, Delower wrote to the MLA for the Kimberley that he might 'just as well walk out' of the country as he could not develop the station without Aboriginal labour:

> For the advancement and development of the country it needs as many small men as possible and if my permit is cancelled it will be in sheer spite on the police behalf as the natives are always well treated and supplied with clothes tobacco and rations in my employ.[53]

In the same year, Scotty Sadler at Tableland station was charged with cattle stealing, and police threatened to remove his Aboriginal stockworkers. The Commissioner of Native Affairs also refused to release his trained half-caste stockman from Moola Bulla government station. Sadler wrote to the commissioner explaining that he was dependent on Aboriginal people as he could not afford the wages for white labour.[54] He pointed out that government intervention had resulted in his 'boy', young Jack Carey, being removed to Moola Bulla, escaping and returning to Tableland station, and then being removed a second time on the orders of the Commissioner of Native Affairs but against the wishes of the Moola Bulla manager. Sadler stated that he had pleaded guilty to a charge of cattle stealing to stop police removing his workers in the middle of a muster. He added that the information drawn from his workers was given under the threat of the police shooting their dogs. On previous visits to Tableland station, police shot and scalped dogs near the homestead and in view of the camp. Sadler wrote:

> It was my cheapest way out if they had brought all my stockmen into Halls Creek they would of been no more

good to me when they returned they would of been real
red ragers [sic] & all had Union Tickets.[55]

The police dismissed Sadler's comment as a 'pathetic' excuse which
was not borne out by the experience of other station managers in
the region who regularly brought Aboriginal stockmen and women
to towns without their being 'spoiled'.[56]

Control of food

In talking about food, informants used certain standard terms and
phrases, almost to the point of becoming cliched. The stories of
learning to hunt a kangaroo or crocodile had repeated lines and
themes, told over and over in extraordinary detail. Such emphasis
reflects the importance of the almost ritualized first spear-making,
the hunting and cooking, which are marks of transition to manhood.
And from the sphere of work, 'shirt, trouser, stick a tobacco' was
reiterated each time wages were mentioned.[57] This referred to their
payment but also to a relationship of servility, with reward in rations
controlled by the Bosses.

On 'holidays' the dignity of controlling food and openly
expressing cultural knowledge was restored. Morndingali was nos-
talgic for some aspects of station life, which provided social stability
to him when he was young. He recorded a long narrative about the
leaders he had grown up with on the stations, who could hunt, fight
and make important decisions about marriages and the country.[58]
These were leaders who stood at the head of large groups of men,
women and children when they gathered during holidays at sites
and dancing grounds, and told them all how to sit, who with and
how to relate to each other. Each of these leaders could feed themselves and their groups and distributed food according to set
obligations and respectful relationships.

Morndingali, Campbell Allenbrae and the majority of other
informants also recalled station work such as horseriding, moving in
the bush and holidays with pride. For them, tobacco was comparatively accessible as they became entrenched into the workforce. But

food and tobacco were cut and controlled by managers, reminding them of their powerlessness to survive without the manager's
patronage:[59]

> *Morndingali*: See the scar from carrying posts longa
> shoulder. Poor fella I been half killing myself. I didn't
> know what I been doing but I reckon I'm quite happy for
> that dried bread and meat … I like my horse, I like my
> cattle, like my new saddle …
>
> *Allenbrae*: It was fun, only the horse side and the
> cattle side …
>
> *Morndingali*: They reckon we was a bloody good
> man. Manager used to reckon 'He's a good man that one.'
> But he used to still feed us with a tucker, cutting one [one
> slice of bread and meat handed out] … just a drink of tea,
> just a little bit of sugar.
>
> *Question*: Tobacco?
>
> *Morndingali*: Ah tobacco was alright, give one stick a
> tobacco. Not tin of tobacco; stick, Nicky Nicky. Nigger
> they callim. Nigger my name.
>
> *Allenbrae*: Nigatine.
>
> *Morndingali*: My name nigger now. You didn't know
> that name, Womba?
>
> *Allenbrae*: Blackfella, well he's a nigger.[60]

Frank Lacy wrote of his 'trouble' in 1966 when a worker
whom he had trained from childhood threatened to kill him over
slices of bread.[61] He was bewildered at the 'trivial' nature of the
conflict. Informants often mentioned being handed food and having
it rationed in a limited and mean way. Tins and storerooms were
locked, flour was carefully measured out, and tobacco was counted
and guarded. When conflicts began to emerge in the 1960s, food
was a significant element of the conflict. Handing over food brought
Boss and 'boy' face to face on these northern stations where
managers handled rations.

Them and us —'a friend for sure'

The boundaries between white men and Aboriginal people were reinforced by legislation that encouraged race-based distinctions between station populations. Ned Delower, for instance, told of his first sexual encounters with Aboriginal women in the east Kimberley in the early 1930s, but would not be drawn on the subject of intimacy of any kind with Aboriginal people once he became a manager. Instead he repeated well-worn phrases alluding to the complete separation of all spheres of life on the stations:

> *Ned Delower.* That's where I first met Billy Munro [Morndingali] and he worked for me years after on Kimberley Downs, marvellous isn't it?
>
> *Question*: Why did you get on well with them?
>
> *Delower.* I never used to try and bully em and I never used to be brother brother with em. This was my camp there and that was their camp there and that was it. In those days they used to be a bit bad if you got familiar with them. They could be bad.
>
> *Question*: But there were men who had Aboriginal women though?
>
> *Delower.* Oh yes there were plenty of those, not plenty but a few ... You been reading the 'Drover's Boy' have you? [laughing][62]

Delower viewed the social and physical separation of Aboriginal people from the homestead and the Bosses as a necessary means of controlling Aboriginal workers:

> *Question*: When you arrived on Napier first up, how did you go with the workers there?
>
> *Ned Delower.* Very good. I've always been good with me natives. I've never been, not like you, brother brother with them. Those days you'd call us racist, I suppose, really racist ... Natives were there, that's their

side, whites were this side and that was it. You had your
own meals, they had their own meals. You didn't sit
down with them. You didn't talk to em, except working
talk and things like that. You didn't hold a conversation
with them like you do now. They're different altogether.
I had that drummed into me when I first went to
Kimberley [in 1930]. In those days when I first went
there things could of been a little bit bad if the whites
hadn't a been strong and conservative ... There could've
been some bad natives in those days ... You just didn't
associate with them, that was it. You kept your place,
they kept theirs.[63]

Even those Aboriginal men and women who were selected
by white men to work in the house or with their children maintained a respectful distance from the Bosses. In the wet season of
1942 Delower moved into the Leopold Ranges prospecting for gold.
He was accompanied by Banjo Woorunmurra for the next ten years,
during which they tracked and rescued a lost white stockman, and
rescued the crew and civilians on an Air Force plane that had crash-
landed at Napier Downs in 1943.[64] But Delower would not admit
Banjo inside the homestead:

> *Ned Delower.* Banjo a friend for sure; he'd been with me
> for years.
> *Question:* Did you treat him differently?
> *Delower.* No no no, they were just natives and that
> was it. I took him to the pub [to work] after. Took him to
> Derby. He used to look after the kids ...
> *Question:* Well he was a bit different then wasn't he?
> *Delower.* In what way?
> *Question:* He was with you more often, in the house
> and everything?
> *Delower.* Oh no, no, no! He was never in the house,
> never in the house. He came up from the camp to work.
> He wasn't treated any different.[65]

Jim Kelly also recalled the social distance between white people and Aboriginal people that existed on northern Kimberley stations in the 1940s:

> ... you never spoke, you know, the only time was you gave an order sometimes. He wouldn't talk to you unless he had to come up and tell you something. In those days in a stock camp, a blackfella wouldn't come up and talk or anything like that.[66]

Changes in living and working arrangements occurred in the late 1930s and '40s which conformed with government policy to prevent Aboriginal women from cohabiting on a permanent basis with white men. The changes also coincided with the leprosy epidemic and the increased surveillance by the leprosy patrols. Police and a medical inspector noted each half-caste child at station camps and any diseases. In 1936 an itinerant pearler notified the Chief Protector of Aborigines that the young girl who had been removed from the doggers' camp north of Kunmunya and sent to an institution had been replaced by another.[67] Scotty Sadler, Jack Connaughton, Jack Wilson and Scotty Salmond also reported each other to the Aborigines Department for breaking the anti-cohabitation clauses of the 1905 Act.

After the introduction of the 1936 Act Regulations, employers in the Derby region dropped most Aboriginal women from their employment lists.[68] Employment figures fell sharply because of this from thirty general permits for 781 people in 1938 to sixteen general permits for 279 people in 1939.[69] The UAM missionary Howard Coate recalled the tension between some police and single white men living with camps of Aboriginal people. The Aborigines Department file on Mount Barnett mission noted in 1940 that Coate had married a white woman who was moving with him to the Mount Barnett lease.[70] In the same period, managers and lease owners like Fred Russ, Dave Rust, Fred Merry and Alec Thompson moved from casual relationships with full-blood local Aboriginal women to enter formal marriages with white or light-skinned mission trained women who then became the station Missus. The first wives who had been taken from the bush were sent away to the camps. Older women at Gibb River and Kurunjie remembered:

> *Jilki Edwards*: His [Susie Umungul's] promise one been die. Alright Dave been got her. And went to station and go to Kurunjie. And this troubling for the, you know, native girl married. This government not like to marry to white people. That was a long time ago … All right she been give to his brother.
>
> *Question*: He didn't hang on to her?
>
> *Maggie Ghi*: Whole lot, he been chuckem out this lot.[71]

Jack Dale welcomed the arrival of white women to the stations because it marked the end of shootings and extreme violence. It was the time when white men settled down, not when Aboriginal people settled down:

> We never know white ladies and kids. All we know these old hard bloke, that's all. First white Missus was Mrs Bell, she the first one we seen. Used to be in this Mount Bell. They used to live there. Done a bit of mining this old bloke, old Ned his name. They had donkey, pack. They'd come in with the donkey to Mount House. That's the first white woman we seen. Then after that Mr Coate had his wife out there. Mr Faulkener. Got bigger and bigger then. More white woman. Not many. They had a mob of half-caste wife all up this way. Two white woman three white woman. Mrs Blythe, Mr Coate's wife and Mr Faulkener's wife. They were living out there. They were really good too. Everything was settling down then. All this wild business they settled down, give it away. 'Missus there, no noise down the camp there, Lady there.' That's what they said. They gotta be very careful.[72]

Jilki Edwards' mother and father stayed outside the missions and stations in the north and central Kimberley until after the Second

World War by exchanging scalps for rations with road workers, dingo shooters and missionaries.[73] During the war, Jilki and her parents moved to clear land for old Scotty Menmuir at Ellenbrae station adjacent to Kurunjie. They worked for a short time, then travelled through the east Kimberley with two visits to Forrest River mission to pick up older relations (including Dickie Udmorrah) and one long walk from there to Mount House for a large law ceremony. Before the end of the war, Jilki's father died, and she and her mother decided to 'settle down' at Kurunjie and work. A white drover picked her mother up from the camp, and they all travelled once again from Tableland to Wyndham. She was trained to ride and work camels but did not like the constant cooking and night watches of droving.

Jilki Edwards described watching the cook hitting Aboriginal men for not jumping to their feet when ordered to move. Her white stepfather intervened on one occasion, stating that the aggressor didn't have a permit for thrashing his workers with sticks. At the Kurunjie camp, another fight occurred over a stockman's wife, and the same white man locked himself in the store while he bashed the Aboriginal husband senseless. He then tied him to a tree and whipped him. Jack Edwards intervened again with the warning that white men were not allowed to be with black women and would lose their work permits if found out. Jilki Edwards was picked up by a leprosy patrol in 1956 and spent three years in Bungarun. Her uncle, Dickie Udmorrah, who moved with her family for years and was at Mount Elizabeth in 1992, and her mother and brother were already there.[74]

Morndi Munro and Jack Dale also told stories of beatings and deaths that were never reported to police. After one fight with the manager at Meda station in the late 1940s, a young stockworker died:

> *Morndi Munro*: All Aborigine fellas, all the blackfellas, they never try to put up a report in the policeman. That's the time. And they used to thought that boy goin to get out [of hospital], get over that sick. But he, they bust his guts out with the boot. He was a big man that [white man] …

> *Jack Dale*: No we had no police then. Not even welfare.
>
> *Morndi*: Today you report people. But early day they was frighten [of] that Gardia, they didn't want to report. They been frighten to do it. And the poor fella got pain on his own and he never got over that. And he got killed then, this boy died then in the hospital here.[75]

According to oral tradition, the dead man's relatives 'sang' the manager, who was killed when his horse fell on him. Morndi Munro and Jack Dale stated that Aboriginal people stopped talking to police about murders because so many people went to gaol; the police did not understand them when they explained that the victims had been 'sung' on behalf of the group.[76] When questioned by police about events, they tried to explain the complex inter-connections of obligations and relationships, of who was responsible in law for 'crimes', thus increasing rather than decreasing the amount of incarceration.

Harry Howendon was chased by police in 1944 for the murder of his second wife. The transcripts of evidence suggest that Aboriginal women stated in evidence that because his wife had broken Aboriginal marriage rules, Howendon was able to punish her according to his rights and abilities in law—not that he did it. Another man, Rajilla, was convicted and gaoled.[77] The deceased woman had asked police for protection from punishment by Aboriginal men, including Howendon, and they had left her with Bob Muir at Mount Barnett dogging camp. Bob Muir ignored the risk and left her with two other women to look after the camp. Howendon and Dutchie Bungarrt had only just been hunted from Munja station for allegedly trying to steal other men's wives.

George Renton lived on the fringes of settlement in the northern ranges and provided an important ration alternative during the war. His camp, Pine Grove, was near the northern border of Mount Hart and Mount Barnett. He was a dingo scalper who attracted Aboriginal people from Munja and surrounding stations to his camp. In 1945 he was reported to be 'harbouring all and sundry' and living 'just like a blackfellow',[78] the fear of 'going native' continuing into the 1930s and '40s. W.C. Connell and his sons, who were at Beverley Springs between Munja and Mount Hart, reported to the Commissioner of Native Affairs that Renton 'had a bad influence on the blacks and they are getting out of hand, just because they take liberties with him they think they can do the same with every other white man'.[79] After enquiries in Perth, the police found that Renton had a previous charge of murdering an Aboriginal person. His permit to employ Aboriginal people, which he had been given in Derby by Lawrie O'Neill, was cancelled by the commissioner. The police raided Pine Grove camp, finding twenty-five people they had been looking for for three years. Eileen Ungundan and Nita Goonjal, Morndingali's younger 'sisters', were also there as little girls and were being trained to hunt dogs and look after the camp. They moved to Napier Downs and became part of the women's muster team in the late 1950s.[80]

Jack Dale worked for Bill Connell at Beverley Springs from about 1945 to '49 and stated that Connell was a loner who found Kimberley Downs too close to town. He was one of the small number of white men who lived with an Aboriginal woman, with the permission of her brothers. This continued the pattern of the 1920s for senior men to call white managers their 'brothers', thus incorporating them into a range of convenient obligations and responsibilities, including training boys, and sharing land and access to wives' sisters. Harry Howendon explained the system as it developed for older stockmen in the late 1940s:

> We been work for him but he got a girl friend. That all.
> Staying one time, that's all. One man gardia been chasim
> [a wife] I go to everybody, 'How we can lettem him do
> that?' Like that you know. They been run around longa
> that girl. Single girl, go round longa that girl, well that his
> business, we can't do nothing. He been married woman,
> well two fella fight that man, like that.[81]

Aboriginal women riders were common in the northern ranges. Government attempts to stop them living with white men as their wives began to have some effect in the 1940s. When women with children gradually moved out of stockwork, they were replaced by younger men, or in the instance at Napier Downs and Kurunjie, with younger women. Some women without children who had also been trained to ride during the early days—like Maggie Gudaworla (Mount House and Glenroy), Weeda Munro (Mount Hart, Napier Downs and Kimberley Downs), Maggie Ghi (Kurunjie and Gibb River), Daisy Angajit (Napier Downs and Kimberley Downs), Barbara Midmee (Tableland) and Susie Umungul (Kurunjie and Gibb River)—continued to work as riders throughout the 1940s and '50s.[82] Their prowess in the saddle and as ringers, roping and cutting young cattle, was the subject of many narratives.[83] They described their clothing as men's clothes—boots, a man's shirt, trousers and hat—but there was no indication that they were hidden from police or government protectors, despite some of them working as contract drovers and riding into townships as late as the 1950s. These older women had, however, moved out of their dual role as riders *and* wives for white men and were living with Aboriginal husbands who also rode or worked in stock camps. During the 1940s only a handful of full-blood Aboriginal women lived and worked with white men as their spouses and as stockwomen. Most had moved away from the homestead to the camps.

When Maggie Gudaworla referred to her group's return to their clan country, Kupingarri, she spoke of a gradual process of travelling north from Mount House to Mount Barnett spanning several years of visits and meetings with relatives, culminating in their reoccupation with the United Aborigines Mission in 1935.[84] The process of returning was gradual, revolving around holidays from stationwork and movements between white men's camps in the region. When the missionaries left during the war, she stayed in the ranges at Bob Muir's camp.[85] In 1946 the missionaries returned with tobacco, dresses and their wives to begin a mission station. They bought Muir's leases at Mount Barnett and Echo Hills but were again refused official mission status or support by the state government. When they applied to open a school, they were also refused.[86] Gudaworla and her relatives went back to Mount House where they could receive rations. Even the white doggers who occupied the pockets of the Kimberley were leaving the northern ranges.

CHAPTER SIX

'To jingle a few coins in their pockets':
the arrival of welfare, 1948–1959

Welfare came in '50 giving hand out of food and rations,
finding a job and helping out giving a tent. When a bad
manager was 'round people couldn't tell police because
police and managers a bit too close. When welfare came
they were more on Aboriginal side.

Maggie Scott, Halls Creek, 1989[1]

IN the 1950s significant changes occurred in legislative
controls over Aboriginal people, coinciding with a policy
shift from segregation to assimilation and a substantial
increase in Commonwealth activity and funding in the area of
Aboriginal Affairs.[2] The West Australian government adopted an
assimilation policy in 1951 but did not substantially alter its policy of
segregating full-blood station people under the benevolent supervision of the Boss and the Missus. In the Kimberley, unlike the
Northern Territory or Queensland, the government closed or otherwise divested itself of all settlements and institutions for Aboriginal
people. This preserved the status quo, leaving pastoralists in the
north and central Kimberley with a virtual monopoly over station

labour, as well as continuing responsibility for feeding everyone on their pastoral leases. Again unlike the Territory, the government did not pay some of the larger stations for rationing Aboriginal people. Nor, as in Queensland, did it provide large settlements for centralizing them.

The state government's partial commitment to assimilation on pastoral stations extended and reinforced the Kimberley's regional difference within Western Australia's pastoral areas. Pastoralists in the Kimberley negotiated with the state over wages and minimum conditions for Aboriginal people living on stations, with the first unofficial agreement for a small amount of cash 'pocket money' occurring in 1950. The subject of equal wages for full-blood people in the Kimberley was carefully avoided by government officials, station managers and Native Welfare officials throughout the 1950s and early '60s.

The Department of Native Affairs, known as the Native Welfare Department after 1954, consistently drew back from open conflict with pastoral employers over conditions for Aboriginal people on stations. They were understaffed and apprehensive that they would become financially responsible for a large group of town-based 'indigents' if they interfered. Negotiations between managers and Welfare over the implementation of new policies were aimed at a gradual transformation in station people's lives without any significant alteration in the locus of power on the stations which might disrupt the ration system and encourage 'unrest'. Special reference was made by Native Affairs Department officers and managers to preventing alleged communistic influences taking hold. They were keen to avoid unionization of the Kimberley workforce and a repetition of the 'problems in the Pilbara' which had resulted in the pastoral strike of May 1946 and ongoing conflict with the department in the 1950s.[3]

In 1947, after seven years at the head of the Department of Native Affairs, Commissioner Bray had retired, without having resolved the Pilbara pastoral strike or reformed the administration of Aboriginal affairs in Western Australia. He had managed to oversee the introduction in 1947 of a State Farm Workers' Award, which for the first time included Aboriginal people—but only those living in the south of the state and they were subject to a 'slow workers' clause.[4] Ex-Police Constable Lawrie O'Neill, who returned to the Native Affairs Department from the army at the close of the Second World War, was the officer responsible for dealing with the Pilbara strikers, while another police officer, Jensen, was appointed to inspect and report on the west Kimberley from 1944 to '49. O'Neill had reported to Bray in late 1945 that Aboriginal people in the Pilbara district were not capable of the unity required to threaten the pastoral industry. This added to the government's surprise when about 800 people walked off stations in 1946, with large numbers staying out until 1949 and forming their own mining enterprise.[5]

On Bray's retirement, Charles McBeath, travelling inspector for the east Kimberley and another ex-policeman, became Acting Commissioner of Native Affairs. In early 1948 he attended a Commonwealth and State conference on Aboriginal affairs, the first since 1937.[6] The conference was partly a response to Western Australia's request to the Commonwealth for an annual £50,000 grant for the department. But it was also a response to increased pressure in the Eastern States—from Aboriginal people, church bodies and other interested academic and private groups—for the repeal of strict legislative controls over Aboriginal people which excluded them from the increasingly important Commonwealth grants for health, education, housing and welfare benefits.[7] A.P. Elkin was present at the meeting and again took a prominent part in the discussions. He pushed for increased services to full-blood people in isolated regions, and minimum wages and conditions on pastoral stations.[8]

McBeath refrained from voting on the recommendation, adopted by all other members, that as well as clothes and standard accommodation, a minimum cash wage be paid direct to Aboriginal employees on pastoral stations. He was 'not prepared to come into line' on the recommendation that all states endeavour to pass uniform legislation and to professionalize departments through anthropological training of all staff. He also declined to vote on the recommendation to pay workers' compensation to Aboriginal people in the pastoral industry. He argued that Western Australia was different from other states in size, its large Aboriginal population and, most importantly, its coverage of northern and southern zones.[9] The department saw the south as predominantly a half-caste and increasingly 'civilized' population, while the north was characterized as a 'full-blood' population, many of whom were viewed as 'primitive'. Only local knowledge and experience could successfully straddle the needs and requirements of two different populations.

While the West Australian government was not willing to alter its policy of nonintervention in northern employment conditions, the possibility of securing Social Security funds was attractive. McBeath supported the principle and argued that Social Security benefits be extended to Aboriginal people, including those resident on pastoral stations, with the exception of 'full-blood aboriginals living under primitive or nomadic conditions.'[10] Payment of Social Security benefits for Aboriginal people could help to resolve the tensions between the department and pastoralists over who was responsible for rationing and maintaining 'indigents'. As early as 1942 the Commonwealth had received a submission from the Graziers' Federation Council of Australia, supporting the extension of the child endowment benefit to station people on the condition that it be paid to station management. They justified this by stating that it was the stations who supported the children and that the parents were not capable of handling cash. Commissioner Bray supported this move, which would help to 'preserve the supply of labour' for the pastoral industry.[11] The suggestion was not accepted by the Commonwealth, however.

Neither the state nor Commonwealth governments wanted Social Security benefits to interfere with Aboriginal people's employment or lessen the government's capacity to control their 'social development'. Restrictions on child endowment benefits were lifted in 1943 on the proviso that they be paid only to 'detribalized' Aboriginal people who had an exemption from the Native Administration Act and did not live on an Aboriginal reserve, attend a state Aboriginal institution or mission, or live on a station where they were still classified as 'semi-tribalized'.[12] The Commonwealth refused to support people on government reserves or institutions on the grounds that these people were dependent on the state and not capable of spending their money in an appropriate manner. All Aboriginal women were excluded from the maternity bonus, known as the 'baby bonus'.[13]

The commissioner was keen for the endowment program to expand and supplement departmental funding. The Western Australian Citizenship Rights Act of 1944 made citizenship holders eligible for age, invalid, child endowment and maternity benefits. In addition, the Commonwealth agreed to pay child endowment to the government for Aboriginal children at approved state institutions. By 1945 the department received £3,000 for children at southern reserves and £4,500 for children at settlements and institutions. This money represented almost half of the £15,000 budget for relief and rations to Aboriginal people in 1945. It also enabled Commissioner Bray to start Udialla ration station eighty miles south of Derby, on the Fitzroy River, for training half-caste boys for pastoral work. It became a ration depot for desert people coming into the Fitzroy River stations, but it closed in 1949 after heavy criticism from pastoral neighbours that it interfered with their labour and was unproductive. The Department of Native Affairs was also reprimanded by the Commonwealth, just before Udialla closed, for paying wages to staff from child endowment money.[14] Child endowment benefits were a significant financial boost for Moola Bulla settlement and the Derby Leprosarium.

Until the late 1940s therefore, when restrictions were lifted on payments to Aboriginal women, only a small number of people in the south of the state and those in northern institutions were eligible for Social Security benefits. As a result of Social Security guidelines and the state's definition of 'Aboriginal', children from Kimberley stations came into a payment category only if they were in an institution, not if they were with their parents on stations or in towns. This focus on the child apart from the family increased during the 1960s, to become an important part of the manager's paternalism and the disintegration of the station mob.

The Bateman Commission: benevolent supervision with a twist

The prospect of increased financial support from the Commonwealth contributed to the government's decision to review the administration of Aboriginal affairs in Western Australia with the

1948 Bateman Royal Commission.[15] The commission provided a range of recommendations which ensured that full-blood people on Kimberley pastoral stations continued to be 'protected' and segregated on the stations under the control of the Boss and the Missus, and only partially incorporated into the emerging welfare system and assimilation policy.[16] Bateman recommended an overall policy of 'gradual' change towards the 'eventual assimilation' of half-caste people on stations, including a special Aboriginal minimum wage in the pastoral industry in the Pilbara and Murchison, and improved housing and education for half-caste children. Despite warning the government that 'sustenance in return for service [was] not in accord with modern civilisation', he believed that full-blood station people in the Kimberley should be given a small wage as store credits but excluded from receiving cash, as they had 'no sense of money values whatsoever and they would become prey to the unscrupulous hawker who would persuade them to spend their money on useless articles'.[17]

Bateman recommended a tough application of the 'neglected' child category in order to completely isolate half-caste Aboriginal children from their 'verminous', 'squalid' fringe camps and those 'lazy', 'unclean, idle and useless creatures' who were their parents and relatives.[18] Full-blood people on stations would have their standard of living raised by training the children in hygiene and the value of money, and regular inspections by departmental staff to assist the managers to supervise the camps.[19] But Bateman did not recommend that full-blood children be removed from the stations to missions or institutions for further education:

> In regard to the pastoral districts generally, in my view it is most undesirable to remove the native children from the stations to the towns for schooling. The influence of the town spoils the native for future employment on the stations and they should not be encouraged to enter the towns if it is at all possible to educate them otherwise. The pastoral industry is an important one to the State and it is almost entirely dependent on native labour. So long as the natives receive fair treatment on the stations it is in

their best interests, as well as the State's, that they should
be employed in the pastoral industry.[20]

Bateman was adamant that the department could improve its
system of supervision of Aboriginal people by increasing its regional
staff and ensuring that it was led by someone with anthropological
training or at least some background in the colonial administration
of Indigenous affairs. This suggestion was taken up, and, with the
support of Elkin, Stanley Middleton was appointed commissioner in
September 1948. He had anthropological training and previous
experience in New Guinea, from where he recruited four of his
colleagues for the Department of Native Affairs.[21] Two of them,
Dave Pullen and Jim Beharrell, took up the positions of Senior
Administrative Officer, Northern District, and District Officer, Derby,
in 1949 and 1950 respectively.

Lawrie O'Neill was 'returned' to the police department in
1949, shortly after Middleton declared that O'Neill's views were
'diametrically opposed' to those of the new staff and the Native
Affairs Department in general.[22] O'Neill's return to the police
marked an important shift in departmental policy, from capture and
punishment to assistance for Aboriginal people. Dave Pullen was
remembered by older Aboriginal informants as the first 'Welfare'
officer in Derby and the west Kimberley, while O'Neill, who worked
as an official Aboriginal protector for at least fifteen years, four of
them as a travelling inspector, was remembered as a 'hard' and
efficient policeman from whom it was difficult to escape. O'Neill
was intimately involved with punitive actions against Aboriginal
people, both explicit, in the capture of beef thieves and suspected
murderers, and implicit, in the capture and chaining of lepers and
bush people. Weeda Munro recalled being frightened of Lawrie
O'Neill when he asked her in the early 1930s to remove her clothes
so he could take her photograph, which was later captioned the
'wild girls of the hills' in Idriess's *Over the Range*.[23] Having made the
transition from bush to station, Weeda Munro was not keen to
remove her clothes and risk being classified a bush woman.

O'Neill's replacement by Pullen and return to the police force
was part of the department's separation from the police, which had

been suggested by each of the Royal Commissions in 1904, 1934 and 1948. Bateman's 1948 criticisms were convincing. He wrote that the concept of police protectors was 'contradictory' and 'universally condemned', adding that in 'isolated districts the police officer wields a great deal of power. His word is law and if he happens to be unsympathetic towards the natives then it is a poor look-out for them.'[24] He wrote that the lack of departmental officers in the Kimberley meant that it was the 'police who administer native affairs', and this was 'entirely wrong in principle.'[25] The practice of employing ex-police officers as travelling inspectors was also impractical because Aboriginal people 'usually fear police' and were unlikely to approach them for assistance.[26] The number of police protectors declined from seventy-seven in 1950 to twenty-nine in 1956, and clearer distinctions developed between police and 'Welfare' from that period.

'Not to encourage unrest'

Dave Pullen was in the Kimberley for only two years. His death in 1951 deprived the department of his enthusiasm and experience— and his unusual literary asides about the region and its white and black residents. One of these, reproduced for the 1950 Annual Report, was a quote that Pullen believed reflected the attitudes of Kimberley residents to missions and missionaries and to change:

> A Mission station boy is no use to anyone for he has acquired the vices of the white man without his virtue. In return for a smattering of education and Christianity he is liable to become conceited, insolent and secretly disloyal. He has learned that all men are equal in the sight of God without the useful corollary that they are not equal in the sight of man and that the world conforms to the latter usage.[27]

This quotation was taken from J.H. Curle's *Shadow Show*, published in 1927. Curle was an English travel writer and journalist for *The*

Times who, like Ion Idriess, brought the excitement of racial difference and savage passions of the post-war British Empire to a large
and enthusiastic audience in the cities. He wrote of his observations
while travelling in the late 1920s and '30s in New Guinea, Africa and
Australia, providing expatriates like Pullen with reading material, as
well as adding to their own exotic image at 'home'.[28]

The fact that Middleton, commissioner from only 1948, chose
to reproduce such comments in a published report was a reflection
of his respect for his New Guinea colleague and their shared vision
for reforming the department and changing white Australian attitudes to Aboriginal people. Middleton himself wrote in the 1949
Annual Report that it seemed:

> incredible that the experiences with native peoples in
> other countries have apparently been entirely lost upon
> most of the people of Western Australia. Obviously the
> familiarity which has bred so much contempt has become
> congenital, and is therefore noticed only in otherwise
> unavoidable circumstances.[29]

In 1950 he commented that the fieldwork task of assimilating
Aboriginal people into white society defied 'lucid description' and
taxed his officers too greatly. He mentioned the perennial problems
of lack of funding and inadequate staffing, and the variation in
the living conditions and experiences of Aboriginal people. But he
also mentioned the existence of white community prejudices, which
blocked the reform program. This was a significant change in policy,
indicating that the department would identify what it believed to be
Aboriginal interests and, to a greater extent than before, support them
against detractors. Middleton reported that departmental officers in
the field were treated by residents and station managers with a 'lack
of respect', as if they were 'of little more account than the coloured
people who are their responsibility'.[30] His officers endured their poor
treatment from the community with the 'patient toleration of men
who know that what they are doing is right, meet, just and overdue'.[31]

The transition from patrolling the frontiers of an external
colony like New Guinea to administering the internal frontiers of

Western Australia had brought both Middleton and Pullen into conflict with pastoralists and parliamentarians, with little support from the public.[32] By 1953, after five years as commissioner, Middleton was accused in parliament of being 'frankly propagandist' for alleging that state Aboriginal affairs legislation:

> approved of [Aboriginal people's] pauperisation on the one hand and on the other directed a form of control which bordered on unwarranted interference with personal liberty unparalleled in the legislative treatment of any other people of the Commonwealth or Pacific territories. Its effect on aborigines was to create in their minds a state of degradation, or at least inferiority, and it appears to have gradually driven most of them into a state of passive resistance which may take years of patient and painstaking effort to remove.
>
> … We, who are charged with the unpleasant duty of administering it, regard it as repugnant to basic humanitarian and welfare principles devoid of any common ground with the people we are trying to help and creative of more misunderstanding, dissatisfaction and abuse than any other piece of similar legislation known to the free world today.[33]

Middleton was particularly critical of the prejudice he found in the northern pastoral industry, where even people who claimed to be 'pro-Aborigine' believed an Aboriginal person 'must be kept in his place'. He openly claimed that police officers reinforced this view and that to attempt to fight against discrimination was to 'fight the entire recognised social system of the white community'.[34]

The conflict between Middleton and Don McLeod, spokesman for the Pilbara strikers, further eroded departmental support. Lawrie O'Neill's advice to Middleton about the situation in the Pilbara was flawed, but Middleton also made his own mistakes. He attempted to force McLeod away from the strikers using the 1936 Native Administration Act to gaol white and black organizers, and to prohibit contacts between Aboriginal people and outside supporters from church or political bodies.[35] The publicity from supporters helped to raise the public profile of the strikers and to discredit Middleton.[36] He in turn sought to ensure that industrial unrest and 'communism' did not spread to the Kimberley.

The 'unrest' of the Pilbara strike was also evident in the Murchison and the Ashburton, where some Aboriginal workers turned from station work to mining.[37] According to McLeod, Aboriginal stockmen from three Kimberley stations near Broome were also supposed to walk off in 1946 but failed to do so.[38] In 1948 Bateman wrote that the problem in the Pilbara stemmed from McLeod's influence, as well as resentment by Aboriginal people towards the department, which they felt failed to support them, dealing only with station managers.[39] He made it clear that the same discontent was becoming a factor in the Derby area, where some Aboriginal people had told him they would also strike for better conditions. He suggested that 'Communistic influences' in the Kimberley would bring about the same divisive situation as in the Pilbara, and that the departmental officer in Derby should 'forestall any such influence as soon as it appeared'.[40]

Middleton did not have to deal with the same scale of organized walk-offs and public scrutiny of departmental actions in the Kimberley as he had in the Pilbara. The situation was different. First, there were no mining alternatives to supplement or replace station rations.[41] The Kimberley was also a region of many different languages and cultural blocs, and only a short time had elapsed since the chaos and terror of the frontier.[42] Vast station holdings for cattle and sheep were rarely fenced or developed to significantly reduce pastoralists' dependency on resident groups of Aboriginal people.[43] Leprosy patrols and the leprosy epidemic also added to the region's isolation. Furthermore, there were no McLeods or other outsiders willing to advocate and assist with strike action. Between 1949 and '59 there were only two recorded official visits to the west Kimberley by a union representative interested in station working conditions for Aboriginal people.[44] And the ban on Aboriginal people joining the Australian Workers' Union was not lifted until 1964. Finally, in the 1950s the state Native Welfare Department provided the most significant critique of conditions on Kimberley stations, but its policy of assistance was not designed to fracture station relationships. It was aimed at encouraging pastoral paternalism, which in turn would save Aboriginal people from abject poverty and extinction, as well as ensuring their future employment.

In 1949, at the peak of national and international publicity about the Pilbara strikers, the Anti-Slavery Society of London also questioned Middleton about slave labour on Kimberley stations. Middleton defended Kimberley pastoralists, referring to pastoral paternalism as the only means of survival that catered for Aboriginal people's inherent cultural dependency. Middleton wrote that it was not a matter of not paying wages, but rather:

> a matter of the stage in the natives' development in the handling of money, of which to a large extent they have no real knowledge, and the possession of which will disadvantage them ... You are no doubt aware that on the stations in the Kimberleys the administration is paternal in nature, in that a considerable number of natives and the relatives of those who work are maintained in food and clothing and other necessaries by the Station owners.[45]

In his reports to Middleton in 1949 and '50, Pullen provided the commissioner with information that undermined such generalizations about Aboriginal people on west Kimberley pastoral stations and questioned the benevolence of the paternalism he found there. Pullen wrote that, on arrival, he:

> came up against the well-rehearsed opinions that the natives should not be interfered with, that they were getting all they needed to keep body and soul together, that they were happy, that money would spoil them and make them more sophisticated and that the pastoral industry would be upset and the stations would have to resort to white jackeroos and thus throw the responsibility of providing for the natives back on the Government. Also I had been led to believe that the stations

were, great heartedly, maintaining hundreds of aged and
indigent people.[46]

After two visits to station camps, Pullen found that Aboriginal
people, particularly stockmen and domestics, began to approach
him and ask for changes in their living and working conditions.
They understood money and wanted a wage. He checked some
station books and found that most stockmen were in debt to the
stations, while in only a few cases were women paid.[47] One
manager had indicated that at the 'end of the year he magnani-
mously wiped off the debts'.

Pullen called on Middleton to implement the 1936 Aborigines
Act and Regulations to improve living conditions on the stations,
suggesting that the 'Administration, through the years, has been very
tolerant … and has not insisted on the carrying out of anything
which might tend to upset the industry'.[48] On the other hand,
Aboriginal people's requests had not been considered by the
department or by Bateman in his report:

> I think that the most important factor was not mentioned,
> the natives themselves. They appear to me to be keen to
> get wages—to jingle a few coins in their pockets, to be
> able, when they feel inclined to buy something for the
> wife and kids and to feel that they are an important unit
> on the station.[49]

Pullen reported that he had 'yet to see the hawkers' who
allegedly threatened to exploit Aboriginal people, and found that
there were very small numbers, about seven or eight, old and sick
people on each of the stations who could be classed as 'indigents'.
Old people watered gardens, tended goats and otherwise contributed to the station economy. He was unwilling to class women
as indigents as they performed some employment duties and most
were the wives of workers and were therefore the responsibility of
the pastoral employers. On offering to remove the old and injured to
the ration station at Moola Bulla, he was told by managers that they
should not be moved as they were 'an important link between the

employer and the young, active workers'.[50] If they left, the young people would not want to stay and work. This was a concern to managers as there was a severe shortage of labour on almost every station in the west Kimberley in 1949 and '50.[51] White labourers were reportedly asking for £8 and £9 a week for muster work, while a well-paid Aboriginal stockman received a maximum of £2 a week.[52]

After his 1949 survey of the stations near Derby and along the Fitzroy River, including Kimberley Downs where Morndingali and his family were working, Pullen described living conditions on the stations. He had seen compounds of flattened tin huts or bush-pole and blanket tents with earth floors where flies sat on piles of bones. There were no ablution facilities at the camps: water was usually brought by women, in buckets hung from a wooden yoke, from nearby rivers or waterholes (thus the classic images of station women). A bush shower was set up for women who worked in the homesteads, but men were expected to wash in the open, which 'embarrassed' them. Medical facilities were just basic kits for minor ailments, and sore eyes were widespread throughout the camps. There was 'almost an entire absence of young children' at the stations, which he believed was partly due to the inadequate diet of flour, meat and tea. Some pre-cooked soups and stews were handed out at the kitchen, collected in billy cans and taken back to the camps or eaten while squatting on the ground or on the logpile behind the kitchens.

Pullen suggested that a dietary survey be undertaken to assist with the implementation in the future of a fixed minimum ration scale, pointing out that the permit system required only 'adequate and sufficient' food, which made 'provisions rather elastic'.[53] To his amazement, although station camps were sometimes as little as 200 yards from the homestead, managers rarely visited them and knew very little about the camps or Aboriginal people's lives. According to Pullen, they were 'just there when they were needed and so long as the tucker was kept up to them, their sores attended to and a handout at Christmas, nothing else mattered'.[54]

In some of his more frank and private exchanges with Middleton, Pullen referred to extremely difficult conditions in the

Kimberley as well as hostility towards him from white Kimberley residents. He reported one incident where the manager told him he was wasting his time because Aboriginal people 'had no intelligence and would never learn the value of money'. Pullen replied that 'it seemed remarkable ... how a lot of unintelligent people could completely run sheep and cattle stations as they are doing throughout the Kimberleys'.[55] Even after driving hundreds of miles, Pullen was not assured of an open and friendly reception from the Boss, especially if he mentioned wages:

> There is no doubt at all that the natives themselves want wages and that this demand will continue to grow in strength. A major upset could easily be caused in the pastoralist areas if a mining or other company offered wages and good living conditions to the natives there would be a general exodus by the natives from their present employment. Most of them are already 'wages conscious' but don't know how to outwardly express their views. They are not encouraged to do so on the stations and any white man who mentions wages in the vicinity of a station is branded a Communist.[56]

To avoid the open conflict with pastoralists and the public scrutiny being afforded the Pilbara, Pullen assured Middleton that he was engaging in a '"cold war", keeping the employers on their toes and, by ceaseless propaganda, making it clear that we have laid down a path and shall not deviate from it'.[57] He referred to pastoralists' goodwill and support once they understood that the department's aim was to separate punishment and police from welfare, not to introduce 'revolutionary' change.[58] They also had to be convinced that the department would not try to force them to adopt a wage system in the Kimberley. After Pullen's first tour of stations near Derby in April 1949, Middleton sent extracts from Pullen's journal to the Minister for Native Affairs to 'allay fears' among pastoralists that the department was pressing for wages.[59] He also sent extracts showing that Pullen had brokered an agreement with an AWU organizer who had visited Derby and the Pilbara in

1950. This ensured that unions would not get involved but wait and see if the department could introduce its own wages-cum-ration scheme. Three days later, Middleton telegrammed Pullen instructing him not to push too hard for the introduction of wages in the Kimberley, adding 'we must be cautious, do not have staff to supervise'.[60]

It is likely that the minister had received word from a Kimberley pastoralist that Pullen was creating trouble in the region. Such was the power of the pastoral lobby in Western Australia that Pullen was immediately instructed to curb his activities and proceed with more conservative goals. The Pastoralists and Graziers Association history, published in 1979, bemoaned the gradual 'lengthening of the lines' of communication between it and the government in comparison to the earlier period, when 'dealings with governments and officialdom were usually direct—only a phone call or a deputation between friends away, if the politicians weren't actually at the [Association] meetings.'[61]

At the end of 1949, Pullen amalgamated ration and wage scales from the Northern Territory, New Guinea and a plan drawn up by McBeath for Moola Bulla in late 1948, to produce a detailed list of conditions and minimum wages for Aboriginal people on Kimberley stations.[62] He asked the commissioner what should be done about children working at missions and was instructed in a circular to all staff in late 1949 that the Masters and Servants Act did not apply to children if they were not 'commanded' or 'ordered' to work. The point was that, where children were not directed to work, there was no employment relationship: 'they are not employed'. So Pullen did not need to concern himself about their working conditions or 'employer's' complaints.[63] Pullen's list of wage rates and conditions for adult workers included a wage for half-caste workers which was higher than that for 'ordinary natives', to encourage them to retain 'different standards'. It also set a minimum wage for men and women working in towns and on pastoral stations, a trainee wage, and a proviso that all employers of Aboriginal labour 'provide adequate and suitable living accommodation for the workers and their dependants, which includes quarters, kitchen, dining room, ablution and sanitary facilities'.[64] The suggested allowance was:

Male stockmen: <u>Annually</u> 4 trousers, 4 shirts, hat, boots, belt, mosquito net, blankets, ground sheet, swag cover, sweater, coat, pocket knife, enamel knife, pannikin, spoon, 2 handkerchiefs.

<u>Weekly</u> 2 soap, 1 matches, 2 sticks tobacco.

Females as domestics: <u>Annually</u> 4 dresses, 6 yrds calico, 1 sweater, 4 towels, 4 handkerchiefs, 1 mirror, 2 combs, 1 blanket, needles and thread, plate, pannikin, spoon.

<u>Weekly</u> 2 soap, 1 matches, 2 sticks tobacco.[65]

'Rations' were also to be given out for three weeks' annual holiday. There was no food ration scale, although Middleton had forwarded the standard scale for New Guinea native workers to Pullen. This included meat, fruit, vegetables, oils, fats, tobacco, rice, wheatmeal, tea, sugar, matches and soap.[66]

The wages scale called for departmental involvement in supervising the initial agreement between each worker and employer, checking books to be kept by stations recording pay and ration scales to individual employees, advising on the rate of pay, and administering a compulsory trust account for a fixed portion of all station workers' wages. The plan attempted to initiate a scale of wages and conditions for a range of workers: male, female, senior, junior, trainees, caste, town and station. Pullen believed that a wage scale 'could prove an important step in the emancipation of native women' by ensuring that they received their own money rather than the usual practice whereby they were handed some cloth or a present by stockmen when they returned from a droving trip.[67] The plan divided workers by caste but left room for lower payments to any 'half-caste' living in 'native' conditions. They, according to the department, did not require incentives or payments to live otherwise. Only 'half-castes' who wanted to spend money on housing or clothing needed to be paid at the top rate for Aboriginal workers.

This plan went a step further than that suggested by J.J. Rhatigan, who had joined the department in 1949 as patrol officer for the Halls Creek region. He was a Kimberley resident who left the department in 1953 to replace A.A.M. Coverley as the Kimberley MLA. Rhatigan's views on wages mirrored Bateman's and those put by the pastoral lobby. He warned of the risk of hawkers, the financial burden to the government when employers decided to keep only the waged workers, and the ridiculousness of paying wages to people who had no idea of money.[68] He suggested introducing a wage that operated only 'of theory': to give some coins regularly to each worker in return for their labour. It was a simple scale involving three levels of money in addition to keep for men and women with no caste distinctions. Men could earn either £1, 15s or 10s per month. Women, who were assumed to be domestics could earn 10s, 5s or 2s 6d. No one under sixteen or over sixty would be included in the scheme unless they were performing 'hard labour'.

The more complex departmental plan, which included incentives for caste workers and departmental supervision, was put to the Pastoralists and Graziers Association of Western Australia in Perth in November 1949, and debated at other association meetings in January and February 1950. Middleton briefed the minister prior to these meetings, reminding him of the need for caution in view of the previous 'attacks' on the department by pastoralists. He noted that A.O. Neville had warned the Fyfe Royal Commission in 1940 that there would be trouble in the Kimberley if Aboriginal people were not paid for their work, that the Commonwealth advised on a base wage in 1947 for the Northern Territory, and that some employers wanted to pay cash but were concerned about the impact it would have on smaller and less wealthy stations who could not afford a competitive cash system.[69] Middleton's notes included a quotation from Sir Hubert Murray, warning that people who 'understand the natives thoroughly' were a 'very dangerous class for they really believe what they say and are quite unconscious of their limitations'. Also included in the briefing documents was part of a 1947 letter from Elkin, warning that the 'new rates of pay for aboriginal employees in the Northern Territory will have its indirect effect on Western Australian native employment, and the employers will have to come out of the dark ages of 50 years ago'. Elkin's advice proved incorrect.

At the Perth meeting the minister explained that the state had to do something because the pressure from the Commonwealth to alter wage scales for half-caste pastoral workers in the Northern Territory would disrupt Kimberley stations.[70] Middleton reassured employers that unions had 'no wish to accept natives', so any agreement would not be subject to formal arbitration: it would be an informal agreement between the state and pastoralists. Pastoralists, on the other hand, wanted the department to police the agreement to ensure that it was fixed and that there would be 'little or no enticing of natives from one station to another'.[71]

The outcome of these meetings was a simplified informal agreement between the Native Affairs Department and the Pastoralists and Graziers Association of Western Australia to pay, in addition to their keep, monthly pocket money of 10s for women, £1 for drovers and 10s to all other men, regardless of their caste or skill. Departmental staff would ensure that the agreement for a flat rate was upheld, thus putting a stop to potential unrest in the pastoral industry. The cash amount could be paid as store credits or extra rations at the 'discretion of the manager'. Only two station owners from the northern ranges attended the meeting: Bob Rowell, who owned Tableland and Napier Downs stations, and Doug Blythe, part-owner of Mount House and Glenroy. They were assured that a cash component would not be enforced.[72] Kimberley pastoral employers were not willing to accept any regulation of living or working conditions, such as compulsory provision of bathing and sanitary conveniences, holiday pay, written agreements or trust accounts. Nor was the state government willing to force their hand. The department backed down from its plans to regulate wages and conditions on stations, and the Pastoralists and Graziers Association was able to advise all its members, including Frank Lacy at Mount Elizabeth, that there would be few changes to the existing system, except in areas near Derby where workforce stability was threatened by alternative employment and cash was beginning to change hands already.[73] In those cases it was in the employers' interest to introduce wages on some stations.

Middleton telegrammed Elkin immediately, triumphant that pastoralists had agreed to a 'wage scale' and formally accepted their

responsibility for all dependants and pensioners on pastoral stations.[74] The minister went to the newspapers to announce the 'pay'
breakthrough for Kimberley Aboriginal people.[75] Charles Rowley
repeated these claims in his book *The Remote Aborigines*, saying that
Kimberley Aborigines were paid wages from 1950 as a flow-on from
the Pilbara strike.[76] In negotiating with the department, pastoralists
had managed to implement a plan that provided a flat-rate pocket
money component—a 'few coins to jingle in their pockets'—which
was lower than the amount already being paid to some workers.[77]
Stockwomen such as Weeda Munro, Daisy Angajit, Maggie Ghi and
Maggie Gudaworla were not accounted for at all in the new scheme.
Rather than agreeing to a 'wage' for Aboriginal workers, pastoralists
and the department had come to an agreement to allow some
employers to break the existing wage-fixing system. They also
reinforced the rhetoric that pastoralists were 'protecting' Aboriginal
people from themselves, announcing to all members that:

> the consensus opinion of the meeting was that the
> present system, whereby both working natives, their
> dependants and pensioners were provided with all the
> necessities of life, virtually from the cradle to the grave,
> was the one best suited to the present stage of develop-
> ment of the natives, and one moreover calculated to avoid
> the evils which are invariably associated with the circu-
> lation of money, among a native people not generally
> educated to its value.[78]

Paying cash to Aboriginal people who lived on isolated stations ran contrary to the non-cash economy, and, as some pastoralists
submitted to the meetings in 1949 and '50, cash was useless where
there was nowhere to spend it. When the agreement was made, there
were no stores on northern Kimberley stations, just storerooms from
where everyone was rationed. Most stations had a system of 'gifts',
after musters, of nominated items like tobacco, cloth, razors, mirrors,
biscuits, lollies and hats. Domestic, garden, butchering, clearing or
goat-herding tasks were completed for rations. The idea of paying
money to Aboriginal people also cut across existing relationships

between Bosses and 'their mob', challenging notions of cultural dependency which underpinned departmental and pastoral negotiations. The debate over paying wages included statements from pastoralists like, 'there are not any decent people who would stoop to bribing natives' and 'bidding for a good Aboriginal stockman must be avoided at all costs'.[79] Aboriginal people were unpaid servants whose culture would be destroyed by the evils associated with money.[80] An Aboriginal person making a demand of a Boss was inconceivable, yet it was this aspect of station relationships that Pullen hoped to change.

Pullen immediately informed the commissioner that the scheme would not work to 'fix wages' in the Kimberley because the rate was too low and did not recognize the variation in skills on the stations. Some managers were embarrassed at the prospect of paying top stockmen 5s a week, while others near Derby and Broome, including Kimberley Downs and Napier Downs (where Morndingali and Weeda Munro and their families worked), intended paying more than 5s a week to keep the best workers from moving to other stations.[81] Pullen added that if managers stuck rigidly to this scheme, £1 would not cover the cost of clothing for a man and his family, they would increase their debt to the station, and this in turn would open the way for 'agitators'.

Maintaining control of cash circulation

The wage system that Pullen envisaged included changing Aboriginal people's relationships with their Bosses, not just providing 'a few coins to jingle in their pockets'. He wanted to assist workers to see their economic value within the pastoral industry and to tackle the Bosses themselves, instead of patiently waiting for change.

One aspect of station life that puzzled him, and which he aimed to change, was 'the extreme loyalty of a native to his Boss—it has almost the quality of the absurd loyalty between a much cuffed dog and his master'.[82] Pullen did not attempt any analysis of the origins of this form of 'loyalty' and made no explicit mention of instances of violence that occurred at the time or in previous years to reinforce servile behaviour. But he did not believe that Aboriginal people were happy with their conditions and tried to understand why more of them did not complain. He noted that the situation on stations had merits for those who could live with their older relatives, marry whom they wished and have children. He believed that compared to missions and fringe camps, pastoral stations offered social stability without the same level of interventionary regulation of family lives. Women in station homesteads were better fed than some town-based women and had access to clothes and a sewing machine from the Missus. He suggested that he had uncovered a 'stoicism' and unwillingness to complain which was part of a Kimberley 'type' and philosophy:

> The aboriginal appears to be a most discerning bloke and he knows when something is in the air and stoically awaits results. Employers are taking much more notice of him, are more solicitous of his welfare and he appears to be lapping it up. And he is shrewd enough to realise he is a pretty important unit on the community and not easily discarded.[83]

Despite his patronizing tone and tendency to typecast, Pullen was unusually reflective and accepting of Aboriginal people's skills and interest. He remained optimistic, writing in his annual reports that all he needed to do was to assist station owners to introduce reforms which, if not welcomed by them with open arms, were inevitable and would have to be accepted eventually. He felt that Aboriginal men shared his and other white Australian workers' interests in wages, housing, caring for children and the Missus, and hoped to implement a new and 'enlightened' welfare philosophy in which the role of the welfare officer was as a 'friend, philosopher and guide' to Aboriginal people.[84] To this end, he produced a strategic plan for overcoming pastoralists' 'blatant antagonism' and resistance to change by focusing his attention on specific stations where changes in wages and living conditions were most likely to succeed. Each of those stations would then provide an example to

Aboriginal people on surrounding stations, who would demand improvements in their own living and working conditions.

Pullen gave Kimberley Downs station as his first example of a station where changes needed to happen, and where the Aboriginal stockmen and women and the general manager, Jack Lee, were willing to change. He reported enthusiastically that 'word appears to have got around' when Tim Munro (Morndingali's older brother and leading hand at the time) visited the Native Administration Office in Derby after a droving trip to ask when the housing would be improved on the station.[85] The 'boys' there had also asked Pullen if they could move to another station where they had heard they could receive a 'few bob'.[86] He suggested that they wait. When the manager heard they wanted to move, he produced the weekly pocket money. This was the kind of change that was acceptable to Pullen: it showed that Aboriginal people were moving towards assimilating with white workers without the department having to confront managers on their behalf. He reported on one small 'spot of unrest', though, when a stockman was 'promptly dismissed by his employer' for asking for better living conditions, and, instead of waiting at the camp before returning to work, the stockman took the unusual step of leaving for a different station.[87]

While Pullen aimed for a change in worker–employer relations, he did not want to support 'unrest' of the kind experienced in the Pilbara. His approach was to encourage Aboriginal people to speak for themselves 'politely' and 'quietly', not to openly challenge the Bosses' power over them. Kimberley Downs showed signs of success, within the limits of expected behaviour for Aboriginal people:

> When employees get to the stage where they are courageous enough to voice complaints in the presence of their employers the gate was opened to freer and easier relations between the natives and their bosses. This is perhaps one of the outstanding changes noticed in the West Kimberleys during the year. A slow but not yet truculent awakening of the native to their importance in the industry is evident. The danger of this developing the

wrong way is appreciated but with our officers covering the whole district it should be noticed and controlled quickly.

… The trends which must be watched are, any sign of truculence on the part of the natives and any subversive influence working amongst them, but these Kimberley natives do not appear to be very pliable material for agitators.[88]

After six months of the new 'wages' scheme, Pullen reported that station workers were 'seldom in credit' and conditions were improving in only a minority of station camps.[89] Complaints from Aboriginal people had increased, but they were mostly about insufficient food, with no 'serious assaults' by employers being reported. Pullen believed that rumours that Aboriginal people would leave the stations to work in towns were unfounded. The majority of Aboriginal men did not wish to leave stations where their families were and where they had a predictable source of work and rations.

Pullen wanted to develop a scheme for skilled town-based Aboriginal people who were doing carpentry, loading and driving trucks, and assisting builders.[90] He also tried to improve conditions for female domestics who worked under permit at businesses and private houses for white women. They were rarely paid more than the 5s flat rate agreed, lived in huts behind white people's houses and worked without breaks. Middleton replied by telegram that it was 'not Department's role to protect or control [but] merely to streamline welfare support. Wages for town workers outside our brief.'[91] He added that the disputes which were occurring in the Pilbara and on the Darwin wharves were not going to occur in the Kimberley as the 'Communistic element' was 'not in Kimberley yet'.

Middleton also reversed his stance on child endowment payments to Aboriginal women in the Kimberley because of the potential impact the money would have on employment relations on pastoral stations at a time when they were negotiating 'wages' and aiming to control the circulation of cash in Aboriginal communities. He may also have realized that the department had insufficient staff to police its expenditure to the extent required by Social Security.[92] The system that had been put in place in the south of the state from 1944 was for police protectors to buy rations from child endowment money and distribute them to eligible Aboriginal people.[93] By 1947 this was the crux of complaints from Aboriginal people. The police working as protectors for the department had taken on the role of trustees for the parents, in order to 'discipline the natives to industrious habits' and regulate aspects of their lives 'such as the care of children and better camping conditions'.[94] In so doing the department came under scrutiny from the Commonwealth and drew some criticism for not having officers in the field, relying too much on police and being 'out of step with other States'.[95]

When Middleton came to office in 1948 he immediately sent circulars to all field officers to 'spread the news' of changes to Social Security guidelines to 'all Natives who do not know their rights', including Kimberley station women.[96] Child endowment could be paid for all Aboriginal children in government institutions, missions and on pastoral stations, and to the mothers themselves if an officer of the department or policeman vouched for their ability to handle the money.[97] By 1950 Middleton noted that the £12,000 of child endowment money paid to missions in Western Australia was the 'saving of Mission activity in this State', adding that they were also a 'great saving to the government'.[98] They were also a potential saving to stations and a large sum of money for recipients, made even more significant by the rationing system of the stations in the 1950s. Child endowment of 10s per week for one child sat in stark contrast to the 5s and 10s per month pocket money which women were allocated under the 1950 'wages' agreement. It was also twice as much as the proposed 5s per week pocket money for stockmen. This was pointed out to the Commissioner by the Director of Social Security in late 1950:

> The payment of Child Endowment to natives living on stations in the Kimberley area is likely to have grave repercussions insofar as employment of natives in the cattle industry is concerned and is certain to cause anxiety to the pastoralists throughout the Kimberley.[99]

To ensure that the money was spent according to Social Security and departmental guidelines, it was paid directly to managers on pastoral stations, and Native Affairs Department officers were discouraged from pushing too hard for Aboriginal women's practical inclusion in the child endowment scheme. Middleton informed the Federal Office of Social Security that the matter of 'spreading the word' to Aboriginal women about their right to child endowment 'could best be disregarded' because they had 'not yet reached the standard' to spend the money appropriately.[100]

Child endowment payments were not taken up by many of the station managers in the north Kimberley, probably because there were very few children on the northern stations. But other stations in the Kimberley were quick to ask for child endowment. Vestey's, which owned five pastoral stations in the east Kimberley, received payments for sixty-five children in 1950 and seventy-two in 1960.[101] The money, in accordance with Social Security guidelines, was distributed by the manager as rations. Patrol officers' reports on stations during this period did not question the expenditure or distribution of these funds until after 1960, when Social Security exclusions were again lifted and stations came under further scrutiny.[102]

The impact of child endowment payments on station relationships in the 1950s was minimized by the state's policies in that period, which ensured that management controlled its distribution in their communities. Managers were responsible for filling in the forms and distributing the money as rations. This was not only acceptable to the state government—it was preferable. Social Security guidelines did not allow for station women to receive or control their child endowment until after 1959. Middleton interpreted Aboriginal people's use of benefits and increasing use of rations as 'exploitation' of the state and missions. He claimed in a circular to all field staff, designed to reduce costs and rations, that parents intentionally placed their children in missions and then lived off the department.[103] This was 'wrong in principle and financially disastrous'.

In 1959, when restrictions were lifted on Aboriginal people's access to Social Security, Native Welfare officers voiced concerns that there was a 'degree of antipathy' from pastoral employers towards Social Security payments to individuals because of 'fear that it would upset current scale of wages' and weaken 'proprietary interests manifested by these stations'.[104] Native Welfare officer Kevin Morgan pointed out that a man with three children could receive three times a stockman's wage in child endowment. This situation fuelled fears among some employers that workers might leave stations and move to town. Morgan added that the department required pastoral employers' support because stations would have to provide the stores which could be bought with the extra cash. They were also the main source of information about the Aboriginal people on their stations.

Name, age and station

Middleton changed departmental reporting practices in 1949 as part of the new patrol officer system. The report forms were five-page documents which had changed from the previous half-page of numbers 'under permit'— male, female, adult, child, half-caste, full-blood—to a more detailed but standard patrol report.

Patrol officers were supposed to visit station camps yearly or every six months if the station was closer and more accessible. On arrival at the stations the officers often found them deserted and the majority of the camp people off at a muster or working away from the homestead. So, in practice, they went to the homestead first and relied on management to provide most of the information in their reports. Although this was expected and soon became standard practice, it developed into a subject of conflicting interest as an increasing number of departmental officers and missionaries began to visit station camps.[105] In 1965 a recommendation was passed by the Pastoralists and Graziers Association to warn missionaries that they must not visit station camps 'without prior notice to station authorities'.[106] The station managers' role as gatekeepers of station mobs emerged in the 1950s as they negotiated with the state over responsibility for Aboriginal people.

When welfare officers went straight to station managers for help with their reports, they received information such as names, ages, whereabouts, family relationships, living conditions and employment details. Their reports included information about accommodation, ablution facilities, rations, hygiene, medical facilities, wages which followed the recommended scale, 'recreation' which was invariably 'hunting and fishing', and 'relations with employer' which were rarely anything but 'satisfactory', 'good' or 'very good'.[107] From 1949 to '59 the reports also included a section for patrol officers to comment on 'behaviour of natives' which was usually recorded as 'quiet and respectful'. Although this formal section was dropped from reports after 1959, similar concerns about Aboriginal people 'knowing their place' and showing 'respectful deference' to their Bosses continued until 1972.[108] A 1962 patrol report stated that Oobagooma station 'natives [were] clean, well spoken, self assured, without arrogance'.[109] In the same year the Kimberley Downs manager was described in the yearly report as giving the impression that he 'yearns for the day when natives could be shot with impunity', but the patrol officer added that he was really a very 'soft touch' who maintained 'sympathetic yet firm control over them'.[110]

Welfare reports rarely included information that came straight from Aboriginal people. The tone and type of information reflected the distance between the administrators of Aboriginal Affairs and Aboriginal people and the almost contemptuous and fearful attitudes that developed in the 1950s. The style of welfare practice worked to silence Aboriginal people, ensuring that the 'unrest' among workers didn't eventuate. The impact on Aboriginal people was to distance them from the pastoral employment system rather than providing them with 'welfare' support. They fell between the stools of being 'employed' and being on welfare. The attitudes of welfare officers and white station personnel was such that unrest or objections that might have emerged in this period had nowhere to be heard or expressed. The information in the welfare reports show this process of not accepting Aboriginal people as workers or providing for them as welfare recipients.

After Pullen's death in 1951, Jim Beharrell, also from the New Guinea Native Administration, took over as district officer and struggled to make yearly visits to stations. He worked without a patrol officer until 1956, when two Aboriginal men were employed as patrol assistants. The lack of staff and resources between 1951 and '56 made it difficult for Beharrell to follow up reports and check on whether conditions were improving for Aboriginal people. Stations closer to towns were visited at least once a year, and those that had airstrips received visits from police and doctors who collected and returned leprosy patients. But others, like Gibb River, Kurunjie, Mount Barnett and Mount Elizabeth, were not visited until after 1957.

After 1951 managers from most stations filled in the report forms themselves and sent them into town on the flying doctor and mail plane or handed them to police patrols. They did not provide plans for upgrading work or living conditions for Aboriginal people, but this did not matter to Beharrell, who wrote in 1952 that the 'battlers' needed to be shown tolerance as they were little better off than their workers.[111] Welfare officers rarely visited the northern stations and did not challenge or worry the managers. Both Theresa Lacy, who was the Missus at Mount Elizabeth from 1946 to about 1972, and Ned Delower, who managed Napier Downs, Oobagooma, Tableland and Kimberley Downs, stated that 'welfare never troubled us'.[112] Delower added that he asked police to make a yearly patrol to kill dogs in the camps but had only two visits from Welfare between 1956 and '67, and they were for age pension investigations.[113] Frank Lacy's journals record visits from the department every second year from 1962 to '70.

The Mount House and Glenroy air beef scheme, which started in 1949, meant that planes were often calling at Glenroy. Nevertheless, it was only in 1959 that the Mount House manager 'heard' from the police that he could apply for child endowment for the children on the station. He was unable to produce the necessary age and birth dates because he had only noted dates of deaths of Aboriginal people, not births.[114] He was instructed by the welfare officer to estimate ages and record birthdays as the first of June in the approximate year.[115] Because Social Security would not provide benefits to anyone with only one name, station children were either given their mother's name as a surname or provided with a white one.

The patrol reports provide interesting details about Aboriginal people's entry into the welfare system and some valuable ethnographic information. For many people this was the first time their names or ages were recorded in writing. It was also the beginning of their taking a white name or even a surname. These records need to be taken seriously but with reservations. They were constructed by white people for the purpose of bringing Aboriginal people into the welfare system. Some managers, patrol officers or institutional staff members knew more than others, could hear more language than others or had better advice from Aboriginal people and managers about names, relationships and ages. An example of a list of names which correlates to a high degree with Aboriginal people's language names is that of the Derby Leprosarium admission books.[116] This was probably a result of long-term acquaintances between the St John of God Sisters and inmates, and some literacy skills among the long-term language-speaking inmates.

Conversely, there were numerous examples of misunderstandings and mistakes in naming and labelling which confused managers and patrol officers, and which Aboriginal people have carried from that time. Some misguided attempts to provide language names resulted in women's names being given as a surname for male children, or questions, statements of fact and body parts being recorded as names. In 1957 the Director of Social Security instructed departmental officers to give the husband's Christian name as a surname for all wives who had only one name.[117] Alternatively, station managers and bookkeepers sometimes gave fanciful surnames to Aboriginal people, such as Hitler, Roosevelt, Michael Angelo, Don Bradman, Roly Poly and Ginger Mick. Peter Lacy remembered that when his father chose names for Aboriginal people at Mount Elizabeth, the children had just finished reading *Treasure Island*, so they suggested Friday (which Frank Lacy later changed to Freddy).[118] Another young stockman on Mount Elizabeth, Scotty Martin, received his surname from the store order for Martin's biscuits. This may also account for the common occurrence of the Martin surname in the north Kimberley. Biscuits were sought-after items and the irony may not have been lost on managers.

From 1963 the departmental policy of naming children with their father's Christian name was stopped, to avoid passing on 'absurd names such as Jimmy Whisky' to children.[119] These disjunctures between eras of naming policies had the effect of reducing the likelihood that non-Aboriginal naming systems in the Kimberley would reflect meaningful Aboriginal relationships. For instance, Curlywig, Quartpot, Nipper and Bandy were dropped, while others that welfare officers thought less offensive became surnames of large family groups who were not necessarily related. For example, Morndingali and Weeda Munro's son became Jack Dann, which was a shortening of his bush name, Dandayi, and not an indication of his relationship to the large Dann family at Beagle Bay Mission. His children, in turn, were listed under their mother's name in the 1960s, when policies changed again to giving children the mother's surname.

From 1965 a policy was also put in place not to use the father's Aboriginal name because it had to be changed as soon as he died.[120] After seeking expert advice from the Anthropology Department at the University of Western Australia, welfare officers were instructed to use approximate English names instead. They were also told that 'undignified, unsuitable or derogatory' names must be avoided, and the 'practice of conferring names inviting ridicule must be eliminated'.[121] The example in the 1965 instruction manual for Native Welfare officers to change Nyunma to Newman was followed on more than one occasion, despite the original names coming from distinct language groups. This created further anomalies between names from Welfare and names from Aboriginal families, and left a confusing trail of misinformation for children to return to if they sought to trace their families at a later stage.

Welfare, blankets and tobacco

The Native Welfare Department depended on managers such as Fred Russ, Frank Lacy and Ned Delower to bridge the gap between the stations and the emerging policy of integrating station people into welfare services. Russ reported to Beharrell in 1954 that he was fed up with all northern Aboriginal people who were discharged from the leprosarium, gaol or the Native Hospital being dropped off at Gibb River station without rations or support from the department.[122] They usually moved from Gibb River into the bush and the Mount Hann reserve area if there were bush groups in the region, but if they were disabled he had to feed them because the department refused to provide rations or subsidies to stations.[123] He complained that the tax exemption for 'native dependants' of £1 per week or £50 per year did not cover the cost of feeding and clothing the extra people who were not directly related to Gibb River workers but were gathering at the station.[124] He suggested that the department remove people to the government ration depot at Moola Bulla station or feed anyone who was not directly related to station workers. Beharrell replied that he needed to send people back to stations to keep the younger ones 'settled' at the stations and allay fears in the communities that people never returned home from the leprosarium.[125]

The department refused to remove adults to towns or provide rations for them at the stations, despite requests from many of the station managers in the north Kimberley. The situation in the 1950s was such that old Aboriginal people were left to live off communal rations at stations while missions on the coast focused on children. At Mount Hart the manager complained to Beharrell in 1955 that there were groups of bush people in the region who were not part of his station camp but were coming in for tobacco and rations (as they were at Mount Elizabeth). They refused to go to missions on the coast because these were outside their country. These old people may have been the last people speaking Unggumi or Worrora to come into a pastoral station. In 1957, after the closure of the coastal missions, Munja and Kunmunya, bush people stayed in the region around Mount Hart station, and the department refused to take responsibility for feeding or removing them.[126] In 1959 the manager would not accept a woman from the leprosarium because she could not work. He added that he wanted all indigents removed, but Beharrell did nothing.[127]

The managers of pastoral stations were not interested in supporting Aboriginal people who did not work. In the 1950s the country and the pastoral stations in the north experienced a severe drought. The old people who had begun their relationship with white managers in the early part of the century were attracted to work partly because they wanted tobacco. Even after they had grown old and worked only occasionally, old people continued to visit stations looking for tobacco either from their younger relatives or as a reward for work. For the younger workers tobacco was the closest thing they had to a wage, and they used it in the same way as money.

The importance of tobacco in the north Kimberley was in evidence from the time of first contact to the 1980s and '90s, when storytellers asked for a tin of tobacco as payment for work. It was a key factor in the transition from bush to station work and then in the rise of the importance of welfare and towns in the 1950s and '60s. The government recognized the power of tobacco to keep people quiet and attract them to settle at a rationing point. When Moola Bulla station was opened in 1910, Travelling Inspector Isdell reminded the Chief Protector of Aborigines to hand out tobacco to bush people:

> tobacco is an item that must not be lost sight of, all these natives would give their food and clothes away for tobacco. An allowance of two sticks to men and a stick to women per week is not too much ...[128]

At Munja rations station in 1943, during wartime tobacco rationing, the manager was challenged by Aboriginal people because he was withholding their tobacco rations and exchanging them for dog scalps. He had buried a quantity of tobacco as punishment for stealing and then had feared for his life after the men threatened him. Howard Coate made the comment while driving to Mount Barnett in 1989 that, in the early years, the Mount Barnett missionaries had trouble attracting labour because they would not provide tobacco. Further north at Kalumburu, the Benedictines also relied on tobacco to attract bush people into the mission. In 1934 Ion Idriess wrote that the small leaseholder Bob Thompson talked of the basic requirements for developing a lease:

one hundred pounds, a couple of pack-mules, a saddle, a few old bags and a bit of wire, a case of nigger twist tobacco, an axe—and a rifle thrown in ... Tobacco is money out here, without it no nigger would work in the Kimberleys.[129]

Black stick tobacco was made in the south of Western Australia from the 1930s by the Michelides company only for the Native Welfare Department. The tobacco leaf was sprayed with a mixture of honey, gum arabic, rum, sugar, glicerine, liquorish, caramel, coconut, walnut and almond essences. The Native Welfare Department received a tax exemption on imported tobacco for producing black stick tobacco commonly called 'nigger twist'. In 1949 Middleton wrote to the Michelides company to ask them to speed up production of black stick tobacco. He had been warned by a pastoralist from the Fitzroy valley region that Aboriginal labour was almost impossible to get partly because of the break in the supplies of black stick tobacco after the war.[130]

Government-sponsored 'native tobacco' was provided to state-funded institutions and to some missions, but detailed records of whether any reached pastoral stations cannot be found. Government rations were withdrawn from pastoral stations around 1911 and not replaced. Station record books for Napier Downs have consistent entries for tobacco from the early 1900s through to the 1950s.[131] In 1920 the ledger shows more than £30 per month paid to H.O. Wills tobacco company. In 1933 the Emanuel-owned Christmas Creek station recorded £20 per month to H.O. Wills for tobacco. On Mount Elizabeth, Frank Lacy detailed his ration items each year, always including black stick chewing tobacco and each 'haul of fish' from the nearby river to supplement station stores. In 1950 he recorded his order of '1 ton flour, 4 bags fine salt, 5 bags sugar, 1 case jam, 4 bags rice and ten pounds native tobacco'.[132] Tobacco was expensive and recorded with care each time Lacy distributed one or two sticks of tobacco to people for work, to return from holidays, to take mail to neighbouring stations, to take to a corroboree or in exchange for dog scalps.[133] Dicky Udmorrah, Emu and his three wives, and Billy and his five wives all moved between

Kalumburu and Mount Elizabeth in the 1950s and went to Frank Lacy for tobacco. Peter Lacy recalled Aboriginal people 'craving' black stick tobacco and the excitement of workers returning to camp when they had mustered at a well-known bush tobacco site near Mount Matthew.[134] Stockmen filled saddlebags with bush tobacco and rode into camp shouting of their acquisitions as they approached. Like other Aboriginal people, they mixed the tobacco with ashes of burned gum-tree bark and chewed it into gobs, which were saved behind their ears.

After the 1950 agreement was made between the Pastoralists and Graziers Association and the Native Affairs Department, Lacy continued to pay workers in kind, feeding a regular group and handing out extra items after droves or musters but recording their cost as part of the 'wage'.[135] Days after noting the new 'wage' scale, he recorded a list of items handed to the leading stockman, whom he had 'borrowed' from Bedford Downs to help muster and drove cattle to Wyndham. The stockman received 'Naga [cloth], tomahawk, handkerchief, wool, pipe, shirt, trousers [and a] dress'. In 1962 Lacy recorded his order for £18 11s worth of fine cut and black stick tobacco.[136] At Oobagooma the head stockman's store list for January to June 1960 showed that he paid £8 for tobacco and £1 for pipes, out of a cash wage component of £90. The rest was spent on a leather belt, a hat, hair oil, toothbrush, mirrors, matches and razors.[137] Boots, shirts and trousers were paid for by the station.

Tobacco rations in Derby became a problem for Native Welfare officers. After following the official dietary survey of 1951, which suggested that one or two sticks of tobacco needed to be given to people on rations, they found that by the late 1950s they were distributing boxes of tobacco to growing numbers of people collecting in Derby. In 1958 officers were instructed to withdraw tobacco from standard rations and not distribute it to missions unless missionaries approved. They were warned that tobacco was not a 'right'; it needed to be given as a 'comfort' and not at stated times but at the officers' 'discretion'.[138] The ration in towns during the 1950s was: '3lb flour, sugar, tea, meat, liver, table margarine, potatoes, meat and veg tinned, fruit or veg tinned, rolled oats, honey, milk, salt, soap'. Meat was distributed at the officer's discretion and could be withheld if game was available.[139] Each rationee also received 5s pocket money and assistance from a departmental officer to spend it.

Camp numbers at the Derby town reserve between the police station and the Native Hospital began to increase from 1950. Prior to that there was strict enforcement of regulations from 1911, prohibiting Aboriginal people from entering towns unless they were under an employment permit. As a result, there was a camp four miles from town where stockmen and unemployed Aboriginal people were permitted to stay for short periods. Native Welfare officer Pullen had intentionally tried to lift the standard of reserve housing and rationing in Derby, partly to improve the general standards in the district by Welfare showing an example to others.[140] He also instigated a scheme for town employers to pay a small weekly rent for their employees to live on the town reserve instead of in humpies in back yards, vacant blocks or having to walk into town each day from a fringe camp. But there were complaints from pastoral employers that workers were not returning after a visit to town or to the Native Hospital, preferring to stay in the reserve on rations; or if they did return, their 'morale for work deteriorate[d] in the camp'.[141] Beharrell defended attempts to improve rations and housing, and assistance with pocket money, stating that the majority of station people wanted to return as soon as possible but a few would not because their living conditions compared badly with the reserve.[142] He nevertheless found that placing people on the flying doctor plane to northern stations also drew complaints from employers.

Beharrell also began to voice suspicions about the motives of large companies and absentee owners who made promises about improving living conditions but were reluctant to outlay any capital. Drought conditions between 1950 and '54 engendered sympathy for small owners. However, he found that managers working for large companies were not permitted to spend money on workers or their families, even where the hygiene was 'deplorable' or housing was a 'disgusting' pile of tins, blankets or rubbish from tips. In these cases he believed there was 'no room for tolerance … his ruthlessness and penny-pinching, in regard to his native labour, reduces them to the point of being slaves'.[143] Beharrell gave a particularly clear statement of the emerging conflict of interest between departmental officers and pastoral employers when he wrote in his annual report that:

> The resources of this country have been developed at the cost of the labour employed. Men have added to their worldly possessions at the cost of other men. Such development has only one true name, and that is exploitation. It should not be permissible for any industry to depend for its success in keeping labour poor … As a Christian people we will never be able to evade the moral issues involved.[144]

He believed that children on these stations were being denied the education that was essential to assimilation because there was:

> strong resentment to allow these children to leave the station to attend the nearest school, for they are selfishly looking to them to provide the station with future labour as stockboys etc, and think that once they receive education they may not desire that form of employment.[145]

He suggested that as Aboriginal people's 'natural place was with cattle', schools should be placed at stations and not in towns, which would disrupt the pastoral industry and Aboriginal people's residence at stations. But after a survey of stations the following year, he decided that most west Kimberley stations did not have enough children to warrant such a scheme and that they should be placed in existing missions or brought to towns as soon as hostels could be built.[146] The hostel scheme began officially in Derby in 1957 and expanded through the 1960s. It was a significant factor in the movement of Aboriginal people to towns and away from stations during that period.

Beharrell reported changes in housing and living conditions at stations in the early 1950s, when the worsening labour position forced pastoralists to either raise the standard of living for workers or lose the trained Aboriginal labour force:

> The economic position is literally compelling the employer
> to become less apathetic towards his native employees, for
> most realise that the numbers of employable natives
> available are insufficient for the needs of all, and it is with
> some concern we learn that the rate of decline amongst
> the aborigines in contact with civilisation, estimated by the
> well known Anthropologist, Mr. Tindale, to be a reduction
> in numbers by 50 per cent every ten years.[147]

The barest minimum for survival remained the benchmark for good practice on stations, with Beharrell stating in 1953 that 'satisfactory' rationing, hygiene and clothing were the most that could be expected for Aboriginal people on stations. Even so it was doubtful that the rations were adequate.[148] Reports from the Health Department about diet and eye diseases confirmed his concerns that living conditions on stations were not good.[149]

The 1954 Native Welfare Act lifted a range of exclusions and controls from some Aboriginal people's lives, particularly those who were of part-descent. Town prohibitions were lifted. The Act marked the end of employment permits, repealed the Aboriginal Medical Fund and allowed for workers' compensation to apply to Aboriginal people on stations, but it did not provide minimum conditions or wages for Aboriginal people. The regulations were only slightly changed from those of 1940, which called for 'suitable substantial and sufficient food and drinking and bathing water'. Employers were to 'provide accommodation, including such sanitary conveniences as may be deemed necessary, to the satisfaction of the commissioner' and a 'mosquito net and bedding if necessary'. All goods were to be sold at current market rates, or no more than the price they would be sold to a white employee, and accounted for in books which were to be kept for departmental officers' perusal.[150] The Act did not significantly alter working and living conditions for full-blood station people whose 'place' as servants and dependants on stations was not challenged by state welfare policy and practice. It was only with the entry of Social Security into station communities in the early 1960s that expenditure and station accounts came under sustained scrutiny.

In 1956 Middleton wrote that the system of Native Welfare patrols to stations was not working. This, he believed, was due to the 'lack of legislative backing to effect, by official direction, improvement in native employees' living conditions', and the 'reluctance on the part of most employers to accept our advice and recommendations'. The 1954 Act had not improved conditions for station people. Middleton appealed to departmental officers to stop their 'reconnaissance and survey' method, which resulted in 'expensive and time consuming travel, a short visit to the station, an even shorter visit to the Native camp', and no effective change. Complaints had been received that there was little contact between Aboriginal people and Native Welfare officers:

> With few exceptions the patrolling officer meets with the same promises and lack of action ... and the same lack on the part of the natives themselves of the desire to improve their own conditions.[151]

The government shifts its focus

In 1958 Frank Gare, who became Commissioner of Native Welfare in 1961, produced the *Report of the Special Committee on Native Matters*, in which he reiterated the field staff's concerns that employers did not respond to departmental appeals and were 'apathetic' and occasionally 'antagonistic towards any improvement in the lives of the natives'.[152] The report referred to submissions that argued for the introduction of the standards in work and living conditions for Aboriginal people required by the Universal Declaration of Human Rights and the International Labor Organization Convention of 1957.[153] Submissions were also made by anthropologists Catherine and Ronald Berndt, who had researched Aboriginal people's working and living conditions on Vestey's stations in the Territory in 1944.[154] The Berndts' statement to the committee presented a bleak picture of station life for Aboriginal people and laid the blame at the feet of wealthy pastoralists:

> Pastoral station managers have it birtually [sic] all their
> own way. Some of them are relatively 'enlightened',
> others the reverse. The general picture in certain areas is
> reminiscent of a feudal situation, epitomised in the com-
> mon statement 'my Aborigines', or the little cluster of
> sordid humpies to one side of the large modern premises
> of many cattle and sheep stations.[155]

The Gare Report argued that Aboriginal people were not
socially 'ready' to accept equal rights and equal access to services,
but that the time had come for the state arbitration court to appoint
a special commissioner to look at the provisions of award wages to
all Aboriginal people. It also detailed the state's requirements for
grants in aid from the Commonwealth and the need for a hostel
scheme to board children in towns while they attended school. It
was no longer acceptable to segregate children on stations for their
labour. The report indicated that Aboriginal people on northern
pastoral stations were no longer to be exempt from departmental
policies designed to encourage their assimilation into white society.
Middleton had already begun that process in 1957, when he
circulated a statement from the minister to all his staff:

> In view of the progress made elsewhere in these modern
> times and in view of the fact that natives in the North
> West, particularly in the Kimberleys, do not seem to have
> been treated as liberally as in the Murchison and South
> West Land division, I am recommending to Cabinet that
> action be taken to improve wages and standards gener-
> ally, more particularly in relation to accommodation,
> ablution facilities etc.[156]

Gare recommended a tougher approach by government to
intervene on stations, and to demand better conditions and greater
inclusion of full-blood people in the welfare net, after the government had closed its own institutions for Aboriginal people to force
them to live independently of state settlements and ration depots.
This placed pressure on Aboriginal people to stay on stations or to

move to towns or missions where there was some support. From 1949 to '59 the government dismantled its policy of segregation and rationing, even of the isolated Worrora, Wunambal and Ngarinyin people, and closed or withdrew from settlements, missions and ration stations.[157] Udialla ration station, which had opened in 1944, was closed in 1949, with all inmates trucked to La Grange ration depot south of Broome.[158] In 1955 La Grange was transferred to the Pallottine Order to complete its separation from the state. Munja ration station was also closed in 1949, and residents were gradually moved to the Presbyterian mission at Kunmunya and then to another site at Wotjulum on the coast south of Munja. In 1956 149 residents of Munja, Kunmunya and Wotjulum were moved into Derby to form the Mowanjum community ten kilometres from the town.

In 1954 all missions were offered ninety-nine-year leases over 1,000 acres of land held at that time, with no qualifications that the land would revert to the Crown if the mission was disbanded.[159] The government also cancelled large reserves, including the Mount Hann reserve, parts of which were opened for pastoral selection in 1955. This reserve, just north of Mount Elizabeth and Gibb River stations, had been mooted in 1916 by A.O. Neville as a ration station for northern bush people, and opened in 1934 in response to Idriess's letters to the police and newspapers about the extraordinary rock art in the region. Pastoral leases north of Gibb River station were opened as a result of this final push for pastoral occupation of the land in the far north Kimberley.

In 1954 the Morgan survey report was made.[160] During the survey work, a mining company representative made his first visit to the region, while W. Fyfe, author of the 1940 Fyfe Commission report into the beef industry, flew to the north to view the new country as Surveyor General. Morgan was led by Aboriginal guides who provided local language names for places and led him to recently used bush camps in the region. He nevertheless reported that pastoral development was possible:

> ... [in the] remote North Kimberley area, the north western tip of the continent commonly referred to as

'Over the Range'. Its previous seclusion from pastoral settlement may be attributed to the existence of natural barriers of rough sandstone ranges to its South-West and South-East and until early this century, the large number of Natives who inhabited the region would have undoubtedly resulted in losses of cattle. However, the numbers of these Natives has declined rapidly and apart from those associated with the Missions on the coast, there are not many in the area.[161]

The UAM missionaries were finally assisted by the government in this period. They were granted land and a permit to begin a hostel for children at Fitzroy Crossing in 1953 and a children's hostel at Derby in 1957. Both projects benefited from child endowment payments and additional state subsidies to missions, which increased rapidly from 1953 to '58 as the state withdrew from institutions and settlements. In 1955 the small UAM hostel and mission experienced a large increase in inmates when the government extended its program of offloading all institutions for Aboriginal adults and sold Moola Bulla pastoral lease to private owners. Two hundred and fifty residents were trucked off the station to Halls Creek and then to Fitzroy Crossing.[162] Middleton experienced a great deal of public criticism over the closure of Moola Bulla in 1955, and again in 1961, when it was alleged that babies from Moola Bulla died of disease at Fitzroy Crossing and that the new owners had made large profits by stripping the property of assets, which included a school, storeroom and other institutional structures.[163]

Moola Bulla was closed because of the government's policy decision not to encourage separate state-run Aboriginal communities. This was in line with assimilation policy, which directed that the government should not encourage Aboriginal people to stay in a tribal or uneducated condition unless they were working on stations. The part-descent workers and their families at Moola Bulla were supposed to assimilate after the closure of the institution by moving to work for private employers. As early as 1948 Bateman had reported that Moola Bulla was in a disgraceful condition, which made it difficult for the government to insist that pastoral stations improve conditions on their own properties.[164] There were also problems with staff and conditions at the institutions. Wotjulum, Munja, Moola Bulla and Forrest River staff all came under suspicion of cohabiting with Aboriginal women in their care at different times from 1936 to '53. Allegations of torture of inmates at Moola Bulla had also been investigated and assault charges laid.[165] The fact that a school and housing for certain workers had recently been established at Moola Bulla was ignored by policy-makers. The government wanted to divest the department of its institutional responsibilities.

Fear of 'McLeodism' emerged again in 1955, after Don McLeod offered to run Moola Bulla for the private leaseholders and retain the large Aboriginal community who lived there. His travels through the Kimberley were again closely watched and reported by pastoralists and Native Welfare officers. A station manager from the Broome district telegrammed the department that 'the notorious Donald McLeod ("Whiskers") and one full-blood native passed here about mid day yesterday, August 29th, heading north for Halls Creek'.[166] A month later, District Officer Beharrell reported that they were resident at Moola Bulla and had asked for a permit to remove Aboriginal people from the state to muster and drove cattle to Queensland.[167] Middleton attacked McLeod in the 1955 departmental annual report for attempting to start a strike team in the Kimberley to disrupt the industry. The new owners of Moola Bulla refused McLeod's help, and the station was sold after much of the cattle and infrastructure was disposed of.

The closure of Moola Bulla was welcomed by surrounding pastoralists. Middleton quoted the Vestey's field superintendent to defend the move, stating that it had 'resulted in a much more equitable distribution of skilled station and domestic labour'.[168] The closure also contributed to the increasing number of children in hostels in the Kimberley. In 1956 there were 116 children resident at the UAM mission in Fitzroy Crossing.[169] Their parents did not receive rations from the government and were encouraged by patrol officers and mission staff to seek work on surrounding stations. The Fitzroy Crossing mission superintendent reported in 1956 that:

> Many were the telegrams received from managers of
> cattle and sheep stations throughout the Kimberleys,
> seeking employees ... The demand was so great that not
> all the stations could be supplied with labour.[170]

One of the important consequences of increased staffing levels and subsidies to missions and the closure of government settlements was an increase in the numbers of Aboriginal children removed from their families and placed in missions.[171] In 1958, Gare suggested in his report that:

> the removal of children should be limited in recognition
> of the emotional damage done to children without a
> home life. Children at missions should be encouraged to
> go home, despite the environment they will return to. But
> if the home is likely to do damage they can stay at the
> mission.[172]

Conditions on stations and in town camps were not always 'suitable'. By 1958 'almost half of all known children' in the Kimberley were in missions where they were subsidized by child endowment funding.[173] One quarter of adults were also at missions, and almost half of them were also being subsidized by the Native Welfare Department. According to Beharrell, old people were not moving into missions because they 'prefer to exist with their relatives and within their tribal areas rather than proceed to an institution'.[174]

The initial entry of Aboriginal affairs administration into the area of 'Welfare' support for Aboriginal people on northern Kimberley stations was an exercise aimed at station managers retaining responsibility for them in exchange for Social Security being integrated into the existing system of localized patronage and control. With the Gare Report, policies began to change even further in the 1960s, and conflicting interests between Welfare and pastoralists emerged, to the disadvantage of Aboriginal people.

CHAPTER SEVEN

Pastoral paternalism turns sour,
1959–1972

Up north, a whole lot of people got shot by White Man, and some were burned in a fire. That was before the station was built up. The Aboriginal people didn't do no harm, they were just chased out of the country for the cattle. We didn't fight for the land, we didn't have any Bosses like White people did. The station was holding the country pretty strong; those days we didn't have anybody ahead of us, but now we've got Native Affairs.

Sam Woolagoodja, Derby 1976[1]

IN the early 1960s state and federal policies began to include full-blood station people in the Australia-wide assimilation project, providing the social and economic conditions for dismantling the station system without providing an institutional alternative for people who left or were forced to leave the stations. Important legislative changes came with the lifting of exclusions to Social Security payments to Aboriginal people in 1959, the 1963 Native Welfare Act and the application of the Pastoral Industry Award to Aboriginal workers in the Kimberley from late

1968.[2] In 1972 the last of the overtly restrictive legislation was lifted from full-blood Aboriginal people in the Kimberley, and they no longer had to apply for citizenship status to exempt them from the Act. From that date they could consume alcohol, manage their own work and financial arrangements, or move interstate without permission from the Commissioner of Native Affairs.[3]

A discourse of intervention and conflicting interests emerged with Welfare's focus on changing living conditions for station people, particularly housing, schooling, health and wages. In the period from 1959 to '72, the Boss and the Missus came under increasing pressure from Native Welfare and the Social Security Department to implement assimilationist ideals on their stations. Their roles as gatekeepers for their communities increased, yet their benevolence came into question as they failed to meet the complex demands from various welfare agencies and Aboriginal people to make significant alterations to living conditions.

The removal of children to hostels and missions and the introduction of age pensions in the early 1960s were key factors underpinning the movements of Aboriginal people towards towns and reserves, where Social Security became the means of survival. By the time equal wages and Aboriginal people's protests about living conditions were blamed for the dismissals and walk-offs of the 1970s and '80s, the social and economic foundations of the old rationing system on most of the stations in the northern Kimberley were already crumbling. The equal wages decision and debate in the late 1960s signalled the end of the long struggle between Welfare and pastoralists over their moral obligation to manage and maintain station communities. The longstanding argument between pastoralists and the government over rations was transformed into an issue of Aboriginal people's cultural inability to work or be productive and 'civilized'. At the same time their land relationships and pastoralists' obligations to them as landowners or assistants developing the country were subsumed into a welfare discourse of deserving and undeserving poor.

'Family welfare'

At the 1961 Commonwealth and State Aboriginal Affairs Ministerial Conference, assimilation policy was formerly advanced by Minister for Territories Paul Hasluck and adopted by all other states. 'Our Aborigines' pamphlets, with black stockmen on the cover, were distributed around Australia to encourage white Australians to accept Aboriginal people as equals.[4] Assimilation policy was again 'accepted with reservations' by Western Australia's representative, Minister Charles Perkins, who stated that the government needed to keep control of information about Aboriginal people's living and working conditions, in order to protect itself against 'left wing elements' using Aboriginal issues to advance their own political interests.[5] He questioned the proposal to go out to desert or isolated regions to bring in tribal people, adding that in the Kimberley 'semi-tribal' people on stations were often on land 'where the natives had lived long before the white man went there' and 'have played a useful part in developing the pastoral economy'.[6] He believed that criticisms of their treatment on the stations may have been well founded in the past, but 'today pastoralists pay more attention to their welfare'. The majority remained illiterate because of isolation and lack of facilities and the fact that compulsory education applied only where there was access to a school. School of the Air was available for the white station children only, because those few Aboriginal children who could benefit did 'not live close enough to the station homesteads'. There were schools at Gogo station and at Camballin and Ivanhoe research stations, but they were mostly used by white children. The minister announced that the new policy that would bring Kimberley station people into the assimilation era was for the expansion of the hostel system in towns, where the children would attend school and receive the 'basic three R's':

> They are not taken from their parents. We are trying to insist that the parents remain on the properties where the children came from. We do not want to see a shift in population. At the end of the school term the children go back to the homes they came from just as our white children return home from boarding school.[7]

Nevertheless, hostel children were not always transported home for holidays because transport was either difficult in the wet season or too costly for parents, or the 'homes' to which they were being sent were not considered 'suitable' by welfare officers, missionaries or managers.[8] Bringing children home for holidays therefore became another task for managers to negotiate on behalf of their communities. The result of this policy was that some managers' children spent more time on the stations than Aboriginal children.

The minister advised the conference delegates in 1961 that 'prominent pastoralists' served on the committees of the hostels, which were financed by the Native Welfare Department. Derby Hostel was the first of its kind in the Kimberley. It was to provide domestic and stock training for young Aboriginal people: 'To put it shortly, the objective is to fit them into the workforce in the area to which they belong.'[9] He also stated that the transitional housing scheme, which formed the backbone of assimilation policy in the south, had not been advanced in the Kimberley.[10] There the department had two transitional houses and twelve tin sheds on the Derby reserve, which provided an alternative to the 'primitive native quarters found in most employers' back yards throughout Derby town site'.[11] State government policy was to close all settlements and 'have done away with any that looked like developing'.[12] Where the Commonwealth Department was funding an assimilation policy framed by employment on housing programs at reserves and settlements, the state was funding a hostel system and refusing to build houses on Mowanjum and Derby town reserves in case they continued to develop independently. Instead, Middleton allowed 'qualified segregation' by making one town reserve a transients' camp and another into an 'intermediate' reserve where non-permanent huts would be erected.[13] This enabled the department to have greater 'authority to ensure a satisfactory standard of living' and the hoped-for transition to a suburban lifestyle.

In 1961 Middleton misleadingly termed this period as the time of 'family welfare' policy. He had returned from a tour of all states, reporting afterwards that he was pleased with Western Australia's 'family welfare' policy, which meant there were and would be no large segregated institutions, stations and settlements which either became 'shanty towns' or 'glittering expensive closed communities of 12 to 15 hundred gloomy natives'.[14] Middleton admitted that, 'more through accident than design', Western Australia was in an advantageous position for assimilating Aboriginal people into the white community. The closure of state institutions and settlements for whole communities had left Aboriginal people living in small groups in town reserves, missions and stations, without permanent housing or facilities. These people were able to be placed elsewhere and were more physically fragmented than those who lived under the collective institutional policies of other states and the Northern Territory. The policy was a negative one, of not encouraging large settlements and not supporting others on stations or near towns. Middleton felt that this was a quicker and 'more cost effective' path to assimilation than having to decentralize Aboriginal people from institutions. Ironically, an important aspect of family policy was removing children from pastoral stations to place them in hostels.

Native Welfare patrol officers struggled to convince managers and Aboriginal parents that schooling in towns was beneficial to them and their children.[15] Instances of parents refusing to send their children to school decreased in the early 1960s, but some managers and parents continued to resist Native Welfare's advances because:

> Parents believe one of the three following theories
> (1) If [my] child goes to school, it will go mad.
> (2) If my child goes to school it will never come back, the white people will take it away.
> (3) Schooling teaches my child white ways, so that when they come home they will sneer at their parenst [sic] and their 'black fellow beliefs'.
>
> No. 3 has been heard before and is a very real and sincere belief.[16]

One patrol officer reported that the owner of three stations was actively discouraging children from going to school because he believed he would lose his labour force if the children were removed. His wife was quoted as saying that 'nobody was going to dictate what I do with my blacks'. The patrol officer later reported that the owner was frightened he would lose the child endowment money.[17] The officer countered by telling the Aboriginal people on the stations that their children would become the 'odd man out' in the Kimberley and would be 'relegated to the blacks' camp' if they didn't go to school.[18] This was not an isolated incident. In 1963 a patrol officer in the east Kimberley was called to attend the Cattlemen's Association meeting, where he was asked to convey their antagonism towards the department for not providing schools on stations instead of 'carting them' to towns and missions.[19] He was also asked to police contracts of employment and 'enforce' them. Pastoralists complained that Aboriginal people were walking off stations and leaving debts at the stores. The officer replied that he always checked a man's past employment to see if he was leaving a situation, and if he had debts he would 'send the native back'.[20]

There were many tensions in this period between some parents and Native Welfare over access and control of their children and access to Social Security benefits. The hostel records have lists of children who 'ran away with parents', did not return after a Christmas holiday, 'absconded' mid-term or were expelled because of breaking rules.[21] Increasingly, as relatives moved to town in the late 1960s, children were able to find a 'parent' nearby at Mowanjum or in one of the two town reserves. In 1964 Commissioner Gare, who had replaced Middleton three years earlier, sent a terse circular to all field staff that the policy for the custody of Aboriginal children had changed in 1960 to ensure that children were treated as:

> part of the family rather than the only part of the Aboriginal race worth saving. From now on institutionalisation for education or removal from parents must be watched and care taken.[22]

The Kimberley Downs station school was opened in 1964 to provide for the families who worked there and on Napier Downs.[23] The population expanded rapidly to eighty-five adults and twenty-four children in the stockwork season of 1968. Families with children moved there from Napier Downs, Mount Hart, Leopold Downs and other stations to join relations at Kimberley Downs. Single men from

Halls Creek and Fitzroy Crossing also moved to the station to work on a temporary basis. It was a time when Morndingali, as head stockman, had widespread influence over a range of people as leader for work and for ceremonies. For a short period the families at Kimberley Downs also lived with their older relatives who were being supported by Commonwealth pensions. In 1966 Native Welfare officers noted that Aboriginal people from the central ranges, Mount House, Mornington, Napier Downs and others from the Derby reserves were congregating at Kimberley Downs. Morndingali was recorded as earning $10 a week as head stockman, with Weeda Munro earning $5 a week as a domestic. There were nine pensioners from Mount Hart, Mount House, Napier Downs and Kimberley Downs, seventeen children and twenty experienced working couples, making a station population of sixty-eight Aboriginal people.[24]

The population on Kimberley Downs dropped sharply in late 1968 and early 1969. This coincided with the closure of the station school after the Department of Labour and Industry representative reported that the children were doing more work than schooling. The children were moved to the UAM hostel in Derby. The same pattern emerged for Meda, Napier Downs and Mount Hart. The children moved to a hostel and gradually the women followed, leaving small groups of working men, a few women and a camp of old people as permanent residents. When the old people also moved to town, the social stability of the station communities disintegrated.

'Making a quid out of pensioners'

An important factor that undermined pastoral paternalism in the Kimberley region was the extension of Social Security benefits to Aboriginal people in 1960. Before that, only a few people in the north received an age pension. Larry Kunnumurra, who had received a Queen's Coronation Medal for fifty years' service to the police force as a tracker, was an exception.[25] He was granted an age pension in 1957, but first he had to be given exempt status from the Native Welfare Act because he was a full-blood Aboriginal person living on an Aboriginal reserve and thus excluded from receiving a pension. In

1957 District Officer Beharrell actively pushed for age pensions for Aboriginal people in the west Kimberley, seeking their mass exemption from the Act to make this possible. After assisting Larry Kunnumurra, he applied for exemption status for elderly people in the leprosarium and Mowanjum mission on the outskirts of Derby. Middleton instructed Beharrell to 'stop interfering and causing resentment' and leave it to Social Security.[26]

In February 1959 Middleton asked for a report from Beharrell on the number of people living on pastoral stations and reserves in the west Kimberley who might be eligible for invalid, age and widows pensions if the Social Security Act was liberalized.[27] Beharrell's estimate of at least 300 people received the response that he had better be careful, as an over estimation would cause embarrassment to the department.[28] Middleton reminded him that the system of paying pensions would involve station managers and mission superintendents as warrantees, thus placing them in positions of 'great trust'. He concluded that not everyone would be accepted, and it was the department's responsibility to prevent 'sponging'.[29]

On 24 December 1959 Middleton wrote a long confidential circular to all field officers, outlining the distribution of maternity, age and disability pensions. These were to be payable from 2 February 1960 to all Aboriginal people (including full-blood) living in 'benevolent homes' or 'controlled communities on missions, reserves and pastoral stations'.[30] Individual missions had negotiated an agreement with Social Security authorities to pay either a portion to the mission superintendent and the remainder to the mission headquarters, or the whole to the mission, with a prescribed 'pocket money' allocation to be distributed by the mission staff. Mowanjum mission authorities opted for a small portion of 10s to be sent to the mission in Derby and the remainder to their head office in Melbourne. Kalumburu mission received the whole £9 10s per fortnight. Pastoral station managers were to receive the whole of the pension with 10s to be given to the pensioner as pocket money and the remaining £9 for the manager's use for the 'pensioner's maintenance and improvements in accommodation and general welfare'. Maternity allowances were to be paid direct to the mission superintendents 'in all cases and they will exercise control in the disbursement of the allowance either in cash or in kind to the mother'.[31] On pastoral stations the manager, his wife or the book-keeper received Aboriginal women's maternity allowances unless the mother demonstrated her ability to manage the money. Aboriginal people living on the fringes of towns in reserves or camps were to be paid direct if Native Welfare officers advised Social Security officers that this was appropriate. Aboriginal people classed as 'nomads', who occasionally lived in the bush or desert, were also brought under the Social Security umbrella if they were 'within the sphere of mission influence'.

Having argued that Aboriginal people could not understand money, the government extended the trustee system by making station managers official warrantees for Social Security benefits for station people, and pastoral stations became 'controlled communities'. Minister Charles Perkins rationalized the trustee or warrantee system as:

> [a] means of keeping those, who have been living at some out of the way place, where they normally belong. If that is not done they will drift into towns and become a problem.[32]

He was reassured by the Federal Minister for Social Security that unemployment benefits were not intended for Aboriginal people, nor were they intended to encourage unemployment as a full-time lifestyle. People would have to register and meet guidelines; they would not be sought out.[33] Perkins replied that if unemployment benefits were available to Aboriginal people, he 'could imagine that many natives would never do any more work for the rest of their lives, and by one means or another would make themselves unattractive to employers'.[34]

Restrictions on Aboriginal people receiving unemployment benefits continued in 1964. Divisional officers were instructed by the state Director of Social Security that benefits were unlikely to be extended in the Kimberley region because there was no representative in the region and it was difficult to establish Aboriginal people as 'genuine workers':

> It is not sufficient to establish full employment for only
> three months of the year which would mean the SSD
> [Social Security Department] subsidising, by way of
> benefit, for nine months of the year at a figure more than
> the natives could earn. This could encourage natives to
> be dependent on the benefit rather than looking for
> employment.[35]

Stations acted quickly to ensure that their old people received age pensions. Kimberley Downs, Bedford Downs, Mornington, Kurunjie, Tableland, Mount House and Gibb River stations all applied for pensions one week before the new guidelines were introduced.[36] £9 10s fortnightly was a significant amount of money in 1960.

The pastoral economy remained unpredictable in the north and central Kimberley throughout the 1960s, despite the opening of the United States hamburger beef market and the provision of trucking roads to Mount House and Glenroy from 1963 and to Gibb River in 1969.[37] Herd management, distances and the environment continued to limit pastoral profits in the north and central Kimberley. In a good year, a small station like Mount Elizabeth might turn off 300 head to make around £7,500 from cattle sales to cover all living and development costs. Even the larger and better resourced stations in the Kimberley, such as Mount House, could expect a beef sales profit of only about £10,000 from 1960 to '62.[38] Frank Lacy, for instance, noted that he was owed only £216 for his cattle sales for 1963, after costs.[39]

The age pension was at least three times an Aboriginal stock-man's 'wage' and compared favourably with a white stockman's award wage of around £12 plus keep of £4.[40] In 1963 fortnightly rations for pensioners at Mount Hart, including transport, were estimated to cost below £4.[41] Again, the system relied heavily on managers to identify recipients, collect the necessary details to meet eligibility requirements, receive the money and disburse the goods. Problems of naming and eligibility were almost farcical, as managers, missionaries and Native Welfare officers attempted to fit older Aboriginal people from isolated stations into Social Security guidelines. Correspondence between Native Welfare, the Social Security Department and station managers covered a range of issues, including: placing a cross on forms instead of signatures; indicating sex of applicants, as staff processing the forms had no idea from language names whether the individuals were men or women; trying to ascertain a birth year from the managers instead of just writing 'sighted' as proof of old age; providing a medical certificate for invalids, proof that they had not left Australia, and proof that only the wife living longest with a man would receive a wife's or widow's benefit; and finally, ensuring that child allowances for widow's pensions were paid to only one wife's children.[42] Each Native Welfare field officer was also reminded of their responsibilities, as agreed with Social Security, to see that Aboriginal people were 'not exploited or imposed upon by their own acts of omission or commission, misspend or mal-handle the money'.[43]

A.O. Day, Native Welfare officer for the Port Hedland district in the north-west of Western Australia, pointed out that the method of establishing eligibility, especially age, was problematic. He wrote that having suggested a birth date to an old Aboriginal person who had no idea of dates and limited English, he or she would simply agree, and this would be backed up by their manager who had a vested interest in their receiving a pension. The field officer would then place the estimated age in the census list, which in turn became proof of age for Social Security to enrol the pensioner and for other health or police enquiries.[44] As to the proof of residency, Day wrote that, as it was 'unlawful for an Aborigine to travel interstate it would be unlikely that anyone broke the residency rules'. To overcome some of the difficulties experienced because of the extreme lack of certification and continued lack of staff to cover the region, a 'reputable referee' (generally a station manager or owner) was accepted as adequate for proving name, age, marital status, family relationships, and whether Aboriginal people were able to 'understand money'.[45] Disability required a doctor's certificate.

In June 1960 the Director of Social Security asked that all Native Welfare officers take 'extreme care in obtaining claims from natives'.[46] Two months later all staff were asked to 'count all' Aboriginal people and 'name them', as the statistics were 'inaccurate and misleading'.[47] Station populations increased after Social Security guidelines were broadened. Managers had not previously notified departmental officers of all pensioners or children on their stations because they were not workers under permit, there were no government rations available for them, and few services were offered or utilized which required registration with Native Welfare.[48] Registering births and deaths of Aboriginal people was made compulsory in 1961, and after 1963 all Native Welfare field staff were instructed to ensure managers knew this.[49] They were also asked to check station books, which were supposed to show any earnings, the amount of board and lodging being retained by management, and the amount being distributed as pocket money to all pensioners.[50] The Commissioner of Native Welfare circulated a standard pension distribution scale, which had deductions for a list of foodstuffs (including fruit, powdered milk and rice), clothes and board, some pocket money, medical expenses and £2 to be banked in the pensioner's name.[51] £2 was a working man's monthly pocket money in the Kimberley at the time.

The number of age pensioners in the Kimberley increased from one in 1953 to twenty-six in 1958, and 134 in 1959.[52] Within six months of pensions being made available to Aboriginal people on stations, missions and reserves, 667 were being paid in the Kimberley.

The 'flood of money' into the Kimberley, which the Derby Native Welfare officer estimated to be about £5,000 per fortnight for all pensions, had an immediate impact on social and economic relations on stations and in towns.[53] The Native Welfare district officer reported that pensions had 'helped to stabilise employment' and were 'proving a big factor in the improvement of wages and working conditions generally'.[54] The payment of maternity allowances and age pensions were reported as having 'spectacular results', allowing the department to discontinue ration allowances to indigents in towns or at missions. Social Security funds now completely financed ration allowances to Aboriginal adults in the Kimberley. Age pensioners on stations were receiving extra fresh fruit and vegetables bought for them by managers, as well as clothing and extra items like tinned fish and sweet biscuits. In towns pensioners no longer relied on the basic welfare ration which provided for their 'bare subsistence', and they were also buying clothes.[55]

Table 2: Social Security age pensions paid to warrantees in the Kimberley

	Missions	Town/ leprosarium	Stations	Totals
Age	189	138	287	
Invalid	81	235	52	
Widows	25	35	1	
Total 1961	295	408	340 (56 stns)	1043
Total 1962	298	336	259	893
Total 1963	279	399	360 (61 stns)	1038
Total 1965	447	252	331	1030

Compiled from ARAD1961–1966 MS AADL.

The district officer reported jubilantly that pensioners' 'self esteem had risen with their independent income' and they were 'wanted in the community for the first time since their prime as a workforce'.[56] He added that:

> this spending power has made these aged natives desirable members of the community and we find Shire Councils taking an interest in their well-being, probably for the first time for reasons other than hygiene. At Missions and stations we find these old people, often previously only tolerated, now living in relative splendour with everyone taking an interest in them and their welfare.[57]

According to the Pastoralists and Graziers Association, the interest shown in pensioners was not always beneficial. They sent

Painting a new cottage on the Derby reserve, 1965.
From Native Welfare Annual Report 1967, copyright Department
of Native Welfare

a deputation to the Minister for Native Welfare in late December 1960 to argue that pension monies were being misspent, with some pensioners supporting 'a lot of hangers-on'.[58] They asked for station managers to be made responsible for the whole pension, without any cash component, and for the Commonwealth and the state to take greater control of its expenditure where they were trustees. All field officers were instructed to take a closer look at how pensions were being used to ensure that pensioners were not being exploited by their relatives or warrantees at pastoral stations and missions.[59]

Under the warrantee system for age pensions a greater degree of outside scrutiny and accountability was expected by Social Security officers than Native Welfare Department officers had experienced previously, or were able to insist upon. Storekeepers were barred from being warrantees, but the potential conflict of

Pensioners eating in the dining hall on the Derby reserve,
1966. From Native Welfare Annual Report 1966, copyright Department
of Native Welfare

interest for station managers who also sold goods in their stores was disregarded. The 1962 Native Welfare Act Regulations, which stated that goods were not to be sold at inflated prices, applied only to employees.[60] There was no regulation of the prices at which goods were exchanged in lieu of pensions or wages. As Middleton had warned in 1959, trustees were placed in positions of 'great trust'. In practice, managers rationed pensioners and used the extra money for improving living conditions on the stations for everyone, not just pensioners. Native Welfare and Social Security condoned this, as well as allowing the station to deduct a fee or charge for handling or cooking stores for pensioners.[61] Pastoralists were now able to deduct money from pensions for caring for their retired workers or older people who moved in to visit at the station camps. The station lists record pensioners moving around stations during the 1960s, staying a year at one station then moving to the next. Most probably moved with their working relatives, but some walked to different stations.

In 1964 Social Security policy towards stations hardened. The Director of Social Security informed all Native Welfare Department field staff that station workers in the Kimberley were no longer legally excluded from receiving unemployment benefits. But most would not receive them as they did not 'fit the worker category': they had no work history, were not receiving a formal wage and were 'employed' for only a portion of the year.[62] He added that Social Security did not want unemployment benefits 'subsidizing' the stations for their workers. The policy for pension expenditure also changed. Pensions could be used for 'general housing and uplift of the whole community' only in the western desert, where 'tribal' people were moving into missions, but not on stations or missions in the north Kimberley, where 'under no circumstances' were officers to take a liberal view of expending pension moneys. The Social Security Director asked Native Welfare field staff to attend stations at meal times and observe the food being distributed, and then to examine the living conditions. He added that he understood that this could cause 'ill feeling' between the managers and the department, but reports of exploitation of pensioners had come to light.

Departmental staff reported that some managers and missions did not improve pensioners' living conditions at all and were barely even keeping them alive.[63] There were also allegations that stations continued to pay wages from pensioners' accounts and evidence from Native Welfare officers that child endowment money had to be used by Aboriginal people to buy food because rations and wages were insufficient.[64]

In 1965 Kimberley pastoral stations receiving pensions were formally investigated by Special Magistrate M.E. Davies for Social Security. The day he was appointed, a newspaper article by Douglas Lockwood in the *Weekend News* claimed there were £9,000 of pensioner monies held by the Wave Hill station managers in the Northern Territory and that West Australian stations may have been in a similar situation.[65] Station managers were now under public scrutiny, with their benevolence in question. According to C.D. Rowley it was during this period that pastoralists in the Northern

Territory were heard to joke that they were making more money from Aboriginal people than from cattle.[66] In South Australia at the same time, pastoralists were being accused of 'nigger farming'.[67]

Magistrate Davies was accompanied by Kevin Johnson, who worked for Native Welfare from 1959 to 1972.[68] The investigations uncovered alleged overpayments and potential problems at stations throughout the Kimberley, with larger companies like Vesteys and Emmanuels coming under some unwelcome scrutiny. The investigations found evidence for pension overpayments of £9,951 to Kurunjie station alone. Repayments of £681 were made by the owner at Mount Hart for pensions paid for one person who had been dead for two years, and another who had lived at the neighbouring station for ten months.[69] At the time of the investigation, the pensioners were naked and surrounded by more than a hundred dogs. They lived at a bush shelter camp 200 yards from the homestead hut along a footpath that was impassable in the wet season. Most had come out of the bush between 1954 and '62 and had been visited only once by a Native Welfare officer.[70] The owner resided on the station between May and November, and allocated blankets, clothes and pocket money during those months. For the remaining five months each year, one of the pensioners was in charge of the camp while the unschooled and illiterate manager was responsible for ordering stores and caretaking. Davies commented that this was 'an extremely poor example of culture contact with natives being out of sight out of mind'.[71] After discussions with the owner, Davies concluded that the situation did not require the removal of the pensioners. The camp was controlled by a respected leader who was not 'sophisticated' but had 'complete control over the camp and his word was Law on the station'. After the investigation in 1965, the pensioner camp was moved to a small 'island' hillock in view of the homestead—a 'traditional camping place'— and the manager was sacked. The old people stayed.

Davies had already supervised the repayment of pension monies at stations in the Fitzroy valley, and he now found that the system of utilizing pension monies for the general good of the station without noticeable changes to pensioners' way of life was widespread. His general comments were that pensioners on Kimberley stations were in much the same position in 1965 as they had been in 1960. Those on good stations had some improvements in accommodation and water supplies, occasional extra store items or washing facilities, but most continued in the 'same primitive way as they have done for many years'. Aboriginal pensioners had 'little understanding of pensions, no guidance and no desire to change their mode of living'.[72] Davies suggested that they receive 'guidance' to understand that they could receive 'comforts' for their pensions; otherwise the money would 'continue to be absorbed by the stations'.

In June 1966 investigations of station books to assess where the money was being spent brought to light the problem of lack of accountability at many stations. Ned Delower was manager of Tableland station when his station books were investigated. His bookkeeping was reported by the investigating team as 'minutely detailed' and could not be faulted.[73] Delower showed accounts and payments for lollies, biscuits, cloth, tobacco and clothes sent from Perth, which he distributed to pensioners instead of the fortnightly pocket money component. The patrol officer accepted his argument that there was nothing at the station beside staple ration items like flour, tea and sugar, so pocket money was not needed by the pensioners. The next year, after further investigations, Social Security officers calculated that there was $9,840 unaccounted for after food and pocket money costs were deducted from the pension payments. Delower explained that $2,000 was placed into the station account on the orders of the owner. On questioning, the owner produced accounts totalling $5,500 for items like 'transport and freight etc', which were accepted by Social Security as a reasonable record of expenditure in the interests of the nine pensioners who lived at Tableland station.

Kurunjie and Mount Hart stations had no station books at all. Seventy-five-year-old Dave Rust, who had served in the First Light Horse during the First World War and had built Gibb River and Kurunjie station huts in the 1920s with his wife, Susie Umungul, had sold the Kurunjie lease to an absentee owner. Rust lived on the station with Susie and eight pensioners who had lived through the period of first contact. Native Welfare patrol officer Kevin Johnson recalled his amazement at seeing the 'old timers' in the far north living in conditions which he had not seen at other stations near Derby or on the Fitzroy River.[74] The old bark huts and stamped earth floors of the homesteads at Gibb River, Mount Elizabeth, Mount Hart, Beverley Springs and Kurunjie had been upgraded with tin rooves and out-houses, but little else had changed from the 1930s. Aboriginal women lived with white men, with a small camp of Aboriginal elders nearby and large packs of dogs roaming the camps. Although the anti-cohabitation clauses had been dropped from the new 1963 Native Welfare Act, Johnson could have intervened on behalf of the Aboriginal people in the camps by bringing them into town for medical assistance or reducing the number of dogs. But he sympathized with the owners of the northern stations, whom he saw as specially deserving 'battlers' because in each case the station Missus at Gibb River, Mount Elizabeth and Mount Barnett was an Aboriginal woman. He reported that they were living in much the same conditions as the camp people and were unable to pay for improvements. He did not believe the pensioners would accept any changes to their 'primitive' conditions if they were made.[75]

At Mount Barnett, Johnson assisted the managers to complete forms for two women who had been denied a pension because they were the second and third wives of one man. Mary Yulbu was one of them. Having survived the frontier and then the leprosarium, she had been dropped at Gibb River by the flying doctor plane and moved back to the country where she had experienced first contact. One of the pensioners Johnson was appraising was old Mobby, or Larry Murphy, who had helped Jack Carey in the 1920s and had moved to Mount Barnett with Fred Russ and Mary Karraworla's daughter in the early 1960s. Mount Barnett was an out-station of Gibb River and until 1965 was built only of bush materials. Mobby was recorded as a good spearman who hunted most of the meat eaten on the station. Johnson reported that they were in the true sense 'battling' and that even the 'sale of one bullock is an event'.[76] Mobby was granted a pension, but his wife was refused because Welfare recorded her birth date as 1913, which meant she was too young in 1963. She was granted a pension two years later when Russ wrote to the Derby Native Welfare office that he had known one of the applicants since 1916, when he was fifteen years old and the woman Mary was at least his age.[77] Most station pensioners were recorded in 1959 or '60 as born in 1899 or 1900, which was sufficient to include them in pension categories. At Mount Elizabeth there were five pensioners, and Johnson suggested signing on two more women whom he believed were eligible for a pension. Lacy refused to sign them on, stating that 'he did not think it was useful'.[78] They lived together in a bark hut and had few needs beyond meat and occasional rations.

The Director of Social Security was not sympathetic to 'battlers' on the isolated ranges stations, and saw no reason to be lenient towards trustees for Aboriginal people. After the Davies investigation, he warned the Commissioner of Native Welfare that pension guidelines were being broken in the Kimberley, where Aboriginal pensioners were rarely receiving 'reasonable benefit' from their money. He added:

> It seems that some warrantees regard the pension as a form of station subsidy and consider that they are entitled to restrict the value of the benefits flowing to the pensioners for various reasons. One being that wages paid to native station workers will not show adversely by comparison.
>
> The effect is that instead of Commonwealth pension moneys benefiting the pensioner only, they are undeservedly and unnecessarily benefiting the station to the extent to which value is withheld from the pensioner.[79]

He declared that responsibility for Aboriginal people lay with the state, not the Commonwealth, and specifically with the Department of Native Welfare. He appealed to the Commissioner for Native Welfare to follow the practices agreed to by 'all other states in the Commonwealth'— to make state welfare officers trustees for all pensioners, and to provide adequate staff to support the Social Security payments to stations and in towns, missions and reserves.

In response to increased pressure from the Commonwealth to scrutinize stations, the Derby Native Welfare district officer suggested a full-scale review of the Kimberley, adding that inadequate staff and conditions for travel needed to be taken into account before Native Welfare took responsibility for pensions from pastoral station managers and missions.[80] In August 1965 the Commissioner for Native Welfare agreed to undertake a general survey of every pensioner on pastoral stations. Where managers would not agree to follow the guidelines for warrantees, departmental staff would explain to the pensioner that 'if he stays where he is the pension may be cancelled'.[81] If the pensioner agreed to move, departmental staff were instructed to advise where he or she should go and to 'assist with the move and gradual transition to direct payment of their pensions'.

A follow-up report was completed in June 1966, after welfare officers went into camps and huts and observed people eating and then asked them to show what cash and belongings they held.[82] Some managers successfully resisted interference and scrutiny from Native Welfare officers, after taking legal advice that trustees did not have to disclose their books because they spent the money for the pensioner, not for the Social Security Department. The pensioner entrusted them to look after their money, and so their relationship was with the pensioner, not the government, state or federal. For instance, on Gogo station, where there were 200 Aboriginal people and fourteen age pensioners, the owners delayed and then refused to allow officers to see their books. This frustrated welfare officers, who wrote that the 'powerful Emanuel group are almost a law unto themselves', setting a pattern in evidence at other stations not to fully disclose Social Security expenditure to Native Welfare officers.[83] According to the district officer, the situation was unsatisfactory across the Kimberley:

> Other stations have very inadequate or carefully doctored records, but it is all very obvious from what the pensioners say, their condition and clothing, plus accounting by the Department of Social Services and this Department, that they are not receiving full benefit of their pensions.[84]

He believed that stations and missions had similar conditions and supported a 'well worn phrase' in the Kimberley at the time, that 'They are all making a quid out of pensioners.'[85]

From 1966 a direct payment of $9 of the $23.50 pension was made compulsory, whether recipients were on church, government or pastoral properties.[86] The Director of Social Security explained that the Commonwealth was going to transfer to direct payments of the whole pension in the near future, regardless of possible problems, and 'would rather err on the side of too early rather than too late'.[87] In 1966 direct payments were made to 433 pensioners, marking the introduction of a welfare benefits system that paid more cash than could be earned as a worker and bypassed to some degree the old handout from either managers or missionaries. Welfare officers were advised that some pensions could continue to be spent by managers on accommodation, wood, water and repairs to houses on stations, but 'it would be necessary for the pensioner to be assured of security of tenure of the building for as long as he wants it'.[88] This may be the formal understanding to which Morndingali referred when he stated that as a pensioner he was 'supposed' to live in a pension house on the station after he retired:

> ... manager didn't try to help me along didn't try to give me a little bit of a block or a little bit of a house put the pension house for me. I coulda stay in my own country! [tapping the table for emphasis] Now I'm in a different part of country. I'm in a Derby town. This wasn't my place. I s'posed to be settle down in my place, in Kimberley Down and Napier. I should have a homestead that last when I was get pensioned off ... Now that was too late.[89]

Native Welfare officers were also trustees for pensioners, holding a pension bank account and some individual bank books for them. After 1963 the accounts were held in individual pensioners' names and were subject to audit. The Native Welfare office in Derby had a large storeroom where rations were kept and distributed weekly to pensioners. Kevin Johnson, Derby field officer at the time, recalled the detailed bookkeeping he and other officers carried out to account for every pound of flour and every stick of tobacco they distributed to Aboriginal people, in addition to their pension pocket money.[90] The transition from rations for 'relief' to the Social Security system did not alter the type or amount of rations, or the personnel distributing them, until the late 1960s, but it greatly increased the amount of pocket money available to pensioners living in towns. After 1967 it was normal rather than exceptional for town pensioners to receive their own money into their own account. Native Welfare officers assisted with stores and with accommodation at the reserve, but their control over the cash was reduced.

In 1968 Native Welfare officers were instructed not to act as trustees for pensioners and not to interfere in how pensions were being spent.[91] The divisional superintendent for the north warned his colleagues that there seemed to be systematic problems for aged pensioners in missions. After the death of a pensioner, the missions 'invariably' registered 'nil' in their trust account. This was dismissed by the commissioner as an arrangement between missions and individual pensioners, and because individual pensioner accounts were not kept at missions but were paid into general accounts, there was no hope of intervening. By 1969 all pensions were paid direct to pensioners, who in many cases then spent their money at station or mission stores, or asked the managers to assist them to buy goods.[92]

The threat to withdraw age pensions from isolated stations or missions, or to withdraw Native Welfare support for pensioners, forced Aboriginal people to relocate to town reserves. Removing the old people from their country or the station where they had 'settled' undermined the social cohesiveness of the communities. With Aboriginal children from most stations also living in hostels or missions and away from their relatives, the demographic and social balance shifted significantly from stations to towns. Sunday Island people moved to Derby in 1962 and Forrest River people transferred to Wyndham in 1966; in both cases the old people refused to move until Native Welfare officers explained that they would not receive food or pensions if they stayed.[93] The transfer to Mowanjum on the fringes of Derby was also resisted by the old people, and a small group actually left the town and walked north into the bush because they could not settle outside their country.[94]

On pastoral stations in the north Kimberley, age pensions were the issue around which Aboriginal people's individual rights began to be protected by a government body. When pensions were first extended to all Aboriginal people on pastoral stations, there had been a simple Social Security guideline that called for the division of the pension into pocket money for the pensioner and the rest for the station for accommodation and keep. Social Security undertook this and paid portions to missions and the whole to stations. This system had enabled stations to subsidize their workforce without challenging their position as Bosses over cash and goods on the stations. But detailed accounting for pension monies was an onerous task that not all stations were prepared to undertake. Then, as Native Welfare officers responded to Commonwealth directions to pressure managers to allow Aboriginal people to handle their own money and force changes in their living and working conditions, paternalism began to turn sour.

Native Welfare station patrol reports grew increasingly critical of conditions on stations and openly suspicious of managers' motives and interests. Mount House pension camp was reported in 1968 as the 'worst camp' in the Kimberley, when one old pensioner was found dying and another 'frail and senile'.[95] They were 'evacuated' by plane to Derby and placed in the Native Hospital, and the managers were 'warned' that Native Welfare would 'keep a close eye on them'. Complaints continued about Mount House pensioners, fuelled by ex-Mount House workers in the Derby reserve, whose parents were still on the station living in the camp. Mount House management countered criticisms from Native Welfare and applied for more pensions. They sent the ration scale to Social Security, which included meat, sugar, matches, biscuits and a tin of herrings and tomato. But pension monies were held up for months because the scale of rations did not have the required pocket money component, and managers were warned that they were in contravention of Social Security guidelines. Each pensioner received $1.00 each fortnight instead of $9.00 pocket money. A further investigation was ordered, and conflict escalated between management and Native Welfare until the district officer reported that the situation was not so bad as suggested. He drew back from the language of exploitation and abuse of rights to that of personal relations and relative needs of old Aboriginal people. There were iron huts, canvas shelters, bower shelters, an iron cottage for the half-caste head stockman, Billy King, and regular rations which were all accounted for in the station books.[96]

The Missus at Mount House did all the accounting for the pensioners and managed the station store. She was galled by the continuing correspondence and delays over pensioners' details such as their age or proof of marriage, or the distance between town and the station, and wrote to Native Welfare that 'these things could not possibly happen to non-aborigines'.[97] The station was sold in 1969 to become part of King Ranch Holdings, and the old Bosses who had established the station at the turn of the century left for the southern cities. The Missus no longer looked after the domestic sphere—books, pensions, medical chest, radio and station store. By 1972 there were only two pensioners left: two had joined families in town, one was in the leprosarium and the other was in Numbala Nunga, the old age residential care institution built in 1969. The pensioners had sums of around $400 distributed to them, and King Ranch was left with a small working population of two married men and a group of single male stockmen. Billy King walked off in 1972 after an argument with the owners over their management practices, and began work at Numbala Nunga for award wages, caring for around forty elderly and disabled Aboriginal people. He joined Jack Dale, who was working at Numbala Nunga after a life of stockwork in the northern ranges and being head stockman at Beverley Springs. Campbell Allenbrae and other stockmen and women were also living in the Derby town reserve in 1969.

Beverley Springs was not immune to Welfare criticism and conflict. Like other stations, it eventually lost most of its younger workers to the town reserves and was left with a camp of old people.[98] One or two bush groups continued to visit in the 1960s, taking tobacco and rations with them as they walked north towards Mount Elizabeth and Kalumburu. Pensioners and workers lived in better conditions than most stations, and had regular and reliable rations. Their housing was built with $4,500 pension money, which had accumulated in their account prior to 1971. In that year the manager informed the Derby Hostel not to send the children home because they would be 'ruined' in the camps. The next year there was only one Aboriginal woman listed as a worker, and eight pensioners and seven 'others': the married workers had not returned after a visit to town.[99]

The Native Welfare patrol officer questioned management in detail about their expenses for pensioners, and the Missus, who filled the domestic role of looking after the pensioners and store, grew increasingly frustrated, writing that she would start to charge Aboriginal people for a range of services such as butchering their meat. In 1972, when four old Aboriginal people who spoke no English at all walked out of the bush onto Beverley Springs, the manager asked for Native Welfare assistance to feed and care for them because they were too old to work for their keep.[100] They were taken to town instead by Native Welfare, assisted by David Mowaljarlai who had moved to town with the Mowanjum Community and worked with a range of service providers throughout the 1950s and '60s. The old 'bush people's' relatives were either in the old people's home, the Derby reserve, Kalumburu mission or at Mowanjum. The bush from Derby to Mount Hart and west to the coast was not occupied by bush people any more, and old people's residency at stations was under threat.

The paradigm of pastoral estates, with resident Boss and Missus leading the social and economic development of the north while they cared for resident Indigenous groups, began to disintegrate on stations such as Meda, Napier Downs, Kimberley Downs, Mount House and Glenroy in the late 1960s. In 1965 D. Treloar, an agricultural economist, wrote that there was insufficient reinvestment in Kimberley pastoral leases for long-term profitable management of herds and pastures by all sections of owners, whether small, large or absentee. Large companies with outside investments had offset some reinvestment costs as tax deductions, but the majority of resident owners had families living in southern cities with calls on the station income. Homestead improvement costs were also high if owners wished to move from the old style of technology to powered homesteads and fenced paddocks.[101] In the late 1960s they were facing reduced profits. Leaseholders relied instead on open range herd management, natural watering points with trucks allowing increased and easier turn-off of cattle, and Social Security assistance to support workers and non-workers.

During the late 1960s many stations were sold. In 1963 there were 342 leases and 123 businesses in the Kimberley, which contracted to 101 leases and sixty-eight businesses in 1971. The horse musters continued, but droving stopped, except for Tableland and stations over the Phillips Ranges, Mount Elizabeth and Gibb River. There the managers continued to live with small groups of Aboriginal people they had known since their childhood. They did not invest in labour-saving technology, hire white men for stockwork, strip their leases of cattle in response to market deviations or sell out to conglomerates.[102] They started tourism enterprises, with the first group of 'elderly people from Victoria' arriving in 1966 to view the cave paintings, the country and the Aboriginal stockmen.[103]

Napier Downs and Kimberley Downs were sold in 1969 to the Australian Land and Cattle Company (ALCCO), which bought several stations in the west Kimberley. In 1971, at the beginning of a four-year 'boom' in cattle prices, the company held leases over four million acres of the Kimberley.[104] These new American-based conglomerate companies signalled a change in ownership and management practices which contributed to Aboriginal people's dislocation from the stations. They were responding to changing markets for Australian beef, from the predictable but slow-moving European market to the fast-developing hamburger market in the United States.[105] They invested in labour-saving technology such as fences, watering points, helicopter mustering, mobile yards, grain feed and trucks. They developed a system of labour management from Camballin, a central point on the Fitzroy River. Their managers were not paid or expected to cater to the welfare needs of non-working Aboriginal people or to develop a homestead sphere with an 'Indigenous' component to support a residential community.[106] In 1970 the new and young Missus at ALCCO's Napier Downs station was questioned and placed under pressure by Native Welfare to clarify pensioners' payments and expenditure and to clean up the camps. She wrote that she 'tried to get some information from various family groups but it is pretty well impossible—I can't even find out some of the surnames let alone when or where they were born'.[107]

The new Missus at Kimberley Downs had similar problems in 1969 when she wrote to Welfare that she couldn't 'explain or understand how the information about the pensioners was arrived at'.[108]

'A general air of discontent'

In the 1960s, as old age pensions began to provide an alternative to rations and station work, an element of resistance developed to what came to be known as the 'old style' of careless indifference to workers or their living conditions. The managers at Napier Downs and Kimberley Downs were also openly arguing with Aboriginal people over their living and working conditions. The Kimberley Downs manager complained to Native Welfare about the 'lack of grip' he had over workers and the 'decline in discipline'. He was particularly unhappy about the tendency, which seemed to be on the increase, for 'workers to drift from place to place, putting down no roots and acquiring no loyalty'.[109] The teams under the leadership of Morndingali threatened to walk off the station in 1961, and again in 1968.[110] Other walk-offs occurred in the 1940s and '50s, but managers eventually found the workers in the bush or they walked back to their families in the camps.[111]

In 1961, before pensioners had control of some of their money, the stockworkers at Kimberley Downs left the muster camp after Morndingali punched a white stockman who was swearing at workers. The team rode away for an hour, then returned to work because they did not want to risk leaving the station and stock-work.[112] There were no rations in towns for Aboriginal station workers, transport was owned and controlled by the Boss or Native Welfare, and Derby was outside their country. The Native Welfare officer reported that they had been 'reprimanded' for walking off and fighting. A similar situation occurred at Kurunjie station in 1963, when the whole muster team decamped one night and refused to return to work for the new manager, who also had to repay Social Security overpayments.

Harry Howendon, who had worked as a horse breaker at Mount Hart, Napier and Mornington in the 1950s and '60s and returned to Mount Elizabeth, to his own country, to 'retire' in the 1980s, explained the walk-off strategy:

> If gardia no good, that manager, if him no good, well everybody get out, everybody walk-out, finish off that whitefella … One time we can walk out and learnem that gardia. Well he can't do [his work], he been look around. We go back longa him … He do wrong for tucker, for clothes, tobacco anything, anything mean bugger, well every body walk out. Learnem him first.
>
> … He tell me 'You can run the camp, I'm finish I stop home.' Alright I been run the camp, he been stop in the homestead …
>
> I tellim 'I never read and write. You know every read and write. You been longa school. Me, I never been longa school. My father been taken away. Well you can have this country, I'm gone.' I been walk out. He been find me half way.
>
> Same Morndi, he been havem plenty gardia. He been walk out everyfella. Some twofella have a fight, next time he been walk out. I never fight gardia, just walk out … When I want tucker, I go for tucker.[113]

By 1968, when Morndingali and the stockmen threatened to walk off Kimberley Downs for better conditions, they also complained to Native Welfare that the manager treated people like the 'early days', saying that 'bread and meat is good enough for natives' and threatening 'to bush all natives for any more cheek', as he was 'not prepared to argue with natives'. Morndingali complained that domestics worked long hours for no cash and pensioners were not receiving their money, despite working on the station collecting wood and tending gardens. Morndingali was described by the patrol officer as a 'trouble maker' who had problems with the new manager's attitudes, which 'could appear to contain prejudice'.[114] He was labelled as one of the 'chip on the shoulder natives' in the Kimberley who were creating 'a general air of discontent'.

The young manager was replaced in late 1969 by Ned Delower, who had known most of the workers previously when he managed Napier Downs in the 1930s. His wife was also willing and experienced at managing the domestic sphere with Aboriginal women, and when interviewed in 1992 she recalled the English and bush names and relationships of women and children on Tableland and Napier Downs.[115] But Native Welfare continued to report a 'general air of discontent', especially from women over their child endowment payments. They received $5 a week and rations, while their endowment was transferred to the hostels where the children had been directed after the school closed. Again Delower and his wife showed lists of stores and pension expenditures to Native Welfare officers, accounting for items bought and distributed to Aboriginal people.[116] By 1971 there were three pensioners, no children, ten or twelve men and only two women living on the station. Most were not resident there during the wet season.[117] Commissioner Gare asked for an investigation and an explanation from the owners about the wage levels on the station. Delower replied that there were no 'trade unionists' so the award wage decision applicable to the Kimberley in 1969 did not apply to his station.[118]

There were continual labour problems at Mount Hart from 1966.[119] The manager recruited labour from Broome, Port Hedland and Wyndham because the resident workers had left with the pensioners and gone to other stations. The outside workers were reportedly 'sophisticated', and their complaints were taken very seriously.[120] They were expected to eat with their hands and accept verbal abuse from the manager, who on one occasion arrived with a rifle at the stock camp and tied one of the workers to a horse. In 1968 new owners of Blina, Ellendale and Silent Grove (a portion of Beverley Springs), Thiess Holdings, bought Mount Hart and gathered workers from the Derby reserve, including Morndingali, for a short period. In 1969 Native Welfare attempted to recoup ration costs for the wife of an employee at Mount Hart, who was staying at the reserve. The manager wrote to Native Welfare stating that he would no longer accept the 'old system' of rationing dependants of station employees.[121] The officer replied that it was 'hoped' that 'station management will accept moral responsibility of assisting their native employees in such matters'.

Over the next two years telegrams were exchanged between the manager and the district office, attempting to place workers on the station from the Derby reserve or from other stations, but Aboriginal people resisted. They now had an alternative form of subsistence in the form of 'Welfare', as well as the Derby reserves and a rising sense of 'rights', similar to those that Patrol Officer Pullen had aimed for in 1949 and '50, but without the hoped-for concessions from employers or widespread confident self-expression from Aboriginal people. The transition years from frontier to Welfare assistance had not encouraged Aboriginal independence to speak up for themselves to management in order to change their conditions. Individuals who disagreed with government officials or station management were still viewed as potentially dangerous 'trouble makers' if they complained.

From 1968 even the small 'battling' station owners were criticized for not providing adequate living conditions for pensioners or wages for workers. Fred Russ at Gibb River, who had rarely been officially questioned by welfare officers, was described in 1970 as 'patriarchal' and unable to change his attitudes, which allowed old people to live in 'byres' and 'hovels' and dress in 'rags'.[122] Frank Lacy at Mount Elizabeth was questioned about a pensioner account that had built up into a large sum of money, although there were no iron huts or ablutions for people on the station. Lacy wrote that this money was for their benefit and he had known one of them for twenty-four years; they had a record player and all they wanted.[123] In 1970 he was criticized again for not providing any housing for workers and for actively preventing an improvement in living and working conditions for Aboriginal people on the station. The Native Welfare district officer reported:

> As will be seen pay is quite wretched, and clearly, the workers are being exploited, but this is not as a result of evil opinions or a desire to degrade. The manager genuinely believes that money is an evil in the hands of the aboriginal. Something sure to be gambled or drunk

away. The attitude is paternal. 'I've been associating with them for 50 years. I know them better than I know the back of my hand. I look after them when they are sick. We all get on well together. It is your department and the like that is spreading discontent etc etc ...' There seems to be no Labour Code to protect the employee, and it is difficult to see how employers can be made to move with the times.[124]

Commissioner Gare asked for an inquiry into Mount Elizabeth, with detailed answers as to whether Aboriginal people on the station were 'happy' and 'aware of their entitlements and [showed] conscious acceptance of the lesser standard'.[125] In addition he wanted to know if they were on their tribal country and if they were willing to move if offered more lucrative work. District Officer Johnson replied that only one Aboriginal person in the whole central and northern ranges was a member of the AWU and that this station was more isolated than most.[126] He added that, although some workers had said they would move to get better wages and conditions, no fellow Pastoralist and Graziers Association members would accept Lacy's workers; they had no choice. The station utilized and cared for six single men who were placed there by Corrective Services. Old Jumbo, who had come to Mount Elizabeth with Lacy in 1946, was frightened of any prospect of change and more concerned about what would happen to him if Frank Lacy was not there than about improving his conditions by moving elsewhere. Gare referred the matter to the Department of Labour and National Service for investigation.[127] It was dropped three months later as a hopeless undertaking that would not 'do any good'.[128]

'A very effective labour exchange'

Aboriginal people's residency patterns began to change noticeably around 1961, as town-based employment increased, offering wages ten times those on stations, and Social Security benefits provided further income for the community to survive outside the stations.[129]

From 1961 one of the Derby town reserves became known as the pensioner reserve, while an official 'transient' reserve was gazetted nearby. This reserve began to increase in size as bushwalking 'holidays' to the river or another station were transformed into wet season lay-offs to town reserves, and inmates and patients discharged from the leprosarium or hospital were also permitted to camp there rather than being transported to stations. Workers and their families were also being displaced from stations for the wet season breaks by managers who refused to provide rations during work breaks and transported them to town instead. Native Welfare staff were concerned at their lack of control of station people, who formed a 'constant drift of natives in and out of towns' where there were some rations, some age pensioners, children, and women following their children to towns.

Stations were also complaining that they were 'beginning to lose workers' who moved to town to work at the Derby wharf, the Native Hospital, the general hospital, the butcher shop and private houses, and on building projects funded by Commonwealth monies, such as an ablution block and plumbing for sections of the Derby reserve. Visitors from the Gibb River Road stations were also meeting Mowanjum residents who were closely related but had been dispersed because of the frontier and work commitments. The transfer of Sunday Island mission to Derby in 1962 further reinforced the trend away from isolated missions and communities towards towns, where Aboriginal people found opportunities for socializing and reconstituting relationships between Bardi, Nyigina, Worrora and Ngarinyin people.

The 'flood of money' from Social Security benefits alarmed Commissioner Gare, who believed that Aboriginal people were learning the 'worst possible social education' and becoming 'parasites'.[130] He demanded that Native Welfare field officers take 'drastic action' and refuse to provide rations to anyone who was eligible for a Social Security pension and who did not have normal expenditures like rent, power bills and water rates. He specifically targeted single people without children and any Aboriginal person who lived in shared reserve housing, tents, or humpies. This category encompassed most Aboriginal people in the Kimberley in the early 1960s. In 1962 there were only two Aboriginal families in their own housing and one in state housing in Derby.[131] In 1963 there were fourteen pensioner huts and an iron unclad pensioner eating hall on one reserve. The transient reserve had only tin humpies to house all Aboriginal people who worked in town and were 'permitted to live on the reserve' or who were visiting town and permitted to camp for short periods. The transitional housing program, which was designed to move people from reserves to integrated suburbs, was not instituted in Derby until late 1966. Even then it was not directed at station transients for fear that

A typical reserve camp. From Native Welfare Annual Report 1972, copyright Department of Native Welfare

Aboriginal people would stop wanting to work and would sit down on the reserves to live from the communal distribution of pension monies.

Opening a school on Kimberley Downs station in 1964 encouraged some adults from there and stations nearby to stay on the station with their children during the work season, but Aboriginal people continued to move into town for the wet season lay-off. By 1964 the transient camp was overcrowded with at least twenty permanent old age pensioners and twenty extended families living in tents and humpies. Native Welfare officers drew up a list of reserve regulations:

1. No drinking.
2. No gambling for stakes.
3. Cleanliness.
4. Dogs to be kept on chain.
5. Houses to be kept clean and tidy.
6. All residents must be clean and neatly dressed.
7. Proper use of toilets and laundry.
8. Conduct well mannered and orderly, fighting and arguments are not to take place.
9. The reserve is not for idle persons. Each inhabitant must have employment.
10. Each resident must abide by the instructions of the Native Welfare Officer and the Reserve Caretaker.[132]

Native Welfare officers worked to offset movements of people into the reserve by functioning as 'a very effective labour exchange' and using the flying doctor plane for transport to remote stations.[133] The majority of Native Welfare station files have a collection of telegrams, starting in 1959 and finishing in about 1969, from managers seeking specific skilled workers who were camping in Derby at the reserve or were on short-term contracts at other stations. The district officer noted in 1961 that the 'demand for labour in the west Kimberley still exceeds supply, indeed, that for able bodied men is so great as to be embarrassing'. This comment was repeated in 1962 and '63.

As early as 1956, the manager at Blina, next door to Kimberley Downs and adjacent to the main road from Derby to Fitzroy Crossing, asked for any workers at all, 'even elderly people for the garden would be a help'.[134] The manager had sacked Ginger Warrebeen after he was injured while walking in the bush. Warrebeen's parents left as well, walking to Napier Downs and eventually moving to the Derby reserve. Len Connell, who employed Jack Dale for years as his offsider, reported in 1962 that managers needed to be protected from 'these smart blacks' who walked away from muster camps in the middle of the night.[135] He had no workers at all and would not be able to muster unless some were found and flown to Mount Hart. Other managers in the West Kimberley were more specific and demanding. One telegrammed the district office for 'Horsemen preferred with wives no duds' and another for 'clean half-castes' for domestic work.[136] The Kimberley Downs manager asked for one 'good house girl (½ caste to FB)' and four stockboys, 'wives acceptable'.[137]

During this period of extreme labour shortage, Frank Lacy went to Halls Creek with his head stockman, Jumbo, to try to find workers who were related to Jumbo and might therefore be willing to move to Mount Elizabeth for work. Lacy noted that everyone refused to move: 'there was no hope'.[138] A pastoral trainee scheme also failed because pastoralists would not enter into a formal agreement with an Aboriginal worker unless they had greater rights to 'discipline' the trainees.[139] Young pastoral trainees were walking off stations, unwilling to work for a trainee's wage or accept the conditions. According to the divisional superintendent, the trainees' parents did not want them to be placed with station Bosses for long periods without being able to contact their families. Derby and Fitzroy Crossing reserves therefore continued to grow, despite most experienced workers being re-employed for short periods each muster season.

By 1968 the Native Welfare district officer for the Kimberley, who was based in Derby, reported that young men were not staying at stations after being sent there from town.[140] Some officers began to question their role as an employment agency for work at below award wages and award conditions. Their role also increasingly became one of removing and caring for children who had been committed by a court to the care of the Child Welfare Department (represented in the Kimberley until 1972 by the Native Welfare Department). In 1968 there were 1,295 Aboriginal children labelled as Wards of the State, with almost half of them in missions or state-run institutions. The Native Welfare district officer reported that committals were increasing as younger generation parents moved away from the stations because they would not accept the old system of work, attitudes and living conditions.[141] Committals of children increased with the growing number of people moving into the town reserves, where they lived in squalid temporary huts which were not 'suitable homes'. On the other hand, new and improved dormitories were built in 1968 and '69 to increase the capacity of the Catholic hostel, Saint Josephs, and the UAM hostel in Derby to provide for more children.[142]

The Pastoral Industry Award and the concept of employees' rights

The Pastoral Industry Award wages decision, made in 1967 but not applicable to the Kimberley until the 1969 work season, applied to Australian Workers Union members and not to full-blood natives employed as station hands unless they held a Certificate of Citizenship.[143] Women were relegated to the sphere of 'domestics' and were not considered relevant to the award hearings.[144] The Commonwealth and the Pastoralists and Graziers Association had successfully argued during the 1965 hearings that Aboriginal people—especially those in the Kimberley—were not socially or culturally ready for a strict wage system, and that the state and federal governments were not ready to replace the pastoral station welfare system with settlements and town-based services.[145] Kimberley pastoralists were given three years to prepare for the introduction of award wages and conditions and the possible mass movement of Aboriginal people away from stations. In the Kimberley the state and federal governments adopted a policy of 'wait and see', increasing town-based services and surveillance of children and old people, without due consideration for the consequences of their policies on the social fabric of station communities.

Throughout the considerable public debate over award wages for Aboriginal people from 1965 to '69, Native Welfare officers were advised by the commissioner not to get involved in wage issues but to inform Aboriginal people of their rights and 'discretely assist' them to go to a union representative.[146] Similar advice was given when the Derby district officer asked, in 1965, if the Native Welfare Department could enforce a minimum standard of food and living conditions which met health regulations, even if it couldn't enforce a minimum wage. The commissioner replied to all departmental officers that:

> [it has been] proved in principle and practice that it is better for the Department not to interfere. Even if there were regulations to cover these aspects they would be extremely difficult to enforce ... setting minimum standards is all that can be expected.[147]

The department nevertheless recognized some responsibility for informing and assisting Aboriginal people, as stated in the 1963 Native Welfare Act:

> to exercise such general supervision and care in respect of all matters affecting the interests and welfare of natives as the Minister in his discretion considers most fit to assist in their economic and social assimilation by the community of the state and to protect them against injustice, imposition and fraud.[148]

The Native Welfare Department's Instruction Manual stated that it was the department's duty to report any 'glaring case of non-compliance with industrial awards' but not to interfere.

In 1969 the Native Welfare Department, in conjunction with the AWU and the Department of Labour and Industry, printed and distributed thousands of copies of a pamphlet to explain the Pastoral Industry Award to Aboriginal workers.[149] Commissioner Gare was

in this
award
YOU
are known
as the

EMPLOYEE
and
the BOSS

is the
EMPLOYER

CHARGES FOR ACCOMMODATION AND KEEP

If you are employed without keep and the boss provides you with a house or accommodation you must look after it and he will discuss with you how much rent you must pay each week. This will be put in writing, the same as for people that live in houses in town.

If the boss sells you meat from the Station he cannot charge more than 5 cents a pound for it and it must be good meat, but if he buys meat from the store for you, then you must pay the store price.

If the Station has a store the boss must display a list of prices and you should check to see that you do not buy very expensive items when cheaper ones will do; particularly with clothing items.

If you are employed with keep, this includes "Good and sufficient living accommodation and Good and sufficient rations for yourself." Most of the goods you should be given are shown on the list, however, sometimes they are not always available and you have to go without a few things until more stores arrive. All food must be properly cooked and served, although this cannot always be in a dining room because you may be in a mustering camp a lot of the time.

HOUSING   **MEAT**   **STORES**   **CLOTHES**

THE BOSS CAN DEDUCT MONEY FROM YOUR PAY FOR ALL THESE THINGS

Pastoral Industry Award pamphlet: 'Pastoral Industry Award: What it Means to You and What You Should Do'.

Copyright Department of Native Welfare 1969

pessimistic about the award, the pamphlet and union enthusiasm to represent Aboriginal workers. When Father McKelson from La Grange mission wrote of the absence of union representatives on stations in the Kimberley and a 'grave undercurrent of unrest' among Aboriginal people, Gare replied that Native Welfare could not get closely involved:

> heavenly intervention would be of assistance in conduct-
> ing an educational program for Aborigines on the rights
> and responsibilities of union membership and the pro-
> visions of the Pastoral Industry Award.[150]

The pamphlet instructed Aboriginal people that they were now 'employees' and the Boss was now an 'employer'. It described their rights to holiday pay, sick pay and wages, and the Boss's right to deduct wages for food, clothing and housing. In 1970 Native Welfare reported that about 50 per cent of employers paid equal wages to Aboriginal people but very few Aboriginal people were unionized. A large proportion of Aboriginal workers in the Kimberley were on 'slow workers' allowance and not receiving award wages. Officers were reminded that it 'cannot be too forcibly empha-sised that this Department has no jurisdiction over the application of this award'.[151]

There was also confusion among welfare officers about Aboriginal people's eligibility for unemployment benefits. In 1968 Native Welfare officers registered their concern at the increasing trend for stations to lay off workers for the wet season, transport them to town to register for Social Security and then re-employ them for two or three months. Welfare policy at that time was for depart-mental officers not to give out rations, while Social Security guidelines continued to exclude seasonally employed people from receiving a benefit during the lay-off period.[152] Applicants resident on missions were also ineligible for unemployment benefits. Native Welfare officers were told that, after the application of the award in late 1968, no changes were to be made to eligibility criteria for unemployment benefits to provide support for Aboriginal people moving or being dismissed from their stations. Unemployment benefits were for 'normal' communities where people were able to work on a yearly basis. They were also informed that refusal to move to find work outside a tribal boundary or a mission would also preclude applicants from receiving benefits. The same applied if they were not formally employed (but not classed as unemployed either), or not likely to be employed. Departmental officers were informed that this policy 'precludes the payment of Unemployment Benefit or the issue of Departmental relief to persons while they are resident on pastoral properties'.[153]

In 1970, at the beginning of the mineral boom in the Pilbara, there were only four people placed on unemployment benefits out of 176 applicants from the entire north and north-west regions. In January 1971 the number had increased to sixty-six receiving benefits out of 248 registered as unemployed.[154]

The policy of 'qualified segregation', which had been in force from 1961, continued throughout the 1960s, with the result that facilities for Aboriginal people on the Derby reserves and in Derby township failed to keep up with the expanding population. Qualified segregation permitted Native Welfare to manage and control reserves without providing services that met a 'normal' suburban standard, as was demanded under the nationwide policy of assimilation. In 1967 there were fifty-nine state houses in the whole Kimberley region which were occupied by Aboriginal people who had shown that they had reached the 'requisite social standard' to occupy a house. In the 1969 wet season, the Derby reserves held 306 adults and an unknown number of children.[155] One hundred people shared thirteen 'dwellings' in the camping reserve. Although Native Welfare's stated policy was to house families with children, there were not enough houses.

Problems of control, hygiene and perceived laziness pre-occupied Native Welfare officers. In 1970 one officer was severely reprimanded for refusing to supervise a twice-weekly reserve clean-up which was initiated prior to a ministerial visit.[156] She wrote that it was an invasion of privacy to check that a woman with six children, in a one-roomed hut with no furniture, 'cleaned up'. The reserve clean-up went ahead to ensure that 'indiscriminate "camping" of un-employed ranks' was discouraged and to improve 'living conditions'.

Despite assisting people on the reserve to appoint ex-head stock-men as 'councillors' to manage community affairs, the senior men were seen to be:

> no more able than other members of the group except that they possess some authority amongst their people—The blind may lead the blind only as long as he is himself led.[157]

Native Welfare officers used their authority to control Aboriginal people so that conditions on the reserves did not continue to deteriorate. Car bodies were forcibly removed from the reserve, although the department sought Crown law advice in case they were infringing reserve dwellers' rights. The advice was that, although Section 23 of the Native Welfare Act stated that consent should be given by a 'Native' prior to the commissioner disposing of his or her property, the Derby reserve was also an institution under the Act. This meant that all residents were inmates and were liable to punishment or eviction if they refused to follow the directions of the reserve manager or Welfare officer.[158]

During the next wet season, 1970–71, 200 people came into Fitzroy Crossing for the wet season break after station managers refused to provide them with rations. They had no accommodation, work or food. Fitzroy Crossing had no facilities for visitors and a very small number of reserve huts for adults attached to or visiting children at the UAM hostel. Social Security conceded to benefits being paid to the workers who had been laid off. In an attempt to prevent further mass lay-offs for the wet season, the Native Welfare Department informed all station owners in 1971 that:

> Social Security (unemployment benefits) will be paid to Aborigines on stations to avoid the wet season layoffs which have accompanied the pastoral award for native workers. Benefits will allow them to stay on property and be ready and on hand for start of season.[159]

Unfortunately, all the paperwork was again the responsibility of station managers, as there were few patrols to the stations and a

Social Security office was not opened in the Kimberley until 1975. Very few managers were prepared to continue their welfare support role for a community of Aboriginal people on the 'dole' and other benefits, and under the potential scrutiny of Social Security. The cases of inquiries into management's abuse of the Social Security system in the mid-1960s had left deep resentment among leaseholders.

At the same time, Aboriginal people were trying to maintain social continuity with their children and old people. Women, in particular, stayed in towns in camping reserves. In 1966 there were 373 women recorded as employed in the pastoral industry in the west Kimberley region, dropping to 230 in 1970[160] and none in 1971. Once again, with a shift in station and government relations, women were written out of work in the pastoral industry. The total number of people employed by the pastoral industry in the Kimberley dropped accordingly from 1,003 in 1970 to 685 in 1971. At that time Aboriginal women were receiving from $2 to $5 per week plus keep as domestics on a pastoral station and from $10 to $20 in hotels.[161] Aboriginal men received $20 to $30 per week for the increasing amount of fencing work undertaken in the region, which was changing the nature of pastoral shepherding and stockwork.

'Fresh scandals from home'— social dislocation in the towns

Campbell Allenbrae came to the Derby reserve for the first time in about 1955.[162] He had been in the leprosarium from 1949 to '55 and was discharged to the reserve.[163] He and his wife, brother and family had dispersed from Kurunjie to Gibb River and Beverley Springs in 1957 after their first Boss, Scotty Salmond, died.[164] His wife was old Charcoal's daughter, and her family still worked at Beverley Springs, near her mother's country. Her own country, like her father's, was in the vicinity of Gibb River station on the Mount Hann reserve.[165] She had also been trained as a stockwoman by Scotty Salmond in the 1930s but was crippled in a horse fall while Allenbrae was in the leprosarium. They were reunited at the Derby reserve. From 1958 Allenbrae was moved from station to station, working for managers who had telegrammed Native Welfare in Derby for workers. He described each move as a move to various relatives and their country, not as a move for work.[166] Another move to Mount House brought Allenbrae close to some of his own relatives from Kurunjie who worked under Billy King as head stockman, but his wife asked to move back to her mother's family at Beverley Springs.

To get to Beverley Springs, Allenbrae accepted work with Native Welfare, plumbing a new section of housing in Derby so that he might buy a vehicle. From there he was sent out alone to the east Kimberley to break horses, and then on to the coast to Oobagooma station.[167] The station was owned by Drs Elphinstone, Holman and Davidson, with a fourth share owned by the manager, Doug Stewart. Allenbrae knew the doctors from the leprosarium. They asked him to work at Oobagooma for them and flew him out on the flying doctor plane from Halls Creek, arranging for his wife to follow.[168]

He came to the reserve again during a wet season in the late 1960s and found his classificatory brother-in-law, Jack Dann, also at the reserve. Dann's father, Morndingali, had been taken from the Isdell River region in the early days by police and had not returned to his country to meet up again with his brother Charcoal. Dann (who was Morndingali's and Weeda Munro's classificatory son) and his wife, Rita Laylay, had moved from Kimberley Downs in about 1967, after the school closed. They also had trouble with transport and arranged to leave the station after a race meeting in town, without confronting the manager. After the races they simply disappeared for a few days until the Boss's patience wore thin and he found other workers or left town for the station.

Allenbrae had not met his brother-in-law before, but had brother-in-law obligations to Dann:

> *Campbell Allenbrae:* We sitting down, at reserve. There was one house, long one. He got a kitchen front. Nother quarter camp, small house on that boab tree … Jacky didn't let me go. That his sister, you know, what I married. I couldn't go, we only just meet first time. I couldn't go anywhere. I was staying there. Right, this welfare, one old fella.
> *Question:* Pullen? Beharrell?

Allenbrae: Beharrell, that's it. He give me ration. And he said 'I got some one looking for boy. You want to go out to work on station, Christmas Creek?' …

Well I work there, finish. Well he [manager] said 'You got any other work? Some one looking for boy. You can go to next bloke.'[169]

Increasingly, during the 1960s, Allenbrae's wife found herself in the reserve surrounded by other women stockriders like Weeda Munro, Daisy Beharrell, Mabel King from Mount House and Maudie Lennard from Meda, and their children and old people. Native Welfare officers noted, however, that there was a process of 'urbanisation of women and children' occurring in Derby in 1961.[170] Able-bodied and skilled stockmen took temporary contract work at different stations and were being treated like independent units of labour by Native Welfare and by employers, but without access to unemployment benefits or award wages.[171] Allenbrae was torn between being 'humbugged' by Welfare to work anywhere across the Kimberley, and leaving his wife and relatives on the reserve:

I told my wife, I gonna go back to station. Wife was thinking all the time, he didn't want to go back. He thinking some one give me job somewhere, he lost me. He on his own.

He think hard all the time 'What I gonna do?'

'Alright I look around what I gonna do.'

My wife was make me sorry.[172]

Weeda Munro had come to the Derby reserve in 1966 and applied for child endowment to look after her foster children from Kimberley Downs station. When the station school closed in 1966, Welfare placed the three children in the Derby Hostel and on a nearby station as a trainee domestic and stockman.[173] Weeda Munro lived at the Derby reserve in a ten-foot-square iron hut with a cement floor. She gained access to one child for a short period but was also asked to pay more than she had received in endowment money for the child's clothing bill at the hostel. Morndingali was offered work as a contract musterer at Mount Hart station in 1967 where Weeda Munro was born; she soon followed. She, like Harry Howendon, Maggie Gudaworla and Susie Umungul, were examples of a pattern that emerged for old people to return to their country if the opportunity arose.

Other older stockmen and women along the Gibb River Road took up paid work in the 1960s at Native Welfare's insistence. Morndingali described work as a plumber's assistant on the reserve and for Main Roads during his 'holiday break' from the stations. Without unemployment benefits or housing and the Native Welfare Department trying to rid their office of rationees, he had little choice about accepting work, despite the social costs of leaving families at the Derby reserve. In 1972 Morndingali was sent by Native Welfare to Kuri Bay pearl farm with thirty-six other Aboriginal men. He worked for a $50 wage, which was higher than the pastoral award of $32, and in conditions he had not experienced before: 'three cooked meals per day, beds, sheets, a beer ration and regular breaks from work'.[174] The Native Welfare officer reported that although pearl farm employees were not paid award wages, which would not satisfy 'the ardent trade unionist', pay was better than at the stations. Nevertheless, Aboriginal workers from Derby decided to leave the pearl farm and return to the reserve because of 'news of fresh scandals from home', which reflected serious social dislocations in the towns. The communities on reserves were refugees who had begun to focus on trying to get back to their country and away from the problems of being crowded together on land which they did not own.[175] This was trivialized by Native Welfare officers, who described the news as a disruptive and worrying influence on the men at Kuri. In response to the men refusing to return to Kuri Bay, the welfare officer in Derby was instructed that he could not direct Aboriginal people to work anywhere if they did not agree to go.[176] This signalled a significant shift away from coercion, or the threat of it. However, because the men had left their place of work through choice, they were ineligible once again for unemployment benefits.

Evelyn Bidd was another stockwoman from the north Kimberley whose mother was cook for the Isdell police camp on the frontier. She was a trained stockrider but stayed in camp from the 1950s to look after a growing number of children. She tried to keep working with her husband during the early 1970s, but, despite at first taking work wherever it was offered—at Mount Hart, Mount House and then Mount Barnett—she and her husband came to town in 1973 to be near their children: 'Only for kids we come to town.'[177] She was adamant that she and her husband wanted to stay on the stations, regardless of pay and conditions, but they could not risk leaving the children in dormitories and hostels.

Weeda Munro applied for an old age pension in 1971, but her Native Welfare file listed her as only forty-seven years old.[178] She was also refused a disability pension on the grounds that she was fit and able to work. She felt she was too old to work and she wanted to live in town near her foster children who were at the hostels. Her husband, Morndingali, was also spending more and more time in town, between employment contracts arranged by Welfare. For Weeda, however, and many other Aboriginal people, her age was not recognized by authorities because there was no accurate documentation created by either Welfare or station owners that could help her get an age pension. In 1952 she and Morndingali were listed as fifty-two and forty-eight years old respectively.[179] In 1962 they were listed as fifty-four and forty-eight years old. Each assessment reduced Weeda Munro's age and placed her outside Social Security benefits. Morndingali was granted a Citizenship Certificate in 1969, which allowed him to claim award wages if he joined the Australian Workers Union, and to drink alcohol.[180] Weeda Munro was granted a Citizenship Certificate in 1970. Like so many Aboriginal people, she had no idea of her age and relied on either station managers or Welfare to help her apply for Social Security benefits. They in turn consulted their files or other pastoralists or missionaries who might help with information. A confusing range of birth dates, names and sometimes family members reflects the department's own confusion and the process of Aboriginal people's entry into the welfare system.

The social and economic conditions of the pastoral industry changed dramatically on most stations in the 1960s, and managers and owners who held large leases near towns opted for a fencing program and temporary, unencumbered labourers who worked for a maximum four months of the year. The financial costs of providing adequate support for a dispossessed population of Aboriginal people were never realistically addressed or contemplated by governments. Despite being granted a special exemption from the application of the Pastoral Industry Award so that government services in towns and settlements could be provided for previously segregated station communities, the West Australian government adopted a wait-and-see policy, and failed to provide adequate or appropriate staff, housing or support for Aboriginal people moving away from stations. Issues of control dominated state and federal welfare policies throughout the period from 1903 to 1972, while fear of what might happen next undermined Aboriginal people's relations with non-Aboriginal people.

The Aboriginal Affairs Planning Authority Act of 1972, which replaced the 1963 Native Welfare Act, lifted legal restrictions on employment, movements out of the state, and access to alcohol and to the full range of Social Security benefits for all Aboriginal people—even the older full-blood station people like Weeda Munro and her contemporaries. The Act catered for formalized consultation with Aboriginal representatives and leaders, reflecting the shift in government policy from assimilation to community development.[181] Clauses in the 1963 Act Regulations, which had made it legal for anyone acting in the protective interests of Aboriginal people and on behalf of the Native Welfare Department to have access to Aboriginal people at all times, were barely altered.[182] The new 1972 Act narrowed the access provisions for all AAPA staff:

> in the exercise of his powers and duties, ... to enter at any time into or upon any land or premises, ship or vessel, where natives are in any circumstances or where he has reasonable cause to suspect that natives may be found.[183]

This clause gave expression to the continuing 'protective' and invasive relationship between all 'gardias' and Aboriginal people in the Kimberley, whether managers, Welfare, police or health, and in turn underpinned the whispered warnings that could be heard on my approaching the reserve in 1989 to begin this research: 'Gardia coming, Gardia coming!'[184]

CONCLUSION

THE early days in the Kimberley ranges were a time of dramatic change for Indigenous people, when Aboriginal men were gaoled in a systematic and intensive campaign against them by pastoralists and police. To survive the rise of the station system, Aboriginal men and women aligned themselves and their families with white men through unspoken and unequal contracts of ownership and protection. In the 1920s a second wave of violent confrontation occurred, when Aboriginal men were identified by police and stockmen as 'trouble makers' for threatening to compete with them over women, children or resources. Intra-group conflicts, which could be mistaken for pre-contact violence, peaked in the late 1920s and early 1930s in the northern region, in response to women's captivity in white stockmen's camps and the changing social dynamics of the region. The station 'mob' was a complex entity formed over a period of ten to twenty years around a white Boss and his Aboriginal assistants. The pastoral system encouraged Aboriginal people to live on or near their own land, and supported a range of cultural continuities, but it forced changes in social relations which many people could not resolve.

In untangling the complex processes of small group and individual negotiations that characterized the early days of contact in the north and central Kimberley from 1903 to 1936, there were not many pastoralist winners of the classic kind. These 'pioneers' from 'over the range' lived on the geographic and social fringes of Australian society, occupying but not 'civilizing' the region. They were not wealthy; they lived mostly with Aboriginal people including their own Aboriginal children.

Government policies not only failed to protect Aboriginal people, but also provided the legislative context for a climate of fear to emerge in the early days. In the northern and central ranges region of the Kimberley, the leprosy epidemic and isolation campaign at the Derby Leprosarium extended the process of forced dispersals of bush people, which had begun in 1903, into the 1940s and early '50s.

State and federal Aboriginal affairs practices and policies quarantined pastoral station groups from education, housing, rationing and other provisions which may have interfered with Aboriginal people's role on the stations or threatened the Bosses' patronage and the fragile peace they had established by 1940. Policy developments from 1934 to '48 also failed to recognize Aboriginal people's investment in the pastoral system or active engagement with pastoral work, reducing their role on stations to group dependency on managers. When the first cash payment to Kimberley Aboriginal pastoral workers was negotiated in 1950, it resulted in a wage-fixing system with a 'pocket money' allowance and no minimum employer obligations for station managers or owners. It was part of a system of 'benevolent supervision' of Kimberley Aboriginal people which resulted in welfare authorities negotiating with pastoral interests over who was responsible for rationing Aboriginal people. Their role as workers was diminished and their attachment to land began to be replaced by a welfare system that was based on a cash handout without roots in a place or a country.

Government programs for removing children to hostels and missions and the introduction of age pensions, both in the early 1960s, precipitated the movement of Aboriginal people towards towns and reserves where Welfare and Social Security became the means of social and economic survival. Child endowment and age pensions were the first of the allowances given to Aboriginal people. Unemployment benefits were not provided until the 1970s. Some Kimberley Aboriginal people experienced sudden and forceful eviction from stations, while others were able to reorient their relationship towards towns and a welfare economy more gradually. Welfare and the restructuring of the pastoral industry contributed to these changes. By the 1960s the station system in the north and central Kimberley was an anachronism, although the isolation of the far north continued to allow the small communities there, like Mount Elizabeth and Gibb River stations, to make the transition to welfare without challenging the Bosses.

Like the process of coming onto the stations, women's roles were again significant in the move off the stations and the dismantling of pastoral paternalism. In the 1960s women were categorized as non-workers, and obligations to their children were challenged and diminished by government policies and practices. As the old people and children became a focus for welfare intervention, moving to town reserves was a strategic response by communities to manage the new interventionist practices of the state and the lack of support on the stations.

Aboriginal people used early days narratives to explain what happened in their lives, in order to fashion their collective and individual histories in the pastoral industry and their relationship with white people after the early days and in the 1960s and '70s. Through oral testimony, the period sometimes invoked by employers, writers or Aboriginal people themselves as the golden era of settled working relationships on the stations in the 1940s and '50s emerged as an era of fragile relationships and gradual recovery in a context of authoritarian control. The extent and significance of the violence, uncertainty and recency of the early days were not recognized by incoming welfare authorities or the wider Australian public who looked north to a strange and remote frontier. Instead, policy-makers continually focused on keeping Aboriginal people quiet and contained. As late as the early 1970s, Native Welfare patrol officers were recording whether Aboriginal workers showed respect to their white employers. This fear of an Aboriginal anger and disrespect echoed through the frontier, the period of hard work and 'settled' relations, and on the reserves in the 1960s, producing a significant 'continuity' of practice through times of blood, sweat and welfare.

EPILOGUE

AFTER 1973 the Commonwealth and state governments increased their spending on Aboriginal affairs but did not keep up with demographic shifts which began in 1960 and swelled to resemble a refugee movement in the 1970s and '80s. The lack of housing and other facilities in towns and settlements in the 1970s magnified the ill effects of moving off the stations. In the early 1980s, when Aboriginal people walked off five east Kimberley stations, they refused to leave their country and move to town but camped nearby at a soak. Their actions were described in newspapers and by Aboriginal people as 'mass walk-outs' in protest against the living conditions on these stations. Television and newspaper coverage presented southern readers and viewers with a shocking contrast to their own urban expectations: humpies, car bodies and no water. Issues of exploitation and workers' and civil rights, which had been raised in the late 1940s as a result of the Pilbara Aboriginal pastoral workers' strike, were now being openly discussed in the Kimberley forty years later.

From 1975 to '79 the Kimberley cattle industry went into 'crisis' following the collapse of the European beef market and price falls for hamburger beef to the United States. This caused a sharp downturn in activities on all stations which did not lift until the late 1980s, when live cattle markets were opened to Kimberley producers who could meet the standards required for that product.[1] Muster activity on the leases declined to caretaking with minimal turn-off and maintenance. Cattle herd numbers reached their highest levels ever at 812,000 head, but resident Indigenous and European populations on the leases plummeted as Aboriginal people sought refuge in towns, where they could survive on Social Security and be near their children and old people. A transitional housing scheme in Derby's 'back streets' began to service some of the 1,175 Aboriginal people in 1977, while the old reserves each held an average of 150 people.[2] Over 300 people lived at Mowanjum reserve, and Broome's reserves held almost 900. At Fitzroy Crossing 500 people were registered as living in town camps and Junjuwa reserve, with 700 people remaining on stations; in the Halls Creek region, 620 people lived on stations and 2,809 were officially resident in towns or reserves.[3] By 1977 only a minority—15.6 per cent—of the Kimberley Aboriginal population were still resident on pastoral stations.

In the late 1970s Commonwealth and state governments began to support Aboriginal people's movement away from towns and back to the land they had occupied as station or mission communities. Small excisions were also made on some stations to allow communities to remain on their land without having to move to towns. Looma Aboriginal Community, for instance, was formed in 1974, fifteen kilometres from Camballin, where Australian Land and Cattle Company staff were housed. In 1978 the Emanuel company agreed to small excisions on Christmas Creek and Gogo for Indigenous communities to live on their properties, with community infrastructure provided by government grants and non-workers receiving Social Security benefits. Pantijen, near the old Munja settlement, was also transferred in 1975 to Aboriginal owners living at the Mowanjum reserve in Derby.

Owners of under-resourced stations took the opportunity to sell out using the safety net offered by the Commonwealth's Aboriginal Land Fund.[4] Tick eradication programs in the 1980s, soil erosion and cattle prices added to pastoral industry woes. A small

Gibb River Station, 1995: Aboriginal stockmen mustering on their station. Copyright M.A. Jebb

Workers' cottages at Mount Elizabeth Station, 1992.
Copyright M.A. Jebb

Phillip Krunmurra in his cottage at Gibb River Station, 1992. Copyright M.A. Jebb

The old pensioner huts at Mount Elizabeth, 1992.
Copyright M.A. Jebb

---

northern station earned as little as $4,500 from cattle in 1984, while a large station made $117,000. The Kimberley Pastoral Industry Inquiry in 1985 estimated that only 17 per cent of Kimberley workers could be employed in the industry at its seasonal peak. It added that a large pastoral station could provide employment for fifteen to twenty men, but the support needed for sixty or more women and children who would form Aboriginal communities on stations had not been seriously considered. The stations over the ranges were finally recognized as especially marginal:

> the original optimism held for the North Kimberley could not now be justified ... Even operating costs may not be covered unless these are kept to an absolute minimum, as in the case of small family-operated concerns ... The Department of Agriculture believes the only feasible options for this area are ... release of parts of the area to

> family operators who are prepared to exist at near-subsistence levels ... The result of thirty years of optimism, backed by significant research effort and plenty of true pioneering endeavour, is one of complete disappointment if one uses economic criteria to measure success.[5]

Gibb River station was transferred in 1987 to traditional Aboriginal owners, and Mount Barnett in 1988. In 1994 Tableland was bought back by the government for Jack Jowan and Mick Jowalji's group, which had never made the transition to town. In 1993, 28 per cent of Kimberley pastoral stations were Aboriginal owned, but many leases had been further alienated from Aboriginal people.[6] For instance, in 1971 AMAX Bauxite Kimberley consortium bought two northern pastoral leases, Doongan and Mitchell, to 'help open up' the north and support proposed mining activities on the Mitchell Plateau between Gibb River station and Kalumburu on the far north coast. The company planned a $100m township where 3,500 residents would 'command uninterrupted views' of 'bright blue waters dotted with islands' off the rugged northern coast.[7] The project did not develop beyond the initial temporary camp and exploration stage, despite a special Act of Parliament to enable it to proceed. Oobagooma and Kimbolton stations on the west coast were transferred to the Australian Armed Services in the mid-1970s, with sections re-gazetted as freehold in the process. Windjana National Park was excised from Kimberley Downs in 1975. Drysdale River National Park was created from the northern leases and parts of old Mount Hann reserve in 1978. Mount Hart and Beverley Springs stations were placed under the Department of Conservation and Land Management control in the early 1990s. Indigenous owners of the northern ranges now had new Bosses to deal with, whose interests were now conservation and ecotourism rather than pastoralism.

Morndingali and Weeda Munro were finally 'retired' to the Derby reserve in 1975 after fifty years of pastoral work. They moved into pensioner housing in 1976 with workers from Meda, Kimberley Downs, Mount House and Napier Downs. Later that year Morndingali spoke to the State Minister for Community Welfare,

Changes in government policies brought politicians to the Derby reserve to consult with Aboriginal elders. From Native Welfare Annual Report 1975, copyright Department of Native Welfare

Norman Baxter, and the Federal Minister, Senator Cavanagh, as an 'Aboriginal elder' rather than a 'trouble maker'. However, while respect from government and white people for Indigenous cultural knowledge increased in this period, Morndingali, his wife and their respective families were not able to return to live in their country. The social and economic basis of pastoral paternalism had disintegrated. They did, however, have a vehicle and a small excision on Napier Downs, where young men and women went each dry season to get out of town and conduct ceremonies.

The Boss and Missus remained at Mount Elizabeth, negotiating the changing expectations of the 'mob' who were now an 'Aboriginal community' but without separate title to their living area. There, the divisive topics of independence, rights and exploitation by station owners and managers, which had helped fracture relations between managers and communities on the majority of stations in the Kimberley, were still being worked out in the 1990s. But

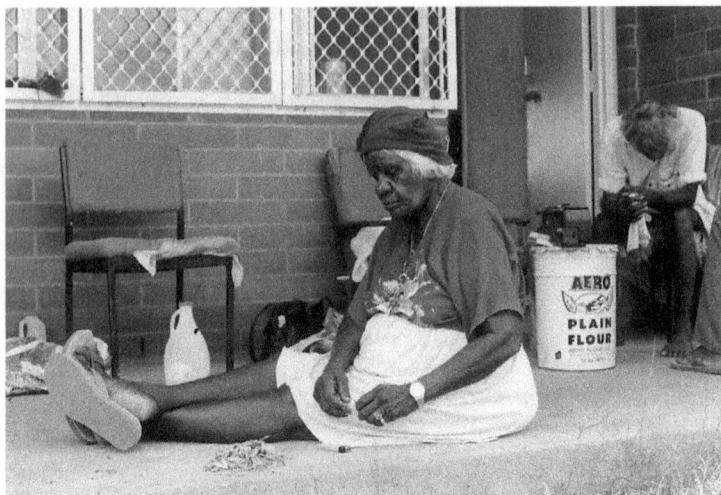

Weeda Munro (Nyanulla) on the front verandah of their
new pensioner house on the Derby reserve, making 'ashes'
for mixing with tobacco to chew; Billy Munro
(Morndingali) sitting behind, 1991. Copyright M.A. Jebb

rather than being directed at work, wages and the pastoral industry, these issues related now to tourism and cultural knowledge. Next door, at Gibb River and Mount Barnett stations, white employees and Aboriginal communities continued to struggle with the demise of the pastoral industry, an 'invasion' of tourists, and fears and expectations which were forged during the very recent frontier and honed by years of segregation.

NOTES

Introduction: The region, the project and the people

1   Cattle Station Industry (Northern Territory) Award 1951, CAR case no. 830-f 1965, evidence Kerr, 10 August 1965. See especially pp. 527, 576, 1144 and 1173.

2   ibid., p. 527.

3   A.P. Elkin, 'Reaction and Interaction: A Food Gathering People and European Settlement in Australia', *American Anthropologist*, no. 53, 1951, pp. 164–86.

4   AD62/1965, *Australian*, 9 March 1966.

5   AD62/1965. Whole file provides press clipping coverage.

6   Ann Curthoys and Clive Moore, 'Working for the White People: An Historiographic Essay on Aboriginal and Torres Strait Islander Labour', in Ann McGrath and Kay Saunders (eds), *Aboriginal Workers*, special edition *Labour History*, no. 69, November 1995, pp. 1–29.

7   G.C. Bolton, 'A survey of the Kimberley pastoral industry from 1885 to the present', MA thesis, University of Western Australia, 1953; Ann McGrath, *Born in the Cattle: Aborigines in Cattle Country*, Sydney, Allen and Unwin, 1987; R.M. and C.H. Berndt, *End of an Era: Aboriginal Labour in the Northern Territory*, Canberra, Australian Institute of Aboriginal Studies, 1987; Tim Rowse, *White Power White Flour: From Rations to Citizenship in Central Australia*, Cambridge, Cambridge University Press, 1998.

8   Rowse mentions this in his analysis of the Durack stations in the east Kimberley. Tim Rowse, 'Tolerance, Fortitude and Patience: Frontier Pasts to Live With?', *Meanjin*, no. 1, 1988, pp. 21–9.

9   Leigh Edmonds, *The Vital Link: A History of Main Roads of Western Australia, 1926–1996*, Nedlands, University of Western Australia Press, 1997, pp. 169–72.

10   'Summary of Permanent Counter Station Data', Registration Site no. 9120 Gibb River Road, Main Roads Department Statistics. 27,589 campers travelled from Derby to the Napier and King Leopold Ranges in 1996.

11   'Frank Lacy Diaries 1923–1970', private collection, Mount Elizabeth, 18 December 1969.

12   Kim Ackerman, "The Renascence of Aboriginal Law in the Kimberleys', in R.M. and C. Berndt (eds), *Aborigines of the West: Their Past and Present*, Nedlands, University of Western Australia Press, 1979, pp. 234–42.

13   Ion L. Idriess: *Over the Range: Sunshine and Shadows in the Kimberley*, Sydney, Angus and Robertson, 1937; *Outlaws of the Leopolds*, Sydney, Angus and Robertson, 1952.

14   Ackerman, 'The Renascence of Aboriginal Law in the Kimberleys', pp. 234–42; Ian Crawford, *The Art of the Wandjina: Aboriginal Cave*

Paintings in Kimberley, Western Australia, London, Oxford University Press, 1968.

15 David Mowaljarlai and Jutta Malnic, *Yorro Yorro: Spirit of the Kimberley*, Broome, Magabala Press, 1993; Alan Rumsay, 'Aspects of Native Title and Social Identity in the Kimberleys and Beyond', *Australian Aboriginal Studies*, no. 1, 1996, pp. 2–10.

16 Patrick Sullivan, 'Colonising the Kimberley: An Ethnohistory', paper submitted to the Northern Australian Research Unit, Canberra, 1995.

17 Morndi Munro (with Mary Anne Jebb as editor) *Emerarra: A Man of Merarra*, Broome, Magabala Books, 1996. He was the last full grammar speaker of Unggumi and spoke Worrora, Nyigina, Bunuba and Ngarinyin.

18 Morndi Munro, David Mowaljarlai, Tape 38, 10 March 1991.

19 NB1, pp. 21–5. Notes taken at Meda station with Willie and Rosalind Lennard, 18 May 1991.

20 Kim Ackerman, Nicholas Green, Patrick Sullivan and Barbara Dobson all produced anthropological reports with Gudaworla's assistance.

21 'Summary of Permanent Counter Station Data'.

22 Pat Lacy, interview notes, NB7, p. 38, 12 August 1991.

23 Eugene Genovese, *Roll Jordan Roll: The World the Slaves Made*, New York, Pantheon Books, 1972, p. 79. This point is more explicitly made in a book by the manager of Louisa Downs station, west of Fitzroy Crossing, which stated that it 'seemed we actually worked for them and were employed as managers to look after their well-being'. L.A. Schubert, *Kimberley Dreaming: The Century of Freddy Cox*, Words Work, 1992, p. 67.

24 'Gardia' means 'whitefella' or 'outsider'.

25 William McGregor, 'Jack Bohemia and the Banjo Affair', *Meridean*, 1988, pp. 46–58.

26 Nicholas Thomas, *Entangled Objects: Exchange, Material Culture, and Colonialism in the Pacific*, Cambridge (MA), Harvard University Press, 1991, p. 35.

27 Some tapes provide a sound bite of community life as well as samples of the difficulties of oral history recording in isolated Aboriginal communities. See further for standard interviewing techniques: Ronda Jamieson, *How to Interview for Family History: For Young, Old and In Between*, Perth, Library Board of Western Australia, n.d.; Ronald J. Grele (ed.), *Envelopes of Sound: The Art of Oral History*, Chicago, Precedent Publishing, 2nd edition 1985.

28 Mixing narrative storytelling and interview is also discussed by Cruikshank in her work with Yukon native women. Julie Cruikshank et al., *Life Lived Like a Story*, Lincoln, University of Nebraska Press, 1990, pp. 1–20.

29 Deborah Bird Rose, 'Remembrance', *Aboriginal History*, vol. 13, part 2, 1989, pp. 135–48.

30   Native Welfare Department Northern District General (NDG), WAS46, acc 3412. File on each station created 1948.

31   J.R.B. Love, *Stone-Age Bushmen of Today: Life and Adventure Among a Tribe of Savages in North-Western Australia*, London, Blackie, 1936; A.P. Elkin, 'Rock Paintings of North-West Australia', *Oceania*, vol. 1, no. 3, 1930, pp. 257–79; Elkin, 'Social Organisation in the Kimberley Division, North-Western Australia', *Oceania*, vol. 2, no. 3, 1931, pp. 296–333; Elkin, 'Studies in Australian Totemism', *Oceania*, vol. 4, no. 2, 1933, pp. 113–31; P. Kaberry, *Aboriginal Women: Sacred and Profane*, London, Routledge, 1939; H.H. Coate and A.P. Elkin, *Ngarinyin–English Dictionary*, Oceania Linguistic Monographs no. 16, 1974; Arthur Capell and H.H.G. Coate, *Comparative Studies in Northern Kimberley Languages*, Research School of Pacific Studies, Australian National University, 1984. Kaberry worked from Moola Bulla.

32   Ion L. Idriess: *Over the Range*, 1937; *One Wet Season*, 1949; *Man Tracks: The Mounted Police in Australia's Wilds*, 1935; *The Nor'Westers*, 1954; *Tracks of Destiny*, 1961. All published in Sydney by Angus and Robertson.

33   Idriess, *Over the Range*, p. 36.

34   Beverly Eley, *Ion Idriess*, Sydney, ETT, 1995, p. 298.

35   ibid., p. 244.

36   Deborah Bird Rose, 'Nature and Gender in Outback Australia', *History and Anthropology*, vol. 5, no. 3–4, 1992, p. 419; Nicholas Thomas, *Colonialism's Culture: Anthropology, Travel and Government*, Carlton, Melbourne University Press, 1994, p. 15.

37   Thomas, *Colonialism's Culture*, p. 35.

38   Eley, *Ion Idriess*, p. 227.

39   Idriess, *One Wet Season*, p. 135.

40   ibid., p. 19.

41   ibid., pp. 62–3.

42   ibid., p. 117.

43   Rose, 'Nature and Gender in Outback Australia'.

Chapter 1: Battle for the New Country, 1903–1914

1   ARAD1906, Henry Prinsep CPA, MS AADL.

2   PD1588 special item, Isdell Police Station Journals 1903–1908, BL.

3   PD4987/1914, US to Col Sec, 7 August 1903.

4   Cathie Clement, 'Australia's north-west: a study of exploration, land policy and land acquisition, 1644–1844', PhD thesis, Murdoch University, 1991, p.43.

5   ibid., p.45.

6   Cathie Clement, 'European settlement and industries, 1863–1886', unpublished MS.

7   Alex. Forrest, 'Nor-West Exploration, Journal of Expedition from DeGrey to Port Darwin', *WAVP* vol. 3, 1880, p. 21.

8   G.C. Bolton, 'A survey of the Kimberley pastoral industry from 1885 to the present', MA thesis, University of Western Australia, 1953.

9   Andrew Gill, 'Aborigines, Settlers and Police', *Studies in WA History*, vol. 1, 1978, pp. 1–28; Neville Green, *The Forrest River Massacres*, Fremantle, Fremantle Arts Centre Press, 1995, pp. 33–52; Howard Pedersen and Banjo Woorunmurra, *Jandamarra and the Bunuba Resistance*, Broome, Magabala Books, 1995.

10   F.S. Hann, diary transcript, acc. 4308A item HS26, vol. f, 9 September 1897 – 5 September 1898.

11   ibid., p. 17. On 31 December 1897 Hann experienced 'loneliness and poverty' in Nullagine, 'out of food, refused credit'. Isdell's support indebted Hann to him: 'How am I going to pay him back ... He is a real white man.'

12   Frank Hann, 'Explorations in Western Australia', read to Royal Society of Queensland, 7 April 1900, typescript BL, p. 11.

13   ibid., p. 10.

14   ibid., p. 16.

15   Hann, diary transcript, acc. 4308A item HS26, vol. f, 12 June 1898.

16   ibid., vol. f, 17 June 1898.

17   ibid., vol. a, 17 June 1895 – 17 July 1896; see entries for 14 July and 4 November 1895 and 7 and 27 March 1896. Hann was accused of stealing Aboriginal women from their husbands: Dryblower, 'Don't Use Force. Just Flog 'em', *Kalgoorlie Sun*, 19 July 1908.

18   Hann, diary transcript, acc. 4308A item HS26, vol. f, 10–11 June 1898.

19   ibid., 25 June 1898.

20   Hann, 'Explorations', p. 9.

21   Bolton, 'A survey of the Kimberley pastoral industry', p. 122.

22   F.S. Brockman, 'Report on Exploration of the North-West Kimberley 1901', *WAVP* vol. 2, 1902. Brockman's diaries for the north Kimberley exploration were missing from Battye Library. See also J.S. Battye (ed.), *The History of the North West of Australia*, Perth, V.K. Jones, 1915, pp. 53–4.

23   Geoffrey Bolton, 'The Kimberley Pastoral Industry', *University Studies in History and Economics*, vol. 11, no. 2, July 1954, pp. 1–53, p. 23.

24   Peter Biskup, *Not Slaves Not Citizens: The Aboriginal Problem in Western Australia, 1898–1954*, St Lucia, University of Queensland Press, 1973, p. 99.

25   Gill, 'Aborigines, Settlers and Police', p. 21.

26   ibid., pp. 20–1.

27   W. Roth, 'Report of the Royal Commission on the Condition of the Natives', *WAVP* vol. 5, 1905; P. Troy, 'Report on Investigations into Isdell Police Post to the Colonial Secretary', WAS1243 cons 481, BL, 30 May 1905.

28   DOLA4610/1902, vol. 01 acc. 541, 20 April 1902. Copy of *GG*, 9 May 1902.

29 Annual Report Police Department, *WAVP* vol. 15, 1902.

30 ibid., no. 17, 1903–04.

31 PD4987/1914, Isdell Police Station, US to Col Sec, 7 August 1903.

32 Roth, 'Royal Commission', p. 15; PD4987/1914, Isdell Police Station.

33 Roth, 'Royal Commission'; Troy, 'Report on Investigations into Isdell Police Post'.

34 Ion L. Idriess, *Over the Range: Sunshine and Shadows in the Kimberley*, Sydney, Angus and Robertson, 1937.

35 Daisy Angajit, in Morndi Munro (Mary Anne Jebb ed.), *Emerarra: A Man of Merarra*, Broome, Magabala Books, 1996, ch. 5.

36 Jack Dale, pers. comm.; Banjo Woorunmurra, NB4, p. 30; Mabel King, NB9, p. 71.

37 Maggie Gudaworla, NB11B, p. 32.

38 Roth, 'Royal Commission', p. 89.

39 The role and craft of black trackers in the Kimberley is described in Jack Bohemia and William McGregor, *Nyabayarri: Kimberley Tracker*, Canberra, Australian Institute of Aboriginal Studies Press, 1995.

40 W.V. Fitzgerald, 'Report of the Trigonometrical Survey Expedition of the North Kimberley', *WAVP* vol. 19, 1907, p. 887.

41 ibid., p. 21.

42 AD940/1908, Travelling Inspector James Isdell, diary, August–September 1908.

43 Troy, 'Report on Investigations into Isdell Police Post'.

44 Many of the names on the police lists were recognizable as familiar places in the northern landscape. Some people alive in the 1980s carried the same name as those in the police files. Others are not recognizable. Police developed their own orthography and relied on informants to name prisoners. It is doubtful that they invented names and more likely that they simply made mistakes in naming and orthography.

45 PD690/1906, PC Napier to CPA, 29 December 1905.

46 CSO2973/1905, Wace to US, 10 September 1905; see also Wace's evidence to the Roth Royal Commission, CSO822/1908.

47 Troy, 'Report on Investigations into Isdell Police Post', Nimbandi's statement, 9 February 1905.

48 ibid.

49 AD95/18, Moola Bulla original file, folios 80–2.

50 PD1588 special item, op. cit., PC Wilson, 26 May 1905.

51 ibid., PC Forbes, 10 November 1905.

52 ibid., PC Forbes, 10 March 1906.

53 ibid., PC Forbes, June 1906.

54 ibid., PC Napier, November 1906. David Mowaljarlai and Wunambal men living at Mowanjum and Kalumburu retold stories of a large-scale massacre on the Charnley River. This incident is likely to be part of that tradition.

55   ibid., PC Forbes, October 1907.

56   ibid., PC Napier, January 1905.

57   Fitzgerald, 'Report of the Trigonometrical Survey Expedition', p. 35.

58   Barry Morris, 'Frontier Colonialism as a Culture of Terror', in B. Attwood
       and J. Arnold (eds), *Power, Knowledge and Aborigines*, special edition
       Journal of Australian Studies, 1992, pp. 72– 87.

59   PD1588 special item, PC Wilson, May 1904.

60   ibid., PC Wilson, 26 August 1905.

61   Troy, 'Report on Investigations into Isdell Police Post', PC Forbes'
       statement.

62   ibid., Nimbandi's statement, 9 February 1905. See also Wace's scathing
       comments in note form on the statement that locking women's hands to
       their neck chains 'could have some advantages'.

63   Biskup, *Not Slaves Not Citizens*, p. 60; Roth, 'Royal Commission'.

64   Roth, 'Royal Commission', p. 15.

65   ibid., pp. 14–15.

66   Gill, 'Aborigines, Settlers and Police', pp. 20–1.

67   Troy, 'Report on Investigations into Isdell Police Post', Nimbandi's
       statement, 9 February 1905.

68   H.H. Coate, *A Grammar of Ngarinyin: Western Australia*, Canberra, Aust-
       ralian Institute of Aboriginal Studies (Linguistic Series no. 10), 1970,
       p. 388.

69   Ion L. Idriess, *Nor'Westers*, Sydney, Angus and Robertson, 1954, pp. 1–26;
       PD7551/1925; Munro, *Emerarra*.

70   Troy, 'Report on Investigations into Isdell Police Post'.

71   ibid., statement by A.E. Love, 20 May 1905.

72   Troy, 'Report on Investigations into Isdell Police Post'.

73   Daisy Angajit in Munro, *Emerarra*, ch. 5.

74   PD1588 special item, PC Napier, 8 September 1905.

75   Fitzgerald, 'Report of the Trigonometrical Survey Expedition'.

76   ibid., p. 35.

77   ibid., p. 54.

78   ibid., p. 24.

79   PD1588 special item, PC Forbes, 11 August 1905.

80   Idriess, *Over the Range*, p. 69.

81   PD1588 special item, PC Forbes, 16 June 1905.

82   Weeda Munro, NB12, pp. 15–16.

83   PD1588 special item, PC Forbes, 6 July 1905.

84   Fitzgerald, 'Report of the Trigonometrical Survey Expedition', p. 24.

85   PD1588 special item, PC Forbes, file note, November 1905.

86   Morndi Munro, NB2, pp. 33–4; Billy King, interview notes, 20 May 1992;
       Jack Jowan, Mick Jowalji, Tape 35, 5 March 1991; Wallace Midmee, NB9,
       pp. 71–2.

87   Kaberry recorded similar information about leadership and the same term, Ngowerung. See Phyllis Kaberry, *Aboriginal Woman: Sacred and Profane*, London, Routledge, 1939, pp. 178–9.

88   King, interview notes; Jack Jowan, Mick Jowalji, Tapes 35 and 36, 5 March 1991; Midmee, NB9; Campbell Allenbrae, Tape 12, 2 April 1996; Scotty Martin for Mount Elizabeth, NB6, pp. 56–7; Maggie Ghi, Susie Umungul, Rosie Mamangulya, with occasional translations and assistance by Jilki Edwards, Tapes 43 and 44, 17 May 1992.

89   PD1588 special item, PC Napier, 14 September 1905.

90   King, interview notes.

91   Evelyn Bidd, NB8, p. 95.

92   PD1588 special item, PC Napier, 24 September 1905.

93   ibid., PC Napier, September 1905.

94   ibid., PC Napier, September 1905.

95   ibid., PC Forbes, file note, 26 November 1905.

96   ibid., PC Napier, 19 December 1905.

97   ibid., PC Napier, 3 February 1906.

98   Morndi Munro, transcript of Balmaningarra story. Undated confidential transcript held by Gulingi Nganga Aboriginal Corporation, Derby.

99   NB11B, p. 23, and Weeda Munro genealogy. Coombool travelled with Constable Fletcher to Mount House and then to Mount Barnett as the bullock team driver with stores for the Isdell police station. Morndingali said Coombool was a Nyigina-speaking person who married a Ngarinyin woman. Morndi Munro, Jeffrey Jamieson, Freddy Marker, Tape 22, 31 July 1990.

100   PD1588 special item, PC Napier, 2 March 1906.

101   PD2412/1906, McQueen RM, Derby, 14 April 1906.

102   PD1588 special item, PC Forbes, 4–15 June 1906.

103   ibid., PC Napier, 24 June 1906.

104   *Hedland Advocate*, 4 August 1906.

105   ARAD1906, MS AADL.

106   David Mowaljarlai, Lawrie Uttamorrah and Wilfred Gunak from Mowanjum reserve told a story of a Charnley River massacre, but it was not for the purposes of this research, and I was not able to record it on tape or in note form.

107   Maggie Ghi, Phillip Krunmurra, Tape 29, 6 June 1995.

108   Harry Howendon, Tape 41, 15 April 1992.

109   PD1588 special item: PC Wilson, 24 September 1905; PC Robinson, 9 October 1906; PC Forbes, 4 May 1907.

110   Mary Anne Jebb, 'Isolating the "problem": Aborigines and venereal disease in Western Australia 1908–1924', BA Hons thesis, Murdoch University, 1987.

111   ARAD1907, MS AADL.

112   Prof. Herman Klaatz, 'Some Notes on Scientific Travel Amongst the Black Population of Tropical Australia 1904–1905, 1906', *Australian Association for the Advancement of Science*, vol. 11, 1907, pp. 577–83. Klaatz's report to the Australian Scientific Conference and his allegations against northern white men and police were reproduced in London newspapers in 1907 (AD599/1907, Secretary of State Elgin to Governor Bedford, 26 June 1907). The northern press reported that Klaatz had said that 'police were paid by those interested to get as many blackfellows as possible, and they captured young women, ostensibly for purposes of evidence, but the real purpose everyone knew'. *Hedland Advocate*, 12 January 1907.

113   *Hedland Advocate*, 12 August 1908, p. 3.

114   *Hedland Advocate*, 25 January 1908, p. 3.

115   Dryblower, 'Don't Use Force. Just Flog 'em'. The verse was directed at Frank Hann. The *Kalgoorlie Sun* verse, 11 April 1909, is entitled 'Frank Hann-Guish' and describes tales of beheading corpses for a museum bounty.

116   Aborigines Act 1905, no. 14 of 1905.

117   AD940/1908, James Isdell, diary, August–September 1908.

118   ibid.

119   ARAD1909, MS AADL.

120   AD95/1918, Isdell to CPA, 31 July 1909.

121   ibid., Col Sec to CPA, 1909.

122   AD359/1910, Isdell to CPA, 19 May 1910.

123   PD1289/1910, PC Forbes jrnl, 16–24 December 1909.

124   ibid., 17 December 1909.

125   PD1290/1910, PC Forbes jrnl, 10–17 January 1910.

126   *Hedland Advocate*, 26 February 1910, p. 5.

127   PD738/1924, Derby Police Letterbook 1910–1913, 28 March 1910.

128   *Hedland Advocate*, 13 August 1910.

129   ibid., 5 August 1911; AD359/1910, Isdell to CPA, 19 May 1910.

130   ARAD1909, MS AADL.

131   ARAD1910, MS AADL.

132   ARAD1912, MS AADL.

133   AD1782/1914, PC Forbes to CPA, 30 June 1914.

134   Biskup, *Not Slaves Not Citizens*, pp. 99–100.

135   M.A. Jebb, 'The Lock Hospitals Experiment: Europeans, Aborigines and Venereal Disease', in R. Reece and T. Stannage (eds), *European–Aboriginal Relations in Western Australian History*, Studies in West Australian History, vol. 8, 1984, pp. 68–86; see also PD738/1924, Derby Police Letterbook 1910–1913, for transport of people from Isdell police post to Derby Hospital for transfer to the Lock Hospitals.

136   The police camp north of Broome continued.

137   PD4987/1914, Sub-Inspector Houlahan to CoP, 21 September 1914. Spong reportedly walked into the bush in 1916 and was found dead by his Aboriginal assistants: *Hedland Advocate*, 30 September 1909.

138   PD4987/1914, Sub-Inspector Houlahan to CoP, 21 September 1914.

139   AD1782/1914, PC Forbes to CPA, 30 June 1914. 'Venereal disease' would have included yaws and leprosy.

140   PD4987/1914, Sub-Inspector Houlahan to CoP, 24 July 1916.

141   Bolton, 'The Kimberley Pastoral Industry', p. 31.

142   Biskup, *Not Slaves Not Citizens*, p. 32.

Chapter 2: 'Stone blind in their need of Christ': the early days Bosses, 1915–1930

1   PD1193/1916, Murder of George Aukland; PD7410/1915, Aukland Murder; PD7871/1921, Murder of Harry Annear.

2   PD8466/1920, Murder of Bass and Smith; Ulbrick and Renland (Russian Jack), reported in *Norwest Echo*, 6 November and 10 December 1920.

3   Fred Russ, interview notes, NB9, pp. 38–48, 3 June 1992.

4   ARAD1919–21, MS AADL.

5   Neville Green, *The Forrest River Massacres*, Fremantle, Fremantle Arts Centre Press, 1995.

6   AD237/1935, Reid to CPA, 31 May 1935.

7   AD195/1929, Extract *United Aborigines Mission Messenger*, 1 September 1935.

8   This is not the late Jack Carey of Halls Creek. Research into probate, births, deaths and marriages has shown that Alexander Campbell Carey, known as 'Jack', was a pearler and Kimberley station owner who died in 1913 and left everything to his brothers, Stewart, Roy and Harry Edward (Henry). Harry bought four pastoral leases in the Kimberley in 1913 on his and his younger brother's behalf (probate file 278/13, vol. 20, no. 3436). He joined the Light Horse and was injured at Gallipoli. It is uncertain whether Jack Carey is one of the brothers.

9   DOLA, acc. 1384 an 3/9, 3944/1920

10   Morndi Munro, Campbell Allenbrae, Tape 11, 1 April 1990; Peter Lacy, interview notes, NB8, pp. 67–8, May 1992; Evelyn Bidd, interview notes, NB9, pp. 55–62, 5 June 1992; Jack Jowan, Mick Jowalji, Tapes 35 and 36, 5 March 1991; Mabel King, Wallace Midmee, interview notes, NB9, pp. 67–85, 8 June 1992; Russ, interview notes; Jack Dale, interview notes, NB9, pp. 96–8, 10 June 1992; Barbara Midmee, Tape 23, 1 August 1990; Harry Howendon, Tape 40, 4 April 1992; Phillip Krunmurra, Maggie Ghi, Tape 60, 29 June 1995.

11   Morndi Munro, Tape 11, 1 April 1990.

12   Munro, Allenbrae, Tape 11; Derby Leprosarium Admission Books, 1935–1981, unpublished, West Kimberley Public Health Department.

13   Aborigines Act no. 14 of 1905, clauses 12 and 13.

14   Peter Biskup, *Not Slaves Not Citizens: The Aboriginal Problem in Western Australia 1898–1954*, St Lucia, University of Queensland Press, 1973, pp. 77–8.

15   ibid., pp. 76–7.

16   ibid., p. 77.

17   See especially ARAD1916–19, MS AADL.

18   Travelling Inspectors: G.S. Olivey 1899–1902, C.G. Fartiere 1907–08, J. Isdell 1907–09, J. Olivey 1916 (Pilbara), E.C. Mitchell 1924–29, C.L. McBeath 1939, L. O'Neill 1941, 1945–48.

19   Aborigines Act no. 14 of 1905, clause 22.

20   ibid., clause 25.

21   AD940/1908, Travelling Inspector James Isdell, diary, August–September 1908.

22   Queensland Charlie may have accompanied Hann to the Kimberley in 1898.

23   AD940/1908, Travelling Inspector James Isdell, diary August–September 1908, 16 September 1908.

24   W. V. Fyfe, *Report of the Royal Commission Appointed to Inquire into and Report upon the Financial and Economic Position of the Pastoral Industry in the Leasehold Areas in Western Australia*, Perth, West Australian Government Print, 1940, p. 158.

25   ARAD1913–19, MS AADL; see also Geoffrey Bolton and M.A. Jebb, 'On the Stations 1905 to 1965', in S. Yu (ed.), In Our Own Country, MS, Kimberley Land Council Library.

26   ARAD1930, MS AADL.

27   ARAD1916,1919, MS AADL. The informal system of selling leases with Aboriginal labour was referred to by the ex-magistrate of Cossack and Halls Creek, Lambden Owen, as a 'jumble-up' of bizarre values and attitudes characteristic of the northern districts around the turn of the century. He wrote that pastoralists asked three questions before buying a pastoral lease: 'How many acres? How many miles of fencing? How many niggers? The niggers always went as part of the stock. If there were no niggers or not enough, the sale was off or the price was dropped.' W. Lambden Owen, *Cossack Gold: The Chronicles of an Early Goldfields Warden*, Sydney, Angus and Robertson, 1933, p. 149.

28   Maggie Gudaworla, Tape 62, 10 November 1995.

29   G.C. Bolton, 'A survey of the Kimberley pastoral industry from 1885 to the present', MA thesis, University of Western Australia, 1953, p. 23.

30   PD1903/15, Skinner to CPA, 10 March 1916.

31   PD1903/15.

32   Gudaworla, Tape 62.

33   Ion Idriess, *Over the Range: Sunshine and Shadows in the Kimberley*, Sydney, Angus and Robertson, 1937, pp. 53–6. Backsen is called Peter Bextram by Idriess.

34   PD1903/15, CoP, file notes, 19 July 1916.

35   PD1193/1916, PC Jury jrnl, 12 December 1915 – 2 February 1916;
        PD1197/1916, PC Napier jrnl, 15 December 1915 – 29 January 1916.

36   Gudaworla, Tape 62.

37   *Nor'West Echo*, 15 April 1916.

38   See Morndi Munro (Mary Anne Jebb ed.), *Emerarra: A Man of Merarra*,
        Broome, Magabala Books, 1996, pp. 54–6, for the Limestone Spring
        massacre.

39   PD70/1916, PC Jury jrnl, 2 November 1915.

40   PD1193/1916, PC Jury jrnl, 23 December 1915.

41   PD1197/1916, PC Napier jrnl, 29 December 1915.

42   PD1903/1915, Skinner to CPA, 10 March 1916.

43   PD7410/1915.

44   PD1903/1915.

45   AD64/1920.

46   AD248/1932, Extract *Longreach Leader*, 24 March 1932, and A.O. Neville,
        Correspondence and file notes.

47   PD1903/1915, Skinner to CPA, 10 March 1916.

48   ibid., Skinner to CPA, Note on Skinner's Letter by Resident Magistrate
        Elliot, 28 June 1916. See also Green, *The Forrest River Massacres*.

49   ibid., PC Napier, Statement, 6 July 1916.

50   ibid., Drewry to CoP, 19 July 1916.

51   ibid., Drewry to CoP, 26 August 1916.

52   ibid., Skinner to CPA, 21 July 1918.

53   ibid., Resident Magistrate Elliot to CPA, 22 August 1919.

54   ibid., Skinner to CPA, 10 March 1916.

55   This is Landarr, clan land which, according to Jack Dale, was her country.

56   PD1903/1915, PC Jury, 4 August 1916.

57   ibid., Skinner to CPA, 10 March 1916.

58   ibid.

59   ibid.

60   PD1531/1917. See also *Nor'West Echo*, 30 June 1917, 4 July 1917 and
        19 January 1918.

61   PD1531/1917, Detective Inspector Mann, Report into the Murder of Bert
        Bowers, n.d. (approximately October 1917).

62   ibid., Frank Gardiner, Statement to Police, 1917.

63   ibid., Frank Gardiner, Statement to Police, 1917.

64   ibid., Jack Dale, Statement to Police, 1917.

65   ibid., Constable Capstick, Statement to Police.

66   ibid., Coomie, Statement to Police.

67   ibid., Detective Inspector Mann, Report into the Murder of Bert Bowers.

68   PD1588 special item, Isdell Police Station Journals 1903–1908, BL,
        PC Forbes, 16 June 1905.

69   Idriess, *Over the Range*, p. 94.

70   PD2665/1927.

71   PD1531/1917, Detective Inspector Mann, Report into the Murder of Bert Bowers.

72   PD1531/1917, Frank Gardiner, Statement to Police.

73   PF770/1947, Sadler to CPA, 30 March 1938.

74   Biskup, *Not Slaves Not Citizens*, p. 97.

75   Jack Wilson shot Scotty Salmond in the throat over the custody of a young half-caste boy, Daisy Angajit's brother (PD1950/1928). Wilson moved to an abandoned station hut with the boy to avoid police (AD298/1930). The issue was resolved in 1935 when the boy was handed to UAM missionaries and removed to Sunday Island mission.

76   AD440/1925.

77   ibid.; Jack Dale, Tape 45, 29 May 1992.

78   ibid.; Billy King, interview notes, 20 May 1992.

79   AD440/1925, PC Walter to CPA, 25 August 1928.

80   ibid., CPA to Police, 11 September 1928; see also PD1345/1927, Fitzroy Patrols vol. 4.

81   Dale, Tape 45; King, interview notes.

82   Ion Idriess, *One Wet Season*, Sydney, Angus and Robertson, 1949; Dale, Tape 45; King, Interview notes.

83   AD417/1925.

84   AD267/1926, Mitchell to CPA, 1 March 1925.

85   ibid., US to CPA, 20 November 1930.

86   Morndi Munro, NB2, p. 7.

87   Maggie Gudaworla, NB11B, p. 21.

88   Morndi Munro, Tape 38, 8 March 1991; Munro, *Emerarra*, pp. 3–5.

89   Munro, *Emerarra*; see PD1168/1916, PD243/1920, PD310/1920, PD2156/1920 for deaths by spearing which were investigated by police.

Chapter 3: 'Taught to kill': soldier settlers and the station 'family'

1   Peter Biskup, *Not Slaves Not Citizens: The Aboriginal Problem in Western Australia, 1898–1954*, St Lucia, University of Queensland Press, 1973, p. 103.

2   *Nor'West Echo*, 6 March 1920.

3   William R. Easton, *Report on the North Kimberley District of Western Australia*, Perth, West Australian Government Print, 1922, p. 6.

4   ibid., p. 50.

5   ibid., p. 52.

6   Pat Jacobs, *Mister Neville*, Fremantle, Fremantle Arts Centre Press, 1990, p. 100.

7   DOLA, acc. 1384 an 3/9, 3944/1920, Russ F.A.

8   DOLA, acc. 1632 an 3/2, 1478/39, Kurunjie Station.

9   Death Register, Derby Courthouse; A.B. Sadler, DOLA lease print-out.

10   Wallace Midmee, interview notes, NB9, p. 74, 8 June 1992.

11   ibid., p. 76, 8 June 1992.

12   ARAD1920, MS AADL.

13   Wallace Midmee and Mabel King, interview notes, NB9, p. 77, 8 June 1992.

14   Mick Jowalji, Tape 35, 5 March 1991.

15   ibid.

16   Barbara Midmee, Tape 23, 1 August 1990.

17   F.S. Hann, diary transcript, acc. 4308A item HS26, vol. f, 9 September 1897 – 5 September 1898, 27 April 1898.

18   Jack Jowan, Tapes 35 and 36, 5 March 1991. This may be Cundra, or Rosie, who joined Connaughton in 1918 and in 1925 was reported by Scotty Sadler as being held without her consent (AD57/1925).

19   Jack Jowan and Mick Jowalji, Tape 36, 5 March 1991.

20   Jowalji, Tape 35.

21   Jowan, Tape 36.

22   Maggie Gudaworla named George as her uncle and the first stockboy for Gibb River. He also worked at Mount Elizabeth and Mount Barnett.

23   Jowan, Tape 35.

24   *Countryman*, 7 May 1970, 'Westraliania' section, pp. 22–3.

25   *Northern Times*, 17 January 1957.

26   *Countryman*, pp. 22–3.

27   PD8466/1920, Murder of Bass and Smith. See also *Nor'West Echo*, 4 September, 2 October and 18 December 1920.

28   District Medical Officer, 14 February 1925, reproduced in W.S. Davidson, *Havens of Refuge: A History of Leprosy in Western Australia*, Nedlands, University of Western Australia Press, 1978, p. 165.

29   Biskup, *Not Slaves Not Citizens*, p. 104.

30   Neville Green, *The Forrest River Massacres*, Fremantle, Fremantle Arts Centre Press, 1995.

31   Rosie Mamangulya, Maggie Ghi, Susie Umungul, Tapes 43 and 44, 17 May 1992.

32   Campbell Allenbrae, Tape 11B, 2 April 1990, notations on draft from Allenbrae.

33   *Countryman*, pp. 22–3.

34   PD7871/1921.

35   Green, *The Forrest River Massacres*, p. 76.

36   Campbell Allenbrae, Tape 11, 1 April 1990; Maggie Ghi   and Jilki Edwards, NB7, pp. 48–52.

37   Green, *The Forrest River Massacres*, pp. 75–7.

38   PD7871/1922, Coomie, Statement to Police, 13 September 1922.

39   Allenbrae, Tape 11.

40   AD1044/1943; AD457/1944.

41   Maggie Gudaworla, NB11B, p. 21.

42   Maggie Gudaworla, Tape 62, 10 November 1995. Jack Dale also told this story but with detailed recollections of the methods used to call up a rainbow, along which they all escaped. These were not recorded on tape.

43   Gudaworla, Tape 62; King, NB9, pp. 67–85.

44   Gudaworla, Tape 62.

45   Gudaworla, NB11B, p. 33.

46   *Nor'West Echo*, 30 August 1924.

47   PD1346/1927, Inspector Douglas to CoP, 3 August 1925.

48   PD1345/1927, vol. 4, Fitzroy Police Patrols.

49   Morndi Munro, Campbell Allenbrae, Tape 11A, 1 April 1990; Peter Lacy, interview notes, NB8, pp. 67–8, May 1992; Evelyn Bidd, interview notes, NB9, pp. 55–62, 5 June 1992; Jack Jowan and Mick Jowalji, Tapes 35 and 36, 5 March 1991; Midmee and King, interview notes, pp. 67–85, 8 June 1992; Fred Russ, interview notes, NB9, pp. 38–48, 3 June 1992; Jack Dale, interview notes, NB9, pp. 96–8; Midmee, Tape 23; Harry Howendon, Tape 40, 4 April 1992; Phillip Krunmurra and Maggie Ghi, Tape 60, 29 June 1995.

50   PF770/1947.

51   David Mowaljarlai, *Yorro Yorro: Spirit of the Kimberley*, Broome, Magabala Books, 1993, p. 154.

52   King, interview notes; Russ, interview notes, pp. 46–7; Lacy, interview notes, p. 66.

53   Campbell Allenbrae and Morndi Munro, Tape 11, 1 April 1990.

54   Harry Howendon, Tapes 40 and 41, 4 April 1992.

55   Howendon, Tape 40. Howendon drove the first flock of sheep across the ranges from Noonkanbah to Sale River in 1935.

56   Ion L. Idriess, *Over the Range: Sunshine and Shadows in the Kimberley*, Sydney, Angus and Robertson, 1937, pp. 200–21.

57   Mamangulya, Ghi, Umungul, Tapes 43 and 44.

58   'Promised husband' refers to arranged marriages: see Phyllis Kaberry, *Aboriginal Woman: Sacred and Profane*, London, Routledge, 1939, for descriptions of 'marriage' relationships in the central and northern ranges.

59   Maggie Ghi, Tape 61, 30 June 1995.

60   Ghi and Umungul, Tape 44.

61   Ghi, Tape 61.

62   Ghi, Tape 44.

63   Maggie Ghi, Susie Umungul and Rosie Mamangulya (Tapes 43 and 44) talked of 'marrying' as single incidents as well as long-term relationships.

64   Jack Campbell travelled with Alexander Forrest's exploration party in 1879; however, I am not sure if this is the same man or perhaps a son.

65   Ghi, Tape 61.

66   Ghi, Tape 44.

67   Jowalji, Tape 36.

68   ibid.

69   Patrick Sullivan, 'Colonising the Kimberley: an ethnohistory', paper submitted to the Northern Australian Research Unit, Canberra, 1995.

70   Allenbrae and Munro, Tape 11.

71   Idriess, *Over the Range*, pp. 30–1.

72   Weeda Munro, NB13, 23 January 1996.

73   PD1168/1916, Circular to all Police in Isolated Regions, 30 March 1916.

74   See PD1168/1916, PD243/1920, PD310/1920, PD2156/1920, PD323/1921, AD480/1025, PD5345/1925.

75   PD5345/1925.

76   This is Howendon's sister.

77   PD5345/1925, PC Bandy jrnl, September 1925.

78   Barbara Midmee, who was born and 'grown up' at Tableland station with Scotty Sadler, retold a story of white men at Gibb River and Mount Barnett disposing of an Aboriginal man and claiming his wife. He was lured to the station for work and then clubbed with a hammer and his body burned. I have not been able to untangle the names of the people involved, although, according to Barbara Midmee's narrative, Fred Russ knew of this event (Midmee, Tape 23).

79   Krunmurra and Ghi, Tape 60.

80   Maisie McKenzie, *The Road to Mowanjum*, Sydney, Angus and Robertson, 1969, pp. 128–9.

81   Bidd, interview notes.

82   *Nor'West Echo*, 10 April 1926.

83   Idriess wrote that a rumour went through the camp that Murphy had been killed somewhere near the coast. This fits with the oral account that Mobby, known to white people as Murphy, was going to be punished (Idriess, *Over the Range*, p. 45).

84   NDG36/55.

85   Russ, interview notes, pp. 46–7.

86   *Nor'West Echo*, 5 and 6 November 1926.

87   ARAD1927, MS AADL.

88   AD412/1927, CPA Strictly Confidential Minute to US, 29 July 1927.

89   Jacobs, *Mister Neville*, pp. 157, 168 and 169.

90   AD195/1929, Mount Barnett Mission.

91   ibid., Neville to Minister, 20 November 1933.

92   AD237/1935.

93   ibid., Salmond to Reid, 23 April 1935.

94   ibid., Reid to CPA, 2 June 1935.

95   AD195/1929, Mount Barnett Mission.

96   ARAD1930–1935, MS AADL; PD6975/1932, PC O'Neill.

97   Russ, interview notes.

98   *Countryman*, pp. 22–3.

99 Maggie Gudaworla, Tape 66, 15 November 1995. Maisie McKenzie also wrote of Reverend Love's pleasure when immediately following the wars of 1926 and 1927, senior men decided not to kill after the death of a clan member (McKenzie, *The Road to Mowanjum*, pp. 128–9).

Chapter 4: The big round-up: the leprosy campaign and its aftermath

1 W.S. Davidson, *Havens of Refuge: A History of Leprosy in Western Australia*, Nedlands, University of Western Australia Press, 1978, pp. 104–5.

2 M.A. Jebb, 'Surviving Bungarun', in S. Yu (ed.), In Our Own Country, MS, Kimberley Land Council Library.

3 Derby Leprosarium Admission Books, 1935–1981, unpublished, West Kimberley Public Health Department; Davidson, *Havens of Refuge*, p. 109, records about 400 people speaking Ngarinyin, Wunambal and Worrora admitted into the leprosarium from 1929 to '75. I have included people from Oobagooma, Mount House, Tableland and Glenroy who were recorded as Nyigina, Unggumi or Bunuba.

4 Ion Idriess, *Over the Range: Sunshine and Shadows in the Kimberley*, Sydney, Angus and Robertson, 1937; see particularly chapters 9 and 12.

5 Jack Dale, interview notes, NB9, pp. 96–9.

6 *WA*, 21 June 1934, p. 17; Davidson, *Havens of Refuge*, p. 45.

7 Davidson, *Havens of Refuge*, pp. 52–3.

8 ibid., pp. 124–7; Derby Leprosarium Admission Books, 1935–1981.

9 ARAD1936, Kunmunya Report, MS AADL.

10 ARAD1937, MS AADL.

11 Morndi Munro, Tape 14, 5 April 1990.

12 ARAD1937, Davis Report, MS AADL.

13 ibid.

14 PD7005/1935, vol. 7, Wyndham Police Patrols.

15 ARAD1938, MS AADL.

16 PD2200/1938, PC Cooper jrnl, 15 May – 31 July 1938.

17 PD5321/1940, O'Neill to Tredgold, 10 August 1934.

18 PD2200/1938, PC Cooper jrnl.

19 Petri, Frobenius, Fox, Lommell, Schultz and Gerta Kleist from Germany and Pentony from the University of Western Australia. Capell was also in the region undertaking linguistic research. ARAD1938, MS AADL.

20 Morndi Munro, Tape 22, 31 July 1990.

21 PD2200/1938, PC Cooper jrnl.

22 Davidson, *Havens of Refuge*, p. 71.

23 ARAD1938, MS AADL.

24 Davidson, *Havens of Refuge*, p. 72.

25 PD2200/1938, PC Rowe jrnl, 3 June – 5 September 1939.

26 Derby Leprosarium Admission Books, 1935–1981.

27 ARAD1939, MS AADL.

28 ibid.

29   Maisie McKenzie, *The Road to Mowanjum*, Sydney, Angus and Robertson, 1969, p. 158.

30   ARAD1939, MS AADL.

31   ARAD1939, Kunmunya Report, MS AADL.

32   Derby Leprosarium Admission Books, 1935–1981.

33   AD195/1929, H. Reid to CNA, 1 September 1940.

34   AD195/1929, PC Mason jrnl, 9 August 1940.

35   The Abbot of New Norcia made representations to the commissioner in 1934 to stop the UAM from entering the north as it would cause 'antagonisms' with their mission further north. Neville refused to provide subsidies or support the central ranges mission. AD195/1929, Abbot of New Norcia Catalan Superior of the Drysdale River Mission to Minister, 21 September 1934.

36   Tom Street, 'In the Interior', *The United Aborigines Messenger*, 1 October 1933.

37   Howard Coate, NB1, p. 42, 24 May 1989. See H.H. Coate and A.P. Elkin, *Ngarinyin–English Dictionary*, Oceania Linguistic Monographs, no. 16, 1974; H.H. Coate, *A Grammar of Ngarinyin: Western Australia*, Canberra, Australian Institute of Aboriginal Studies, Linguistic Series no. 10, 1970. See further William McGregor (ed.), *Studies in Kimberley Languages: In Honour of Howard Coate*, Munchen/Newcastle, Lincom/Europa, 1996.

38   AD195/1929, Reid to CNA, 1 September 1940, and Police Reports on file.

39   Tom Street, 'Mr Street on the Track', *United Aborigines Messenger*, 1 September 1935.

40   Fred Russ, interview notes, NB9, pp. 38–48.

41   AD195/1929.

42   ARAD1940, MS AADL.

43   Davidson, *Havens of Refuge*, p. 88.

44   I was unable to tape this story. Mabel King, NB1, 19 May 1989, p. 21.

45   Derby Leprosarium Admission Books, 1935–1981.

46   Neville Green, 'Government Stations', in S. Yu (ed), In Our Own Country, MS Kimberley Land Council Library.

47   Munro, Tape 22.

48   AD268/1945, O'Neill Report to CNA, 22 September 1945.

49   Phillip Krunmurra, Tape 60, 29 June 1995.

50   AD1032/1943, Brigadier Hoade Western Command to CPA, 29 March 1943.

51   AD1032/1943, CPA to Brigadier Hoade, 10 April 1943.

52   PD3906/1944; AD268/1945.

53   PD3906/1944, PC Box Report to Inspector Reid, January 1945.

54   ibid.

55   ibid.

56   AD268/1945, PC Carr to Inspector O'Neill, 12 February 1945.

57   PD3906/1944, O'Neill to CNA, 12 November 1944.

58   AD268/1945, O'Neill to CNA, 22 September 1945.

59   ibid.

60   PD3906/1944, PC Box Report to Inspector Reid, January 1945.

61   AD1117/1945, CNA Bray to Inspector O'Neill, 9 October 1945.

62   AD268/1945, CNA Bray to Oldmeadow, Forrest River Mission, 2 November 1945.

63   'Vermin Control in Western Australia', MS, Agwest Library, Derby.

64   PD2691/1927 vol. 5, Derby Patrols, for instance. But most patrol files from 1915 have accounts of killing dogs in camps.

65   PF770/1947, Sadler to CPA, January 1944.

66   PD408/1936 has correspondence surrounding the killing of a white man at Cape Voltaire. Aboriginal men are accused, and one is convicted and jailed, but letters from police and a man called 'Nick the Greek' show that the white man was probably killed by other beachcombers for his 150 dog scalps. He had exchanged the scalps with local Aboriginal people, but relations with them soured when he demanded a woman from the leading man and then shot camp dogs for the scalps. See DOLA1384/1921 on trading scalps for rations at Munja government station.

67   Jilki Edwards, Tape 55, 4 April 1992.

68   James Kelly, interviewed by Michael Adams, 1982–83, transcript BL, OH540, p. 301. Kelly recalled receiving £2 per scalp.

69   ARAD1947, MS AADL.

70   Theresa Lacy, interview notes, NB12a, 17 December 1994; Scotty Martin, interview notes, NB8, pp. 52–6.

71   Davidson, *Havens of Refuge*, p. 178.

72   H.D. Moseley, 'Report of the Royal Commission upon Matters in Relation to the Condition and Treatment of Aborigines', *WAVP* vol. 1, 1935.

73   Davidson, *Havens of Refuge*, p. 45.

74   ARAD1933, MS AADL.

75   Moseley, 'Report of the Royal Commission', p. 10.

76   ibid., p. 4.

77   ibid.

78   ibid., p. 5.

79   ibid. These comments mirrored those in the 1933 debate about the 1898 Land Act Amendments to reduce Aboriginal people's access to water-holes and fenced paddocks on pastoral leases (see *WAPD*: 13 November 1934, pp. 1276–9; 29 November 1934, pp. 1672–6; 20 December 1934, pp. 2244–8). The Minister for Lands warned parliamentarians that Aboriginal people would be forced to leave their country and move to reserves and ration depots in order to survive (*WAPD*, 20 December 1934, p. 2246). Aside from the financial burden to the state, he argued that it was 'not fair' to restrict Aboriginal people's access to water, a right which they had held since 'time immemorial'. Parliamentarians with

pastoral interests stated that the amendments would not be applied in practice except in the case of 'outlaws' (*WAPD*, 29 November 1934, p. 1675).

80   Anna Haebich, *'For Their Own Good': Aborigines and Government in the Southwest of Western Australia, 1900–1940*, Nedlands, University of Western Australia Press, 1988, p. 277.

81   Peter Biskup, *Not Slaves Not Citizens: The Aboriginal Problem in Western Australia, 1898–1954*, St Lucia, University of Queensland Press, 1973, p. 105.

82   *WA*, 16 June 1934, p. 19; *WA*, 21 June 1934, p. 17; PD6875/1932, PC O'Neill, June 1934.

83   Moseley, 'Report of the Royal Commission', p. 5. Mount Hann Reserve no. 20120, gazetted 1929, extended to 1,520,000 acres. Degazetted 1954. See also DOLA01931/1934: Mount Lyell Reserve no. 8215, 1,000,000 acres near coast and Admiralty Gulf.

84   Moseley, 'Report of the Royal Commission', p. 24. American ethnographers S.D. Porteus and R. Withington visited all coastal communities near Broome in 1934, taking photographs and motion pictures. Ralph Piddington and his wife were at La Grange. Professor Clark from the USA and Livingstone from Sydney applied to go to Sunday Island but stayed in Broome, and Kaberry undertook research in 1934.

85   Phyllis Kaberry, 'Do They Justify Their Existence?', *WA*, 9 December 1935.

86   Phyllis M. Kaberry, *Aboriginal Woman: Sacred and Profane*, London, Routledge, 1939.

87   Biskup, *Not Slaves Not Citizens*, pp. 105–6.

88   Kaberry, 'Do They Justify Their Existence?'

89   ARAD1934, MS AADL.

90   ARAD1920, 1921, 1930 to 1937, MS AADL.

91   Frank Stevens, 'Parliamentary attitudes to Aboriginal affairs, 1936–1965: Intervention by the state', unpublished MS, 1968, AADL; Biskup, *Not Slaves Not Citizens*, pp. 171–3.

92   Native Administration Act, 1905–1936, Regulations, section 106Q, *GG*, 8 September 1939; AD307/1937, circular no. 186, 26 August 1939; Peter Biskup, *Not Slaves Not Citizens*, p. 172.

93   Native Administration Act, 1905–1936, Regulations, sections 86a, 86b, 87, *GG*, 8 September 1939; AD307/1937, circular no. 186, 26 August 1939.

94   Biskup, *Not Slaves Not Citizens*, pp. 177–8; A.P. Elkin, 'Aboriginal–European Relations', in R.M. and C. Berndt (eds), *Aborigines of the West: Their Past and Present*, Nedlands, University of Western Australia Press, 1979, pp. 285–323, p. 313.

95   Moseley 'Report of the Royal Commission', p. 5.

96   ibid.

97   AD237/1935, Reid to CPA, 31 May 1935.

98   W.V. Fyfe, *Report of the Royal Commission Appointed to Inquire into and Report upon the Financial and Economic Position of the Pastoral Industry in the Leasehold Areas in Western Australia*, Perth, West Australian Government Print, 1940, p. 162.

99   A.O. Neville, *Australia's Coloured Minority: Its Place in the Community*, Sydney, Currowong Publishing, 1947, pp. 193–4.

100   ibid., p. 198.

101   ARAD1939, MS AADL.

102   Fyfe, *Report of the Royal Commission*, p. 608.

103   ibid., p. 87.

104   ibid., p. 160: Biskup notes that Moola Bulla was particularly irksome to pastoralists, as it was central to pastoral stations and a working station itself. By 1940 Moola Bulla had approximately 200 men, women and children, with forty-eight children attending school. Biskup, *Not Slaves Not Citizens*, pp. 139, 200.

105   Fyfe, *Report of the Royal Commission*, p. 156.

106   ibid., p. 157.

107   ibid., p. 88.

108   ibid., p. 630.

109   ibid., p. 161.

110   'Proceedings of Commonwealth and State Aboriginal Welfare Authorities Meetings', 1937, AADL.

111   ARAD1938, MS AADL.

112   ARAD1944/1945, MS AADL.

113   ibid.

114   Moseley, 'Report of the Royal Commission', p. 4.

115   'Proceedings of Commonwealth and State Aboriginal Welfare Authorities Meetings', p. 33.

116   ibid., p. 604.

117   ibid., p. 596.

118   ibid., p. 604.

119   ibid.; see also NWD749/1938, Louisa Downs, for an example of this.

120   'Pastoral Industry Award: Variations', CAR vol. 53, 1944, pp. 212–57.

121   ibid.

Chapter 5: The struggle for authority: settling down

1   Morndi Munro, Tape 21, 24 April 1990.

2   Ann McGrath, *Born in the Cattle: Aborigines in Cattle Country*, Sydney, Allen and Unwin, 1987.

3   PD408/1936, Alleged Murder of Whiteman.

4   PD2665/1927.

5   Robert Hall, *The Black Diggers: Aborigines and Torres Strait Islanders in the Second World War*, Sydney, Allen and Unwin, 1989, p. 172.

6   Morndi Munro (Mary Anne Jebb ed.), *Emerarra: A Man of Merarra*, Broome, Magabala Books, 1996, p. 125.
7   In 1938 and 1942 the managers from Louisa Downs and Christmas Creek asked for government support to remove people who would not or could not work, but they were also refused. AD308/1930 Christmas Creek; AD749/1948 Louisa Downs; 249/31 Margaret River Station.
8   ARAD1941, MS AADL.
9   ARAD1939, MS AADL.
10   Phyllis Kaberry, 'Do They Justify Their Existence?', *WA*, 9 December 1935.
11   Phyllis Kaberry, *Aboriginal Woman: Sacred and Profane*, London, Routledge, 1939, pp. 11, 246.
12   Morndi Munro, Tape 5, 7 October 1989.
13   Jack Dale and Morndi Munro, Tape 28, 28 February 1991; Jack Dale: Tape 45, 29 May 1992; Tape 46, 29 May 1992; Tape 47, 28 May 1992.
14   Ion Idriess, *Over the Range: Sunshine and Shadows in the Kimberley*, Sydney, Angus and Robertson, 1937, p. 5.
15   Dale, Tape 45.
16   AD308/1930, Police Report, 14 September 1943.
17   Jack Dale and Morndi Munro, Tape 27, 28 February 1991.
18   Dale, Tape 27.
19   Dale, notes on transcripts of Tapes 27 and 28.
20   Dale, Tape 27, 28 February 1991.
21   Idriess, *Over the Range*, pp. 14, 303.
22   Morndi Munro, Tape 10, 1 April 1990.
23   See Banjo Woorunmurra and Morndi Munro in Munro, *Emerarra*, pp. 80–6.
24   Maggie Ghi, Tape 43, 17 May 1992.
25   Campbell Allenbrae, Tape 12, 2 April 1990.
26   ibid.
27   Mick Jowalji, Tape 25, 5 March 1991; Ginger Warrebeen, Tape 27, 28 February 1991; Daisy Angajit, Tape 29, 26 February 1991.
28   Munro, Tape 28, 28 February 1991.
29   Harry Howendon and Dickie Udmorrah, Tape 40, 4 April 1992.
30   Munja manager to CPA, 20 August 1943, Mowanjum Research Notes, 'Mission Lands Review', unpublished MS, Aboriginal Affairs Planning Authority, 1988.
31   Theresa Lacy, interview notes, NB12a, 17 December 1994.
32   'Frank Lacy Diaries 1923–1970', private collection, Mount Elizabeth station, 12 January 1949.
33   ibid., 15, 17 and 18 February 1950, 8 February 1955, 21 September 1968.
34   ibid., 8 February 1955; also told by Scotty Martin, NB6, pp. 56–7.
35   Tim Rowse, '"Were You Ever Savages?" Aboriginal Insiders and Pastoralists' Patronage', *Oceania*, vol. 58, no. 1, December 1987, pp. 81–99.

36   Dale, Tape 45, 29 May 1992.

37   Peter Lacy, interview notes, NB8, p. 74, 18 May 1992.

38   ibid., NB6, pp. 53–4.

39   Fred Russ, interview notes, NB 9, pp. 38–48.

40   Morndi Munro, Tape 12, 23 April 1990.

41   Morndi Munro, NB3, pp. 47–50.

42   Ned Delower, Tapes 50 and 51, 22 July 1991.

43   Ned Delower, Tape 48, 8 July 1991; Tom Ronan, *Once There Was a Bagman*, Melbourne, Cassell Australia, 1966, pp. 190–3.

44   PD1903/1915, Skinner to CPA, 21 July 1918.

45   Cecil James Kelly, transcript OH540 1982–1983, interviewed by Michael Adams, BL, p. 259.

46   ibid., p. 151.

47   Banjo Woorunmurra, Tape 14, 5 April 1990.

48   Billy King, interview notes, 20 May 1992.

49   NDG36/58.

50   Delower, Tape 51.

51   Morndi Munro, Tape 26, 22 February 1991; Ned Delower, Tape 49, 8 July 1991.

52   Munro, *Emerarra*, pp. 128–34.

53   AD298/1930, Delower to R. Coverley, 24 September 1944.

54   PF770/1947, Sadler to CPA, January 1944.

55   ibid.

56   PF770/1947, PC Bond to CNA, 4 March 1944.

57   Morndi Munro, NB6, pp. 124–5. Howendon stated: 'Before, no pension. Only bread and meat and shirt and trouser, we been work, tobacco. We never get a money olden time' (Tape 51, 5 April 1992). Weeda Munro stated: 'blanket, trouser, shirt, boot, hat, tobacco. Every month flour, meat, kangaroo, when we go la bush' (NB1, 18 June 1989).

58   Morndi Munro, Ginger Warreebeen, Freddy Marker, Tape 31, 6 March 1991, translated by David Mowaljarlai, 8 August 1991.

59   Elizabeth Povinelli explores the value and meaning of food in Aboriginal culture in the Darwin region. Her findings echo north Kimberley informants' consistent mentions of food as an important item of exchange and as evidence of the 'proper' relationship of people to the environment. Elizabeth Povinelli, *Labor's Lot: The Power, History, and Culture of Aboriginal Action*, Chicago, University of Chicago Press, 1993.

60   Munro, Tape 10.

61   'Lacy Diaries', 21 June 1966.

62   Delower, Tape 50.

63   Delower, Tape 49.

64   Munro, *Emerarra*, pp. 126–7.

65   Delower, Tape 50.

66   Kelly, transcript OH540, p. 258.

67   PD408/1936.

68   ARAD 1939, MS AADL.

69   ARAD1939, MS AADL.

70   AD195/1929, file note, Derby Police, 29 November 1940.

71   Maggie Ghi, Susie Umungul, Rosie Mamangulya, with Jilki Edwards
      translating, Tape 43, 17 May 1992.

72   Dale, Tape 46.

73   Jilki Edwards, Tape 55, 4 April 1992.

74   See further M.A. Jebb, 'Surviving Bungarun', in S. Yu (ed.), In Our Own
      Country, MS, Kimberley Land Council Library.

75   Dale and Munro, Tape 28.

76   Munro, *Emerarra*, p. 97.

77   PD4458/1944.

78   AD195/1929.

79   ibid.

80   Daisy Angajit in Munro, *Emerarra*, p. 103.

81   Harry Howendon, Tape 41, 5 April 1992.

82   Maggie Ghi, Susie Umungul, Rosie Mamangulya, Tapes 43 and 44,
      17 May 1992; Weeda Munro and Daisy Angajit in Munro, *Emerarra*,
      pp. 99–109; Maggie Gudaworla, Tape 63, 14 November 1995; Barbara
      Midmee, Tape 23, 1 August 1990.

83   See the women's stories in Munro, *Emerarra*.

84   Gudaworla, Tape 63.

85   Maggie Gudaworla, Tape 65, 15 November 1995.

86   AD195/1929, Commissioner Bray to UAM, 15 October 1946.

Chapter 6: 'To jingle a few coins in their pockets': the arrival of welfare, 1948–1959

1   Maggie Scott, interview notes, NB3, p. 10, 23 September 1989.

2   See Peter Biskup, *Not Slaves Not Citizens: The Aboriginal Problem in
      Western Australia, 1898–1954,* St Lucia, University of Queensland Press,
      1973; C.D. Rowley, *The Remote Aborigines,* Harmondsworth, Penguin,
      1970.

3   ARAD1955, MS AADL.

4   ARAD1947, MS AADL.

5   Biskup, *Not Slaves Not Citizens,* p. 214. See also J. Wilson, 'Authority and
      leadership in a "new style" Australian Aboriginal community: Pindan,
      Western Australia', MA thesis, University of Western Australia, 1961;
      Kingsly Palmer and Clancy McKenna, *Somewhere Between Black and
      White: The Story of an Aboriginal Australian,* Melbourne, Macmillan,
      1978; Andrew Markus, 'Talka Longa Mouth: Aborigines and the Labour
      Movement, 1890–1970', in Ann Curthoys and A. Markus (eds), *Who Are
      Our Enemies? Racism and the Working Class of Australia,* Sydney, Hale
      and Ironmonger, 1978, pp. 138–57; D.W. McLeod, *How the West Was Lost:*

The Native Question in the Development of Western Australia, Port Hedland, Western Australia, self-published, 1984.

6   Proceedings of Commonwealth and State Welfare Authorities meeting, Canberra, 3 February 1948, AADL.

7   Paul Hasluck, *Black Australians: A Survey of Native Policy in Western Australia, 1829–1897*, Carlton, Melbourne University Press, 1942, pp. 76–7.

8   Proceedings of Commonwealth and State Welfare Authorities, 1948, AADL.

9   ibid., pp. 4, 14, 17, 20.

10   ibid., p. 8.

11   Quoted in William de Maria, '"White Welfare: Black Entitlement": The Social Security Access Controversy, 1939–59', *Aboriginal History,* vol. 10, no. 1–2, 1986, pp. 25–39, p. 34.

12   AD1104/1939, whole file relates.

13   De Maria, '"White Welfare: Black Entitlement"', pp. 25–39; William G. Sanders, 'Access, administration and politics: the Australian social security system and Aborigines', PhD thesis, Australian National University, 1986.

14   AD932/1943, Acting Clerk in Charge, Native Welfare, 25 February 1949.

15   Biskup, *Not Slaves Not Citizens,* pp. 219–22.

16   F.E.A. Bateman, 'Report on Survey of Native Affairs', *WAVP* vol. 2, no. 19, 1948.

17   ibid., p. 16.

18   ibid., p. 26.

19   ibid., p. 16.

20   ibid., p. 25.

21   ibid., pp. 229, 232; Kevin Johnson, Tape 59, 17 May 1994.

22   Biskup, *Not Slaves Not Citizens,* p. 237.

23   Morndi Munro (Mary Anne Jebb ed.), *Emerarra: A Man of Merarra*, Broome, Magabala Books, 1996.

24   Bateman, 'Report on Survey of Native Affairs', p. 22.

25   ibid., p. 35.

26   ibid., p. 36.

27   ARAD1950, MS AADL.

28   See W. Lambden Owen, *Cossack Gold: The Chronicles of an Early Goldfields Warden,* Sydney, Angus and Robertson, 1933, preface by Curle.

29   ARAD1949, MS AADL.

30   ARAD1950, MS AADL.

31   ibid.

32   A.O. Neville noted that as Administrator to Aboriginal people, he received less direction and support than his colleagues who worked with Indigenous peoples in other parts of the world. Pat Jacobs, *Mister Neville*, Fremantle, Fremantle Arts Centre Press, 1990, p. 229.

33   ARAD1953, MS AADL; comments and debate at *WAPD* vol. 136, pp. 2761–6, 16 December 1953.

34   ARAD1953, MS AADL.

35   Biskup, *Not Slaves Not Citizens,* pp. 220–2, 235–41.

36   McLeod, *How the West Was Lost,* ch. 5.

37   Biskup, *Not Slaves Not Citizens,* p. 236.

38   Don McLeod, Tape 67, 16 May 1994.

39   Bateman, 'Report on Survey of Native Affairs', p. 18.

40   ibid., p. 18.

41   Rowley, *The Remote Aborigines,* pp. 251–7.

42   'Blocs' refers to regions as described by Kim Ackerman, 'The Renascence of Aboriginal Law in the Kimberleys', in R.M. and C. Berndt (eds), *Aborigines of the West: Their Past and Present,* Nedlands, University of Western Australia Press, 1979, pp. 234–42.

43   D.W.G. Treloar, 'Investors and Kimberley Cattle', *Australian Journal of Agricultural Economics,* vol. 9, no. 1, 1965, pp. 53–66.

44   AD34/1949, Pullen to CNW, 18 July 1949.

45   AD34/1949, Minister for Native Affairs to Anti-Slavery Society London, 12 September 1949.

46   ARAD1950, MS AADL, also published in *WA,* 24 June 1950.

47   AD34/1949, Pullen jrnl, 20 June 1949.

48   AD34/1949, Pullen to CNA, 28 September 1949.

49   ibid.; also quoted in Biskup, *Not Slaves Not Citizens,* p. 241.

50   AD34/1949, Pullen to CNA, 28 September 1949.

51   See ARAD1949, ARAD1950, MS AADL.

52   AD34/1949, McGaffin Superintendent La Grange to CNA, 2 June 1949.

53   ARAD1949, Pullen Report, MS AADL.

54   ibid.

55   AD699/1949, Pullen Report, 9 August 1949.

56   ibid.

57   ibid.

58   ARAD1950, MS AADL. A similar argument was recorded by Coralie Rees in 1953: Coralie and Leslie Rees, *Spinifex Walkabout: Hitch-hiking in Remote North Australia,* Sydney, Australian Publishing Company, 1953, pp. 126–7.

59   AD34/1949, CNW to Minister, 17 May 1949.

60   AD34/1949, CNW to Pullen, 20 May 1949.

61   Neva Maisey, *No Man Alone: The Pastoralists and Graziers Association of Western Australia (inc) 1907–1979,* Perth, Westcolour Press, 1979, pp. 92–3.

62   AD34/1949, Pullen to CNA, 28 September 1949; AD34/1939, McBeath to CNA, 14 January 1949.

63   AD699/1949, circular memo, 13 December 1949.

64   AD34/1949, McBeath to CNA, 14 January 1949.

65   AD34/1949, Pullen to CNA, 28 September 1949.

66   AD699/1949, Territory of Papua and New Guinea. Department of Native Labour Circular no. 112, 7 December 1949; see 'Dietary Survey of Aborigines in Western Australia', Department of Health, Commonwealth, 1951, AADL.

67   ARAD1950, MS AADL.

68   AD34/1949, Rhatigan to CNW, 8 March 1949.

69   AD34/1949, file note, Middleton to Minister, n.d.

70   AD34/1949, Minutes of Meeting PGA, 2 November 1949.

71   AD34/1949, Minutes of Meeting PGA, 3 February 1950.

72   AD34/1949, Pastoralists' Association of Western Australia Inc., Notification of 'Payment of Native Employees —West Kimberley Stations', 3 February 1950.

73   'Frank Lacy Diaries 1923–1970', private collection, Mount Elizabeth station, loose note, June 1950.

74   AD34/1949, 10 February 1950.

75   AD34/1949, Extract from *WA*, 14 February 1950.

76   Rowley, *The Remote Aborigines*, p. 261.

77   AD34/1949, CNA to Pullen, 20 May 1949.

78   AD34/1949, PGA of Western Australia Inc., 'Payment of Native Employees —West Kimberley Stations', 3 February 1950.

79   AD239/1930, 15 July 1930; AD745/1938, O'Neill Report on Liveringa Station, 3 May 1946; AD34/1949, Minutes of Meeting PGA, 2 November 1949.

80   Paternalism was imbued with the notion that it was not socially appropriate to discuss money in public, nor morally responsible to discuss it with inferiors who had no understanding of it.

81   AD34/1949, Pullen to CNW, 26 April 1950; AD34/1949, Pullen Report to CNA, 16 June 1950.

82   ARAD1949, Pullen Report, MS AADL.

83   AD699/1949, Pullen Report, 9 August 1949.

84   ARAD1950, MS AADL.

85   AD34/1949, District Officer Derby jrnl, 1 November 1949.

86   ARAD1950, MS AADL.

87   ibid.

88   ibid.

89   ibid.; ARAD1951, MS AADL.

90   AD34/1951, Pullen to CNW, 23 January 1951.

91   AD34/1949, Middleton to Pullen, 26 January 1951.

92   AD932/1943, whole file relates.

93   AD932/1943, CNW to CoP, 5 April 1943.

94   AD932/1943, note, Bray to Minister, 4 May 1943.

95   AD932/1943, Prime Minister Curtin to Premier, 2 March 1943.

96   AD1058/1946, CNA Circular Instruction no. 3, 29 November 1948.

97   Sanders, 'Access, Administration and Politics', p. 94.

98   ARAD1950, MS AADL.

99   NDG33.2, DSS to CNA, 19 October 1950; see also AD705/1950.

100 NDG33.2, CNA to DSS, 24 August 1950.

101 AD178/1961, Patrol Report, 15 October 1960.

102 ibid.; Sanders, 'Access, Administration and Politics', p. 105.

103 NDG1/1/1a, Circular Instructions no. 56, 24 November 1956.

104 AD932/1943, K. Morgan Regional Report, 23 September 1958.

105 Kevin Johnson, Tapes 58 and 59, 17 May 1994.

106 NDG18-1, Minutes of Meeting, PGA West Kimberley District, 4 July 1965.

107 WAS46 acc. 3412, NDG files created in 1948 for all Kimberley stations.

108 AD298/1930, Patrol Report, 1962.

109 ibid.

110 NDG36/36, Patrol Report, 1962.

111 ARAD1952, MS AADL.

112 Theresa Lacy, NB12a, 17 December 1994; Ned Delower, Tape 51, 22 July 1991.

113 Delower also told a detailed narrative about the first vote for Aboriginal station people in the state elections in 1965. The story shows how he enrolled Aboriginal people from the station and then, as official polling booth officer, assisted them to vote. According to Delower, each station did the same thing, and consequently the votes always followed the manager's preferences. Delower, Tape 51.

114 NDG36/58, D. Blythe to Beharrell, 15 September 1959.

115 NDG36/58, Kevin Johnson to Blythe, 17 December 1959.

116 Derby Leprosarium Admission Books, 1935–1981, unpublished, West Kimberley Public Health Department; Morndi Munro, notes on leprosarium lists, NB4, p. 53, 31 July 1990.

117 AD1058/1946, Humphreys, DSS to CNA, 24 July 1956.

118 Peter Lacy, interview notes, NB6, p. 60.

119 NDG33-2, RS Mauger, DO Halls Creek to DO Derby, 14 November 1963.

120 'Department [OF?] Native Welfare Instruction Manual, 1965', AADL, B21-2.

121 ibid., B18-2.

122 NDG36/37, Russ to Beharrell, 20 April 1954.

123 NDG36/79, Sturt Creek Station file.

124 NDG36/37, Russ to Beharrell, 20 April 1954. I have not found the extent to which this rebate was claimed, although it may have been claimed throughout the pastoral industry for many years. Advice from the Taxation Office Canberra was that 'Natives' were arguably 'dependants' of the stations under section 79 of the Income Tax Assessment Act 1936, which gave concessions of £50 per year for children under sixteen. This accords with Russ's deduction.

125 NDG36/27, Telegram, Beharrell to Russ, date obscured.

126   NDG36/57, Fraser to Beharrell, 23 January 1957.

127   ibid., 20 May 1959.

128   AD95/1918, Isdell to CPA Gale, December 1909, Moola Bulla.

129   Ion Idriess, *Over the Range: Sunshine and Shadows in the Kimberley*, Sydney, Angus and Robertson, 1937, p. 239.

130   AD745/1938, acc. 1733, Middleton to Michelides 21 January 1949, Noonkenbah.

131   M.C. Davies Ledgers, Kimberley Downs and Napier Downs, MN183A/19, BL.

132   'Lacy Diaries', loose note, 1950.

133   'Lacy Diaries', 1949, 1950 and 28 January 1955.

134   Lacy, interview notes, p. 55.

135   'Lacy Diaries', 25 June 1951, states: 'Jack: legions spurs 1.10.0 hat pipe brush towel trousers riding trousers credit muster one pound. Jumbo: trousers cash 1.10.0 hat 2.10.0 spurs 1.15.0 riding trousers 1.10.0 credit muster 1.0.0'.

136   ibid., invoice, 1 April 1962.

137   AD298/1930, Oobagooma was then owned by three doctors— Elphinstone, Holman and Davidson—and D. Stewart, manager.

138   NDG1/1/1a, Circular no. 64, 17 April 1958.

139   NDG1/1/1a, Circular no. 69, 27 November 1958.

140   ARAD1950, MS AADL.

141   AD780/1949, US to CNA, 23 November 1953.

142   AD780/1949, Beharrell to CNA, 9 December 1953.

143   ARAD1952, MS AADL.

144   ARAD1955, Beharrell DO Derby, MS AADL.

145   ARAD1952, MS AADL.

146   ARAD1952, ARAD1953, MS AADL.

147   ARAD1954, MS AADL.

148   ARAD1953, MS AADL.

149   'Dietary Survey of Aborigines in Western Australia'. See the AADL for papers by Ida Mann on eye diseases in the Kimberley region.

150   Native Welfare Act Regulations, *GG*, 9 October 1962.

151   NDG1/1/1/a, CNW Circular no. 53, 14 August 1956.

152   Frank Gare, *Report of the Special Committee on Native Matters (With Particular Reference to Adequate Finance)*, Perth, West Australian Government Print, 1958, p. 53.

153   ibid., p. 10.

154   R.M. and C.H. Berndt, *End of an Era: Aboriginal Labour in the Northern Territory*, Canberra, Australian Institute of Aboriginal Studies, 1987.

155   'Material Set Out by R. and C. Berndt in Reply to Questions Put by Special Committee on Native Matters, Parliament House, 18 April 1958', AADL.

156   AD843/1941, CNW to District Office North, 8 January 1957.

157   Biskup, *Not Slaves Not Citizens*, p. 264.

158   ARAD1950, MS AADL.

159   Biskup, *Not Slaves Not Citizens*, p. 253.

160   J. Morgan, *Report on the Central North Kimberley Region*, Perth, Western Australian Department of Lands and Surveys, 1955.

161   ibid., p. 35.

162   See further H. Rumley and S. Toussaint, 'For Their Own Benefit? A Critical Overview of Aboriginal Policy and Practice at Moola Bulla, East Kimberley, 1910–1955', *Aboriginal History*, vol. 14, no. 1–2, 1990, pp. 80–103; Kimberley Language Resource Centre, *Moola Bulla: In the Shadow of the Mountain,* Broome, Magabala Books, 1996.

163   Mary Anne Jebb, 'Moola Bulla: Historical Issues for Native Title', unpublished report for the Kimberley Land Council, 1993.

164   Biskup, *Not Slaves Not Citizens*, p. 230.

165   Rumley and Toussaint, 'For Their Own Benefit?', pp. 80–103; Bruce Shaw, 'The Discrimination Was So Thick', in Bill Gammage and Peter Spearitt (eds), *The Australians 1938*, Sydney, Fairfax Syme and Weldon, 1988, pp. 54–63: Kimberley Language Resource Centre, *Moola Bulla: In the Shadow of the Mountain.*

166   AD226/1955, M. de Marchi to Beharrell, 30 August 1955.

167   AD226/1955, Beharrell to CNW, 9 September 1955.

168   ARAD1955, MS AADL.

169   ARAD1956, MS AADL.

170   ibid.

171   NDG1/1/1a, Native Welfare Circular no. 93, 11 July 1960.

172   Gare, *Report of the Special Committee on Native Matters*, p. 27.

173   ARAD1958, MS AADL.

174   ibid.

Chapter 7: Pastoral paternalism turns sour, 1959–1972

1   Sam Woolagoodja in R. Layton, 'Coastal Story Places in the Western Kimberlies' [sic], unpublished report, 1976, p. 2.

2   Social Services Act 1959, no. 57 of 1959; Native Welfare Act 1963, no. 79 of 1963; CAR Case nos 536 of 1964, 270 and 289 of 1965, were successfully appealed in 1967 for delayed application of the Pastoral Industry Award 1965 to the Kimberley to December 1968.

3   Natives Citizenship Rights Act Repeal Act 1972, no. 24 of 1972; Liquor Act Amendment Act 1972, no. 76 of 1972.

4   See also 'Our Aborigines' pamphlets mentioned in Tim Rowse, 'Assimilation and After', in A. Curthoys, A.W. Martin, Tim Rowse (eds), *Australians: From 1939,* Sydney, Fairfax Syme and Weldon, 1987, pp. 133–49.

5   Proceedings of Commonwealth and State Aboriginal Welfare Authorities Meetings 1961, AADL, p. 69.

6   ibid., p. 36.

7   ibid., p. 37.

8   Native Welfare Instruction Manuals have sections on procedures for returning children to their homes for holidays. 'Department of Native Welfare Instruction Manual, 1969/70', AADL, B-2-13 and B-6-15.

9   Proceedings of Commonwealth and State Aboriginal Welfare Authorities Meetings 1961, AADL, p. 37.

10   ibid. p. 40.

11   AD780/1949, Health Department Inspector to CNW, 28 August, 1956.

12   Proceedings of Commonwealth and State Aboriginal Welfare Authorities Meetings 1961, AADL, p. 41.

13   NDG1/1/1a, Circular no. 73, 26 June 1959; Aboriginal Affairs Planning Authority, 'Mission Lands Review', unpublished report, 1988, p. 250(e).

14   NDG30/5, Circular Report, CNW to all DOs, 28 June 1960.

15   NDG36/8, Blina Station,18 July 1961; NWD749/1938, Louisa Downs.

16   NWD749/38, Mauger Patrol Report, 1963.

17   ibid., 24 March 1964.

18   ibid., 1963.

19   NDG18-1, 13 March 1963.

20   ibid.

21   NWD143/1961, Derby Mission Centre Register of Inmates; NWD23-13-4. Amy Bethel Hostel functioned as a base for preaching along the Gibb River road twenty years before its official gazettal as a mission institution in 1957.

22   NDG1/1/1a, Circular no. 142, Custody of Native Children, 1 May 1964.

23   NDG36/36, Patrol Report 1964, Kimberley Downs Station.

24   NDG36/36, Patrol Report 1966 and 1967.

25   AD1058/1946, notes on file for Annual Report 1957.

26   AD1058/1946, Beharrell to CNW, 19 June 1957.

27   NDG33/3/1a, CNW to Field Officers, 10 February 1959.

28   NDG33/3/1a, Beharrell to CNW, 25 February 1959.

29   NDG33/3/1a, CNW to Beharrell, 7 April 1959.

30   AD1104/1939, Confidential Circular no. 272, CNW to all Field Officers, 24 December 1959.

31   ibid.

32   Proceedings of the Native Welfare Conference Commonwealth and State Authorities, January 1961, AADL, pp. 105–6.

33   ibid., p. 112.

34   ibid., p. 106.

35   Divisional Superintendent's Conference Meeting Minutes, 10 to 14 February 1964, AADL.

36   NDG33/3/1a, 25 January 1960.

37   Kimberley Pastoral Industry Inquiry, Department of Regional Development and the North West, Perth, 1985.

38   *Report of the Pastoral Leases Committee*, Perth, Western Australian Govern-
      ment, 1963, Appendix G.

39   'Frank Lacy Diaries, 1923–1970', private collection, Mount Elizabeth
      station, 11 March 1963.

40   C.D. Rowley, *The Remote Aborigines*, Harmondsworth, Penguin, 1970,
      p. 226.

41   NDG36/57, DSS to Telford, 9 June 1965.

42   NDG1/1/1a, Circular no. 83, 28 January 1960; see also NDG3/3/1a.

43   NDG1/1/1a, Circular no. 83, 28 January 1960.

44   AD1104/1939, A.O. Day to CNW, 9 February 1960.

45   NDG1/1/1a, NWD Circular no. 97, 14 September 1960.

46   NDG1/1/1a, NWD Circular no. 92, 8 June 1960.

47   NDG1/1/1a, NWD Circular no. 96, 22 August 1960.

48   NDG36/79 is a good example of this.

49   'Department of Native Welfare Instruction Manual, 1965', AADL, B18-3.

50   AD1104/1939, Circular no. 97, CNW to all Field Staff, 14 September 1960.

51   NDG33/3/1a, CNW, 10 August 1960.

52   NDG33/3/1a, List of Pensioners.

53   ARAD 1960, MS AADL.

54   ibid.

55   ibid.

56   ARAD 1961, MS AADL.

57   ibid.

58   AD1104/1939, Minister for Native Welfare to CNW, 15 December 1960.

59   ibid.

60   Native Welfare Act 1954, Regulations, *GG*, 9 October 1962.

61   Report of the District Welfare Officers' Conference, February 1963, Perth,
      AADL, p. 13.

62   Divisional Superintendent's Conference Meeting Minutes, February 1964,
      AADL, p. 14.

63   NDG33/3/1a, Special Magistrate M.E. Davies for DSS to CNW, 19 May
      1965.

64   NDG36/36, Kimberley Downs; ARAD1963, MS AADL.

65   NDG33/3/1a, *Weekend News*, 13 March 1965.

66   Rowley, *The Remote Aborigines*, p. 304. Kimberley pastoralists did not
      receive government rations or 'maintenance' funding as did pastoralists
      in the Northern Territory. See further Owen Stanley, 'Aboriginal Com-
      munities on Cattle Stations in Central Australia', *Australian Economic
      Papers*, vol. 15, no. 27, 1976, pp. 158–70.

67   Tim Rowse, 'Rethinking Aboriginal "Resistance": The Community
      Development Employment (CDEP) Program', *Oceania*, vol. 63, no. 3,
      March 1993, pp. 268–86, p. 275.

68   Kevin Johnson, Tape 58, 17 May 1994.

69   NDG36/57, DSS to Telford, 9 June 1965.

70   NDG36/57, Patrol Report, May 1965.

71   NDG36/57, DSS to Telford, 9 June 1965.

72   NDG33/3/1a, Special Magistrate M.E. Davies for DSS to CNW, 19 May 1965.

73   NDG33/3/1a, Pensioner Survey Report, 4 June 1966.

74   Johnson, Tape 58.

75   NDG35/36, Patrol Report, 1965.

76   NDG36/35, Patrol Report, 10 June 1965.

77   NDG36/35.

78   NDG36/56.

79   NDG33/3/1a, Humphreys DSS to CNW, 2 July 1965.

80   ARAD1965, MS AADL.

81   NDG33/3/1a, CNW to Director of DSS, 3 August 1965.

82   NDG33/3/1a, Pensioner Survey Report, 4 June 1966.

83   ibid.

84   NDG33/3/1a, Kevin Johnson Report re Pensioners, 8 August 1966.

85   ibid.

86   NDG33/3/1a, LB Hamilton DSS to WA SS, 7 September 1966.

87   ibid.

88   'Department of Native Welfare Instruction Manual, 1967', AADL.

89   Morndi Munro, Tape 12, 23 April 1990.

90   Kevin Johnson, Tape 59, 17 May 1994.

91   Divisional Superintendent's Conference Meeting Minutes, 1968, AADL, p. 20.

92   NDG36/79.

93   See NDG31/1 and NDG31/4/1 for Forrest River Mission transfer to Wyndham. See Michael Robinson, 'Change and adjustment among the Bardi of Sunday Island, North Western Australia', MA thesis, University of Western Australia, 1973, pp. 180–9, for Sunday Island; see further AAPA, 'Mission Lands Review'. The Louisa Downs manager also wrote of older residents moving to Halls Creek to receive their pensions and young men moving to receive unemployment benefits. L.A. Schubert, *Kimberley Dreaming: The Century of Freddy Cox*, Perth, Words Work, 1992.

94   AAPA, 'Mission Lands Review', pp. 250d–f; David Mowaljarlai and Daisy Uttamorrah, *Visions of Mowanjum: Aboriginal Writings from the Kimberley*, Adelaide, Rigby, 1980, pp. 22–6.

95   NDG36/58, Patrol Report, 1966.

96   NDG36/58, District Officer Report, 26 January 1967.

97   NDG36/58, Manager Mount House, 10 February 1969.

98   NDG36/6.

99   NDG36/6, Patrol Report, 20 June 1972.

100   NDG36/6, memo, Derby District Office, 21 September 1972.

101   D.W.G. Treloar, 'Investors and Kimberley Cattle', *Australian Journal of Agricultural Economics*, vol. 9, no. 1, 1965, pp. 53–66, p. 59.

102   Kimberley Pastoral Industry Inquiry. See DOLA, acc. 1764, files 3931/1964 and 3930/1964, for warnings from pastoral board members that companies were allegedly stripping assets from leases.

103   'Lacy Diaries', 2 July 1966.

104   W.D.Scott and Co., 'An Assessment of the Needs and Opportunities for the Aborigines of the Kimberley', vols. 1 and 2, 1971, AADL.

105   Kimberley Pastoral Industry Inquiry.

106   See Frances Crawford, 'The story of Looma', MA thesis, University of Western Australia, 1976.

107   NDG36/61, R. Wells to Derby District Office, 22 June 1970.

108   NDG36/36.

109   NDG36/61, Patrol Report, 20 May 1969.

110   NDG 36/36.

111   See Morndi Munro (Mary Anne Jebb ed.), *Emerarra: A Man of Merarra*, Broome, Magabala Books, 1996; Harry Howendon, Tape 41, 5 April 1992; Jack Dale, Tape 28, 28 February 1991; Banjo Woorunmurra, Tape 13, 5 April 1990.

112   NDG36/36, Patrol Report, 25 July 1961.

113   Howendon, Tape 41.

114   NDG36/36, Patrol Report, 24 August 1968.

115   Dot Delower, interview notes, NB7, p. 13, 11 May 1991.

116   NDG36/36, Patrol Report, 28 November 1969.

117   ibid., 17 May 1971.

118   ibid., May 1972.

119   NDG36/57, Patrol Report, 19 April 1966.

120   NDG36/57, file note, 1 August 1966.

121   NDG36/57, Thiess Bros to Welfare Derby, 19 September 1969.

122   NDG36/35, Patrol Report, 1970.

123   NDG36/56, Lacy to Welfare Derby, 4 October.1966.

124   NDG36/56, Patrol Report, 1970.

125   NDG36/56, CNW to Northern Division, 21 June 1971.

126   NDG36/56, Kevin Johnson to CNW, 1 July 1971.

127   NDG36/56, CNW to Arbitration Inspector, Department of Labour and National Service, 7 January 1972.

128   NDG36/56, Welfare Derby CNW, 18 April 1972.

129   ARAD1961, MS AADL.

130   NDG1/1/1b, Native Welfare Circular, 11 November 1962.

131   ARAD1961, MS AADL.

132   NDG31/1, Regulations Derby Reserve, 4 August 1964. See also Haebich's description of a similar process for Katanning reserve, when an agreement was drawn up in 1913 to control behaviour of reserve residents and counter-protests by white town residents. The regulations stated that 'they must be good', no drinking, no gambling, no firearms, no 'loafers' and no young men to eat old people's rations. Anna Haebich, *'For Their*

Own Good': Aborigines and Government in the Southwest of Western Australia 1900–1940, Nedlands, University of Western Australia Press, 1988, pp. 145–6.

133   ARAD1961, MS AADL.

134   NDG36/8, Welfare to Blina Manager, 15 February 1956.

135   NDG12/8, Len Connell, Silent Grove, to Native Welfare Derby, 23 February 1962.

136   NDG12/4, Manager, Mt Anderson, 2 December 1962.

137   NDG12/4.

138   'Lacy Diaries', 12 December 1966.

139   Divisional Superintendent's Conference Meeting Minutes, 19–23 June 1967, AADL.

140   NDG12/4.

141   ARAD1968, MS AADL.

142   ibid.; ARAD1969, MS AADL.

143   'Department Native Welfare Instruction Manual, 1967', AADL.

144   'Variation: Pastoral Industry Award', CAR case no. 1669 of 1969, p. 6.

145   'Cattle Station Industry (Northern Territory) Award 1951', CAR case no. 830 of 1965, p. 1173.

146   NDG11/3/b, CNW to Derby District Office, 17 March 1967. Extensive press coverage collected as newspaper clippings on AD62/1965.

147   Divisional Superintendent's Conference Meeting Minutes, 21–25 June 1965, AADL, p. 12.

148   Native Welfare Act no. 79 of 1963, section 7f.

149   AD62/1965, 'Pastoral Industry Award: What It Means to You and What You Should Do', NWD, 1969.

150   NDG11/3b, CNW to Fr McKelson, 23 July 1969.

151   NDG1/1/1c, Instruction to Field Officers, 1967.

152   Divisional Superintendent's Conference Meeting Minutes, 1968, AADL.

153   NDG1/1/1c, Instruction to Field Officers, 1967. This is followed by Circular Instruction to all Field Officers, no. 1 of 1968, which calls for the registration of all employed Aboriginal men turning twenty in the next six months for National Service. Unemployment benefits were not granted to Aboriginal people living on stations in the Northern Territory in 1976. Stanley, 'Aboriginal Communities on Cattle Stations in Central Australia', p. 164.

154   Scott and Co., 'An Assessment of the Needs and Opportunities for the Aborigines of the Kimberley'.

155   NDG31/1. Children were not officially recorded.

156   NDG31/1, Kevin Johnson to Field Officer Derby, 17 June 1971; continuing correspondence on NDG1/4/1b.

157   NDG31/1, Kevin Johnson to Field Officer Derby, 17 June 1971.

158   NDG1/4/1b, Crown Law to CNW, 14 November 1969.

159   NDG36/57, Kevin Johnson, Circular to all Stations.

160   ARAD1967, ARAD1970, MS AADL.

161   Scott and Co., 'An Assessment of the Needs and Opportunities for the Aborigines of the Kimberley', pp. 11–17.

162   Campbell Allenbrae, Tape 57, 2 March 1992.

163   Derby Leprosarium Admission Books, 1935–1981, West Kimberley Public Health Department.

164   Campbell Allenbrae, in Munro, *Emerarra*, pp. 35–42.

165   Campbell Allenbrae, interview notes, NB3, p. 39.

166   Allenbrae, Tape 57.

167   NDG36/67. Noted as Campbell Cambellay in 1960 and Campbell Allinbar in 1962.

168   Allenbrae, Tape 57.

169   ibid.

170   ARAD1961, MS AADL.

171   ARAD1970, MS AADL.

172   Allenbrae, Tape 57.

173   PF821/1963.

174   Munro, *Emerarra*, pp. 141–5; NDG11/2/b.

175   NDG11/2/b.

176   NDG11/2/b, CNW to Welfare Derby, 21 February 1972.

177   Evelyn Bidd, interview notes, NB9, p. 62.

178   PF821/1963.

179   NDG26/51, Patrol Report, Meda Station, 1952.

180   Certificate granted to Bill Munro, *GG*, 8 August 1969; Munro, *Emerarra*, p. 139.

181   Scott Bennett, *Aborigines and Political Power*, Sydney, Allen and Unwin, 1989, pp. 28–9.

182   Regulations of Native Welfare Act 1963, clauses 14(4) and 15, MS AADL.

183   AAPA Act Regulations, *GG*, 30 June 1972, clause 4(2).

184   This was the title of my seminar paper at Murdoch University in 1991 introducing my research topic. David Trigger also draws attention to this warning in Queensland and uses it as a metaphor for Aboriginal people's responses to Europeans and government agencies in north-west Queensland. See further David, S. Trigger, '*Whitefella Comin': Aboriginal Responses to Colonialism in Northern Australia*, Cambridge, Cambridge University Press, 1992.

Epilogue

1   Kimberley Pastoral Industry Inquiry: Final Report, Department of Regional Development and North West, Perth October 1985, p. 35.

2   ARAD1977, MS AADL.

3   ibid.

4   S. Hawke and M. Gallagher, *Noonkanbah: Whose Land Whose Law*,
     Fremantle, Fremantle Arts Centre Press, 1989; E. Kolig, *Nookanbah*,
     Canberra, Australian Institute of Aboriginal Studies, 1987.
5   Kimberley Pastoral Industry Inquiry, pp. 191, 192, 193.
6   Patrick Sullivan, *'All Free Man Now': Culture, Community and Politics in
     the Kimberley Region North-Western Australia*, Canberra, Australian
     Institute of Aboriginal Studies, 1995, p.15.
7   W.D. Scott and Co., 'An Assessment of the Needs and Opportunities for
     the Aborigines of the Kimberley', 1971, section 14-5, AADL.

SELECT BIBLIOGRAPHY

Books, articles, reports and theses

Ackerman, Kim, 'Material Culture and Trade in the Kimberleys Today', in R.M. and C. Berndt (eds), *Aborigines of the West: Their Past and Present*, Nedlands, University of Western Australia Press, 1979, pp. 243–51.

———, 'The Renascence of Aboriginal Law in the Kimberleys', in R.M. and C. Berndt (eds), *Aborigines of the West: Their Past and Present*, Nedlands, University of Western Australia Press, 1979, pp. 234–42.

Anderson, Christopher, 'Aborigines and Tin Mining in North Queensland: A Case Study of Contact History', *Mankind*, vol. 13, no. 6, April 1983, pp. 473–98.

Attwood, Bain, 'Review Article. Aborigines and Academic Historians: Some Recent Encounters', *Australian Historical Review*, vol. 24, no. 94, April 1990, pp. 123–35.

Bateman, F.E.A., 'Report on Survey of Native Affairs', *WAVP*, vol. 2, no. 19, 1948.

Battye, J.S. (ed.), *The History of the North West of Australia*, Perth, V.K. Jones, 1915.

Berndt, R.M. and C., *End of an Era: Aboriginal Labour in the Northern Territory*, Canberra, Australian Institute of Aboriginal Studies, 1987.

Biskup, Peter, *Not Slaves Not Citizens: The Aboriginal Problem in Western Australia, 1898–1954*, St Lucia, University of Queensland Press, 1973.

Blundell, Valda Jean, 'Aboriginal adaptation in north west Australia', PhD thesis, University of Wisconsin-Madison, 1975.

Bohemia, Jack, and William McGregor, *Nyabayarri: Kimberley Tracker*, Canberra, Australian Institute of Aboriginal Studies Press, 1995.

Bolton, G.C., 'A survey of the Kimberley pastoral industry from 1885 to the present', MA thesis, University of Western Australia, 1953.

———, 'The Kimberley Pastoral Industry', *University Studies in History and Economics*, vol. 11, no. 2, July 1954, pp. 1–53.

———, 'Black and White after 1897', in C. T. Stannage (ed.), *A New History of Western Australia*, Nedlands, University of Western Australia Press, 1981, pp. 124–78.

———, and Mary Anne Jebb, 'Surviving the Stations 1905 to 1965', in S. Yu (ed.), In Our Own Country, MS, Kimberley Land Council Library.

Brockman, F.S., 'Report on Exploration of the North-West Kimberley 1901', *WAVP*, vol. 2, 1902.

Clement, Cathie, *Pre-Settlement Intrusion into the East Kimberley*, East Kimberley Impact Working Paper no. 24, Canberra, Centre for Resource and Environmental Studies, 1988.

———, 'Australia's north-west: a study of exploration, land policy and land acquisition, 1644–1844' PhD thesis, Murdoch University, 1991.

————, *Kimberley District Pastoral Leasing Register 1881 to 1887*, Mount Lawley, WA Heritage, 1994.

————, 'European Settlement and Industries, 1863–1886', in S. Yu (ed.), In Our Own Country, MS, Kimberley Land Council Library.

Coate, H. H., *A Grammar of Ngarinyin: Western Australia*, Linguistic Series no. 10, Canberra, Australian Institute of Aboriginal Studies, 1970.

————, and A.P. Elkin, *Ngarinyin–English Dictionary*, Oceania Linguistic Monographs no. 16, 1974.

Cruikshank, Julie, 'Introduction', in Julie Cruikshank et al., *Life Lived Like a Story*, Lincoln, University of Nebraska Press, 1990, pp. 1–20.

Curthoys, Ann, and Clive Moore, 'Working for the White People: An Historiographic Essay on Aboriginal and Torres Strait Islander Labour', in Ann McGrath and Kay Saunders (eds), *Aboriginal Workers,* special edition of *Labour History*, no. 69, November 1995, pp. 1–29.

Davidson, W.S., *Havens of Refuge: A History of Leprosy in Western Australia*, Nedlands, University of Western Australia Press, 1978.

Doolan, J.K., 'Walk-off of Various Groups from Cattle Stations: Victoria River District Northern Territory', in R.M. and C.H. Berndt (eds), *Aborigines and Change: Australia in the 70s*, Canberra, Australian Institute of Aboriginal Studies Press, 1977, pp. 106–13.

Easton, William R., *Report on the North Kimberley District of Western Australia*, Perth, West Australian Government Print, 1922.

Edmonds, Leigh, *The Vital Link: A History of Main Roads of Western Australia, 1926–1996*, Nedlands, University of Western Australia Press, 1997.

Elkin, A.P., 'Reaction and Interaction: A Food Gathering People and European Settlement in Australia', *American Anthropologist*, vol. 53, no. 2, 1951, pp. 164–86.

————, 'Aboriginal–European Relations', in R.M. and C. Berndt (eds), *Aborigines of the West: Their Past and Present*, Nedlands, University of Western Australia Press, 1979, pp. 285–323.

Fitzgerald, W.V., 'Report of the Trigonometrical Survey Expedition of the North Kimberley', *WAVP*, vol. 19, 1907.

Forrest, Alex., 'Nor-West Exploration, Journal of Expedition from DeGrey to Port Darwin', *WAVP*, vol. 3, 1880.

Furnell, L.C., *Report of the Royal Commission into Aboriginal Affairs Western Australia*, Perth, West Australian Government Print, 1974.

Fyfe, W.V., *Report of the Royal Commission Appointed to Inquire into and Report upon the Financial and Economic Position of the Pastoral Industry in the Leasehold Areas in Western Australia*, Perth, West Australian Government Print, 1940.

Gare, Frank, *Report of the Special Committee on Native Matters (With Particular Reference to Adequate Finance)*, Perth, Western Australian Government Print, 1958.

Gill, Andrew, 'Aborigines, Settlers and Police', *Studies in WA History*, vol. 1, 1978, pp. 1–28.

Goodall, Heather, 'Aboriginal History and the Politics of Information Control', *Oral History Association of Australia Journal*, no. 9, 1987, pp. 17–33.

Green, Neville, *The Forrest River Massacres*, Fremantle, Fremantle Arts Centre Press, 1995.

Grele, Ronald J., 'Movement Without Aim: Methodological and Theoretical Problems in Oral History', in Ronald J. Grele (ed.), *Envelopes of Sound: The Art of Oral History*, Chicago, Precedent Publishing, 2nd edn 1985, pp. 129–54.

Haebich, Anna, *'For Their Own Good': Aborigines and Government in the Southwest of Western Australia 1900–1940*, Nedlands, University of Western Australia Press, 1988.

Hawke, S., and M. Gallagher, *Noonkanbah: Whose Land Whose Law*, Fremantle, Fremantle Arts Centre Press, 1989.

Haydon, A.L., *The Trooper Police of Australia: A Record of Mounted Police Work in the Commonwealth from the Earliest Days of Settlement to the Present Time*, London, A. Melrose, 1911.

Hunter, Ernest, *Aboriginal Health and History: Power and Prejudice in Remote Australia*, Cambridge, Cambridge University Press, 1993.

Idriess, Ion L., *Man Tracks: The Mounted Police in Australia's Wilds*, Sydney, Angus and Robertson, 1935.

——, *Over the Range: Sunshine and Shadows in the Kimberley,* Sydney, Angus and Robertson, 1937.

——, *One Wet Season*, Sydney, Angus and Robertson, 1949.

——, *Outlaws of the Leopolds*, Sydney, Angus and Robertson, 1952.

——, *The Nor'Westers*, Sydney, Angus and Robertson, 1954.

——, *Tracks of Destiny*, Sydney, Angus and Robertson, 1961.

Jacobs, Pat, *Mister Neville*, Fremantle, Fremantle Arts Centre Press, 1990.

Jebb, M.A., 'The Lock Hospitals Experiment: Europeans, Aborigines and Venereal Disease', in R. Reece and T. Stannage (eds), *European–Aboriginal Relations in Western Australian History*, Studies in West Australian History, vol. 8, 1984, pp. 68–86.

——, 'Surviving Bungarun', in S. Yu (ed.), In Our Own Country, MS, Kimberley Land Council Library.

——, and Anna Haebich, '"Across the Great Divide": Gender Relations on Australian Frontiers', in Kay Saunders and Raymond Evans (eds), *Gender Relations in Australia: Domination and Negotiation*, Harcourt Brace Jovanovich, 1992, pp. 20–35.

Kaberry, Phyllis M., *Aboriginal Woman: Sacred and Profane*, London, Routledge, 1939.

Kelly, J.H., *Beef in Northern Australia*, Canberra, Australian National University Press, 1971.

Kimberley Language Resource Centre, *Moola Bulla: In the Shadow of the Mountain*, Broome, Magabala Books, 1996.

Kimberley Pastoral Industry Inquiry, Department of Regional Development and the Northwest, Perth, 1985.

Klaatz, Prof. Herman, 'Some Notes on Scientific Travel Amongst the Black Population of Tropical Australia 1904–1905, 1906', *Australian Association for the Advancement of Science*, vol. 11, 1907, pp. 577–83.

Kolig, Erich, *The Nookanbah Story*, Dunedin, University of Otago Press, 1987.

Lambden Owen, W., *Cossack Gold: The Chronicles of an Early Goldfields Warden*, Sydney, Angus and Robertson, 1933.

Layton, Robert, 'Coastal Story Places in the West Kimberlies', unpublished report, Australian Institute of Aboriginal Studies, 1976.

Long, Jeremy, 'Leaving the Desert: Actors and Sufferers in the Aboriginal Exodus from the Western Desert', *Aboriginal History*, vol. 13, 1987, pp. 9–43.

Long, T., 'The Development of Government Aboriginal Policy: The Effect of Administrative Changes, 1829–1977', in R.M. and C. Berndt (eds), *Aborigines of the West: Their Past and Present*, Nedlands, University of Western Australia Press, 1979, pp. 357–66.

Loos, Noel, *Invasion and Resistance: Aboriginal–European Relations on the North Queensland Frontier, 1861–1897*, Canberra, Australian National University Press, 1982.

Love, J.R.B., *Stone-Age Bushmen of Today: Life and Adventure Among a Tribe of Savages in North-Western Australia*, London, Blackie, 1936.

McGrath, Ann, *Born in the Cattle: Aborigines in Cattle Country*, Sydney, Allen and Unwin, 1987.

——, and Kay Saunders (eds), *Aboriginal Workers*, special edition of *Labour History*, no. 69, November 1995.

McGregor, William, 'Jack Bohemia and the Banjo Affair', *Meridean*, 1988, pp. 46–58.

—— (ed.), *Studies in Kimberley Languages: In Honour of Howard Coate*, Munchen/Newcastle, Lincom/Europa, 1996.

McKenzie, Maisie, *The Road to Mowanjum*, Sydney, Angus and Robertson, 1969.

Maisey, Neva, *No Man Alone: The Pastoralists and Graziers Association of Western Australia (inc) 1907–1979*, Westcolour Press, Perth, 1979.

Maria, William de, '"White Welfare: Black Entitlement": The Social Security Access Controversy, 1939–59', *Aboriginal History*, vol. 10, nos. 1–2, 1986, pp. 25–39.

Markus, Andrew, 'Talka Longa Mouth: Aborigines and the Labour Movement 1890–1970', in Ann Curthoys and A. Markus (eds), *Who Are Our Enemies? Racism and the Working Class of Australia*, Sydney, Hale and Ironmonger, 1978, pp. 138–57.

May, D., *From Bush to Station: Aboriginal Labour in the North Queensland Pastoral Industry 1861–1897*, Studies in North Queensland History Monograph no. 5, Townsville, 1985.

Morgan, J., *Report on the Central North Kimberley Region*, Perth, Western Australian Department of Lands and Surveys, 1955.

Morphy, H. and F., 'The "Myths" of Ngalkon History: Ideology and the Images of the Past in Northern Australia', *Man*, vol. 19, 1985, pp. 459–78.

Moseley, H.D., 'Report of the Royal Commission upon Matters in Relation to the Condition and Treatment of Aborigines', *WAVP*, vol. 1, 1935.

Mowaljarlai, David, and Daisy Uttamorrah, *Visions of Mowanjum: Aboriginal Writings from the Kimberley*, Adelaide, Rigby, 1980.

Muecke, Stephen, 'Discourse, History, Fiction: Language and Aboriginal History', *Australian Journal of Cultural Studies*, no. 1, May 1983, pp. 71–9.

———, A. Rumsay, B. Wirrenmurra, 'Pigeon the Outlaw: History as Texts', *Aboriginal History*, vol. 9, no. 1, 1985, pp. 81–100.

Munro, Morndi (Mary Anne Jebb ed.), *Emerarra: A Man of Merarra,* Broome, Magabala Books, 1996.

Neville, A.O., *Australia's Coloured Minority: Its Place in the Community*, Sydney, Currawong Publishing, 1947.

Nixon, Marion, *The Rivers of Home: Frank Lacy —Kimberley Pioneer*, Perth, Vanguard Press, 1979.

Pedersen, Howard, and Banjo Woorunmurra, *Jandamarra and the Bunaba Resistance*, Broome, Magabala Books, 1995.

Perez, Eugene, *Kalumburu War Diary*, Perth, Artlook Books, 1981.

Povinelli, Elizabeth A., *Labor's Lot: The Power, History, and Culture of Aboriginal Action*, Chicago, University of Chicago Press, 1993.

Read, Peter, 'The Price of Tobacco: The Journey of the Marmala to Wavehill 1928', *Aboriginal History*, vol. 2, nos. 1–2, 1978, pp. 140–8.

Reece, R.H., 'The Aborigines in Australian Historiography', in John A. Moses (ed.), *Historical Disciplines and Culture in Australasia*, St Lucia, University of Queensland Press, 1979, pp. 253–81.

———, 'Inventing Aborigines', *Aboriginal History*, vol. 11, nos. 1–2, 1987, pp. 14–23.

Reynolds, Henry, 'Violence, the Aboriginals and the Australian Historian', *Meanjin*, vol. 31, no. 4, December 1972, pp. 471–7.

———, *The Other Side of the Frontier: Aboriginal Resistance to the European Invasion of Australia*, Harmondsworth, Penguin, 1982.

———, *With the White People: The Crucial Role of Aborigines in the Exploration and Development of Australia*, Ringwood Victoria, Penguin, 1990.

Ronan, Tom, *Packhorse and Pearling Boat: Memories of a Mis-spent Youth*, Melbourne, Cassell Australia, 1964.

———, *Once There Was a Bagman: A Memoir*, Melbourne, Cassell Australia, 1966.

Rose, Deborah Bird, 'The Saga of Captain Cook: Morality in Aboriginal and European Law', *Australian Aboriginal Studies*, no. 2, 1984, pp. 24–39.

———, 'Remembrance', *Aboriginal History*, vol. 13, part 2, 1989, pp. 135–48.

———, *Hidden Histories: Black Stories from Victoria River Downs, Humbert River and Wave Hill Stations*, Canberra, Aboriginal Studies Press, 1991.

———, 'Nature and Gender in Outback Australia', *History and Anthropology*, vol. 5, nos. 3–4, 1992, pp. 403–25.

Roth, W., 'Report of the Royal Commission on the Condition of the Natives', *WAVP*, vol. 5, 1905.

Rowley, C.D., *The Destruction of Aboriginal Society*, Harmondsworth, Penguin 1970.

——, *The Remote Aborigines*, Harmondsworth, Penguin, 1970.

Rowse, Tim, *White Power White Flour: From Rations to Citizenship in Central Australia*, Cambridge, Cambridge University Press, 1998.

Rumley, Hilary, and Sandy Toussaint, '"For Their Own Benefit?" A Critical Overview of Aboriginal Policy and Practice at Moola Bulla, East Kimberley, 1910–1955', *Aboriginal History*, no. 14, vol. 1, 1990, pp. 80–103.

Sanders, William G., 'Access, administration and politics: the Australian social security system and Aborigines', PhD thesis, Australian National University, 1986.

Sharp, Ian, and Colin Tatz (eds), *Aborigines in the Economy: Employment, Wages and Training*, Melbourne, Jacaranda Press, 1966.

Stevens, F., *Equal Wages for Aborigines: The Background*, Victoria, Federal Council for the Advancement of Aboriginal and Torres Strait Islanders, 1968.

Sullivan, Patrick, *'All Free Man Now': Culture, Community and Politics in the Kimberley Region North-Western Australia*, Canberra, Australian Institute of Aboriginal Studies, 1995.

——, 'Colonising the Kimberley: An Ethnohistory', paper submitted to the Northern Australian Research Unit, Canberra, 1995.

Thomas, Nicholas, *Colonialism's Culture: Anthropology, Travel and Government*, Carlton, Melbourne University Press, 1994.

Treloar, D.W.G., 'Investors and Kimberley Cattle', *Australian Journal of Agricultural Economics*, vol. 9, no. 1, 1965, pp. 53–66.

Trigger, David S., *'Whitefella Comin': Aboriginal Responses to Colonialism in Northern Australia*, Cambridge, Cambridge University Press, 1992.

Willis, Peter, 'Patrons and Riders: Conflicting Roles and Hidden Objectives in an Aboriginal Development Programme', MA thesis, Australian National University, 1986.

Unpublished reports and manuscripts

Aboriginal Affairs Departments 1904–36, newspaper clippings, PR2425, BL.

Annual Reports of the Aborigines Departments (ARAD) 1898–1972, MS AADL. The full series of reports from 1898 is only available in manuscript form at the Aboriginal Affairs Department Library.

Davies, M.C., 'Ledgers: Kimberley Downs and Napier Downs', MN183A/19, BL.

'Department of Native Welfare Instruction Manual, 1965' and '1969/70', AADL.

Derby Leprosarium Admission Books, 1935–1981, West Kimberley Public Health Department.

Divisional Superintendent's Conference Meeting Minutes, 1964, February and June 1965, 1967 and 1968, AADL.

Emanuel Station Records, MN1312 A/3, BL.

'Final Report on Pastoral Land Tenure, 1986', Department of Premier and Cabinet WA.

Fitzgerald, W.V., 'Diary of the Kimberley Trigonometrical Survey Expedition April 5 – October 25 1905', typescript, BL.

'Frank Lacy Diaries 1923–1970', private collection, Mount Elizabeth station.

Hann, Frank. 'Explorations in Western Australia', read to Royal Society of Queensland, 7 April 1900, typescript, BL.

——, diary transcript, acc. 4308A item HS26, vol. a, 17 June 1995 – 17 July 1996, and vol. f, 9 September 1897 – 5 September 1898, BL.

Middleton, S.G., 'The Problem of Our Native People', symposium at University of Western Australia, October 1951, AADL.

Proceedings of Commonwealth and State Aboriginal Welfare Authorities Meetings, 1937, 1948, 1951, 1961, 1963, 1966, 1967, vols. 1–2, 1972, AADL.

Report of the District Welfare Officers' Conference, February 1963, Perth, AADL.

Scott, W.D., and Co., 'An Assessment of the Needs and Opportunities for the Aborigines of the Kimberley, vols. 1 and 2', 1971, AADL.

Stevens, F., 'Parliamentary Attitudes to Aboriginal Affairs 1936–1965: Intervention by the State', unpublished MS, 1968, AADL.

Submissions to the Commonwealth Conciliation and Arbitration Commission Regarding Equal Wages for Aborigines in the Pastoral Industry, Sydney, Arbitration Commission, originals viewed in Derby Courthouse. [Transcripts of evidence for, 'Cattle Station Industry (Northern Territory) Award 1951', CAR case no. 830 of 1965.]

Troy, P., 'Report on Investigations into Isdell Police Post to the Colonial Secretary', WAS1243 cons 481, 30 May 1905, BL.

Van De Ruit, R., 'Report on Community Development Work Derby 1981–1984', February 1984, Western Australian Department for Family and Children's Services, Derby.

Government archives

Aborigines Department and its successors all held at the State Records Office WA. Extensive lists from:

Aborigines Department, 1878–1908, 1920–30.

Aborigines and Fisheries, 1908–19.

Aborigines Protection Board, 1886–98.

Department of Native Affairs 1936–54.

Department of the North West 1920–25.

Native Welfare Department 1959–72.

Arbitration Commission Reports: 'Pastoral Industry Award: Variations', 53, 1944, pp. 212–57, 'Cattle Station Industry (Northern Territory) Award 1951', CAR 830 of 1965, CAR 536 of 1964, CAR 1669 of 1967.

Department of Land Administration, DOLA station files.

Native Welfare Department Northern Division General, WAS46, acc. 3412, approximately 400 files including one for each station created, 1948 containing the patrol reports and station lists.

Personal files created by the Aborigines Departments held at Western Australian Department for Family and Children's Services.

Police Department [PD], acc. 430, held at Battye Library, Perth, 1902–48.

PD1588, special item, Isdell Police Station Journals 1903–1908, BL.

Western Australian Acts of Parliament (Statutes), 1886–1972.

Western Australian Blue Books, 1924, 1938.

Western Australian Government Gazette, 1902–54.

Western Australian Parliamentary Debates, 1902–61.

Western Australian Votes and Proceedings, 1902–36.

Newspapers

Australian
Countryman
Hedland Advocate
Kalgoorlie Sun
Northern Times
Nor'West Echo
United Aborigines Mission Messenger
Weekend News
West Australian

Taped interviews (numbered 1–67, dated 1989–94) by the author with:

Campbell Allenbrae, Daisy Beharrell (Angajit), Jack Dale, Jack Dann, Ned Delower, Jilki Edwards, Maggie Ghi, Maggie Gudaworla, Harry Howendon, Kevin Johnson, Mick Jowalji, Jack Jowan, Phillip Krunmurra, Pat Lacy, Peter Lacy, Don McLeod, Rosie Mamangulya, Barbara Midmee, David Mowaljarlai, Morndi Munro, Weeda Munro, Dickie Udmorrah, Susie Umungul, Betty Walker, Ginger Warrebeen, Banjo Woorunmurra.

Research notebooks (numbered 1–13) in author's possession

Referenced with name of informant, notebook [NB] number, page number and/or date: e.g. Maggie Gudaworla, NB11B, p. 32.

INDEX

Photographs are listed in **bold type**.